CW00918299

Oscar Wilde

A Vagabond with a Mission

BY SPECIAL APPOINTMENT

(COPYRIGHT)

ROBERT W. THRUPP   *Photographer to the Queen.*   66, NEW ST. BIRMINGHAM

Wilde in his daywear, Birmingham, March 1884

Oscar Wilde

A Vagabond with a Mission

*The Story of Oscar Wilde's Lecture Tours
of Britain and Ireland*

Geoff Dibb

The Oscar Wilde Society

Published by The Oscar Wilde Society 2013

Copyright © 2013 by Geoff Dibb

Quotations from *The Complete Letters of Oscar Wilde* and the text of Wilde's Essay on Chatterton are reproduced by permission of the Estate of Oscar Wilde

The right of Geoff Dibb to be identified as the author of this work has been asserted by him in accordance with the Copyright, Designs and Patents Act 1988

All rights reserved. Apart from any use permitted under UK copyright law no part of this publication may be reproduced, stored in a retrieval system, or transmitted, in any form or by any means without the prior written permission of the publisher.

First published in Great Britain in 2013 by
The Oscar Wilde Society
63 Lambton Road
London SW20 0LW

ISBN 978-0-9560120-2-9

For my
three marvellous boys
George, Lawrence and Patrick

12 December 1885   Central Station Hotel, Glasgow

I am away in the region of horrible snow and horrible
note paper! Lecturing and wandering – a vagabond with
a mission!

Letter from Oscar Wilde to Henry Marillier

Contents

Illustrations

Plates *between pages 124 and 125*

Wilde's flyer for *Personal Impressions of America* on 10 July 1883

John Ruskin: Wilde disagreed with Ruskin's aesthetics in his lectures.

William Morris: Wilde espoused his theories in *The House Beautiful*

Whistler when Wilde first met him, about 1878

Edward Burne-Jones, about 1882

Wilde in Birmingham, March 1884

Wilde in Birmingham, March 1884

Mary Anderson who turned down *The Duchess of Padua*

Princes' Hall on the right where Wilde gave his first public lecture.

Wandsworth High Street with the Town Hall on the left where Wilde gave his first lecture after the failure of *Vera*

Cliftonville Hotel, Margate

Ramsgate. The Granville Hotel is the building with five gothic gabled windows. The tower is the rear of the hotel.

Lillie Langtry, about 1883

Southport: the sea front. The Winter Gardens is the iron and glass building at the far end of the Promenade

Southport Winter Gardens

Flyer for Wilde's Southport lecture, August 1883

Marie Prescott who starred in *Vera*

Wilde whilst assisting with rehearsals for *Vera* New York, August 1883

Wilde in New York, August 1883

Shelbourne Hotel, Dublin where Wilde stayed in November 1883

Kingstown (now Dún Laoghaire) Harbour, Dublin. Carlisle Pier where the Holyhead ferry arrived is to the right.

Constance Lloyd in about 1884

Wilde in evening dress. Caricature by 'Ape' (Carlo Pellegrini) Vanity Fair May, 1884

Tynemouth where Wilde stayed for a weekend, December 1883

Carlisle. The County Hall where Wilde lectured in February 1884 is centre left.

Friar's Crag, Derwentwater visited by Wilde, February 1884

Railway Station, Scarborough, behind is the Pavilion Hotel where Wilde stayed, February 1884

Flyers for The House Beautiful, 1883
Dorothy Dene: Wilde met her in York, October 1884
Birmingham Midland Institute where Wilde lectured in March 1884
Bradford Mechanics' Institute where Wilde lectured twice in 1884
Wilde in Ryde, 1884, card sent to Philip Griffiths December 1884
Leeds Mechanics' Institute where Wilde lectured four times in 1884
Torquay. The Bath Saloon where Wilde lectured in January 1886 is in the centre of the photograph.
Letter from Wilde complaining to Appleton, January 1885
Letter from Wilde to Appleton, Ulverston, February 1885
Wilde in his fur coat, March 1885. Drawing by Harper Pennington
The Nicholson Institute, Leek where Wilde lectured in March 1885

In the text

Every effort has been made by the author and the publisher to trace the holders of copyrights in illustrations and quotations. Any inadvertent omissions or mistakes will be rectified in future editions.

Acknowledgements

THE RESEARCH for this book began nearly thirty years ago at the Leeds Local History Library and over the years I have visited libraries throughout England. Librarians across the United Kingdom and Ireland have been very helpful by answering many questions and by finding newspaper accounts of Oscar Wilde. I wish to offer my thanks to librarians everywhere who have helped enormously in compiling the research for this book.

Throughout this time I have published many articles in *The Wildean*, the journal of the Oscar Wilde Society, beginning in *The Wildean* numbers 3 and 4 with my article on Oscar Wilde in West Yorkshire. The Society has been very supportive of my work and I wish to acknowledge the considerable help, support and friendship of the Chairman, Donald Mead, and Michael Seeney, the Honorary Secretary. Both Don and Michael have also undertaken their own researches into Wilde's lectures in Southport and Newcastle-upon-Tyne. Peter Vernier, another member of the Society, has helped considerably in tracking down these elusive newspaper accounts. I would also like to thank Horst Schroeder for his continued interest and support of this project. I am grateful to them all.

I wish to thank Merlin Holland for permission to publish my transcription of Wilde's *Essay on Chatterton*. In supporting me in this I also wish to acknowledge the help of Rebecca Fenning Marschall and Scott Jacobs at the William Andrews Clark Memorial Library, University of California Los Angeles, Oliver Howe at Gale, Cengage Learning, and Rachel Foss and Zoe Wilcox at the British Library. For assistance in tracking down Morse's accounts of the 1883/84 lecture tour I wish to thank Suzanne Tatian, also at William Andrews Clark Memorial Library, University of California Los Angeles and for a greater understanding of Richard Ellmann's information on the lectures I am grateful for the help of Lori Curtis of the McFarlin Library, The University of Tulsa.

I wish to thank Jeffrey Kraus of the Jeffrey Kraus Collection at www.antiquephotographics.com for his permission to use the photograph of Wilde taken in Birmingham and, with my editing, as the dust-wrapper of this book. I also wish to thank Isaac Gewirtz of the New York Public Library for permission to reproduce Wilde's letter to Appleton complaining of the lectures to come, and Liam Kelly of The British Newspaper Archive for permission to use images from the brilliant website, The British Newspaper Archive.

Finally, I would like to acknowledge the interest and support of the late Karl Beckson, with whom I wrote the UK lectures entry in *The Oscar Wilde Encyclopedia*, and the late Bryan Connon for his help with Beverley Nichols' story about his family's meeting with Wilde.

Prologue

IT WAS almost Christmas Day, 1884. There had been gales and storms, shipping had been disrupted and lives lost at sea: the west of Scotland was bitterly cold and the snow was lying on the ground, inches thick. The 30 year-old Oscar Wilde was there – in 'the region of horrible snow and horrible note paper!' was how he described Glasgow. On Sunday, 21 December he was to give his final lecture of 1884 to the famously hard-to-please Glaswegian public; or, at least, the few of them he expected to be prepared to emerge from the warmth of their parlours in such conditions. Apart from his honeymoon in June and a summer break, Wilde had been lecturing solidly for fifteen months, cramming in five, six and seven day's work each week and two lectures each day: he was tired and he was cold. With a fur hat on his head and his green, fur lined and trimmed coat wrapped around his ample body, Wilde left his hotel and made the short walk to the lavish St Andrew's Halls. The enormous Grand Hall, where he was to lecture, was claimed to have the best acoustics in Britain. At 6pm the doors were opened and thirty minutes later Wilde walked proudly out onto the platform of this vast hall dressed in his swallow-tailed evening suit, black satin double-breasted waistcoat glistening in the stage lights, black tie and a wide expanse of white shirtfront in the centre of which a solitary diamond stud sparkled. Applause broke out, with a theatrical flourish Wilde bowed his head with his waved auburn hair and the applause increased. The audience was enormous: the Grand Hall was absolutely crammed and all standing room had been taken: 5,000 expectant people had braved the 'horrible snow' to be entertained by the 'Great Aesthete', Oscar Wilde, the young man who had been travestied and criticised for some years, and all across the world. This was something special for both audience and performer: it was the largest audience Wilde would ever have and for ninety minutes these 5,000 people listened to him, rapt, laughing and applauding every jest, every perfectly exaggerated story and every unique observation of this droll and extremely clever young man. This evening was a most brilliant end to what had been an eventful two years for Wilde and the next day he would catch the

Wilde lecturing in Glasgow

train and return to his wife, Constance, for a few days precious relaxation.

Oscar Wilde's lecture tours of the United Kingdom began almost two years before this brilliant evening but to see their origins we have to look back to the influence of Oxford University and his coming up to London in 1878.

Introduction

At every single moment of one's life one is what one is going to be no less than what one has been.

Oscar Wilde, *De Profundis* (1897)[1]

OSCAR Fingal O'Flahertie Wills Wilde was born in Dublin on 16 October 1854, attended Trinity College where he excelled at Greek and in 1874 he was awarded the Berkeley Gold Medal for his studies. He won a scholarship to Magdalen College, Oxford where he made a name for himself. There he fell under the twin influences of John Ruskin[2] – the Slade Professor of Fine Art – and Walter Pater[3] – Fellow of Brasenose College. These two men had an enormous influence on him which lasted for the rest of his life. He graduated from Oxford in 1878 with glorious academic results and the Newdigate Prize for poetry and moved on to London, where he met James Whistler,[4] an American-born, British-based artist, dandy and wit:[5]

> Whistler demanded admiration bordering on sycophancy and gave in return domination bordering on enmity.

It was about this time that Whistler asked his friend, the architect and all-round aesthete, Edward Godwin,[6] to design a house with studio for him on Tite Street, Chelsea. In parallel he sued Ruskin who had libelled him in a review of his painting *Nocturne in Black and Gold: The Falling Rocket*. Whistler won his case but a derisory farthing damages were awarded, costs were shared and combined with the cost of building his White House he was bankrupted in 1879.

Sir Rennell Rodd[7] writes:[8]

> It was in '82, '83 that I saw most of him [Whistler] in Tite Street, not the White House. That had already passed into the hands of Quilter.[9] But there was another house nearly next door where he had a studio. Frank Miles,[10] Waldo and Julian Story[11] Walter Sickert,[12] Harper Pennington,[13] and, at one time, Oscar Wilde, were constantly there. Jimmy, unlike many artists, liked a

Walter Pater. Lithograph by William Rothenstein

camarade about the place while he was working, and talked and laughed and raced about all the time, putting in the touches delicately, after matured thought, ten yards away, with preternaturally long brushes.

For two or three years, Oscar Wilde was so much with Whistler that everybody who went to the studio found him there, just as everybody who went much into society saw the two men together. Wilde had come up from Oxford not long before the Ruskin trial, bringing with him a reputation as the most brilliant undergraduate who had ever flashed upon the University, as the winner of the Newdigate prize, and as the apostle of "beauty". Many a reputation is lost on the way between Oxford and London, but his was only strengthened. He was brilliant among men of the world, witty sayings of his were repeated eagerly and his youth seemed to excuse the affectation of his pose as reformer. He was at once sought after, and had the world of London at his feet. It was natural that, of all the men he met, none should appeal to him more powerfully than Whistler.

It was as natural that Whistler, on his side, should be flattered by the homage Wilde paid him. He was looked upon as the world's jester after his return from Venice when Wilde's devotion drew them into closer intimacy. The younger men who were now gathering about Whistler, had still to make their name and reputation. Wilde's name was in every man's mouth, he had not outworn the reputation brought from Oxford, he shone with the splendour of the great work he was expected to produce. He was the most promising poet and man of letters of his generation. To be singled out for his allegiance was flattering. More than this, to have his companionship was amusing. There is no question of the charm of his personality.

For a time Wilde lodged with the artist Frank Miles at his house, also on Tite Street and also designed by Godwin.

In London Wilde became the personification of Aestheticism even though the satirising of this intense philosophy of art appreciation was initially aimed at Dante Gabriel Rossetti,[14] one of the founding members of the Pre-Raphaelite Brotherhood. Wilde became the visible incarnation of aesthetes and was impersonated in Burnand's[15] play *The Colonel,* the longstanding butt of the satirical magazine *Punch* and the merciless caricatures of George Du Maurier,[16] showing Wilde as a limp young man 'living up' to his blue and white porcelain. This porcelain had been first popularised by Whistler and Godwin who were great collectors. Wilde was purported to be the main character (Bunthorne) of Gilbert and Sullivan's[17] *Patience,* a comic opera about the Aesthetes, one of which was a:

> Greenery-yallerey
> Grosvenor Gallery ...
> Young man

who would famously:

> Walk down Piccadilly
> With a poppy or a lily
> In his medieval hand

Years later, when Wilde was asked about this, he replied:[18]

> To have done it was nothing, but to make people think one had done it was a triumph

As Wilde's fame as an aesthete grew, Richard D'Oyly Carte,[19] whose company was about to tour the United States of America with *Patience,* hit upon the idea of having Wilde tour ahead of his company in order that that the American public could understand exactly what the play parodied. Wilde took the opportunity and spent virtually the whole of 1882 on a lecture tour of the United States and Canada, wearing the aesthete's garb of a velvet suit with knee-breeches, silk stockings and buckled shoes. The fact that Wilde had the temerity to lecture in America on artistic matters rankled with Whistler, who felt that *he* was the ventriloquist and Wilde, whom he saw as his puppet, should not stand up on his own and start lecturing. Whistler started to believe that Wilde was stealing all his ideas on art and, from 1882 onwards, these thoughts increased and their relationship began to deteriorate.

It is at the end of his American lectures that we meet Wilde in this book. Biographies in the past have paid scant attention to his lectures in the United Kingdom but this book sets out to give detailed information about them, covering the period 1883 to 1889. I have drawn heavily upon contemporary accounts of Wilde and have used quotations from newspapers and other sources. Through these we see him from a new perspective, one we rarely have, our visions of Wilde being obscured by over a century of hindsight and interpretation.

The consensus view of Wilde's lectures in the UK has been that they were ephemeral events, even being subjects of which he was ashamed. However, I feel that the evidence is that this is far from being the case. These lectures took as their subject matter important social topics of the day. Because of this and the controversy which was never far from everything he said or did, they gave Wilde his opportunity to re-enter the world of journalism which, in turn, led to his editorship of *Woman's World* in 1887. They also had significant implications for Wilde's artistic development, giving him an opportunity to apply his own ideas – whatever Whistler felt about their ownership – to these great matters of the day. In doing so we can see in these lectures not only the development of Wilde's views, but Wilde begins to use the actual lexicon and phraseology of his mature works.

I have three objectives in writing this book:

1. to give details of the towns and cities Wilde visited on his lecture tours;

2. to give detailed transcriptions of the lectures he gave; and
3. to show how these lectures fit into the gestation of his mature works.

This book provides a unique six-year window on Wilde. It is Wilde before, and at the outset of, his major writings: it is Wilde in transition from the aesthetic, unemployed young man to the controversial author, active homosexual and famous playwright.

CHAPTER 1

January to August 1883

The Lectures Begin

NEW YEAR'S Day 1883 dawned with Wilde at sea: he was on board the SS Bothnia in the middle of the Atlantic Ocean, returning from New York. When travelling in the opposite direction almost a year previously he had famously described the Atlantic as disappointing and he was probably feeling disappointed now, sailing back to London after spending almost the whole of 1882 travelling, and being fêted, all over North America. What did 1883 hold for him? Later in the year he would become twenty-nine years old, although he would not admit it. He was no longer the young man he posed as and his significant academic achievements at Oxford University — which had failed on the purely utilitarian measure of providing him with a career — were well behind him. Soon he would be in London, yet again, and without an income, yet again.

The newspapers across the United Kingdom reported his departure from New York on 27 December: this was news, even if only a little piece of news:[1]

> Mr. Oscar Wilde sailed for home by the Bothnia yesterday. He left sorrowfully. He says his mission to reform the tastes and dress of the Americans has been a failure.

But the newspapers were strangely mixed-up about his arrival: some reported he had disembarked at Queenstown (now Cobh) in Ireland, but whilst the Bothnia did stop there, it then steamed on to Liverpool where Wilde finally arrived on Saturday 6 January, reporters at the ready. The *Liverpool Post* was able to interview Wilde[2] on board where he had had plenty of time to re-evaluate the success of his American venture, finally concluding that, perhaps, it had not been quite that much of a failure after all:

> Mr. Wilde said his lecturing tour was the most successful undertaking of the kind ever known, and that he has "lectured to more people than any one else who has visited that country."

The correspondent continued:

> Mr. Wilde was then questioned on the crucial point – the report that had been spread regarding his expressions of opinion on the subject of the Atlantic Ocean. Had he been accurately reported in the statement that he was 'disappointed with the Atlantic?' 'Certainly I was disappointed,' said Mr. Wilde, with an imperturbable gravity, relieved only by the faintest glimmer of a smile. 'The Atlantic,' he proceeded to explain, 'is greatly misunderstood.'

The enigma not having been solved for the interlocutor, he pressed Wilde further:

> 'Everything one says should be in mystery, more or less.' After this oracular statement, the unhappy interrogator saw no means of pursuing the argument ...

Later on Saturday the big question of the Atlantic Ocean was finally cleared up:

> Oscar was bound to admit ... that his previous criticism on the Atlantic was "possibly somewhat harsh"

He returned to London: [3]

> Quite a flutter prevailed in aesthetic circles ... in anticipation of the appearance in some of his old haunts of the high priest of the order. Mr. Oscar Wilde will, I understand, deliver some lectures in the metropolis upon his American experiences.

Reporters were keen to move on from the Atlantic to the admittedly lesser problem of Wilde's future:[4]

> From Park street he goes straight to Paris, where he means to work out some new and startling notions of a literary, and possibly dramatic, character ... He goes back to America in the "fall," then to Australia, and ultimately to Heaven.

So, even though he had been back in England for less than one day, the whole of 1883 had, however vaguely, been mapped out by Wilde, although Australia and Heaven would drop off his agenda.

The immediate *frisson* of return faded and, in need of escape, Wilde left for decadent Paris and set about meeting writers and artists, and being a poet, *flâneur* and playwright. He had begun to write his latest play, *The Duchess of Padua*, and completed it whilst in Paris. He was also negotiating an American run for *Vera; or, the Nihilists* which was his first play and had been many years in gestation, originally being published in 1880.[5] Marie Prescott[6] liked it and agreed terms with Wilde in February, promising a New York first night in August.

Early in March, Wilde dined with a group of English and American artists at the Paris Pen and Pencil Club and was asked to speak:[7]

> at dessert he made a little speech on his American experiences.

This little speech picked out some of the highlights of 1882 and his anecdotes included a story which he made famous and, with a few lexical adjustments, was to become part of his future lectures and the standard defence for a pianist:

> "When I arrived at Leadville, in the evening I went to the Casino. There I found the miners, and the female friends of the miners, and in one corner a pianist sitting at a piano over which was the notice, 'Please do not shoot at the pianist; he is doing his best.'" Mr. Wilde was struck with this recognition of the fact that bad art merits the penalty of death …

This phrase became so famous that it was used, with minor variation, as the title of an album by Elton John ninety years later.[8] This little speech was an embryonic version of his first public lecture which he was to give in July: *Personal Impressions of America.*

By May, though, things were worse: he had received bad news. *The Duchess of Padua* was turned down by Mary Anderson:[9] 'this is tiresome' he said to his friend Robert Sherard[10] when he received the message. Sherard had met Wilde in Paris and remained a friend for the rest of Wilde's life. He is, therefore a valuable witness to Wilde's life at this period, although his apparent 'innocence' blinded him to any inappropriate behaviour on Wilde's part. Eventually, when Paris had exhausted the windfall from his American adventure, the wonderful city had to be quitted: Sherard to the Lake District and Wilde back to London, with such few means that he could only live beyond them.

Wilde moved into rooms on Charles Street close to the very fashionable, and wealthy, Grosvenor Square in Mayfair. Shortly afterwards Sherard joined him and described their rooms in his biographies of Wilde.[11] What he has to say gives an interesting insight into Wilde's lifestyle at this important time:

Mary Anderson. Drawing by Harry Furniss

The lodgings, which were for single gentlemen of distinction, were kept by a Mr and Mrs Davis. They were most excellent people, the kind of landlord and landlady that one so very rarely meets in the dreary Sahara of London Lodgingdom. Mr Davis had been a butler in good families; his wife had been a cook, and a real cordonbleu she was. Mr Davis used to go out to banquets in the city to super-intend the waiting, and had a standing arrangement with the Governors of the Bank of England.

They were both devoted to Oscar Wilde, though he was often in their debt, and could not speak too highly of his cleverness, kindness and consideration …

Oscar's rooms were on the top floor, an oak-panelled sitting-room, with a small bedroom opening out of it. When Oscar was at home, I used to sleep in a bedroom on the ground floor, when he was en voyage I was allowed to use his bedroom. I remember that the bed was no sybaritic couch; it was a particularly hard camp bedstead, and reminded me of those we had at Oxford. There was no bathroom in the house, an inconvenience which troubled Oscar Wilde but little. He was not addicted to the daily bath …

The arrangements at the lodgings in Charles Street were distinguished and comfortable. Our newspapers were invariably aired before they were brought, with the early cup of tea, to our bedsides. The valeting was what one is accustomed to in the best houses. As to the catering, it was incomparably the best I have ever met with in any lodgings. We used to déjeuner in the French fashion about eleven o'clock, and it was as good a breakfast-lunch as any that could be got anywhere in London. The Davises had some excellent claret, and the coffee that Mrs Davis made reminded one of the café noir that used to be served at the "not at all bad little place in the Avenue de l'Opéra" where we used to dine with the Duchess.

('The Duchess' was Wilde and Sherard's in-joke name for the source of their funds when they ate in Paris: Mary Anderson's hoped-for taking of *The Duchess of Padua* … until she refused it.) Despite the camp bed and the lack of a bath, Wilde's aired newspapers and eleven o'clock *déjeuner* with Parisian quality coffee and some excellent claret hardly sounds as if it was too harsh and demanding a lifestyle.

Wilde needed funds to see him through until *Vera* triumphed in New York and he scouted for opportunities, but there was little available. What there was came from Colonel W. F. Morse who had managed his American lecture tour and was now in London: he could offer more lecturing. Morse promised Wilde a healthy number of lectures across the United Kingdom[12] although without the level of income of the American tour:[13]

> Mr. Wilde had come from Paris, where he had been since returning from America, having found it necessary to earn money for his current expenses. He called at my office, about the middle of June, and there was then arranged a preliminary lecture in London, to be followed by others throughout the country should the results of this first effort prove satisfactory.

Wilde had no other options: this surely was something he could do and do well, the American lectures had been successful in parts and to some extent he could enjoy it, being the extrovert he was. So in the short term lecturing would be a stopgap for just two months or so until *Vera* in New York threw him his lifeline.

He had few preparations to make: before he had gone to the United States he had proposed taking lessons from Hermann Vezin,[14] a famous actor of the day who also gave lessons in deportment and elocution. Sherard — who misremembers this as being just before the UK lectures — writes[15] about Vezin's attitude to tutoring Wilde when asked:

"Vezin, I am to go lecturing in England. I want you to help me. I want a natural style with a touch of affectation."

"Well," answered Vezin, "and haven't you got that, Oscar?"

Since then he had amassed a year's experience of lecturing and had no need of any further guidance. The subject matter would be relatively easy: he could update some of his previous lectures in line with his current thoughts and the British conditions, or even stand there and tell the tale of his many and amusing experiences during that year in America. He had already made a start on that when he spoke at the Paris Pen and Pencil Club. How hard could it be? He was a natural.

In early June, no doubt for social reasons, Wilde accompanied his mother[16] in attending a private lecture John Ruskin gave in Kensington.[17] This must have given him an opportunity to catch up with his old mentor and provided an hour or so of aesthetic revision. Ruskin's lecture was in two halves: the first half was on fairyland (a subject the Wilde family were steeped in, with both of Wilde's parents having studied Irish folklore) and art for children, a subject which interested Wilde and would find its way into his later lectures. The second half of the lecture included a section about 'Francesca's Books' which contained a series of much praised drawings by a Miss Francesca Alexander of whom Ruskin wrote to her mother:[18]

> I wish I could learn an entirely new writing from some pretty hem of an angel's robe - to tell you with what happy and reverent admiration I saw your daughter's drawings yesterday; reverent not only of a quite heavenly gift of genius in a kind I had never before seen, but also of the entirely sweet and loving spirit which animated and sanctified the work, and the serenity which it expressed in the purest faiths and best purposes of life.

This sentence sets out quite concisely Ruskin's theory of art criticism and his view of the overwhelming importance of high moral standards - the entirely sweet and loving spirit as well as the purest faiths and best purposes of life – which he saw as essential to great art.

On this area in particular Wilde now disagreed with Ruskin but the themes of beauty and morality, and their inter-relationship, intertwine throughout the rest of his life and through his writings. As well as Wilde and Speranza, the invitees at this lecture included Sir Frederic Leighton RA,[19] probably the most famous artist of the day and President of the Royal Academy and the Art Student Club where Wilde would be lecturing in just a few days' time; the eminent Pre-Raphaelite, Edward Burne-Jones with his wife;[20] Lord Mount-Temple

Wilde's mother 'Speranza'. Drawing by Harry Furniss

whose wife[21] was to become a friend of the Wilde family, particularly of Wilde's wife Constance, and, as described in the newspapers, many other distinguished members of society. I imagine this was a pleasant evening and Wilde found it food for thought as he prepared for his own forthcoming lectures.

Lecturing to Art Students

FOR HIS LECTURE tour, Wilde had a manager, Colonel W.F. Morse, and his assistant, George Webb Appleton,[22] to handle all his affairs. However, this support team was not in place until mid-June and, earlier in the month, we find Wilde arranging his own lecture to the Royal Academy art students at their club on Golden Square, just around the corner from the Royal Academy of Arts in Piccadilly and close to his digs in Charles Street. The first letter of 2 June[23] is to the students accepting the invitation to lecture at 8pm on 30 June and the next is addressed to Eric Forbes-Robertson[24] agreeing to be at the club at 8:45pm on 30 June. The lecture had clearly been moved to 9 pm and was to be chaired by Forbes-Robertson himself, probably in response to Wilde's request for a student in the chair. However, the time available may not have been sufficient for Wilde to prepare, as Robert Ross[25] suggests:[26]

> Wilde always admitted that, relying on an old and intimate friendship, he asked (Whistler's) assistance on one occasion …

> This I presume to be the Address delivered to the Art Students
> of the Royal Academy in 1883 ...

The full text of this lecture given in Appendix A is based upon that
published by Ross in his *Complete Works* in 1908[27] as *Lecture to Art
Students*. However, Morse states that the lecture's title was *Modern Art
Training* which I have adopted here. Wilde begins in this way:

> In the lecture which it is my privilege to deliver before you to-
> night I do not desire to give you any abstract definition of
> beauty at all...We want to create it, not to define it. The
> definition should follow the work: the work should not adapt
> itself to the definition.

This amounts to Wilde's rephrasing of the opening paragraph of
Walter Pater's *Preface* to his famous, even notorious in its day, *Studies
in the History of the Renaissance*[28] which begins:

> Many attempts have been made by writers on art and poetry to
> define beauty in the abstract. ... Such discussions help us very
> little to enjoy what has been well done. ...To define beauty, not
> in the most abstract but in the most concrete terms possible, not
> to find a universal formula for it, but the formula which
> expresses most adequately this or that special manifestation of
> it, is the aim of the true student of æsthetics.

Pater's book of essays was revolutionary at the time, particularly
where he sets out the clear water between Ruskin's views on art and
morality and his own subjective, impressionistic, amoral focus on art.
Pater's overall views were summarised in this *Preface* and the final
Conclusion which was to become very controversial. In Pater's own
words, he was so concerned that the *Conclusion* 'might possibly
mislead some of those young men into whose hands it might fall' that
he omitted that chapter from the second edition and only published
an amended version in later editions.[29] But the cat was out of the bag
and one young man into whose hands this precious book fell was
Wilde. In *De Profundis*,[30] written in Reading Gaol in 1897, Wilde
writes:

> I remember during my first term at Oxford reading in Pater's
> *Renaissance* — that book which has had such strange influence
> over my life

Whether the strange influence upon the young Wilde amounted to
Pater's worry that it 'might possibly mislead ... young men' is open to
interpretation, but what is beyond question is the importance of
Pater's writing for Wilde. Therefore, at the very beginning of his first

lecture in England, to an audience of art students, we have Wilde's paraphrased tribute to his master, Walter Pater. After his introductory statements he sets out his intentions for the lecture:

> The subject of my lecture to-night is what makes an artist and what does the artist make; what are the relations of the artist to his surroundings, what is the education the artist should get, and what is the quality of a good work of art.

Pater begins his second paragraph of the *Preface* with a famous quotation from Matthew Arnold:[31]

> "To see the object as in itself it really is,"

which he then modifies by:

> … the first step towards seeing one's object as it really is, is to know one's impression as it really is …

Wilde also latches onto this phraseology in this lecture and takes the position a little further:

> Appearance is, in fact, a matter of effect merely, and it is with the effects of nature that you have to deal, not with the real condition of the object. What you, as painters, have to paint is not things as they are but things as they seem to be, not things as they are but things as they are not.

Imagining things as they are not, then, is the way forward for the artist. Wilde considers at great length the impact of nations upon artists and art and ridicules it:

> Such an expression as English art is a meaningless expression. One might just as well talk of English mathematics

and argues that true artists transcend any such considerations. He looks at the nineteenth century and then, in comparison, ancient Greece, concluding:

> … remember that there never has been an artistic age, or an artistic people, since the beginning of the world

Not even ancient Athens under Pericles.[32] The treatment of the great Greek sculptor Phidias[33] is given as an example of this:

> for having introduced into a bas relief, taken from Greek sacred history, the image of the great statesman who was ruling Athens at the time, Phidias was flung into prison and there, in the common gaol of Athens, died, the supreme artist of the old world.

Wilde then draws a parallel between Phidias and Sir Frederic Leighton whom he had seen at the Ruskin lecture a few days previously and may even have been in his audience on this evening:

> What would you say if all the English bishops ... took off Sir Frederic Leighton in a prison van to Newgate?

He then comments more generally:

> And do you think that this was an exceptional case? The sign of a Philistine age is the cry of immorality against art, and this cry was raised by the Athenian people against every great poet and thinker of their day - Aeschylus, Euripides, Socrates.[34]

Wilde will find himself in exactly this position in seven years' time following the publication of his novel *The Picture of Dorian Gray*[35] when his art, and he, will be accused of immorality. This argument about *Dorian Gray* was even re-used during his trials in 1895 as evidence of his guilt.

He then deals with the artist's need for beautiful external conditions: surely these are necessary for great art? Wilde gives a lengthy quotation from Ruskin describing the great beauty of fourteenth century Pisa as experienced by Nino Pisano[36] which he then contrasts with current conditions:

> And then look at the depressing, monotonous appearance of any modern city, the sombre dress of men and women, the meaningless and barren architecture, the colourless and dreadful surroundings.

Following this Wilde demolishes Ruskin's arguments:

> Is it really true that beautiful surroundings are necessary for the artist? I think not; I am sure not. Indeed, to me the most inartistic thing in this age of ours is not the indifference of the public to beautiful things, but the indifference of the artist to the things that are called ugly. For, to the real artist, nothing is beautiful or ugly in itself at all.

This lecture was not reported very extensively, unlike the lectures to come, probably because it was given in a private club to a private audience. However, a number of newspapers did give short reviews and picked up on one small piece of the lecture: a section where Wilde describes Gower Street and The Embankment in London, the latter no doubt partially in homage to Whistler who had painted so many pictures from the Chelsea Embankment. In the published text this section of the lecture is dealt with in one sentence:

> In Gower Street at night you may see a letter-box that is picturesque; on the Thames Embankment you may see picturesque policemen

But the newspapers which did cover this lecture gave long quotations about these parts of London with Wilde commenting far more extensively on his impressions:[37]

> Even Gower Street, one of the most monotonously dull and colourless of formal London thoroughfares has periods when it is actually beautiful. I remember coming home from a party and passing through it when day was breaking when its aspect was most charming and I was forcibly struck by this fact. In the softening obscurity of the morning mist which had filled it with golden and purple hues, softening its outlines, and giving variety to its shadows, with the sunrays piercing it in long golden shafts, the roofs were shining like molten silver, and the vermilion pillar-post shone like a gem. It was a scene of almost fairy-like beauty.

This vivid description could almost be a response to Ruskin's lecture on fairyland, or an impressionistic description of a Whistler townscape. Following the above was the observation:

> On another occasion I found that the weird effect in a fog on the Thames Embankment which gave even such a very commonplace and unlovely thing as a policeman — with cape and helmet and multiplicity of buttons — which was not, under ordinary circumstances, a thing of beauty or a joy forever, but lit up with dusky light was such an expression of Michael Angelesque grandeur in appearance, that a painter might have sought a better subject a long time before he found it.

These statements do add a more typically Wildean flourish to the rather bland sentence that has previously been published. Of course, the idea of Wilde returning from a party at dawn and being forcibly struck by this vision of fairyland drew several sarcastic comments:[38]

> People coming home from a party when daylight does appear may congratulate themselves if they are not forcibly struck by something else.

No doubt this response was exactly what Wilde had hoped for.

Wilde's general theme in this lecture is about the quality of the true artist's perception and the artist's personal impressions. Towards the end he says:

> To paint what you see is a good rule in art, but to see what is worth painting is better. The true artist did not wait until life became picturesque for others. He took care to see life under pictorial conditions always.

> I do not desire that external life should be permanently beautiful but I do know that under certain conditions of light and shade everything would look beautiful. Once in every twenty-four hours everything became beautiful.

Wilde then criticises Ruskin again, this time it is his views on how industry mars a townscape:

> Mr. Ruskin had said many dreadful things about the iniquity of smoke, and I am not going to praise it on sanitary grounds. I would only remind you of the beauty Turner[39] saw in those very scenes which Mr. Ruskin so often ran down. There was no better answer to those who complained of commerce spoiling art that to turn to Turner's pictures.

The value of smoke to a townscape is one Wilde takes up in later lectures[40] and came in for considerable negative comment from reporters, particularly those based in the large manufacturing cities of the north of England where smoke was a constant, and a serious, health concern.

Following this lengthy exposition about the artist and what the artist makes, Wilde asks:

> Who is the artist? There is a man living amongst us who unites in himself all the qualities of the noblest art, whose work is a joy for all time, who is, himself, a master of all time. That man is Mr. Whistler. He is the greatest artist of the day.

This was Wilde's genuinely held, high opinion of Whistler, which he included in later lectures even though their relationship was becoming more difficult. Whistler's irritation at what he saw as Wilde's plagiarism would only get worse as time progressed.

Wilde condemns all archaeological, historical or sentimental paintings:

> As regards archaeology, then, avoid it altogether: archaeology is merely the science of making excuses for bad art

because their primary aim is not to give the observer artistic joy. He disapproves of artists who cling to specialisms in subject matter:

> All such divisions as animal painters, landscape painters, and painters of Scotch cattle in an English mist, painters of English

cattle in a Scotch mist, racehorse painters, bull-terrier painters,
all are shallow

This joke about the painters of cattle of interchangeable nationality in different mists must have been well received by the art students because Wilde repeated it to good effect during later lectures. Wilde then concludes by paraphrasing more of Pater's philosophy:

A picture has no meaning but its beauty, no message but its joy.
That is the first truth about art that you must never lose sight
of. A picture is a purely decorative thing.

Much of this lecture is a statement of Wilde's Paterian sympathies, his growing distance from Ruskin and his admiration for Whistler. I am *forcibly struck*, though, as Wilde was at dawn in Gower Street, by the similarity of this lecture's arguments and those contained in his major critical works, particularly *The Critic as Artist* and *The Decay of Lying*.[41] These dialogues were first published in 1889 and 1890 and later collected for Wilde's volume of criticism, *Intentions* (published in 1891). In these critical dialogues, we find Wilde using very similar phraseology to that he uses here in his lecture, enabling us to see that Wilde's thoughts on aesthetics had crystallised to a great extent by June 1883. The closing pages of Part I of *The Critic as Artist* deal with most of the same matters – in part the views of Arnold, Ruskin and Pater - and in the same terms. In *The Critic* he writes:

the primary aim of the critic is to see the object as in itself it
really is not[42]

which is almost identical to this lecture's suggestion that the primary aim of a painter is to paint:

… not things as they are but things as they are not.

This sentiment is mirrored in *The Decay of Lying*:[43]

No great artist ever sees things as they really are.

Wilde's emphasis in the lecture on the artist's subjectivity and vision:

Do not wait for life to be picturesque, but try and see life under
picturesque conditions.

is restated in *The Critic* as:

rejecting the tedious realism of those who merely paint what
they see, try to see something worth seeing[44]

The sections of the lecture which deal with archaeology in art and where Wilde criticises artists who choose to specialise, are dealt with in similar ways in *The Critic*, Wilde sarcastically calling them 'the anecdotage of painting'[45] because they

> rank with illustrations, and even considered from this point of view are failures, as they do not stir the imagination

Finally, Wilde's emphasis at the end of the lecture that a painting *has no meaning but its beauty, no message but its joy ... is a purely decorative thing*, finds its expression in almost every part of both of his critical dialogues:

> Still, the art that is frankly decorative is the art to live with. ... Mere colour, unspoiled by meaning, and unallied with definite form, can speak to the soul in a thousand different ways.[46]

> Art never expresses anything but itself.[47]

Reviews were few but positive:[48]

> The lecture ... was sometimes epigrammatic, often humorous, and its brilliantly eccentric philosophy seemed to vastly delight the students. Very heterodox from an Academic standpoint were many of the views promulgated, not the least startling being the lecturer's earnest and emphatic laudation of Mr. Whistler's work and method. This delicate sermon, preached to a very remarkable audience of young brushes, promises well for the *American Impressions* on the 10th.

However, Wilde could not relax for too long on this emphatic laudation;[49]

> Mr. Herbert Vivian tells the story of a dinner given by Whistler after Wilde had been lecturing: 'Now, Oscar, tell us what you said to them,' Whistler kept insisting, and Wilde had to repeat all the phrases, while Whistler rose and made solemn bows, with his hand across his breast, in mock acceptance of his guests' applause.

Ellmann feels that Vivian 'cannot have reported the bowing altogether accurately',[50] but if Ross was correct and Wilde had asked Whistler for his assistance, then this story could well have been correct and is illustrative of Whistler's growing enmity. Wilde would not ask for help with a lecture again. Whistler, though, according to Ross, was quietly impressed with Wilde's facility with the English language and took from Wilde what he needed:[51]

> ... Whistler certainly reproduced some of it (*Modern Art Training*) as his own in the *Ten O'clock* lecture delivered subsequently, in 1885. To what extent an idea may be regarded

as a perpetual gift, or whether it is ethically possible to retrieve an idea like an engagement ring, it is not for me to discuss.

But I will discuss it in Chapter 6.

Personal Impressions of America

FOLLOWING his lecture to the 'young brushes', Morse arranged Wilde's first public lecture – entitled *Personal Impressions of America* – for 8:30pm on Thursday, 10 July at the Princes' Hall, Piccadilly. This was a hall for public functions in the new building for the Royal Institute of Painters in Water Colours which had opened in April. It could hold an audience of over 600 and was described in one newspaper[52] as:

> ... the new Prince's rooms in Piccadilly ... are now the lecture rooms par excellence in the metropolis.

This lecture is a light and amusing compendium of his experiences in America and is what we now - and, indeed, then - recognise as an Oscar Wildean production, containing many amusing and idiosyncratic observations. It was reported in newspapers across the UK with many identical reviews being repeated, which indicates just how famous Wilde now was, how newsworthy and how much public interest there was in his words and actions.

Much comment in the press was made of the high price of admission: stalls were 10/6 (half a guinea) and 7/6, the balcony 5/- . Other than that reviews varied, particularly about factors which one would not think could be open to too much interpretation. But the description of the people present, the audience's response to the lecture and the number who stayed to the end were all subject to conflicting reports. The variety of these introduces one immediately to the highly divergent views the press had of Wilde and it is clear that the reporters and newspapers of the day had their own agendas about him and his position: fool, genius or what the *Lady's Pictorial* described him as:

> what any young man might be proud to be, a refined and accomplished gentleman; quiet and unassuming in manner, and, that rarest of all rare things, a really good talker.[53]

Whilst we recognise Wilde as a 'really good talker', the young man, 'quiet and unassuming in manner', strikes us now as slightly at odds with our received impressions. But the range of views about him and, in particular, the views of those who disparaged him, was something which would not change for the rest of his life.

Wilde caricatured wearing the aesthetic dress
he had ceased to wear, with P. T. Barnum.

His clothes and hair always attracted a great deal of comment and all reports of the lecture agreed upon his appearance: now his evening wear varied little from the norm, in contrast to the aesthetic garb he wore for his American lectures. In fact, many reviewers were surprised at this change and it was rumoured that he could have earned far more in fees if only he would have continued to dress as a burlesque Aesthete, straight from the pages of *Punch*. But, as he told Sherard in Paris:[54]

> ... it is now months since I discarded my eccentricities of costume and had my hair cut. All that belonged to the Oscar of the first period. We are now concerned with the Oscar Wilde of the second period, who has nothing whatever in common with the gentleman who wore long hair and carried a sunflower down Piccadilly.

And Oscar Wilde of the second period, refusing to wear fancy dress, actually wore:

> Evening dress, the trousers tightly fitting, a white flower in the buttonhole, the shirt cuffs overlapping the sleeve as a

schoolboy's collar overlaps his jacket, and a heavy seal pendant from the watch-albert of dark material, and a large solitaire in the shirt breast constituted the chief features of his clothing. His hair is still of aesthetic cut, but not as it is known in the comic opera of Patience, nor as it has been made known through pictorial periodicals. It is now cut and trimmed that it may follow the contour of the head – not closely, but thickly, and arching over the ears, and outlining the forehead.[55]

Elsewhere, Wilde's hairstyle was reported[56] as:

His latest development, just now "fetching" the town … with a little lock falling over the forehead, he looks really very nice, if not perfectly like the respected and lamented Prince Regent.[57]

or:

His hair had been cut, and what remained of his more than auburn locks had been curled with irons.[58]

This was a look which was termed elsewhere as 'Byronite' although Wilde himself described his new hairstyle, first conceived and produced in Paris, as 'Neronian'. Wilde relates that he took his hairdresser to the Louvre to see an ancient bust of Nero which bore the style he required and he was pleased with the results:

However, society must be amazed, and my Neronian coiffure has amazed it. Nobody recognises me, and everybody tells me I look young: that is delightful, of course.[60]

This might just be the beginning of Wilde's quest for youth, or, at least, the appearance of it.

The size and 'class' of the audience were seen by the press to be indicators of Wilde's success, or failure, and so were open to different reports depending upon the editorial stance of that particular newspaper. In a minority of reports the attendance was described as poor: 'very ordinary, very sparse who could not be roused to any enthusiasm'.[61] However, in most reports the audience was said to be of a good size, the hall full and, with a degree of hardly contained surprise:

He is still as popular as ever, for the room was absolutely crammed with good folks who paid half-a-guinea apiece to hear a lecture.[62]

Another newspaper reported:[63]

The audience was very large, it was also very fashionable and decidedly aesthetic, especially the female portion of it. Some of the dresses worn by the ladies would in ordinary society be considered a little outlandish ...

One can only imagine. The audience also included students from the Royal Academy, to whom Wilde had given at least six tickets,[64] and, specifically, Whistler, presumably having missed Wilde's debut he wished to be present at this second performance:

"Jimmy" was there — all there, some one remarked; for he jumped about like a cricket, and put himself in evidence all over the hall.[65]

Quite what Whistler could find to complain about in this lecture, a humorous telling of stories from Wilde's tour of America, I do not know, but it is indicative of the state of the Wilde/Whistler relationship which at one time had been so cordial.

Despite the cost of the tickets and the size of the fashionable audience, Wilde was late in taking the stage – the advertised commencement time was 8:30pm but it was fifteen, twenty or even thirty minutes later, depending upon the newspaper you read, before he appeared and began to lecture. The *Daily Telegraph*[66] reviewer asked:

Is unpunctuality capable of being reduced, like murder, to a fine art?[67] Mr. Wilde began his lecture some twenty minutes after the appointed time and appeared on the platform with such a delightful unconsciousness of having anything to apologise for that the audience were disarmed in a moment, notwithstanding a shock of disappointment

But then again, as Wilde would later write: 'punctuality is the thief of time'.[68]

Wilde read from notes, which was unusual because in almost every other lecture he gave he was reported as using no notes of any kind. Despite having a very good memory, Wilde must have felt insufficiently confident of his material for this important public London debut. Of course, in public speaking, it is important to grab the audience's attention from the very start so it must have been rather galling for him to have to compete for the first fifteen minutes with an organ grinder outside in the street. One reviewer commented[69] that some of his audience were amused and distracted:

The incident was a bitter commentary on a remark of Oscar's a few evenings previous at a party. "Music," said he, "to be charming should be unexpected. The man who has the best idea of giving pleasure by music is the organ-grinder."

There was some suggestion that a detractor, having heard this quip, had arranged for the organ grinder to play as the lecture began. But notwithstanding the unexpected accompaniment, Wilde was a very competent lecturer and this was reflected in reviews of his performance:

> The lecture may be described as very "Oscar Wildish."(sic) It was paradoxical, audacious, epigrammatical, it abounded in good stories, well told in picturesque descriptions, it was often humorously nonsensical, and gave plenty of original information.[70]

And the audience was:[71]

> ... pleasantly surprised to find a very sensible and observant young man, who touched on a vast variety of Transatlantic subjects with decided originality, somewhat audacious brilliancy, and a good deal of quaintly quiet humour.

The result was that Wilde was:

> met with a very cordial reception, and was frequently applauded during his lecture.[72]

In fact, for the next few years, this type of positive comment upon his lecturing style, his speaking ability and his audience's response to the content of his lectures was to be repeated in newspapers across the UK. The impression given is that the point was worth making purely because of the negativity of some sections of the press. Of course, there were the doubters who could be very critical:[73]

> ... the lecturette, self-conceit, ridiculous art-jargon, tailoring and all is plaguily dull.

So what did Wilde have to say on the evening of 10 July – 'ridiculous art-jargon' or not? (A full text of *Personal Impressions of America* as delivered in the autumn of 1883 is given in Appendix B). Wilde already held the position of 'wit' and for some time his amusing sayings had been widely quoted in newspapers. This lecture was full of *bon mots* which were reported extensively (all unreferenced quotations which follow are from the published *Impressions of America*.) He began by claiming that his lecture would contain 'very little useful information', which some of the press reported as though it was an affront to their sensibilities: after all, didn't the Victorian public want to be educated, to use their little leisure time profitably? It was a formulation Wilde would use to begin other lectures and he clearly valued its paradoxical style and the pose of studied triviality he could assume. The issues of usefulness and uselessness would occupy him a great deal later, notably in *The Preface* to *The Picture of Dorian Gray*.

Wilde then described his first American experience: the reporters who swarmed on board his ship the moment it anchored in New York, to ask him what he thought of America:[74]

> Not having seen it, I was entirely unbiassed on the subject, and I gave, on the whole, a very flattering account of my experiences of America as far as it had gone.

He considered Americans, if not to be the best dressed people, then the most comfortably dressed. The country, unlike in England, exhibited no poverty. However:[75]

> The second thing was that everyone seemed to be in a hurry, and this made him think it could not be a country of great romance, for romance was difficult where it was a vital necessity to catch a train.

And with the trains and industry came terrible noise:

> It is surprising that the sound practical sense of the Americans does not reduce this intolerable noise. I fail to see why these whistles could not be set to very beautiful notes of music... All Art depends upon exquisite and delicate sensibility, and such continual turmoil must ultimately be destructive of the musical faculty

which to some extent conflicts with his messages in *Modern Art Training* where he suggested that a beautiful environment was not essential for the production of art.

Unlike the best of English cities, such as York or Oxford, Warwick or Gloucester, American cities lacked historical beauty, being:[76]

> great howling cities like Birmingham and like Manchester, very rich and full of commerce, and one who stopped to admire the architectural beauty of any building would be disappointed.

Wilde considered that beauty in American towns came where modern science and engineering had been applied to life and inventors and engineers were given the highest recognition, cities and their wealth depended upon them. Americans had made great technological strides, particularly with the electric light:[77]

> Madison square ... lit by a great mast from which the electric light hung in lanterns, was one of the most beautiful sights one could see. It was in these things one could see the real beauty of America...

And he was particularly impressed in Chicago:

> I have always wished to believe that the line of strength and the
> line of beauty are one. That wish was realised when I
> contemplated American machinery. It was not until I had seen
> the water-works at Chicago that I realised the wonders of
> machinery; the rise and fall of the steel rods, the symmetrical
> motion of the great wheels is the most beautifully rhythmic
> thing I have ever seen

These sentiments about the benefits of engineering and science to
society are quite at odds with the general perception of Wilde,
although he did set out similar views in *The Soul of Man under
Socialism*:

> On mechanical slavery, on the slavery of the machine, the
> future of the world depends...There will be great storages of
> force for every city, and for every house if required, and this
> force man will convert into heat, light, or motion, according to
> his needs.[78]

> Sympathy with consumption does not cure consumption; that
> is what Science does. And when Socialism has solved the
> problem of poverty, and Science solved the problem of Disease
> ...the sympathy of man will be large, healthy, and
> spontaneous.[79]

In America nature was varied because the country was so huge: [80]

> with its variations from the tropical heat of Florida to the chilly
> cold of New York

and its sheer size required that all travelling had to be done by train: [80]

> everything was twice as large and twice as far off as it should
> be.

When he travelled west: [81]

> one had to cross the prairies, which were so ridiculously vast
> that Nature, when it came to decorate them, seemed to have
> become alarmed and given up in despair. It was an expanse of
> monotony, so vast that the train passing over it seemed
> immobile...the train travelled for days, stopping occasionally at
> a small station, where what by some curious process of
> reasoning was called a meal was served. Here he met the
> Indians, who were very picturesque and charming as long as
> they wore their own clothes, and very ugly when they put on
> European dress. Their language struck him as resembling

German metaphysics – very fine as long as it was not understood (laughter). When it was interpreted he generally found it to convey a request for half a dollar or some tobacco.

His views about one famous natural sight in America were quoted extensively:

Niagara, like the Atlantic, was at first sight extremely disappointing ... every American bride is taken there, and the sight of the stupendous waterfall must be one of the earliest, if not the keenest, disappointments in American married life.

In order to appreciate its splendour and strength it was necessary to go under the fall itself in a suit of yellow sealskin, so ugly that he should never have consented to wear it, but that he was informed that a similar dress had been worn by that great artist Madame Sarah Bernhardt [82] (laughter).[83]

Wilde was clearly impressed with California which he thought was beautiful and reminiscent of The Riviera in spring. San Francisco was transformed:[84]

... one passed at night time suddenly into a little city of winding streets lit ... by painted paper lanterns ...

and he was much taken with the Chinese people there:

The people — strange, melancholy Orientals, whom many people would call common, and they are certainly very poor — were a most artistic people, and what was most pleasing about the Chinese was that everything they did and touched was beautiful. Unlike the people of England — who hoarded their beautiful art works in cabinets — these Chinese have determined that they will have nothing about them that is not beautiful for general use. In the Chinese restaurant, where these navvies meet to have supper in the evening, I found them drinking tea out of china cups as delicate as the petals of a white rose, whereas at the gaudy hotels I was supplied with a delft cup an inch and a half thick.

The Chinese lifestyle he witnessed accorded with a William Morris[85] inspired rule of house decoration — 'have nothing in one's house which is not useful and beautiful' — and it impressed Wilde. He referred to these 'china cups as delicate as the petals of a white rose' in his later lecture *The House Beautiful* as an example of how we should surround ourselves with useful things, beautifully made. He admired other aspects of their culture:[86]

What was most pleasing about these Chinese was that everything they did and touched was beautiful. The bills of fare at their restaurants were beautifully drawn with Indian ink upon the finest rice paper. Their poetry was far too delightful to be locked up in books … so the poet wrote his sonnets upon fans and pocket handkerchiefs, and sometimes embroidered them upon beautiful dresses …

He was also impressed by what he saw of Chinese theatre which was:

… the most imaginative and artistic theatre in the whole world. They did not depend on gorgeous scenery and splendid decorations, the actors having their art permanently and entirely in the imagination. I remember on one occasion seeing a young actor preparing for his part. He was first fanned by his servant, then he got his cup of tea, then he sent for a beautiful background in the shape of a yellow satin umbrella, and lastly took two long rods of bamboo with little lamps at the ends, and two masked servants held them up one on each side of his face in order that the audience might feel delighted at his wonderful natural facial expression. That was really imaginative acting – with these preparations the actor felt he could produce the right artistic impression on the audience.

Wilde dealt with his experience of Chinese theatre in considerable detail and his positive comments about its imaginative potential, produced without the need for imitations of natural scenery, contrasts strongly with the rather conservative aesthetic he advocates in his two critical articles about staging Shakespeare plays which were published in 1885.[87] He continued to play with these theories and adapted these articles to produce his final Shakespearian essay — *The Truth of Masks - A Note on Illusion*[88] — published in *Intentions* in 1891, where he assumed a more ambiguous position towards realism at its close:[89]

Not that I agree with everything that I have said in this essay. There is much with which I entirely disagree. The essay simply represents an artistic standpoint, and in aesthetic criticism attitude is everything.

Much quoted was Wilde's experience of train travel:

the boys who infest the cars and sell everything that one can eat — or should not eat — were selling editions of my poems vilely printed on a kind of grey blotting paper, with all the stops left out for the low price of ten cents, or five pence. Calling these boys on one side I told them that though poets like to be popular they desire to be paid, and selling editions of my poems without giving me a profit is dealing a blow at literature which must have a disastrous effect on poetical aspirants. The invariable reply that they made was that they themselves made a profit out of the transaction, that was all they cared about, and that settled the question.

When Wilde visited Utah he met many Mormons and was unimpressed with their architecture:

Salt Lake City contains only three buildings of note erected by the Mormons: the Tabernacle, the Amelia palace, and the co-operative stores. The chief of these being the Tabernacle, which is in the shape of an ordinary tea kettle

and after some description of the Tabernacle and its wall paintings he commented: [90]

This wonderful design and these marvellous decorations were mysteriously communicated to Brigham Young. It is satisfactory to know that no architect of modern times had anything to do with it.

In the Rocky Mountains, after complaining of the advertisements defacing the peaks, Wilde came to Leadville, apparently a rough mining town. He was advised that they may shoot him or his travelling manager:

I wrote and told them that nothing that they could do to my travelling manager would intimidate me.

When he arrived he observed that: [80]

Every man's dress was picturesquely ornamented with knives and pistols

Wilde was invited by the miners to dinner down a silver mine where each of the three courses was whisky. Postprandial entertainment with the miners included a return to his reminiscences of the saloon which he had recounted in his after dinner speech in Paris, but with a little more polish: [90]

They afterwards took me to a dancing saloon at the end of which was a piano and the typical pianist playing, where I saw the only rational method of art criticism I have ever come across. On the wall, right over the piano was printed a notice:

PLEASE DO NOT SHOOT
THE PIANIST
HE IS DOING HIS BEST

In between Paris and London Wilde had improved this anecdote: the wording is tighter and any references to the female friends of the miners, which would have outraged the sensibilities of his UK audiences, had been judiciously dropped.

Travelling south, passing through Virginia, Charleston and New Orleans, Wilde met the more elderly inhabitants who could not forget the civil war:[91]

> ... he found Mr. Jefferson Davis[92] living quietly and simply amidst a most lovely plantation of magnolia trees, and had an opportunity of seeing there some traces of the dignity of the South in antique times.

At Galveston:[93]

> There was one night, when the moon was gilding the bay with silvery streaks, he turned to a gentleman and said, "How beautiful the moon is." and the man replied, "You should have seen it, sir, before the war."

The cosmopolitan nature of American society - the press, women's role, the young people of America - all these impressed Wilde, especially the young women, of whom he was much quoted as saying:[93]

> The American girl was the prettiest despot in the world. She seemed to be a little oasis of picturesque unreasonableness in the desert of common sense.

But his view about their dresses was often derided:[94]

> ... there is too much of the French milliner's handiwork about it ... a dress should be sent home incomplete, and that it should be left to the lady to decide what flower, lace, or ribbon should be used to give the note of tone and colour.

He was struck by the major difference between how women were treated in America and in the UK:[93]

> There, also, the intellectual side of woman's nature was fully appreciated, and no country had ever offered women such a career as America; and in no country had the career of women as fitly justified the opportunity and privileges given them ... women in America held a far higher position in public life and in the possibility of an unmarried woman earning her own livelihood.

Wilde's proto-feminism was not a passing fad. In November 1887 in his *Literary and Other Notes* for *The Woman's World* he wrote:[95]

Nothing in the United States struck me more than the fact that the remarkable intellectual progress of that country is very largely due to the efforts of American women, who edit many of the most powerful magazines and newspapers, take part in the discussion of every question of public interest, and exercise an important influence upon the growth and tendencies of literature and art.

He concluded his lecture by saying:[96]

... that much more important than all he had seen was what he had learned in America. He had learned among other things that poverty was not a necessary condition of a great country, and that he had obtained a fuller conception of the meaning of the word "Liberty."

which was followed by warm applause.[97]

Most reporters considered that however interesting, the lecture was overlong, it stretched to two hours and one review said it was two and a half.[98] Unfortunately, parts of the audience began to leave:[99]

as Mr Wilde's lecture far exceeded the limits announced, and threatened to become wearisome, not a few of his patrons ... by twos, threes, and half dozens, kept up a continual move towards the door during the latter part of his discourse.

Eventually:[100]

the lecturer, who was conscious that he had occupied too long a time, apologised, and compressed some of his most interesting passages towards the close.

Notwithstanding the over-run, not everyone was disappointed by the late finish:[101]

When next he speaks he would ingratiate his audience by commencing more punctually, the hour at which he ceases concerns himself alone, for few indeed would really tire of his

well-modulated voice, his graceful delivery, and the purity and richness of his language.

Alternative views were that before the lecture was suitable for another audience he had to cut it into two or condense it significantly:[102]

There is much in the lecture, and in Mr. Wilde's mode of delivering it, to sustain interest, but it must be greatly curtailed if audiences are not to be exhausted.

Wilde caricatured as an aesthetic drake.

Wilde did opt to edit his text because future, undivided, lectures of *Personal Impressions of America* were kept to approximately one and a half hours.

The Lecture Tour Begins

FOLLOWING THE Princes' Hall lecture Morse and Wilde reviewed the situation:[103]

This introduction of Mr. Wilde to a London audience was deemed sufficient to warrant his presentation throughout the English provinces.

> At that time there was no regular system for placing lectures or making up a connected tour of engagements. The Mechanics' or Literary Institutes of the United Kingdom were usually the agencies by which speakers came into contact with the public, and these were accustomed to provide practical subjects, topics of real every-day interest, or a form of entertainment in magic and legerdemain, dialect monologues, illustrated travels, or musical comedies and concerts. The lectures of Mr. Wilde took their place on the list, and were a part of the series, except in one or two of the larger cities, where they were managed … for the joint benefit of the theatre and speaker.

Wilde had just over two weeks to prepare himself before he gave his first few lectures outside London ahead of departing for New York to help with rehearsals for *Vera*. He began on 26 July lecturing twice on his *Personal Impressions of America*: in the afternoon at the sumptuous

Cliftonville Hotel in Margate and in the evening at the Edward Pugin[104] designed Granville Hotel in Ramsgate. Many years later Wilde wrote to his then publisher, Leonard Smithers:[105]

> I am glad you went to Margate, which, I believe, is the *nom-de-plume* of Ramsgate. It is a nice spot not vulgarised by crowds of literary people.

I can only surmise that Wilde had not given the lecture his undivided attention during his fortnight break as it was as late as the afternoon at Margate, on the Cliftonville Hotel headed writing paper, that he made six pages of notes for the lecture, presumably to help him make all his main points whilst keeping the lecture to well under two hours duration.

Wilde must have been pleased that whatever his notoriety in London, at these first two lectures outside the capital he was able to draw a sizeable crowd. It was reported[106] that:

> There was a large attendance on each occasion

and the reporter considered his lecture:

> was of an interesting character, full of amusing incidents, and delivered in a conversational style. Mr. Wilde seemed at home with his audience, and the audience appeared thoroughly at home with him. The result was that his remarks were very attentively listened to.

A few days later Wilde headed north where he was to lecture on 1 August at The Winter Gardens, Southport, a major seaside resort just north of Liverpool, where he probably stayed. This lecture was advertised and linked with a week's performances by Richard D'Oyly Carte's Opera Company of the 'New and Original Aesthetic Opera.... PATIENCE',[107] also at the Winter Gardens. Lillie Langtry[108] — great beauty, actress, supposed love of Wilde's younger life — arrived in Liverpool from New York on 31 July. Wilde was there the next day in time to present her with a bouquet of roses as she left for London by the 11 o'clock train.[109] Wilde then travelled to Southport and decided to do some shopping. Having a celebrity in their midst, *The Southport Guardian*[110] noted his activities:

> He was at a bookstall in Chapel Street purchasing some pictorial paper and when departing the salesman handed him the plate belonging to the print. Oscar on beholding it started slightly, and observed, "pray spare me." This remark will

Lillie Langtry. Drawing by Harry Furniss

doubtless be handed down to succeeding generations as an utterance of the great aesthetic poet, and treasured as such.

I thank Don Mead, the Chairman of the Oscar Wilde Society, for uncovering this gem and I am delighted to be able to hand it down yet again and continue what seemed to be the reporter's rather optimistic destiny for his story. Wilde was favourably received by a large audience for his afternoon lecture at the Winter Gardens:[111]

Mr. Wilde's entertainment — it can hardly be dignified with the title of lecture — ... is delivered with considerable fluency and freedom. ... Mr. Oscar Wilde has filled a curiously unique niche in the catalogue of crazes ... . To his credit be it that Mr. Wilde saw his opportunity and took it. Whether it will float him to fortune or not the future will unfold ... It remains our province to notice that Mr. Oscar Wilde is a charming entertainer, and if his arguments are specious and lack profundity his extreme good humour and quaintness will almost invariably command an attentive and appreciative audience.

One review of this lecture[112] begins — as ever — by telling its readers that Wilde was not dressed as Bunthorne but:

> the white pointed cuffs turned back over his coat sleeves, and the necktie and handkerchief of the same colour, the latter carefully arranged so that a portion of it protruded from the breast of his buttoned-up, black frock coat. Grey trousers with straps, completed a costume

Here we see Wilde's outfits for the next few months becoming set. This matching tie and handkerchief is the first mention of this combination. It was actually a crushed strawberry coloured silk handkerchief, matching his loosely knotted tie for his daywear, universally commented upon throughout the autumn, winter and following spring. In the evenings he maintained his 'normal' evening wear with a black tie (or stock as it was described) but from now Wilde adds the crushed strawberry silk handkerchief to the ensemble, it being pushed into the top of his black satin waistcoat.

On 2 August Wilde left Liverpool: he sailed for New York, hoping for great things from Marie Prescott and *Vera*.

Table 1. The Lectures: June to August 1883

Date	Town	Venue	Time	Lecture
Sat 30 June	London	Royal Academy Students' Club Golden Square,	9:00 pm	Modern Art Training
Tue 10 July	London	Princes' Hall Piccadilly	8:30 pm	Personal Impressions of America
Thu 26 July	Margate	Cliftonville Hotel Hall	Afternoon	PIA
Thu 26 July	Ramsgate	Granville Hotel Theatre	8:00 pm	PIA
Fri 27 July	Southampton	Philharmonic Hall	8:30 pm	PIA
Sat 28 July	Brighton?			
Wed 1 Aug	Southport	Winter Gardens	3:30 pm	PIA

Key

? Ellmann mentions this (p 227) but no other evidence for it has been found.

CHAPTER 2

September to Christmas 1883

Engagement

The Vera Fallout

THIS was to be an important few months for Wilde. During a sweltering summer in New York, *Vera; Or, the Nihilists* had been a commercial and artistic failure. Wilde was much lampooned in the press in both the United States and United Kingdom and reporters took great delight in ridiculing him. However, at the same time there were some dissenting voices from the gloating chorus and one sceptical report was published in several newspapers:[1]

> On the first night, the representative of one of the leading New York journals expressed a distinctly favourable view of the play in the *entr'acte*, but added, "However, what's the use of that? Look at my orders;" and he produced a cable from the proprietor of the paper, then in England; "No matter what it is, abuse it in two columns." This is a fact.

So was it a conspiracy? There were a few positive reviews but the negative ones outweighed these. Marie Prescott, perhaps not too surprisingly, having invested heavily and starred in the play, leapt immediately to the defence:[2]

> My own feelings in this matter are that Mr Wilde is much superior to the prejudice against him, and I know that *Vera* is a noble play …

Mary Anderson, who had refused *The Duchess of Padua* whilst Wilde was in Paris, had her views:[3]

she thought his new play, "Vera," had been rather harshly dealt with. "I have read it and think it contains some strong situations"

and his beloved Lillie Langtry, last seen in Liverpool but at the present 'living in the most sumptuous style in the Champs Élysées … took up the cudgels valiantly for Mr. Wilde':[4]

Oscar Wilde has hosts of enemies on the other, as well as on this, side of the Atlantic; but he will live them all down like other men of genius. He is a very clever writer, possesses remarkable ability, and is destined to do great things in the near future.

The unpleasantness of the critical assessments of his play — if they could be classed as assessments — must have set some alarm bells ringing for him. One report[5] was more considerate:

The play was not successful; but why should its failure be announced by the dramatic critics in a spirit of exultation, as if its author were a notorious criminal who had at last been convicted... why should Mr. Wilde's mishap condemn him to public scorn as a humbug and imposter?

Wilde had rather created and even courted this relationship with the press and one can only look at what this more kindly notice says about him — his being treated as 'a notorious criminal who had at last been convicted' — with a degree of apprehensive hindsight: we are in the privileged position of knowing how this ends. Even Henry Irving,[6] at a banquet in his honour in New York, in front of five hundred guests and the press, felt on safe ground making a slightly jokey reference[7] to Wilde in a speech when referring to a newspaper interviewer:

The only thing I would quarrel with him for was saying I reminded him of Mr. Oscar Wilde.

Wilde had become fair game.

The Returning Lecturer

THE SS ARIZONA with Wilde on board arrived from New York at Queenstown on Wednesday, 19 September.[8] Wilde then made his way back from the south coast of Ireland to London by train and ferry. It says much about him that after the major set-back of his literary and financial hopes in New York, he returned to the hard

MR. OSCAR WILDE

Has the honour to announce that he will Deliver his celebrated

LECTURE,

ENTITLED

"PERSONAL IMPRESSIONS OF AMERICA,"

IN

HOPE HALL, LIVERPOOL,

ON SATURDAY AFTERNOON, OCT. 6,

Doors open at 2 30. Lecture at 3.
Front Seats, 3s.; Side Seats, 2s.; Gallery, 1s.

THE LECTURE

Will be Repeated in the Evening at Eight o'clock.
Doors open at 7 30. Admission—Front Seats, 2s.; Gallery, 6d.
Plan of the Hall and Tickets at William Lea's Music Warehouse, 50 and 52, Church-street.

PRESS OPINIONS.

"Pleasantly surprised to find a very sensible and observant young man."

"Decided originality, brilliancy, and a good deal of quaintly quiet humour."

"Full of a strong personal interest and an undercurrent of Irish fun."

"It was a decidedly new method of approaching life."

"Amusing fashion of making a vivid sketch-book of the men, women, girls, rivers, theatres, tea-cups, T. moons, that he drifted across in his 'pilgrim's progress.'"

"The voice clear and quiet; the whole thing original and quaint and interesting."

"Mr. Oscar Wilde visited 34 States and Territories and travelled 30,000 miles in his American tour."

"American Life and Character, as seen under all sorts of conditions, pleasant and otherwise."

"His anecdotes are told with abundant humour; his manner is graceful and easy."

N.B.—Mr. Wilde will offer some observations upon dress for both sexes, with special reference to his own personal attempts to influence American taste in favour of the adoption of a more graceful style than that which at present prevails.
        d

A sizeable advertisement for Wilde's Liverpool lectures

labour of a lecture tour of the United Kingdom with so little time to prepare: his first lecture was to be at Wandsworth in southwest London five days after disembarking. However, the reality was that he had no other way of earning a living and had to swallow his pride and get on with it.

Now his lecture tour of the UK got underway properly with two lectures: *Personal Impressions of America* which he had already written, delivered several times and had been able to edit and improve, and a new lecture, *The House Beautiful*. For this lecture Wilde had taken his American lecture of the same title, selected a few of its relevant points and had rewritten the rest to fit with what he currently felt. In the three months or so to Christmas 1883, Wilde was to travel enormous distances across England and Scotland: from Penzance, Cornwall in the south west of England, to Brighton in the south east, to Aberdeen in the north east of Scotland, calling at many towns and cities in between. It has been suggested that the geographical arrangement of his lectures was haphazard, Otho Lloyd, Constance's brother, saying:[9]

> 'He is lecturing still, going from town to town, but in the funniest way, one day he is at Brighton, the next he will be at Edinburgh, the next at Penzance in Cornwall, the next in Dublin; he laughed a good deal over it and he said that he left it entirely to his manager.'

As can be seen from his itinerary at the end of this chapter, this is not an accurate description of Wilde's travels. It is, though, a testimony to Victorian railways that such a tour was possible and that in a world without our technological advantages, this level of organisation – making arrangements with local agents, hiring halls, printing and distributing posters and brochures - was possible at all, carried out only by means of the penny post and the occasional telegram.

During the autumn and winter, Wilde delivered his two lectures fairly equally. The decoration of houses was a subject of great interest at the time, many books were published about it and artistic and social visionaries such as John Ruskin and William Morris had both considered and contributed to the issue. Wilde's lecture on *The House Beautiful* was a response, in part, to the urbanisation of British industrial cities and the expansion of London. This massive transformation of towns and the depletion of the countryside was driven by the enormous labour demands of industry and the major engineering and building projects — houses, factories, ports, railways, roads — which this required. These new sources of employment demanded a ready labour supply 'on the doorstep'. They also needed energy which was supplied by coal, requiring a growth and expansion of coal mines which sprang up wherever the geology was suitable. Industrialisation on this scale led to vast areas of housing being built, much of it the familiar, high density terraced housing of the period, surrounding every major mill and factory. Towns and cities across the nation were expanding at a phenomenal rate to accommodate this surge of population and parts of our larger cities must have been an enormous, continuous building site. All these houses had new occupants — mostly untutored in the arts — who had few ideas about how to decorate them. But never fear, help was on hand: Oscar Wilde was about to tell you exactly how it was done.

The growth in urban areas brought perceived dangers — moral and spiritual — as well as many public health issues which were debated. Transport, sewerage, poor quality housing, education and schools for children were subjects which politicians and the public grappled with. To address these matters, large public exhibitions of industrial products and the fine arts became a feature of the late nineteenth century. The first great international exposition - *The Great Exhibition of the Works of Industry of all Nations* - was held in London in 1851 under the direction of the Society of Arts and its objective was that 'Great Britain made clear to the world its role as industrial leader.' Wilde was not a fan:[10]

> The public clung with really pathetic tenacity to what I believe were the direct traditions of the Great Exhibition of international vulgarity, traditions that were so appalling that the houses in which people lived were only fit for blind people to live in.

Sir Joseph Paxton's[11] Crystal Palace, an enormous exhibition space made entirely of prefabricated units of iron and glass, was built for the Great Exhibition and subsequently removed to Sydenham and extended. Wilde would give his last lecture before Christmas there. Following the Great Exhibition's lead and acting as an inspiration, many Industrial and Fine Art Exhibitions were held across the country and they provided appropriate venues for Wilde's topical lectures.

A Definite Proposal

WHILST BUSY lecturing during the autumn, Wilde became engaged to Constance Lloyd.[12] He had known Constance for some years and after his New York debacle he had given her a copy of *Vera* to read. On 11 November, Constance wrote[13] to him:

> I was much interested in 'Vera'…I cannot understand why you should have been so unfortunate in its reception unless either the acting was very inferior or the audience was unsympathetic … I am afraid you and I disagree in our opinions of art, for I hold that there is no perfect art without perfect morality, whilst you say they are distinct and separate things …

So yet another woman jumped to *Vera* and Wilde's defence. Constance was clearly well versed in Wilde's attitude to art and morality, her opinions falling more on Ruskin's side of the argument.

The engagement happened whilst Wilde was lecturing in Dublin on Thursday 22 and Friday 23 November. *Complete Letters* contains letters[14] from Constance to her brother, Otho, about Wilde and his lectures (she preferred *House Beautiful* to *Personal Impressions of America*). However, over the weekend, Wilde must have made the big decision and asked for her hand in marriage. On Monday, 26 November, when Wilde had sailed from Dublin to Holyhead, Anglesey and caught the train to Shrewsbury for that evening's lecture, Constance wrote to Otho again:

> Prepare yourself for an astounding piece of news! I am engaged to Oscar Wilde and perfectly and insanely happy.

Frank Harris[15], the journalist, became a friend of Wilde's at this time. He and Sherard, though key witnesses to Wilde's life during these years, both have their weaknesses: Sherard seems unable to see anything and Harris — generally regarded as a dissembler — tells about more than he actually saw. Harris writes that the engagement and subsequent marriage had a very humdrum financial justification:[16]

> ... Wilde was extravagant in almost every possible way. He wished to be well-fed, well-dressed, well-wined, and ... was constantly in dire need of cash ...

Undoubtedly Wilde did need money and at the time there was an intended legal action against him 'by the caretaker of some property of his in County Galway, for salary and money expended'.[17] As Lady Bracknell would observe in *The Importance of Being Earnest*:[18]

> What between the duties expected of one during one's lifetime, and the duties exacted from one after one's death, land has ceased to be either a profit or a pleasure. It gives one position, and prevents one from keeping it up.

His property in Galway had clearly ceased to be either a profit or a pleasure.

There were other allegations, expressed in Ellmann,[19] that Wilde made the decision to marry in order to hide his homosexual inclinations, which he felt were becoming increasingly obvious, particularly to the press. Yet from the few letters which do exist between Wilde and Constance, and Wilde to friends,[20] both of them seem very affectionate and genuinely in love with each other.

As with everything he did, Wilde's engagement received its usual sort of treatment by the press[21] including appropriate Gilbert and Sullivan quips:

Bunthorne is to get his bride[22]. Oscar Wilde is going to be married. ... She is a Dublin girl, a Miss Lloyd ... To her other attractions, she adds the important one of money ... There was at first some fear lest London should lose its lion and society its favourite source of admiration and ridicule. A terrible rumour had got about that Mr. and Mrs. Oscar Wilde were to settle down in Dublin. The Grosvenor Gallery might shut up and Mr. Du Maurier retire from *Punch*. Happily this danger is averted. We keep Oscar.

Some reports of the engagement were decidedly strange:

...it is stated tonight that Miss Constance Lloyd ... is the happy, or unhappy, daughter of Eve on whom Mr. Oscar Wilde has bestowed his affections. I say happy or unhappy not out of disrespect to the young lady, because if so be that she is the ideal of the aesthetic one's matrimonial aspirations, she must be no ordinary every-day sort of woman. I say unhappy because most ladies, without being suspected of envy, will declare that to please Wilde long will require more than human perfection.[23]

Reading these observations now makes one wonder quite what the subtext of such an article actually was. Certainly it contains comments about Constance's possible difficulties — she requiring 'more than human perfection' — of some prescience.

Whistler

WILDE'S RELATIONSHIP with Whistler was becoming strained even though Wilde was praising him very highly in his lectures. All over the land he told his audiences that Whistler was the greatest living artist in England, if not the world, and encouraged them to seek out his paintings. But this seemed not to placate Whistler who continued to assail him — hiding his malevolence behind 'friendly' sarcasm. However, whatever Whistler's opinion was of his own opinions, Wilde was extremely well educated and well read: certainly he had an unrivalled knowledge of the philosophy of aesthetics as well as having Charles Baudelaire[24] and Théophile Gautier[25] amongst the writers he admired and whose philosophies on art he had absorbed. At the start of the year he had had the opportunity to meet many writers and painters in Paris and so he knew, if few others in the UK did, that Whistler's ideas were not all his own and were, to some extent, derivative. Notwithstanding this strain on their relationship, Sherard[26] tells us that when Wilde returned to London from his lectures:

SPECIMENS OF THE BUTTERFLY SIGNATURE
OF JAMES McNEILL WHISTLER

Whistler's stinging butterflies: the coin is Whistler's slight
misrepresentation of the farthing he was awarded as
damages in his libel action against Ruskin. Quite
what his butterfly is doing to it is anyone's guess.

We generally dined *en ville*. Oscar was usually invited out; I
dined where I could, not in-frequently with Duke Humphrey.[27]
Sometimes we went to the Café Royal, and on more than one
occasion Whistler was with us. He was not very prosperous in
those days, and used to order the very cheapest claret to take
with his frugal grill. Oscar Wilde showed him the greatest
deference. "Like the grand Virginian gentle-man that you are,"
he sometimes said to him. Whistler seemed to me always to be
nurturing a grievance, either against some individual or against
the social collectivity. I remember once saying to Oscar that the
pre-prandial conversation with Whistler was an excellent
substitute for bitters as an apéritif, and so indeed it was. His
remarks were the *cascara sagrada*[28] of conversation. I was
promptly snubbed by Oscar for my observation. "One does not
criticise a James McNeill Whistler," he said, though later on he
himself was to criticise him, and not without acerbity.

To say that Whistler was 'prickly' would be an understatement: his
was another dimension of prickly and Sherard's 'bitters as an apéritif'
quip works quite well, as does his observation of his constant
nurturing of grievances. Wilde was bringing this aspect out in
Whistler more and more. This is all well documented in Whistler's
Gentle Art of Making Enemies: a truly beautiful book with wide
margins, small blocks of text with even smaller piercing annotations,
sometimes appended with his little, pointedly-tailed, stinging
butterfly.

The title and subtitle say it all about Whistler's pride and pleasure
in argument. It was that careful exasperation which Whistler
perfected, the jabbing of a sensitive spot until there occurred the
welcomed 'unseemliness and indiscretion': all of which was then fully
publicised in his many letters and pamphlets of the time, finally
collected together in this volume.

In November, *Punch* published[29] a few paragraphs of a supposed
overheard conversation between Wilde and Whistler:

> … I suddenly heard the voice of Mr. Oscar Wilde discussing
> with Mr. Whistler and others the attributes of two well-known
> actresses. The criticism is at least expressive. "Sarah Bernhardt,"
> he said, "is all moonlight and sunlight combined, exceedingly
> terrible, magnificently glorious. Miss Anderson is pure and
> fearless as a mountain daisy. Full of change as a river. Tender,
> fresh, sparkling, brilliant, superb, placid."

The article continues in a sarcastic vein, describing the criticism as
having:

THE GENTLE ART

OF

MAKING ENEMIES

AS PLEASINGLY EXEMPLIFIED
IN MANY INSTANCES, WHEREIN THE SERIOUS ONES
OF THIS EARTH, CAREFULLY EXASPERATED, HAVE
BEEN PRETTILY SPURRED ON TO UNSEEMLINESS
AND INDISCRETION, WHILE OVERCOME BY AN
UNDUE SENSE OF RIGHT

A FOURTH EDITION

LONDON MCMVI
WILLIAM HEINEMANN

Title page of *The Gentle Art of Making Enemies*

an indefinite sort of charm in the meaningless mash up of empty adjectives, and inconsequent antitheses…

Wilde sent Whistler a telegram:[30]

Punch too ridiculous. When you and I are together we never talk about anything except ourselves.

To which Whistler, certainly never one to miss the chance of a self-aggrandising riposte, replied:

No, no, Oscar, you forget. When you and I are together we never talk about anything except me.

Both telegrams were published in newspapers and Whistler republished them in his collection. However, Whistler did not see fit to include Wilde's completion of the sequence with his final telegram:[31]

It is true, Jimmy, we were talking about you, but I was thinking of myself.

All this jocularity masked Whistler's exasperation with what Wilde was becoming.

Anticipation

THE BUILD-UP to Wilde's appearance in the many towns he visited varied a great deal. When returning to Dublin in November, the Irish Times described his reception on the day before his lecture:[32]

Mr. Oscar Wilde arrived last evening by the mail steamer from Holyhead. Notwithstanding the bitter cold wind a large number of gentle men assembled on the Carlisle Pier, and remained there until the steamer arrived, when they gave Mr. Wilde a welcome.

In the weeks and days before Wilde arrived to give his lecture, local newspapers' coverage ranged from extensive articles on the forthcoming visit, biographies and large advertisements containing the details, to hardly any mention at all. An example of the first variety was in Derby. Derby was one of the great industrial cities of the English Midlands with three major factories which spanned the entire history of porcelain manufacture in the United Kingdom. It was also the home of the industrial revolution with very early water powered factories and, in the nineteenth century, it became the headquarters of the Midland railways. Wilde's visit there had large newspaper advertisements[33] including an extensive synopsis of the lecture — one of which appeared the day before his lecture — and on the same day in a separate column, Wilde was proclaimed as:

> a man of unquestionable capacity, and his lecture can scarcely fail to be interesting and suggestive

The newspaper also pointed out that he is not 'simply conceited and eccentric', presumably in answer to the critics who thought that he — simply — was. Elsewhere there was an extended biography which begins by getting Wilde's date of birth wrong, having him born in 1853 instead of, accurately, the year after, or even, in line with Wilde's usual practice, a year or two after that. Wilde recognised that his youth was disappearing: 'those whom the gods love grow young'[34] was his aspiration and he spent most of his adult life subtracting one or two years from his age. He did this until his appearance in the dock on 3 April 1895 when he made that misrepresentation one time too many and was caught lying under oath by Edward Carson,[35] pretending to be thirty-nine when he was, in Carson's words, 'somewhat over forty'.[36] The rest of the biography covered his parents' attainments in detail and his education accurately, gave a few personal Oxford reminiscences before covering the publication of *Poems* with a very positive review by Oscar Browning[37] ('England is enriched with a new poet') and it presented the full text of one of Wilde's most famous and touching poems, *Requiescat*, about his dead sister, Isola. Notwithstanding the extensive pre-lecture coverage, the audience on the night was smaller than expected, which was attributed to the poor weather, although it was reported that the audience constituted 'a considerable number of ladies and gentlemen who listened ... throughout with evident appreciation.'[38]

Looking at an advertising campaign which was a little less extensive than that in Derby, Wilde's visit to the industrial north east of England included one of the smallest advertisements for his lectures I have come across.[39] In tiny Victorian typeface it reads, in its entirety:

> OSCAR WILDE
> IS COMING TO MIDDLESBROUGH

No date, time, place or reason was given for this visit: presumably the Teesside cognoscenti would find these details out for themselves. In comparison, in a column close by, was a slightly larger advertisement for *ASHES! ASHES!* available at the chemical works. If the size of the advertisement reflected the subject's importance, then Wilde needed to improve his standing in Middlesbrough. This was underlined when a local reporter queried the reasons for Wilde's appearance in their town:[40]

Why Middlesbrough should have been chosen ... one cannot tell. Of all local towns in unaestheticism we should say it bears the palm. Perhaps, however, it was with the view of inoculating a love of the beautiful into the blast furnace kings and brawny-armed toilers that Ironopolis was selected.

Quite.

Reception

WILDE'S reception at his lectures — even from the more prejudiced audiences — was generally very positive. His audiences soon became interested in the lecture (sometimes much to their own surprise) and were attentive, even rapt. Similarly with the reporters: most of the reviews were positive, particularly when commenting upon Wilde's lecturing style and ability:[41]

Mr. Wilde's charm was mainly that of literary grace. His definition of ugliness as "the immorality of art," for example, was decidedly smart, and his jaunty talk about "the criminal calendar of Europe, which ranges itself under the name of history," was properly calculated to impress people.

Wilde was already famous and many reviews began with a statement about the audience being attracted because of Wilde's notoriety rather than because of their interest in hearing the content of the lectures. Again, in Middlesbrough:[42]

It was evident that many of those who went to hear him ... did so more from a feeling of curiosity than anything else. They wanted to see what the much talked-of "Oscar" was like.

Even in his home city of Dublin, notwithstanding Wilde's reception at the harbour side the evening before:[43]

It was a strictly select audience, that came rather by reason of curiosity, and out of compliment to the notoriety of the lecturer, than any sympathy with, the exaggerated art principle which he is popularly understood pre-eminently to represent.

Among that strictly select audience were Constance with friends and family, and the young W. B. Yeats[44] was also there.[45] The bored or cynical audiences were few in number but there were some. The most awful audience I have come across was described in a review of a lecture in the Free Trade Hall, Manchester in October, where the reporter first writes:[46]

... this famous, or, perhaps, I should say notorious, apostle of culture was going to pay a visit to the head centre of cotton and Philistinism, I determined to spend an evening in listening to the quite too intensely utter style of oratory practised by the would-be regenerator of society, Oscar Wilde.

The sarcastically negative attitude towards Wilde and the similarity of the reporters' views in both Manchester and Middlesbrough, questioning his visit to such philistine towns, illustrates what an uphill task Wilde had. The review continues:

So wending my way to the Free Trade Hall ... paying my humble "bob" at the wicket, proceeded upstairs to the gallery, where, on looking round found the great hall nearly empty ... long rows of forms tenantless, a few people sparsely scattered on the front benches of the various class of seats ... the occupants of the sixpenny seats had evidently put in an appearance simply to have a lark; for, before the performance came off, one exuberant spirit unearthed from out of one of his pockets, a small mouse, which wandered into the front seats to the manifest alarm of such of the fair sex therein assembled, and after looking in terror around slowly made its way to the wall, where it was pounced upon and carried off by one of the attendants amidst a round of applause. During the lecture several of these sixpenny folk rose from their seats and walked off, making as much noise as they possibly could, and annoying both the lecturer and lectured, as far as I am concerned, I consider it a most caddish example of bad taste, and only regret that it occurred in Manchester.

Poor Wilde. At least these bad experiences seem to be at a rare minority of lectures but they must have been very unsettling for him. The reporter, though, abandoned his negativity having listened to Wilde:

... his lecture was rather interesting ... Taking it all round it wasn't nearly as bad as I expected, and I shall go to see him when he comes again.

Sherard is inconsistent in how he describes Wilde's reaction to lecturing, in one biography he says that the lectures were not distasteful to him whereas in another he seemed to dislike the work.[47] It probably depended upon his reception. In contrast to Manchester's 'long rows of forms tenantless,' the curiosity and interest of the general public resulted in some enormously successful attendances. In Hull where the lecture hall held nine hundred:[48]

The Royal Institute was crowded to excess

and in Chesterfield larger accommodation had to be found:[49]

> ... a large audience — an audience comprising well nigh all the leading families of the neighbourhood — assembled ... to hear Mr. Oscar Wilde ... It had been intended that the lecture should be given in the lecture room, but owing to the numerous audience an adjournment had to be made to the large hall

In Ayr:[50]

> ... there was an extraordinary demand for tickets — so much so that the sale had to be stopped before mid-day on Tuesday. Half an hour before the proceedings were to commence the hall was crowded in every part.

In Nottingham[51] just before Christmas, Wilde was described as having attracted a magnificent audience:

> The large hall of the Mechanics' Institution was crowded ... in every part, platform included, with a good humoured and attentive audience ...

and what is more, they were delighted with his performance:

> He is decidedly and emphatically a wag. His aestheticism is all veneer, and underneath there is a good deal of genuine Irish fun.

In Birkenhead, where the young Richard Le Gallienne[52] was in the audience:[53]

> The Music Hall was densely crowded ... there was a very large audience ... as large a number as the hall would hold, and the stewards had some difficulty in finding seats for all who came to hear and see.

Of course, not all his audiences were so large and there were some smaller attendances, but these were usually attributed to the bad weather on those evenings as his lecture tour trudged through the winter.

Whatever the number in the audience, they were generally described as being of a high class: a strictly select audience[54] or of quality.[55] It was clearly seen as important that Wilde should draw an audience from the higher levels of society and in Middlesbrough the review of the lecture[56] stated that Wilde had not attracted the many but:

The principal families of Middlesbrough were well represented, and a good sprinkling of Stocktonians were present.

After he had been in Derby, Wilde wrote three letters[57] to people he had met, and these give us an impression of his activities when not on stage. His reception must have been very positive because Wilde's letters are to thank people for their kindness, providing visits to the Crown Derby Porcelain Company and for the gift of an 'exquisite specimen' of Derby china which 'will always be to me one of the little masterpieces of my collection'. In December, Wilde wrote to William Bemrose[58] of Derby thanking him for an example of the Crown Derby porcelain which he had sent and commenting that:

> The more I see of the English provinces the more confident I get about the future of our handicrafts and decorative arts …

Bemrose had also sent a pamphlet he had written and Wilde wrote to say that it accorded with much he had to say in his lectures. This pamphlet is a brochure published to accompany the *Gladstone Dessert Service* which the company had just produced.[59] This service of twenty-six pieces had been funded by subscription and was from the 'Liberal Working Men of Derby' to be presented to Gladstone[60] on 22 December. The brochure gives a history of the Crown Derby Company and describes the Gladstone Service in great detail. These details include descriptions of the flowers painted on the plates by a venerable master who still worked at the company:

> This floral tribute … consists of simple old-world flowers, of which the rose is the most showy. "Posies" he calls them in his unpretentious way. They are the flowers of William Shakespeare, and not of Oscar Wilde; the blooms of quaint country-gardens, moss-grown and still, and not of aesthetic drawing rooms of the languorous lily and peacock school of art.

I think that we can safely presume that Wilde had actually not come across this sentence before he had replied to Bemrose so positively. Later in the year Wilde wrote to the librarian at Worcester to thank him for showing him around the city:[57]

> I have most pleasant memories of my morning in Worcester with you, and of all the lovely things you showed me from the blue and white Worcester china down to the gilded king before the altar.

For a week in late November the Carl Rosa Opera Company was playing at the Newcastle Tyne Theatre and, on the Wednesday, Wilde lectured on *The House Beautiful* at the Literary and Philosophical

Society, 500 yards away. After his lecture Wilde was invited to the performance and joined the audience, which was crowded almost to excess, and spent the rest of his evening watching Bizet's *Carmen*.[61]

Following these lectures in the north east, Wilde was invited to spend his weekend with family friends — Emily Thursfield and her family — in the lovely seaside town of Tynemouth[62] east of Newcastle-upon-Tyne.

We begin to build up a picture of Wilde's life at this time and the invitations he received. Here, then, is the other side of the lecture tour and the endless nights stuck in hotels: a relatively unknown social life, filling in the empty hours that are a natural accompaniment to travelling on one's own from town to town. I am certain that this did not happen everywhere, but from the invitations he received which we now know of, we get a broader picture of Wilde's life on the road.

With a lecture tour of these proportions there were occasional problems. The first of these was at Bournemouth on 3 November when Wilde failed to show up at the advertised time. One newspaper reported this[63] whilst laying on the puns rather over-heavily:

> On Saturday a large and fashionable audience assembled in the Theatre Royal, Bournemouth, to hear Mr. Oscar Wilde lecture on "The House Beautiful," so it was only right that there should have been "a beautiful house" present on the occasion. Unfortunately, the lecturer did not appear, and after waiting an hour, Mr. Nash, the manager, returned the audience their money, whereat, though there was no Oscar, nearly everyone was "Wilde." Whether the manager was found Nashing his teeth, we know not, as we are unacquainted with his Nationality.

Wilde wrote to Nash to apologise[64] and his letter was published in the local newspaper. He said he had arrived to find that the lecture was planned for the afternoon but:

> through an oversight on the part of my secretary I was led to suppose that my lecture was fixed for tonight.

Appleton probably received a reprimand — assuming it was he who was at fault — and the lecture was hastily reorganised. In fact they added an extra lecture and Wilde appeared at very short notice on the following Friday and Saturday when he lectured to large and appreciative audiences on both occasions.

One should either be a work of art, or wear a work of art.

WILDE'S APPEARANCE always came in for a great deal of comment. In many newspaper reviews these personal observations drowned out a short, almost incidental report of the actual content of the lecture. Reviewers considered the first and most important fact was Wilde's dress because, as virtually every newspaper reported, with a feigned apology, he was not wearing velveteen, knee-breeches, lace cuffs and buckled shoes. In Hull,[65] just as everywhere else:

> Those who came expecting to see a gentleman attired *à la* Bunthorne, and conducting himself after the manner of that character of *Patience* notoriety, must have been much disappointed

Instead, for his daytime wear, Wilde continued with his light trousers, black velvet waistcoat and velvet jacket from the breast pocket of which peeped a crushed strawberry silk handkerchief. He wore a crushed strawberry silk tie and his shirt cuffs — Vandyke cuffs — were turned back over his coat sleeves. He wore it with aplomb, dressing:[66]

> ... of an afternoon like others in his own rank, perhaps with a little more taste: the light trousers, dark frock coat, yellow kids, shirt cuffs that overlap the sleeves of his coat, and an orange-coloured handkerchief in his breast, forming a costume that becomes him to perfection, and harmonises well with his easy, elegant manners.

At the evening lectures his dress was described as being like ordinary men — arrayed as nearly in ordinary evening dress as could be expected[67] — except in the odd particular. And with more details of these odd particulars, in Dundee:[68] his vest, which was double-breasted, was of black satin, and cut to exhibit a liberal display of linen. In the shirt front there was but one large gold stud. From underneath the vest there peeped out a pink silk handkerchief. His tie was of black satin, and his collar a folding one of peculiar design. The cuffs of his shirt overlapped the sleeves of his coat. His boots were patent leather without design. The jewellery he wore consisted of two large-sized signet rings one on the third finger of each hand, and two great seals of uncommon design suspended from a fob pocket by a black silk ribbon.

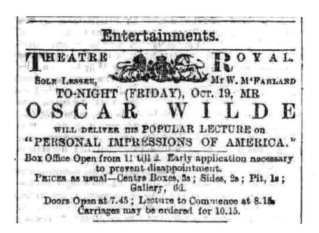

Wilde delivers his popular lecture in Dundee.

In the evening at Galashiels in southern Scotland:[69]

> Mr. Wilde is nothing if he is not a well-dressed and well got-up
> man; from the tips of his ambrosial curls to the tips of his
> beautiful boots he is an harmonious study in black and white …
> Mr. Wilde's revival of the old-fashioned style of dress, the coat
> and the cuffs, the watch-fob and the trouser-straps of our
> fathers has in it something which appeals … because they
> dressed with immensely more care and studied effect than their
> successors in these degenerate times.

His dress was described as being a revival of older styles: of fifty years
ago,[70] or:

> The style might be fairly described as savouring of the George
> III period.[71]

His cuffs, termed 'Van Dyke', and the pink silk handkerchief were
mentioned in almost all reviews. The handkerchief was variously
described as orange, salmon coloured or even terracotta but was
generally accepted to be 'crushed strawberry'. Wilde's delicate little
watch occupied the more modern fob in the waistcoat. As he walked
onto the stage, he carried gloves in one hand and a white
handkerchief in the other (this handkerchief seemingly having a
practical rather than the purely decorative role of his crushed
strawberry silk one.)

Occasionally Wilde wore a buttonhole, a feature for which he was
to become so famous:

> A really well-made buttonhole is the only link between Art and
> Nature.[72]

Examples were at Birkenhead where 'a flower of modest dimensions
adorn(ed) his well fitting dresscoat'[73] and at Hull where he however
displayed a lily in the button-hole of his coat[74] for his evening lecture.
This lily buttonhole was the only floral symbol which Wilde allowed
to link him to his fabled greenery-yallery days.

After his outfits, Wilde's overall physique and hairstyle were the
subject of much comment because both varied from his audience's
expectations, formed by Du Maurier's cartoons in *Punch*. Of course,
Wilde claimed to be very happy with his new hairstyle but something
had happened to it whilst supervising *Vera* in New York: there are
three photographs by Sarony[75] taken in August where Wilde's
hairstyle is definitely not Neronian but cut short and straight with a
fringe. He must have had second thoughts and let it grow again
because his hairstyle's reception on the recommenced lecture tour was
variously reported — and not very flatteringly — as being 'slightly
curly, tousled, long and curly, profusely spread over his head and
forehead, dressed in classic Greek style, brought down in the shape of
a "lunatic fringe" over the forehead' and in Ayr:[76]

> his hair, instead of hanging down upon his shoulders, as it was
> wont to do, is in a frowsy brown mass coming down upon the
> brow, somewhat after the style adopted by some "girls of the
> period".

I am certain that this variety of descriptions of his hairstyle was, in
part, linked to the availability — or, rather, non-availability — of
hairdressers for men in the towns he visited. It must have needed
fairly constant attention to keep it truly Neronian. I imagine there
were few hairdressers up to such a task in Hull, Glasgow and
Middlesbrough (or, to be fair, almost everywhere), which could have
resulted in the self-inflicted frowsy brown mass he seemingly
exhibited at times. Wilde's hair and its maintenance is reminiscent of
Algernon's response in *The Importance of Being Earnest*:[77]

> CECILY: I hope your hair curls naturally. Does it?
> ALGERNON: Yes, darling, with a little help from others

and if he did not get that 'little help from others' it seems he ended up
with a 'lunatic fringe'.

Apart from his hairstyle and clothes, Wilde's overall physical
appearance was scrutinised very closely; he so clearly was not a thin,
lank aesthete. In Aberdeen this dilemma was described in detail:[78]

> No man has been more diversely limned — not to say twisted,

tortured, caricatured — than Mr Wilde ... *Punch* began it with Postlethwaite, Burnand aggravated it with Streyke, and Gilbert capped it with Bunthorne. ... The mental confusion that naturally enough some of us had fallen into with regard to the personal appearance of the typical aesthete might well have accounted for an anxiety, had it appeared, to behold what manner of man he is. Somebody said that all celebrated people lose on a close view. The reverse is the case with Mr Wilde: he gains. No one ... expect(ed), after all one has read, to find that he is a tall, well-built, decidedly interesting young gentleman. ...

And in Chester:[79]

They must likewise have been compelled at a glance to disabuse their minds of the preconceived most erroneous ideas about a "pallid and lean" or "a foot-in-the-grave young man"; for it would be well to understand that Mr Oscar Wilde exhibits no alarming symptoms of becoming the tenant of an early grave.

The newspaper readers were also disabused in Shrewsbury:[80]

his manner is not languid nor does he limp. In stature he is rather above the medium height and he is exceptionally well-built.

This tall, 'exceptionally well-built' aesthete without a limp (it was, of course, suggested that he was 'limp', not that he had one) was described in Middlesbrough as:[81]

a young man of fairly good physique, inclined much more to *embonpoint* than to unnatural sleekness.

Whilst lecturing in Birkenhead, Richard Le Gallienne was in the audience and gives us a good description and impression of Wilde at the time from the perspective of one who first saw him as a lecturer and then got to know him and lived within his artistic circle in London in the 1890's. Of the Birkenhead experience (10 December 1883), in an affectionate yet not uncritical description,[82] he says Wilde:

...was known only as ... a ridiculous, posturing figure, a fantastic laughing-stock, whom no one took seriously. And yet I am glad to record to the credit of that Birkenhead audience, that, after its first bewilderment, it forgot to laugh at him, and soon began laughing with him ...

He describes him on the stage:

… Wilde had abandoned his knee-breeches and was dressed in a sort of Georgian costume, with tight pantaloon trousers and a huge stock. His amber-coloured hair, naturally straight, was not very long, and was unashamedly curled and massively modelled to his head, somewhat suggesting a wig. His large figure, with his big loose face, grossly jawed with thick, sensuous lips, and a certain fat effeminacy about him, suggested a sort of caricature Dionysius disguised as a rather heavy dandy of the Regency period. There was something grotesquely excessive about his whole appearance, and while he was in a way handsome, he made one think of an enormous doll, a preposterous, exaggerated puppet such as smile foolishly from floats at the Nice carnival. But his strong, humorous haughty eyes, his good brow and fine nose must not be forgotten from the general effect, nor his superb and rather insolent *aplomb*, which early dominated his audience. And, of course, his wonderful golden voice, which he modulated with elaborate self-consciousness. Exotic as he was, he was at the same time something entirely different from the dilettante, lily-like "aesthete" we had expected, and the great surprise about him was his impudent humour and sound common sense. That he could talk sense at all was a complete revelation.

Returning to the newspaper accounts we have in Chester:[83]

Mr Wilde looked a poet no doubt, though perhaps not like a great poet, but he was good-looking, plump, yet shapely, and on the whole conveyed the impression that aestheticism had not at all deranged his digestion.

Only the shallow know themselves

IN BRIGHTON, Wilde was seen as:[84]

tall and well-built; and, if it were not for a somewhat effeminate appearance, rendered all the more pronounced by the entire absence of beard or moustache, he may fairly lay claim to a good personal appearance.

This effeminacy was not an isolated observation, it was made by Le Gallienne in Birkenhead (above.) One Middlesbrough reporter was particularly harsh:[85]

a first impression being that a female in male attire was before the audience … of tall stature, finely proportioned, dark, swarthy, clean-shaved visage, with fairly-formed features, and masses of unparted black hair

Here, unlike in most places he visited, Wilde could not win over the reporter who developed this theme and his prejudices remained intact in a very negative review which described Wilde as having the:

> ... manner of a namby-pamby, lackadaisical effeminate type, with head almost continually leaning to either the left or the right; white kids, rolled and unrolled, and twiddled in the hands as a very girlish girl would clasp and play with her handkerchief.

The identification of Wilde as effeminate — the word being used several times — or as assuming feminine characteristics, does form a theme in some newspaper reviews. Sometimes this relates to the 'entire absence of beard or moustache': to be clean-shaven was seemingly an unusual choice for a man in the 1880's. It led me to consider what the word 'effeminate' actually meant to the newspaper reading public of the time. The term did seem to signify not so much the individual's sexuality (as we understand it now) but rather a man's attitude, morals and behaviour: the term is associated with a man who appears to be weak, morally lax, dresses as a dandy and has an interest in the arts. One implication was that the Victorians – including Wilde himself - considered that an effeminate man was attractive to women:[86]

> GWENDOLEN: The home seems to me to be the proper sphere for the man. And certainly once a man begins to neglect his domestic duties he becomes painfully effeminate. Does he not? And I don't like that. It makes men so very attractive...

Although described as a young man, Wilde would be twenty-nine years old in October 1883. Being very intelligent, egocentric and devoted to self-cultivation, I find it difficult to imagine that he could have been unaware of his own sexuality, whatever that was. Many biographers identify Wilde's homosexual activity as 'beginning' (whatever that may mean) in 1886, but to me this seems unrealistic. Whatever the finer tunings of the definition of the word in the 1880's, I feel with these mentions of effeminacy we are seeing some recognition of what the Victorians considered to be Wilde's 'lax morality', which fits, to a degree, with the suggestion that Wilde needed to marry to provide camouflage for his sexuality. From today's perspective we can look again at the comments about Wilde being tall and athletic, nature having been prodigal with her gifts, and re-interpret them. Whilst it is difficult to be certain of the meaning of such reports, the sub-text seems to have been of the 'he is a good looking man but you'd be surprised' variety. His deeper nature was being found out.[87] Combined with Wilde's love of baiting the press, this was producing a lethal combination which would eventually explode at his trials in 1895. Not only was Wilde seen as epitomising effeminacy in the 1880's but he would go on to redefine the term in the mid 1890's.

On the stage

FOR MOST of his lectures, Wilde appeared on an empty stage, alone, entering from the wings or climbing the steps from the auditorium and introduced himself with a bow. On some occasions there was a chairman who made a few introductory comments, not always too helpful to Wilde, but in Ayr he was accompanied onto the platform not just with a chairman but with some of the most high ranking gentry of the area. The local newspaper named them with relish:[88]

> On the motion of Mr Kennedy of Dunure, Major-General Alexander was called to the chair. Amongst the other gentlemen on the platform were - Lord Oranmore and Browne; Sir Archibald Campbell of Blythswood; Mr Campbell of Craigie, M.P.; Colonel Allan, Rosebank; Colonel Hamilton Campbell of Netherplace; Mr Somervell of Sorn; Major Douglass; Mr C.G. Shaw, Mr William Pollock, Mr W.H. Johnstone, Woodside Terrace, Glasgow; Dr Ronald, Dr Somerville, Mr John Murdoch, R.D. Murdoch, &c.

They must have made a terrifically impressive appearance on the stage and quite a statement of Wilde's acceptance by some of the most elevated members of Scottish Society. This must have been very encouraging for Wilde who, notwithstanding his avowed left-wing leanings, seemed to crave the approval of the rich and titled and, indeed, revelled in it later in his life. To add to the overpowering impression, as well as the massed gentry:[89]

> the platform was profusely decorated with pot plants according to the aesthetic lecturer's taste

This was definitely a first: stage or 'artistic' furniture decorated the platform on several occasions, but a selection of the finest pot plants was unique.

Other than at the very earliest lectures, Wilde lectured without notes of any sort and so did not need a lectern, or indeed a table, other than as somewhere to deposit his white gloves. At some venues more had been done with the stage, sometimes local entrepreneurs took the opportunity to illustrate some of the ideas which Wilde would be expounding by exhibiting their own wares. At the desperate lecture at

THE "WILDE" SUITE.

COMPRISING

5FT. ART GREEN SIDEBOARD, with plate-glass panel back.

SIX   „   RUSH SEAT CHAIRS.

TWO   „   CARVING CHAIRS.

6FT. by 3FT. 9IN. ART GREEN DINING TABLE, with patent extending screw.

THE WHOLE COMPLETE

2 2   G U I N E A S.

TO BE SEEN AT

KENNARD'S

FURNISHING WAREHOUSE,

19, GRAND PARADE, ST. LEONARDS.

Advertisement for a "Wilde" dining suite in Art Green

The Free Trade Hall, though, the stage decoration merely amounted to:[90]

> a very small table covered with a dirty crimson cloth, a solitary chair, and a small desk on four ricketty looking legs

However, at Dublin, the stage was more elaborately set:[91]

> it was a morning room ... the prevailing tone or "note", as Mr Oscar Wilde would say...was sober, or, should we say, *pianissimo?* ... the total effect was quite charming and picturesque ...

and in Malvern:[92]

> The hall was profusely ornamented by the aid of screens, tapestry, and other ornamental furniture, kindly lent by various tradespeople of the town.

I do not think that Wilde or his management team had any role in choosing the furniture on the stage but this decoration could lead to slight digs in Wilde's direction. In Dublin the newspaper report[93] moved into a more frivolous tone when contrasting the stage furnishings with the lecture:

> ... it is, however, necessary to notice one unresolved discord which it is curious did not jar upon the delicate nerves of Mr

Oscar Wilde. This was a horribly practical tin coal-scuttle, of a hopelessly commonplace type ... but when later the lecturer passed some severe strictures upon coal-scuttles in general, those who heard him found a little difficulty in understanding how he could tolerate this one in particular.

In Hastings things were taken even further and an enterprising Mr Kennard's shop in Grand-parade exhibited:[94]

> ... the "Wilde" dining-room suite ... comprising six rush-seat chairs, two carved chairs, a dining table, with patent extension, and a sideboard, with plate glass panel. Each is worked in art green, and, being of artistic design, makes a very pleasing effect in a row, while the price is, at the same time, moderate.

This was a time before the question of controlling the use of one's name had been grappled with.

Wilde's Delivery

ACROSS the country, Wilde's delivery came in for many compliments:[95]

> The lecture was spoken without book, and was delivered in a clear, well-cultivated voice, and easy graceful manner, with occasionally a little helpful action of head and hand

Whilst this was a typical description of Wilde's lecturing style, some reporters had their tongues in their cheeks:[96]

> The attitude and style of this interesting young man during the delivery of his lecture were, of course, the acme of perfection. He disposed of his hands – those very awkward adjuncts of the public speaker – in the most ingenious fashion. Now he would be toying gracefully with a crumpled glove, which eventually found its way to the table, and there underwent a series of 'aesthetic' manoeuvres, according to the momentary whim of the owner. Then Mr Wilde — with one foot carefully advanced to give the form the 'line of beauty' — would bring one hand up to the front of his waistcoat and allow it a brief interval of rest, whilst the other found its way to the hip, to be there reposed. The style of Mr Wilde's delivery was graceful and fluent, and, as the lecture was well mixed with 'funniosities', there were frequent rounds of laughter — duly suppressed, of course, so that the Lecturer's refined sense of the 'fitness of things' might not be rudely shocked.

This stance was described elsewhere and is illustrated in some cartoons of the time. In Shrewsbury his easy style as a natural storyteller was described[97] as speaking:

> … to the audience with all the ease, familiarity, and absence of oratorical display that might be expected from a traveller describing his journeyings to a group of friends around a snug fire-side. This, indeed, is one of Mr Wilde's peculiarities, and it is one of his attractions also. If he tells a droll story or perpetrates a good joke, he seems quite unaware of the fact, and makes his audience laugh all the more by a glance at his own immovable features

His style, humour and delivery did win over audiences throughout the UK, many commenting upon his language being 'epigrammatic, eloquent and humorous'; delivered 'clearly and distinctly', in 'clear, pleasing tones, without note or reference of any kind'. He managed to baffle some of his audience with his peculiar power of satire and many commented, as in the extract above, that the funnier his story, the straighter his face. At Nottingham, the suspicion was that he was pulling their legs:[98]

> … a quiet manner of delivery, but he is decidedly original and quaint…in a distinct but humorous manner worked the audience into that state that they wondered whether or not he was patronising and "chaffing" them. He told his drollest stories with the gravest face, and the more improbable became his narrative the more serious was his whole aspect.

His presentation was the well-practised effect of a tried, tested and accurately honed script. However, the lectures were given without notes which I think produces the variations in his delivery as he moves the order of the text around to suit his thoughts on that particular day. He must have relished some variation as a means of keeping himself interested in the subjects he repeatedly lectured about. And in the applause and laughter, which were reported as greeting many of his best lines, we are seeing the play of his witty, off-the-Vandyke-cuff delivery for which he would become so famous. At this stage, he was becoming renowned as a wit and Frank Harris describes him:[99]

> At this time he was a superb talker, more brilliant than any I have ever heard in England, but nothing like what he was to become later.

And he clearly used all his wit and ability to produce the amusing effect upon his audiences that he both desired and achieved.

The House Beautiful

S O WHAT were the messages of *The House Beautiful*? It is true that certain themes had been drawn from his American lectures as his lecture flyers announced. However, the lecture had been significantly recast to suit the circumstances in the UK and to better reflect Wilde's current thoughts. This was a lecture which evolved during the autumn of 1883 and spring of 1884, and a full text is given in Appendix C which illustrates the lecture as it was given in early 1884. Here, though, is a summary of Wilde's main points taken from the lecture given during late 1883.

Wilde had already signalled his interest in housing issues in his lecture to art students, *Modern Art Training,* when he had roundly criticised London developments:

> street after street of the most foolish and stupid architecture that the world has ever seen; architecture, where every lovely Greek form is desecrated and defiled, and every lovely Gothic form defiled and desecrated, reducing three-fourths of the London houses to being, merely, like square boxes of the vilest proportions, as gaunt as they are grimy, and as poor as they are pretentious - the hall door always of the wrong colour, and the windows of the wrong size ...

The pamphlets published by Morse to advertise *The House Beautiful* described the lecture as:

> The lecture, 'The House Beautiful,' is, for the most part, an exposition of the application of the principles of true artistic decoration to the exterior and interior of the homes of the people. He takes up in detail each one of the elements that enter into the complete artistic furnishing of a room, and gives elaborate schemes of colour and art decoration which properly supplement each other. He points out the defects and inconsistencies which, under our present style, produces in many cases a sense of discord and inharmoniousness, not easy to define, but which, if once brought to notice, can always hereafter be avoided. Mr. Wilde will also offer some observations upon style and colour in dress for the house and in the street: on the influence of artistic surroundings upon children: and on the value of handicrafts as the basis of education. The lecture will contain the principal portion of the address delivered by Mr. Wilde during his late American tour, together with much additional matter relative to the present position and future development of art decoration in this country.

This makes it quite clear Wilde is dealing with the 'homes of the people' rather than the more lavish and expensive interior decoration undertaken by, and for, the rich. However, he did use descriptions of rooms decorated at considerable expense by Whistler, Leighton and other artists, particularly those in the new artists' colony in Holland Park,[100] as examples of his general principles of house design and decoration. Wilde is already identifying some of his thoughts upon dress which were to become an important subject for him in the following year, and developing his ideas about education which he would form into a new lecture early in 1884. In summary:[101]

> Mr Wilde took a most searching view of the exterior and interior, and contents of a modern English dwelling, and showed in clear and logical terms how to furnish a house and "how not to do it." In the building and furnishing of a house the chief ends in view were durability, substantiality, comfort, beauty, and harmony, and the faults to be avoided were imitations, superfluous decorations, and discord in colours … the cold-blooded fashion in which the lecturer demolished the "household gods," in the form of the dearly treasured gim-cracks of the model housewife, was enough to drive any maiden aunt of ordinary susceptibilities to distraction.

Lecturing at Derby in October, as well as the extensive advertisements, Wilde was given the most fulsome build-up in the local press. The synopsis of his lecture that the newspaper printed[102] was very detailed and included statements such as:

> … His own observations and experience, together with the complete art training which he has had, have made him an authority upon this subject … He gives elaborate schemes of colour … He points out the obvious defects and inconsistencies, which under our present style produce in many cases a sense of discord and inharmoniousness. … He illustrates all these remarks by descriptions of the most celebrated houses and rooms of the modern painters, Whistler, Millais,[103] Alma Tadema,[104] etc. …

Goodness knows what Whistler would have said had he read this article puffing Wilde with the 'complete art training' which had made him such an authority and enabled him to comment upon Whistler's own designs of house decoration. Whistler's fabulous Peacock Room[105] – entitled *Harmony in Blue and Gold* – was completed in 1877 to the considerable unhappiness of its owner, Frederick Leyland, who

Whistler's *Harmony in Blue and Gold*

felt that Whistler had massively overspent his budget without approval. Of course, this dispute would descend to rancour. Other than this lavish room, Wilde admired Whistler's design and decoration of the room for his exhibition of a second set of etchings of Venice in February 1883:[106]

> a yellow and white room (decorated by the master of course)

The other two artists mentioned in the flyer — Millais and Alma-Tadema — together with Leighton, were involved in building and interior design projects of their own:[107]

> The red brick purpose-built studio-house was a distinctive Victorian contribution to domestic architecture ... they were indeed expressive of their owners in interesting ways. ... Both Leighton and Alma-Tadema were awarded Gold Medals by the Royal Institute of British Architects for their exceptional knowledge of architecture.

Leighton's house must have been influential for Wilde. The interior design:[108]

> ... blended art from different world cultures. In (the) hall for instance, Leighton had Japanese pots standing on a mosaic floor

inspired by ancient Pompeii, under a seventeenth century Turkish wedding chest that had been adapted as a seat for the stairs.

Leighton's Silk Room featured sage green silk wall coverings as a background to the paintings and, in a superb display, in the Arab Hall there were tiles from Damascus, a frieze by Walter Crane,[109] work on the dome involving Burne-Jones and deep blue tiles designed and manufactured by William De Morgan.[110] This hall includes, high up, an extensive latticework window of the overlooking Egyptian mashrabiya[108]. Wilde would mention such features in *The House Beautiful* as perfect examples of interior decoration. The Arab Hall exemplified Leighton and Wilde's love of art and decoration from all times and all cultures: they both believed, as did Pater, that all beautiful things can exist together in harmony.[111]

Wilde was not always complimentary about the halls in which he lectured. For example, when he was speaking in the Banqueting Room of the Royal Pavilion in Brighton,[112] he said:

> he was not quite sure he would not quarrel with the man who decorated that room, for he thought he had mistaken the whole meaning of Art

In his lecture, though, he would be more positive about other buildings and:[113]

> … gave as perfect specimens of decorative art … the Alhambra in Spain, and St. Mark's at Venice

although it was made clear that these rather ambitious examples of interior decoration were ideal expressions of his theories.

In Dorchester Wilde began his lecture:[114]

> I do not desire to give any history of art … nor to give any abstract philosophical definition of beauty. What we in this century desire is to be able to surround ourselves with beautiful things. As to defining what beauty is, we are quite content to leave that to the 20th century.

This was essentially the re-use of his opening lines in *Modern Art Training* where, in turn, Wilde is paraphrasing Pater's *Preface* to *The Renaissance*. During the lecture he dealt with the exterior and interior of a house from a decorative viewpoint, criticising some contemporary architectural styles:[115]

> In London, where South Kensington has made its harrowing inroads among us, with the Corinthian chimney pots, and Doric porticoes, the outside of the houses are extremely ugly.

Wilde recommended red brick as the most desirable material for the outside of a house and his contemporary architectural preference was for the 'Queen Anne' style of exterior design. The Queen Anne style included fine brickwork varied with terracotta panels or tile-hung upper stories. Other characteristics were white woodwork and blond stonework detailing, oriel windows, corner towers, asymmetrical fronts, deeply shadowed entrances and broad porches. All these features were exemplified in some of the houses being constructed in the developments at Holland and Bedford Parks. However, when he lectured in Aberdeen he did recognise how different the local building materials were compared to those available in England:[116]

> ... here in Scotland, where we had a stone country, he did not know that it would be very practical to advise us to join with them in England with their red brick Queen Anne houses ... But he did not see why the white and greystone outsides should not be made far more beautiful than they were by bands of various coloured stones, such as they used in Venice by laying in a shield of coloured marble.

Before moving to the inside of the house, he dealt with doors which:[117]

> Should show as much as possible the character of the wood of which they were made, or they might be painted with a light shade of green

Just inside the door, linoleum or floorcloth were deprecated for the hall floor, Wilde recommended tiled or stone flooring. As regards decorating the walls:[118]

> He would not have pictures in the hall, because to have good pictures there would be injurious; and as for bad pictures, they should be nowhere.

He suggests that William Morris had laid down some sound rules for the decoration of our homes.[119] The first was:

> Have nothing in your house you do not think to be beautiful or know to be useful.[120]

and the second:

> Have nothing in your house you do not think to be a pleasure to the man who made it and do not afford pleasure to you when you look at it.[121]

There was a third rule:

> not to have any imitation of one material in another, not to

paint one wood like another more costly, or to paint wood or
iron like stone

which, while he agreed with it, had been exaggerated by Ruskin, who
declared that it was extremely immoral, reducing the owner of the
house to the permanent telling of falsehoods to everybody who
happened to call. Ruskin felt that was a kind of depravity whilst
Wilde considered Ruskin was taking it a little too far:[122]

> ... the morality of art was beauty, and its immorality was
> ugliness. ...

Wilde contended that the first consideration for the home owner
when decorating a room was to establish a colour scheme. He thought
that all colours were beautiful, just as musical notes were, but it was
their juxtaposition that could be displeasing:[123]

> There should be some scheme of colour predominant in the
> decoration of each room, remembering that, whilst all colours
> were beautiful, it was only the secondary ones which were
> useful for the purposes of house decoration.

It was important to strike a harmonious note throughout a room with
a background of neutral colours predominating:

> As to the use of colours in decoration, ... they should always
> begin with a low tone, and keep the high primary colours in
> reserve for the delicate and more precious materials and a pure
> note of colour was perhaps best left untouched by design.

He was in favour of plain walls instead of wallpaper but he did
speak favourably of Japanese leather and he preferred to break up
the wall with a wooden dado and a frieze at the top:[124]

> Pure colour was often more satisfactory in wall paper than
> recurring pattern. He often wondered that they did not use deal
> wainscoting ... with a stamped leather frieze ... or a plain
> distempered plaster wall would often make a very pretty room.

Wilde highlighted the need for the panelling, not papering, of
ceilings to give interest rather than being a blank, white, flat surface.
Other features which he encouraged were the carrying up of
shelving to the ceiling either around a mantelpiece or doorway so
that the owner's items of china and glass could be exhibited. He also
showed his Eastern influences by supporting the use of fretwork,
lattices and tiles with an Islamic influence.

He then moved on to tell his audiences how 'more ordinary
methods of artistic decoration' could be applied to their houses.

Windows were such important features in a room, they[125]

> ... ought not to be so large as they often are. They create not a proper light, but a glare, which is not what is wanted. Besides, said Mr. Wilde humorously, they only encourage us in that bad habit of looking into the streets to see what our neighbours are doing, and they also encourage our neighbours in the still worse habit of looking in at our windows to see what we are doing.

When Wilde was in Paris in early 1883 he had a hotel room that looked out over the Seine. Sherard commented[126] on the wonderful view but Wilde's response was:

> A gentleman never looks out of the window.

Glare and light were in the same relationship as noise and music. Glare needs to be avoided:[127]

> He advocated smaller panes of glass, and spoke very much in favour of artistically stained glass.

Moving on to the floor of the room:[128]

> The floor should not be carpeted all over, because it looked heavy, and Oriental carpets with a border were recommended.

He became famous for his comments on fireplaces:[129]

> ... the polished steel monstrosity was extremely irksome to the servants to clean ... with regard to the chimney pieces, he abhorred white marble, and would fling it out of the window if he had a chance

and on coal scuttles:[130]

> They did not want a deer of Landseer's or "Tintern Abbey by moonlight" upon the front of their coal scuttles: a plain brass scuttle was sufficiently beautiful.

It is interesting to see how Wilde maintained these views on interior decoration throughout his life. In a letter written almost two years later in May 1885[131] — at this time Constance and he had been living in Tite Street for five months — he picks out key parts of this doctrine from *The House Beautiful*: he emphasises the need to choose a 'scheme of colour ... for the room':

> I hope, and in my lectures always try and bring it about, that people will study the value of pure colour more than they do.

And he gives an example from his own home:

I have for instance a dining-room done in different shades of white, with white curtains embroidered in yellow silk…

He states that he does not like Morris' wallpapers:

They seem to me often deficient in real beauty of colour…[but] he is far more successful with those designs which are meant for textures which hang in folds

A plain wall is preferable and Wilde describes another room in his own house:

… with blue ceiling and frieze (distemper), yellow (oil) walls, and white woodwork and fittings, which is joyous and exquisite, the only piece of design being the Morris blue-and-white curtains, and a white-and-yellow silk coverlet.

He also includes many of these ideas in his description of Lord Henry's library in *The Picture of Dorian Gray*:[132]

It was, in its way, a very charming room, with its high panelled wainscoting of olive-stained oak, its cream-coloured frieze and ceiling of raised plasterwork, and its brickdust felt carpet strewn with silk, long-fringed Persian rugs'. … Some large blue china jars and parrot-tulips were ranged on the mantelshelf, and through the small leaded panes of the window streamed the apricot-coloured light of a summer day in London.

His interest in wallpapers continued to the end, a month before he died he famously complained about his room in the Hotel d'Alsace in Paris:[133]

My wallpaper and I are fighting a duel to the death. One or the other of us has to go.

Following his descriptions of good internal design, Wilde's lecture then moved onto the realm of education and the need for children to understand more of the decorative arts and to learn how to use their own hands. He pokes fun at the 'useful' nature of education at the time and what children were taught:[134]

If, instead of teaching little boys and girls the latitude and longitude of countries that no one wanted to go to — which was called geography — and all that criminal calendar of Europe, which was termed history — we were to teach them simple decorative arts, how much better we would make them, and what a source of knowledge and delight in after-life we would be giving to them …

Despite Wilde's wish to distance himself from Ruskin, this belief was strongly influenced by him. Schools themselves should become the most beautiful buildings in our towns and villages to encourage children to attend. The reporter in Derby approved of these sentiments:[135]

> But perhaps the most widely and permanently useful part of his discourse was that in which, after eulogizing the local prize exhibits in the Art Gallery, he insisted upon the national importance of educating children in various handicrafts. This, we believe, is one of the "questions of the day." Of book education we have enough and to spare. What we want now is a large increase in the means of technical education, both in our elementary schools and in our working-men's colleges and the like.

Wilde was clearly in tune with many, often in the manufacturing centres in the midlands and north of England, in his demands for a more practical education for children. This debate continues into our own day.

Wilde always concluded this lecture in the same way[136], with:

> ... a brilliant peroration, which was loudly applauded

along these lines:

> The mission of art was very simple. It had no very elaborate philosophy about it. It merely claimed to bring into the life of every one of them a little joy, to touch the fleeting hours of day and make them gracious.

Which is another restatement of the closing passage of the infamous *Conclusion* to Pater's *Renaissance*[137]. He then concludes:

> And if men ask me what creed one could get in this mysterious passion for beauty and love of art, I do not know what better answer one could give than what was said by an English poet of this century who loved beauty more purely and passionately than any since Shakespeare: John Keats. Somebody writing to Keats asked him to have reverence for some tradition of prejudice of his day, and Keats wrote back and said "I have not got the slightest reverence for anything in existence except for the Eternal Being, the memory of great men, and the principle of beauty."

This final quotation from Keats[138] was one Wilde was very fond of. What Keats had actually written was:[139]

I have not the slightest feeling of humility towards the public or
to anything in existence but the Eternal Being, the Principle of
Beauty, and the Memory of great Men

Wilde had intended to use this on the title page of his *Poems* and he
did use it to conclude his American lecture, *The English Renaissance of
Art.* In the letter Keats continued with greater acrimony:

... a Preface is written to the public — a thing I cannot help
looking upon as an enemy, and which I cannot address without
feelings of hostility.

Wilde had clearly decided that, whatever his feelings were, he would
omit any references to being hostile towards the public because it
might not go down too well with the very people who were providing
him with his only source of income.

Wilde finished this leg of his tour with a lecture at the Crystal
Palace on 21 December. Constance wrote that after this lecture he had
a week's holiday 'which will be much joy for me'.

Table 2: Lectures September to December 1883

DATE	TOWN	VENUE	TIME	LECTURE
Mon 24 Sep	Wandsworth	Town Hall		Personal Impressions of America
Tue 25 Sep?	Weymouth			
Wed 26 Sep	Exeter	Theatre Royal	evening	PIA
Sat 29 Sep	Bath	Theatre Royal	8:00 pm	PIA
Mon 1 Oct	Sutton Coldfield	Institute	evening	PIA
Tue 2 Oct	Harborne & Edgbaston	Institute		delayed to 3rd
Wed 3 Oct	Harborne & Edgbaston	Institute	8:00 pm	PIA
Thu 4 Oct	Dorchester	Town Hall	evening	The House Beautiful
Oct?	Oxford?			
Sat 6 Oct	Liverpool	Hope Hall	3:00 pm	PIA
Sat 6 Oct	Liverpool	Hope Hall	8:00 pm	PIA
Mon 8 Oct	Manchester	Free Trade Hall	8:00 pm	PIA
Wed 10 Oct	Erdington	Institute	8:00 pm	HB
?	Perry Bar	Institute		
Tue 16 Oct	Hull	Royal Institute	8:00 pm	HB
Thu 18 Oct	Aberdeen	Her Majesty's Theatre	3:30 pm	HB
Fri 19 Oct	Dundee	Theatre Royal	evening	PIA
Sat 20 Oct	Cupar	Union Street Hall	3:30 pm	HB
Sat 20 Oct	St Andrews	Town Hall	evening	PIA
Mon 22 Oct?	Stirling			
Tue 23 Oct	Galashiels	Mechanics Institute	8:00 pm	PIA
Wed 24 Oct	York			PIA?
Thur 25 Oct	Derby	Mechanics Institute	8:00 pm	HB

Fri 26 Oct	Chesterfield	Stephenson Memorial (large) Hall	8:00 pm	HB
Tues 30 Oct	Brighton	Royal Pavilion Banqueting Room	3:30 pm	HB
Wed 31 Oct	Brighton	Royal Pavilion Banqueting Room	3:30 pm	PIA
Thur 1 Nov	Hastings	Gaiety Theatre	3:30 pm	HB
Fri 2 Nov	Exeter?			
Sat 3 Nov	Bournemouth	Theatre Royal	afternoon	HB (Wilde late so cancelled)
Mon 5 Nov	Penzance	Institute		PIA
Tues 6 Nov ?	Budleigh Salterton			PIA
Thur 8 Nov	Torquay	Royal Theatre & Opera House		PIA
Fri 9 Nov	Bournemouth	Theatre Royal		PIA
Sat 10 Nov	Bournemouth	Theatre Royal		HB
Mon 12 Nov	Lichfield	St James' Hall	evening	HB
Tues 13 Nov	Leighton Buzzard	Corn Exchange	evening	PIA
Wed 14 Nov	Burton-on-Trent	St Paul's Institute		HB
Thur 15 Nov	Macclesfield	New Theatre Royal	evening	
Mon 19 Nov	Chester	Royalty Theatre	8:00 pm	HB
Tue 20 Nov?	Lecture*			
Thur 22 Nov	Dublin	Gaiety Theatre	3:00 pm	HB
Fri 23 Nov	Dublin	Gaiety Theatre	3:00 pm	PIA
Mon 26 Nov	Shrewsbury	Theatre Royal	8:00 pm	PIA
Tue 27 Nov ?	Sunderland			
Wed 28 Nov	Newcastle upon Tyne	Amphitheatre, Literary and Philosophical Society	night	HB

Thur 29 Nov	Middles-brough	Oddfellows Hall	evening	PIA
Fri 30 Nov	Newcastle upon Tyne	Lecture Hall, Literary and Philosophical Society	evening	PIA
Mon 3 Dec?	Lecture*			
Tues 4 Dec	Ayr	Town Hall	night	HB
Wed 5 Dec?	Lecture*			
Thur 6 Dec?	Lecture*			
Fri 7 Dec	Glasgow	St Andrew's Hall	8:00 pm	PIA
Mon 10 Dec	Birkenhead	Music Hall	night	PIA
Tues 11 Dec	Southport	Winter Gardens	3:30 pm	HB
Wed 12 Dec	Blackpool			HB
Thur 13 Dec	Stourbridge	Corn Exchange	night	HB
Fri 14 Dec	Malvern	Drill Hall	afternoon	HB
Fri 14 Dec	Malvern	Drill Hall	evening	PIA
Mon 17 Dec	Nottingham	Mechanics' Institution	evening	PIA
Tues 18 Dec	Worcester	The Theatre Royal	8:00 pm	HB
Wed 19 Dec?	Lecture*			
Thur 20 Dec?	Lecture*			
Fri 21 Dec	London	Crystal Palace	3:00 pm	HB

Key

? either a doubtful date or location

*a possible lecture indicated by the summary accounts

CHAPTER 3

January to Summer 1884

Marriage

THE YEAR 1884 began with newspapers reporting[1] that Wilde was the centre of attention in the Supreme Court of the United States of America. This was in a case under American copyright law about the use of one of the famous Sarony photographs taken in January 1882.[2] It was contested for Sarony that the picture which had been printed by the Burrows-Giles Lithographic Company was Sarony's 'invention', Sarony having

> arranged the said Oscar Wilde in a graceful position, and suggested and evoked the desired expression.

The defendants maintained that Sarony could not contend that he had invented or created Mr Oscar Wilde himself, therefore he had no right to protection as the author of the image. That was widely reported across the UK with great humour: reporters with tongues firmly in their cheeks objected with faux outrage that this American, Mr. Sarony, could possibly claim that he had 'invented' Oscar Wilde: our Oscar, Made in England. How dare he? The newspapers seemed to lose interest thereafter as the case wore on and it was in March, and seemingly then of no consequence to the English press, when Sarony won this landmark case, was awarded damages and US copyright protection was extended to photographs for the first time. So here we have Wilde inadvertently making legal history in the USA: as was always the case, anything he became involved with could become newsworthy and create controversy. His manipulation of the press, his perfectly delivered soundbites and his image were all managed in a way we now recognise in the modern cult of celebrity.

The Sarony photograph of Wilde considered by the
Supreme Court of the United States

This was to be a major year for both Wilde and his fiancée,
Constance Lloyd. During the first six months of the year Wilde would
metamorphose from fiancé, to bridegroom and then, in May and June,
to honeymooner in Dieppe and Paris. However, even though the
engagement was now three months old, newspapers were still

fascinated by Constance, the marriage to come and Wilde's plans for the future. In Newcastle it was reported[3] that

> the young lady who is to be married to Mr Oscar Wilde in spring has, it is said, a fortune of something like £18,000 in her own right.

The newspapers commented in a variety of ways,[4] some sarcastically, some not so, about his future:

> This will, I suppose, be the marriage of the season. It is true that since the collapse of aestheticism and the restoration of its votaries to a more rational frame of mind, Mr Oscar Wilde has slipped down from that pinnacle upon which he had perched himself

There would have been a great many matters to attend to, as anyone knows who has arranged a wedding. It is therefore surprising that very little correspondence from this period exists: of the few letters in *Complete Letters* which can be definitely dated to the first five months of 1884,[5] there are no letters from Wilde organising the wedding, just one inviting a single guest and none making arrangements for the honeymoon.

Civilising the Provinces

AFTER his week's break for Christmas, Wilde began January 1884 by immediately departing for a short tour of lectures in Ireland. At this time, Ireland was undivided and in its entirety was seen as part of the United Kingdom of Great Britain and Ireland. Many Irish possibly did not see it in quite the same way. His first lecture was in Belfast on 1 January and his lectures at this time continued to be *Personal Impressions of America* and *The House Beautiful,* both of which had been delivered many times during 1883. However, Wilde did introduce a new lecture — *The Value of Art in Modern Life* — which he gave just a few times before his marriage and he was to significantly revise this in the autumn.

After two nights in Belfast, Wilde began a great circuit of the island and travelled to Londonderry for two evening lectures, then down the west coast via Limerick (two nights) to Cork (another two nights), east to Clonmel then to the south coast at Waterford, north to Dundalk then back to Kingstown, Dublin from where he caught a ferry to Anglesey.

After his visit to Ireland Wilde resumed the lecture tour on the mainland with two lectures in the major industrial city of Sheffield at the southern edge of the West Riding of Yorkshire, then venues

NEW THEATRE ROYAL.
BELFAST.
MR. OSCAR WILDE'S LECTURES IN
BELFAST,
TUESDAY and WEDNESDAY, January, 1 & 2,
1884, MID-DAYS.

Mr. J. F. WARDEN has the honour to announce
that

MR. OSCAR WILDE
WILL DELIVER
TWO LECTURES
AT THE
NEW THEATRE ROYAL, BELFAST,
ON
TUESDAY and WEDNESDAY, Jan. 1 and 2.

On Tuesday Afternoon,
THE HOUSE BEAUTIFUL.

The true principles of Decorative Art as applied
to the exterior and decoration of the homes of the
people.
Doors open at 2. Lecture at 2·30. Carriages at 4.
On Wednesday Afternoon,
PERSONAL IMPRESSIONS OF AMERICA.

An address upon topics suggested by a year's
travel in the United States and Canada.
Doors open at 2. Lecture at 2·30. Carriages at 4.
Private Boxes, to hold 8, 40s; to hold 6, 30s; to
hold 5, 25s; to hold 4, 20s. Balcony Stalls, 4s.
Upper Circle, 2s. Pit, 1s. Gallery, 6d.
Box Office open from 10 till 3, where seats to
Balcony Stalls and Private Boxes may be secured
free of extra charge, or by letter or telegram ad-
dressed Mr. W. BRICKWELL.

Wilde's first lectures of 1884

OSCAR WILDE'S LECTURES.
LEAMINGTON .... *FRIDAY NEXT, March 7.*
CHELTENHAM .... *SATURDAY NEXT, March 8.*
WOLVERHAMPTON.... *MONDAY, March 10.*
WALSALL .... *TUESDAY, March 11.*
LEICESTER .... *WEDNESDAY, March 12.*
BIRMINGHAM .... *THURSDAY, March 13.* [783
AFTERNOON AND EVENING AT MIDLAND INSTITUTE.

Wilde's tour of the West Midlands in 1884

mainly in the north of England and Scotland until the end of February. In this period we have an almost complete listing of his lectures and his journeys make for interesting reading: it appears that an attempt was being made by his managers to try to ensure the lectures were located close to one another. It seems that a route was decided upon, venues booked and then extra lectures, sometimes slightly off that route, were slotted into the already planned series. For example, from Sheffield, Wilde travelled to Huddersfield, Kings Lynn, Lincoln, Halifax; then there is a blank Sunday, probably indicating a return to London to see Constance, followed by a full weeks' lectures: on the Monday, Gainsborough in Lincolnshire, then Harrogate, Chesterfield, York, Scarborough. Whilst the lectures are not too far apart, these routes are not the most efficient (eg Gainsborough — Harrogate — Chesterfield — York forms a rather inefficient criss-cross path across Yorkshire) but they are clearly not a selection of venues chosen at random.

Wilde stayed in the Royal Victoria Hotel next to Sheffield Victoria railway station (now defunct) and from there writes – as a very proud fiancé – two letters to Lillie Langtry and to Waldo Story. In these letters Wilde tells them — in an effusive fashion — about his love for Constance and their engagement. To Langtry he says they will be married in April (which eventually becomes the end of May) and describes how attractive he finds Constance:

> … a grave, slight, violet-eyed little Artemis, with great coils of heavy brown hair which make her flower-like head droop ...

He also reports that lecturing is making him quite rich but he misses Constance and telegraphs her twice a day. To Story he starts his letter by saying 'Amazing of course — that was necessary' which is a slightly odd comment, but Wilde always wanted to amaze people and perhaps he did see his engagement as an amazing response to the negative reports which were circulating. He also writes in a very similar way about Constance and adds:

> We are of course desperately in love. I have been obliged to be away nearly all the time since our engagement, civilising the provinces by my remarkable lectures.

He tells Story 'I am perfectly happy.' These letters read quite naturally and, to me, they undermine the claims that Wilde married purely to divert attention from his sexuality or to save himself from having to earn a living (which the marriage did not accomplish, in any case.) Even if one or both of these motives were present, from the evidence of the letters we do have, these do not seem to be the sole reasons for his marriage.

Anticipation

THERE WAS STILL considerable interest in Wilde and all that he did. The coverage of his lectures during the autumn and winter of 1883 had been widespread and this interest continued into 1884. In Huddersfield it was reported:[6]

> Although Mr. Oscar Wilde does not occupy the prominent position before the world that he did two years ago, his fame is still sufficiently remembered to create a desire on the part of many to see him.

Notwithstanding this reduced prominence, in Preston a preview[7] of *Personal Impressions of America* said:

> the lecture is stated to be an interesting one, and various newspapers have spoken in praiseworthy terms of it, and from what we can gather, it is well-worth hearing. And if it were in the peculiar *rôle* which the lecturer has taken recently in connection with aesthetic matters it would warrant the attendance of many persons.

Wilde had refused to continue with 'the peculiar *rôle*' in July the previous year but, even dressed more conventionally, it was expected that the audience would be drawn quite widely. In the advertisement[8] for the lecture it was reported that:

> The lecture will conclude in time for trains on the East Lancashire Section – for Kirkham and Lytham, for Leyland and Chorley, and all roadside stations

which gives Wilde an eleven mile radius of attraction around Preston.

Comments upon Wilde's appeal could be varied, some being quite sarcastic, as in Southsea:[9]

> It is surely characteristic of the tolerant and catholic spirit of the age that Oscar Wilde is one of its minor prophets. No man leaped into notoriety more easily, or retained it on cheaper terms...(and some are) treating mere eccentricity as an indication of genius.

On the other hand, whilst in Belfast,[10] Wilde was praised very highly as:

> ... one who must be regarded as a most perfect and unique specimen of the order [of lecturers]

and that his appearance 'caused something approaching actual excitement'.

Others were fascinated with what Wilde was to do to earn a living after he had completed his lecture tour. In Middlesbrough[11] it was suggested that:

He cannot decide whether he ought to enter Parliament, (go) on the stage, or marry

This last option is an odd comment as his engagement had been widely reported at the end of 1883. A further suggestion[12] is that

Mr George Rignold[13] contemplates carrying off Oscar Wilde to the Antipodes, where Mr Rignold has himself made a great and very well-deserved success.

There was another Australian theme to comments in February in Scotland:[14]

Edinburgh turned out *en masse* to hear Mr Oscar Wilde lecture on two consecutive nights. He has just completed his hundredth lecture since his return from America, and his "dates are filled" to the end of March; he then resigns the lily for the orange blossom. He thinks of an Australian tour, with a view, he says, of, if possible, reforming the ugly shape of that country as depicted in modern maps, and will come home via Japan. "Bring me storks!"

A visit to Australia seems to have been a theme for Wilde's plans for both 1883 and '84 but his projected piece of geo-engineering would have to wait. Whatever his future plans, Wilde continued to have a very favourable reception to his lectures in the UK. He was invited to Cardiff to lecture as part of its Fine Art Exhibition in March and he had a very positive response:[15]

The committee of the Cardiff Fine Art Exhibition are to be congratulated upon having secured the services of Mr. Oscar Wilde as a lecturer. From more than one point of view it is the best hit they have made. The audiences at both the morning and the evening lectures were unusually large, and, what is of equal importance, must have been charmed with the intellectual treat placed within their reach. I could not help feeling amused at the look of helpless wonder which passed between many of the listeners at the conclusion of the morning's lecture upon "The House Beautiful." It was patent that the majority of them had come there with singularly false views of the mental capacity of Mr. Oscar Wilde, and were prepared for anything rather than the thoughtful, eloquent words which the lecturer poured forth for an hour and a quarter without a single note or reference.

These comments about him overcoming his audience's prejudices are not unique and it says a great deal for his stagecraft. All preconceptions were often cast aside after hearing him speak and reporters reacted against what they saw as the negative exaggerations which were so commonly made about him:

> Any two things wider apart than the coarse caricature of the American press and the real Oscar Wilde it would be hard to imagine. Nor have some of our English journals – especially the comic and satirical ones – been guiltless in this respect. Formed upon these bases, the popular conception of the Prophet of Aestheticism is about as false as anything could well be, and the Cardiff people are fortunate in having had the fallacy dispelled so charmingly to-day. The art of criticism was fearless, the reasoning logical, the satire most refined and pungent, the similes and illustrations poetical to a high degree. In the second lecture the pictures of American life were very graphic, and the analysis of American character remarkably shrewd. I only wish we could sit down to such a "feast of good things" in the way of lecturing more frequently. Mr. Oscar Wilde will always be welcome in Cardiff.

After his popular lecture at The Circus, Newcastle-upon-Tyne on Sunday evening, 17 February, Wilde travelled across the country for a mini-tour of the Lake District and environs.[16] He lectured on Monday in Carlisle then, until Friday, Wilde lectured on each day at Workington, Cockermouth, Maryport, Ulverston and returned to the north-east to lecture in Sunderland on the Saturday. In the advertisements it was recommended that:

> All lovers of Art and Refinement should not miss this opportunity of hearing one of the most noteworthy "Men of the Time."

This was an appellation much used at the time and closely repeated in the May edition of *Vanity Fair*[17] magazine when an illustration by Ape[18] was published with Wilde's potted biography under the heading,

MR. OSCAR WILDE. "THE APOSTLE OF
ÆSTHETICISM.

MR. OSCAR WILDE. MR. OSCAR WILDE'S
LECTURES.

MR. OSCAR WILDE. ASSEMBLY ROOMS,
WORKINGTON.
TUESDAY, FEBY. 19TH.

MR. OSCAR WILDE. Chairman:
C. J. VALENTINE, Esq.

MR. OSCAR WILDE. MR. OSCAR WILDE.

PUBLIC HALL,
MR. OSCAR WILDE. COCKERMOUTH.
WEDNESDAY, FEB, 20TH.

MR. OSCAR WILDE.

MR. OSCAR WILDE.

MR. OSCAR WILDE. ATHENÆUM,
MARYPORT,
THURSDAY, FEBY. 21,
1884.

MR. OSCAR WILDE. Chairman:
WILFRID HINE, Esq.

MR. OSCAR WILDE. MR. OSCAR WILDE.

MR. OSCAR WILDE. TAKING advantage of
a Visit to West
Cumberland, arrange
ments have been made
MR. OSCAR WILDE. with

MR. OSCAR WILDE,
MR. OSCAR WILDE.
Who has been induced
to give a series of his
MR. OSCAR WILDE.
POPULAR LECTURES

MR. OSCAR WILDE. as above. The Subject
at Cockermouth and
Workington will be
MR. OSCAR WILDE. "Personal Reminiscen
ces of a Tour in America;"
at Maryport the Subject
MR. OSCAR WILDE. will be "The House
Beautiful."
All lovers of Art and
MR. OSCAR WILDE. Refinement should not
miss this opportunity of
hearing one of the most
MR. OSCAR WILDE. noteworthy "Men of
the Time."

MR. OSCAR WILDE. Admission, 1s; Reserved, 2s.

MR. OSCAR WILDE. Doors open at 7.30; to
commence at 8.

Wilde 'induced' to give his popular lectures in the Lake District

MEN OF THE DAY:

MR. OSCAR WILDE.

OSCAR, the younger son of the late Sir William Wilde,[19] archaeologist, traveller, and Queen's Surgeon in Ireland, won the Berkeley Medal for Greek in Trinity College, Dublin, and a Scholarship. Migrating to Magdalen College, Oxford, he took two "Firsts" and "the Newdigate." Then he went wandering in Greece; and, full of a Neo-Hellenic spirit, came back to invade social London. He invented the aesthetic movement. He preached the doctrine of possible culture in external things. He got brilliantly laughed at, and good-naturedly accepted. In 1881 he published a somewhat startling volume of poems, and at once went to America to preach his gospel of culture. Then, as an itinerant art-apostle, he wandered from New York to San Francisco, lectured to all sorts and conditions of men, produced a play, and came back to London. Suddenly he gave up dado-Worship for dandyism, cut his long locks, and accepted life. He is a sayer of smart things, and has a rare flow of thoroughly Irish wit and an excellent notion of the advantage that may accrue to any man from drawing attention to himself anyhow.

He has lived through much laughter, in which he has always joined. He has many disciples, and is of opinion that "imitation is the sincerest form of insult." He is twenty-eight years old, comes of a literary family, and is essentially modern. He is to be married next week.

Actually, of course, in the forthcoming October he would be 30 years old, if truth was to be told (which it wouldn't be, if Wilde had anything to do with it.)

During his tour of the Lake District, Wilde visited Keswick[20] on Thursday 21 February, *en route* to Ulverston, and on his arrival was met by Mr. H. L. Jenkinson, a local historian and Mr. R. S. Cahill who was Head of the art school: both were major figures in the arts in the town.[21] Wilde was taken by Cahill to see an exhibition of his watercolours and then they walked to Friar's Crag at Derwentwater, the lake alongside Keswick, which Wilde admired greatly and his response was reported in the press:

"This," said he, "is lovely. And that's Southey's Lodore.[22] The effect of the atmosphere is just right for seeing a picture of this sort. The lake is just large enough for beauty. In America the lakes are like seas, where you lose sight of land, and there are cruel storms which wreck vessels." He thought open footpaths should exist through all beautiful places everywhere, and that it was a mistake to think that the public were ruthless destroyers of property when admitted to private grounds. He inquired very closely into the subject of a railway being injurious to the effect of beautiful scenery, and said, without giving a direct opinion on the matter, "It must be a pleasant thing to look out of a first-class saloon carriage and see the beauties as you pass," and thought they would be better enjoyed when perfectly at one's ease.

Here we get a rare, probably unique, view of Wilde as a champion of ramblers and his assessment of the positive value for travellers of introducing modern transport infrastructure into areas of great natural beauty. A view many – both then and now – would not share and, at the time, many residents of the Lake District did not, amongst them Ruskin and his friend and colleague, Keswick's local Rural Dean, Canon Rawnsley.[23] He was vicar of St. Kentigern church, Crosthwaite on the outskirts of Keswick and had engaged in a local campaign to protect the countryside. Southey's grave is in St. Kentigern churchyard and there is a monument to him in the church: I wonder if, after viewing Cahill's watercolours, Wilde was taken to the church to see the Southey monuments, met the vicar and was thus introduced to the local railway controversy. Interestingly, Canon Rawnsley and his wife Edith, under the influence of Ruskin, established the Keswick School of Industrial Art during 1884 in their parish rooms, specialising in, and becoming famous for, working in metals, especially *repoussé* copper work (which Wilde admired and mentioned approvingly in *The House Beautiful*). The presiding spirit of the School was anti-industrialisation, typical of the Ruskin and Morris inspired Arts and Crafts movement with its attempts to counter the effects of industry and mechanisation upon men by allowing them their self-expression in high quality work. One of the School's aims was:

> To show that here in England an abundance of skill of hand is wasted which, if any education worth its name were given to the whole working man – to his eye, hand, heart, as well as head – could and would help England.

This aim sets out essentially the same views on education as Wilde's which he was preaching at this time in *The House Beautiful* and the emerging lecture *The Value of Art in Modern Life*:

> If ... we would teach them the use of their hands, teach them the simple handicrafts, those beautiful decorative arts, such as carpentry, wood carving in the flat, the use of the potter's wheel, the decoration of pottery, weaving, dyeing, working in

metal, beating out sheets of brass into raised *repoussé* work we would, I am quite certain, to begin with, be making children far happier in school than they were at present.

Keswick School of Industrial Art flourished and its products are much collected today as beautiful specimens of the Arts and Crafts movement.

Dandyism is the assertion of the absolute modernity of Beauty.

W ILDE'S DRESS and hairstyle continued to attract considerable attention. Nobody seemed able to adapt to his non-wearing of the Aesthetic garb of the American tour. Or, at least, the newspapers were unwilling to let it pass unreported. Londonderry[24] had a typical response which was felt to be urgent enough to warrant telegraphing to the newspaper's offices in Dublin:

> There was great disappointment felt among the curious at discovering, contrary to expectation nothing extraordinary in the attire of the lecturer ...

Knowing that Wilde had been lecturing solidly for over three months and had received extensive newspaper coverage, it is surprising that anyone expected anything different to what they got. In one of Sherard's biographies of Wilde[25] there is a photograph of Wilde taken in Birmingham wearing his daywear which was fairly constant from September 1883 until the end of his first lecture tour in April 1884. This tallies exactly with the many written descriptions we now have. Sherard entitled the photograph *Oscar Wilde, Aesthetic Period, About 1884* and it must have been taken on 13 March when Wilde lectured twice at the Midland Institute in Birmingham. He peers out to his left with his downward sloping eyes and his impassive face does have the look of the Asiatic Bacchus André Gide[26] said some compared him with. He wears his favourite green, fur-lined coat with its fur collar and cuffs which he had worn throughout his tour of America. Under this he wears his open black velvet jacket and under this his black velvet waistcoat. There are two associated photographs from the same session[27] which have Wilde facing in each direction, in one he is holding his yellow kid gloves. His pale trousers can be seen and the crushed strawberry handkerchief is just visible in the jacket top pocket and his matching crushed strawberry tie is tied in a large, flamboyant bow beneath his soft shirt collar. His hair in these photographs is not as curled and Neronian as Wilde originally described it, it now having more 'volume' than curl.

After the clothes, reporters soon turned their attention to Wilde's figure - in Belfast[28] on his very first day:

> His handsome, frank features, and his substantially-moulded figure — for nature has not been parsimonious with him — were certainly not suggestive of the ... model when the craze of Mr George Du Maurier was at its highest ...

This is not the only mention of Wilde's inclination to *embonpoint*. Wilde lectured at the Firth College (now Sheffield University) on consecutive days in January — *The House Beautiful* and *Personal Impressions of America* — and was described[29] as one

> whom nature has been prodigal rather than sparing of her gifts. Mr Wilde, in fact, appeared much more like an athlete than either limp or lank

which gives the readers of the *Sheffield and Rotherham Independent* a very different image of Wilde — as a previously unsuspected athletic figure — than is, or was, customarily the case. His athletic appearance seems, to us, now, a particularly odd characterisation of one who is traditionally seen as 'portly' at best and indolent in the extreme, but the word is repeated in a description from Leeds[30] when he gave the impression of being:

> ... not a nerveless, bloodless idealist, but a tall athletic figure.

Turning to his clothing, in Bristol for his evening lecture:[31]

> Mr Wilde was ... clad in the costume of an ordinary Philistine, his frock coat having between it and the patent leather boots a dual garment of broad check material such as Macdermott might have designed for his friend 'Arry.[32]

'Arry was a cheeky cockney character from Punch who wrote letters in verse and was often in cartoons, some of which showed him wearing trousers with a very large check. He was described as:[33]

> 'Arry — as common as he is, dressed in his mustard and cress plaid suit — is aware of the social hierarchy but knows just how close the top and bottom rungs are.

I think 'Arry's suit was probably a little louder than Wilde's tweed trousers but in a few years' time Wilde will demonstrate just *how close the top and bottom* strata of society actually were. Continuing the description from Bristol, though:

> Bright colour was supplied in the shape of necktie and breast handkerchief, affording a compromise between pink and terra cotta. After making his bow the lecturer deposited upon the

table his light yellow gloves and white handkerchief, the latter being caressed alternately with the owner's reversed linen cuffs. Mr. Wilde possesses high elocutionary and histrionic powers, with no more affectation than exists in the average curate

It is difficult to assess the histrionic powers of curates at the time, but Wilde appears to have been considerably less affected than many of the reporters in the UK expected. However, curates seem to have been subjects of interest all of their own,[34] even to Wilde:

LADY MARKBY: I can't understand this modern mania for curates. In my time we girls saw them, of course, running about the place like rabbits. But we never took any notice of them, I need hardly say. But I am told that nowadays country society is quite honeycombed with them. I think it most irreligious.

As well as being 'attired in ordinary evening dress' in Preston[35] the reporter considered that he favoured:

the form of fashion in which the young ladies at present wear their hair ... [he] is a young man, of pleasant countenance, inclining to feminincy.

Wilde may well have objected to this neologism (with Dr Chasuble's 'scholar's shudder'.[36])
In Cardiff, during the afternoon:[37]

Those who expected to find Mr. Wilde looking like one of the poets in "Patience" were doomed to disappointment. His hair was very little longer than that of an "every day young man," and his tall and well-built figure was clad in quite a matter-of-fact morning frock – which allowed a rather liberal display of shirt cuff – and unwhisperables of light coloured tweed, with a tolerably large plaid pattern. Nor did he carry a sunflower or a lily, but simply wore a small white flower in his buttonhole. Mr. Wilde's pose would by most people be considered graceful and easy, albeit scoffers might call it a "stained glass attitude"

These large plaid 'unwhisperables' — one of the many Victorian euphemisms for a man's trousers — sound to be exactly the same pair as he wore at Bristol at the beginning of March and are a minor variation of Wilde's daytime wear.

It was not uncommon for newspapers to give its readers a short biography of Wilde - with the usual year or two deducted from his age - but in Bradford a newspaper[38] gave a biography accompanied with one of the very few illustrations of him published in newspapers at this time. It is a black and white 'portrait' engraved from a sketch

Mr Oscar Wilde.

Wilde in a characteristic pose in Bradford

made from the gallery of the Bradford Mechanics' Institute. In this sketch we see Wilde standing in a characteristic pose: left hand on hip and right hand off picture, but clearly gesticulating. This pose is so often described in reviews, as is his habit of looking slightly upwards, which we also see here. His evening dress is as was described everywhere at this time: the usual evening suit of black with its black satin double-breasted waistcoat, a bunch of seals hanging from it and the famous crushed strawberry pink silk handkerchief peeping out of the breast, not to be confused with the white handkerchief in his left hand (which seems to have a ring on the wedding finger). His shirt cuffs – Van Dyke cuffs – are turned back over his jacket sleeves and the shirt collar is turned over a thin black tie. Wilde's hair is more voluminous than in other images and looks not so much post-Neronian as pre-Hendrixian. This image just precedes the *Vanity Fair* 'Ape' caricature which has the advantage of being in colour.

The Master of Deportment

WILDE KNEW THAT he must attract the audience's attention from the very start and when he had no chairman to introduce him he must have carefully considered his entrance onto the stage. In Sheffield:[39]

> He entered the room with a grace which any master of deportment might have envied, and in reciting...comported himself with an air of aristocratic ease.

and in Leeds[40] during his afternoon lecture:

> ... they awaited the appearance of the typical apostle of aestheticism, Mr. Oscar Wilde. The flutter of expectation swelled almost into an audible titter as the red hanging at the back of the platform was dramatically pushed aside ... Mr. Oscar Wilde is apparently not far behind Mr. Henry Irving in the value he puts upon what is theatrically called an entry. A few seconds' posing gave the spectators an opportunity of scrutinising his personal appearance. It was by no means Bunthornian, or "in the high aesthetic line." He wore neither knee-breeches nor silk stockings, but a pair of tight-fitting light trousers, a short black velvet waistcoat, and a coat of similar material and colour. From the breast pocket peeped an ornamental crushed-strawberry handkerchief, and from his low broad collar hung a crushed-strawberry tie. His cuffs were turned over at the wrists. The only other peculiarity was his hair, which is slightly curly and dressed something after the Florentine *cinque-cento* fashion common to cheap prints of sacred personages.

Were they gazing upon *Saint Oscar*?[41] In the evening in Leeds[42] Wilde wore an evening suit much the same as any gentleman would wear. As in the afternoon:

> His entry was again marked with that dignified grace which would recommend him for a master of deportment.

and in his presentation of his *Personal Impressions of America*:

> ... he was easy and self-confident, as became the apostle of a cult. In the treatment of his subject he was entertaining, paradoxical, and at times a little extravagant.

Which is a good description of the Wilde of public imagination — the wit and raconteur — who described himself whilst he was in prison[43] as 'a lord of language'. Any mistaken impression the public may have had of Wilde being what was known at the time as a fashionable *masher* could not last for long:[44]

> No sooner, however, does he open his mouth than the possibility of such an error is removed. He has a clear musical voice, and an even flow of words, always well chosen, and at times eloquent.

As in Leeds, so it was almost everywhere else. In Huddersfield[45] it was reported that *'Mr Wilde is extremely happy as a lecturer'* and in Belfast,[46] at the beginning of the year:

> Among the many lecturers who have appeared from time to time in this country we have heard none who seemed to know so thoroughly what he was talking about as Mr Oscar Wilde; we have known none whose delivery was so singularly free from affectation...(and who) possessed the power of securing the attention of an audience for so long without resorting to any tricks of style. Mr Wilde is refreshingly natural both in language and delivery. He speaks with a degree of earnestness... Mr. Wilde is very economical of phrases whose application is, as it were, subjective to the thought and feeling of the poets making use of them; his language is of a type that, for want of a better word, we may venture to call "cultured colloquialism."

The Darlington[47] reporter clearly had all his preconceptions wiped away after he had seen and heard Wilde lecture:

> What appears most singular to those who hear him is that such a matter of fact young man should have obtained the reputation of being crotchetty-cracked and utterly-utter, for these are actually the least terms we would employ in describing him.

And in his lecturing:

> His delivery was very graceful, occasionally almost impassioned, his attitude dignified, perhaps at times even a little stiff.

Whilst a little further north in Stockton,[48] Wilde's stance and lecturing style were described:

> with his head thrown back, his eyes for the most part fixed upon the sunlight, and a placid smile playing on his countenance, he spoke for an hour and a half in slow, measured accents, and with aesthetic intonation, but with a touch here and there of the Cockney pronunciation.

I am certain that Wilde would be astonished to have this cockney verbal idiosyncrasy reported (when he relaxed later with a cup of Rosy-Lee.) It was noted that he did not stand stock still whilst lecturing:[49]

> At first he twirled in his left hand a pair of light coloured gloves, which apparently had never been used for the covering of his hands. Afterwards he placed his hands behind, occasionally resting his left hand on his hip and motioning with the other. Towards the conclusion of his lecture he drew out a gold watch, delicately fingered it for a few seconds, and then glanced at the position of its digits. After it had remained on the table or desk at his side for a short time, the same process was gone through, and the watch was then returned to the vest pocket. Throughout he held his body well poised, his head was thrown back, and slightly leaning to the right shoulder...

but this positivity was rather reduced when the reporter turned to Wilde's physical presence:

> ... Probably many of those present ... would be surprised at the almost "massive" appearance of Mr. Wilde, and to think him "much taller and stouter" than their ideal.

The overall impressions were still very positive even when, as in Scarborough,[50] his delivery of *Personal Impressions of America* threatened to become as long as his much criticised Princes' Hall debut the previous summer:

> Mr Wilde appears, indeed, to look upon everything, even the common affairs of social, domestic, and commercial life, from a very elevated art point of view. ... the lecturer retired amid enthusiastic applause. The lecture, which extended over nearly two hours, was listened to throughout with evidently close and rapt attention by the audience. The lecturer's choice flow of language, the charm of his manner, his graphic descriptions, his occasional hyperbole, all contributed to render of the most pleasing character a discourse which from "other lips" might have fallen without a tithe of the effect he produced.

And on the previous day in York[51]

> The few perhaps expected more gush, a manner considerably more theatrical and free, and tricks of dress, style, speech, and surroundings of an extravagant kind. ... His humour is playful rather than broad and flashing. His enthusiasm is of a softened, luxurious and almost non-contagious kind. But his manner of

sketching an oddity, a period or a people, he has more power than could have been expected. The lightness of his touch is here a distinct acquisition though you can never be quite sure whether he is laughing with you or at you.

This final comment is repeated at many venues but the description of his enthusiasm — of the 'almost non-contagious kind' and his 'lightness of his touch' — are highly descriptive of Wilde.

Artistic Furniture

THERE was no consistency about decorating the stage in any particular way. On most occasions the stage was empty except for Wilde and one or two props. An example of a minimalist approach was at Southsea:[52]

> Mr. Wilde stood between the table on the platform and the head of a couch, and assumed an æsthetic pose

However there were a fair number of exceptions to this when local tradespeople decided this was a splendid opportunity to show off their furniture and other decorative wares: at Belfast[53] on his first two days of lecturing, the promoters saw fit to include a reference to the stage setting in the advertisements:

> The Æsthetic furniture used for this occasion is supplied by N. A. Campbell & Co. of Belfast

In Northampton,[54] the home of British furniture making, not only did Wilde make a good impression but the stage was extensively dressed for his lecture:

> Mr. Wilde is what ladies would call a "rather good-looking young fellow," the wealth of hair clustered round his head adding somewhat to his *distingué* appearance. His voice is of a pleasant, mellifluous character, and his enunciation as near perfection as could be desired. His attitude during the hour and a half that his lecture occupied was graceful throughout. Having no notes or manuscript of any kind, he carried in his hands a pair of light kid gloves. Occasionally wringing and crushing these, he was enabled to relieve himself of any awkwardness which might have been displayed if his hands had been unoccupied. He was surrounded on the platform by a number of articles of furniture, kindly lent for the purpose by Messrs. Phipps and Son, of Gold-street. The entrance to the stage was draped with blue Kensington serge and Madras muslin curtains, while on either side were hangings of cross-

over French tapestry and chenille. In the centre of the platform stood a handsome table in the Chippendale style. Other specimens of the same style comprised a "five o clock tea" table and a very beautiful cabinet of Messrs. Phipps' own manufacture. To the latter particular attention was called by the lecturer. There were also a set of real Chippendale chairs and two handsome, six-fold Japanese screens. In the centre of the platform was a beautiful old shumac carpet, and the *tout ensemble* was completed by the artistic arrangement of a number of specimens of Dunmore and other ware.

There was an impressive display at Bristol[35] where the advertisements stated that 'The Lecture will be illustrated by examples of Art Furniture selected at Messrs Trapnell and Gane's, 39, College Green, Bristol' and the reviewer[56] noted:

> In the afternoon the large salon was well filled. Messrs Trapnell and Gane ... enriched the orchestra with exquisite curtained screens, oak cabinet work, and other furniture of their manufacture, to which Mr. Wilde referred in terms of high approval as illustrations of his views. ...

And another Bristol company took the opportunity to publicise their involvement with Wilde:[57]

> We understand that Messrs. Cotterell Brothers furnished a selection of art wall decorations for the lecturer, and that the designs mentioned by him are to be seen in their show rooms.

During *The House Beautiful* at Bristol, when Wilde spoke of mantelpieces, he particularly pointed out that:

> The best were of wood, and the exceedingly beautiful chimney piece on the platform - with small shelves for bright pottery, delicate china, and other pretty ornaments - illustrated exactly what he meant. He was glad to say this and the other beautiful things had been produced in Bristol, designed by Mr. Caleb Trapnell and manufactured by his firm. It afforded one great pleasure to find that in the city where he lectured they made so many pretty things to illustrate his meaning. The Jacobean clock case showed a nice sense of simplicity and refinement, and the ornament, as in all good carving, was kept flat.

Messrs Trapnell and Gane were clearly not inclined to hide their aesthetic light beneath any old-fashioned bushel and they were soon advertising:[58]

ARTISTIC FURNITURE — Messrs Trapnell and Gane have just issued a supplement to their furnishing catalogue, which is profusely illustrated with Queen Anne, Chippendale, Renascence (*sic*), and other designs of furniture, some examples of which met with much merited approval from Mr. Oscar Wilde on the occasion of his recent visit to this city. The various drawings are very beautifully executed.

At the Cardiff Fine Art Exhibition, during the afternoon lecture,[59] Wilde:

> … stood before a background composed of hangings designed and worked by a Cardiff lady — Miss Mabel Fedden — and which, we are informed, satisfied even his critical taste. The platform was also decorated by plants and flowers, lent by Mr. Pettigrew. Of the lecture there could scarcely be two opinions. Delivered with the greatest fluency and distinctness of enunciation, it was replete with good sense and pregnant with artistic suggestiveness …

and he concluded *The House Beautiful* with a reference to the works on display at the Exhibition:

> The great fault of the art of this country, he also remarked, was that it was much too serious. We had not one pure piece of joy and phantasy and laughter, like the Japanese picture of "The Butterfly's Funeral," which could be seen on a screen at the other end of the Exhibition.

Here Wilde's view that the aim of art was to bring 'one pure piece of joy and phantasy and laughter' is clearly derived from Pater with the addition of laughter, which was a particular objective all of his own: Pater did not crack jokes.

Exotic Art

WHILST EXPLAINING his philosophy of *The House Beautiful,* Wilde took the opportunity to acknowledge some of the halls he visited as wonderful pieces of architecture, one particularly being the Birmingham Midland Institute:[60]

> Mr. Wilde seemed to be very much struck by the fact that he had to give his lecture on "Internal Decoration" in a room which afforded a specially remarkable example of the art, his eyes frequently wandering over the fanciful mosaic patterns that adorn the walls; and at an early point of his address he took occasion to speak of the hall as in every way one of the

loveliest bits of art decoration he had had the pleasure of lecturing in front of in England, and as one of the instances that showed that already a great deal had been accomplished in the way of art education in England. ... Mr. Wilde remarked that he had read a very interesting lecture written by the artist who decorated those walls, a lecture on "Exotic Art", in which, as far as he could see, there was a plea for a national art, and also a kind of warning for them not to use ornament that belonged to other nations. He could not acknowledge himself a convert to that view; in fact, he entirely differed from it. It was quite true that we were employing ornament the idea of which had long passed away, but that was only one of the things that showed the complete supremacy of artistic beauty over any philosophical meaning. If they looked at the decoration of that room, they would see various forms that had sprung from amongst eastern nations, many designs invented by natures alien to our own, but which it seemed to us perfectly right to use.

The architect (rather than 'artist') responsible for the completion of the Midland Institute (and not just the decoration of the walls) and, indeed, the lecture *Exotic Art* which Wilde had read and decried, was John Henry Chamberlain.[61] He was an exponent of the architectural ideas of Ruskin who had selected Chamberlain as one of the trustees of his Guild of St George. He designed many of Birmingham's civic buildings including its schools. The greatest of these buildings were acknowledged to be the Mechanics' Institute, which no longer stands, and the School of Art, which does. As well as knowing Ruskin, Chamberlain also knew William Morris who presented him with forty-five wood engravings designed by Burne-Jones to illustrate the 'Cupid and Psyche' story from 'The Earthly Paradise'. One example of Chamberlain's domestic architecture was 'The Grove' in Harborne, Birmingham, which was designed in 1877–78 for William Kenrick,[62] a prominent Birmingham businessman. The V&A acquired the anteroom to the drawing room just before the house was demolished and it reflects the Aesthetic style.[63] It is richly decorated with inlaid, painted and gilded wood and, inevitably, this was used to display Kendrick's collection of blue and white ceramics.

I am slightly surprised that Wilde mentioned Chamberlain and his lecture in such negative terms because Chamberlain had given his *Exotic Art* lecture to a large audience in the same hall in October the previous year and had died at a friend's house within half an hour of the close.[64] Chamberlain's lecture was one of a series of Monday evening lectures at the Midland Institute for 1883/84 which also

included two lectures by William Morris on 'The Gothic Revival';
Edmund Gosse[65] 'The Public and Private Use of Sculpture' and Max
Müller[66] on 'Religious Reforms in India'. Chamberlain's main theme
was the Englishness of much art and architecture — he gave as
examples the cathedrals of England — and what he termed exotic art
influences which he defined as 'foreign art out of place' in
architecture. He accepted the exotic influence in painting and
sculpture but maintained that architecture and decoration should be
free from it. Chamberlain considered architecture was dead until the
revival of English Gothic:[67]

> a style which was not brought from a foreign soil, but which
> was fitted to the wants of the people, which appealed to their
> sympathies and satisfied their passions.

Wilde correctly saw this as an argument for an English school of art
and design, and rejected it on the basis of his (and Pater's) aesthetics.
Wilde's view was internationalist and ahistorical and was expressed
in his lecture *Modern Art Training* and maintained in *The House
Beautiful*. He concluded his criticism of Chamberlain's philosophy
with a statement of his own:[68]

> They must remember that the world and not the country was
> the province of the artist, and the harmony he looked for was
> not the harmony of the country, or of the century, or of history,
> but purely the harmony of the eye.

The Value of Art in Modern Life

ON SUNDAY 17 February at The Circus in Newcastle-upon-Tyne,
Wilde gave his new lecture *The Value of Art in Modern Life* and
it was reported[69] that:

Oscar is an authority on all matters pertaining to art ... and (this
is) a most comprehensive text to preach from. And no one is
better qualified to preach such a sermon but Oscar, and his
being run after wherever he appears in public is an admission
of the fact ... he is regarded almost as a kind of personification
of art.

It is not surprising that Whistler grew increasingly angry about
Wilde's apparent position as art expert — 'no one is better qualified'
— and his pre-eminence, in the eyes of the public and press at least,
on all artistic matters. But to be regarded as a 'personification of art',
to have made his life and art one, was one of the great objectives for
Wilde, deriving from his Paterian sympathies. It is a theme which

runs right through all his mature works: it is the science of life which is applicable to everything, however seemingly trivial:

speaking of the science of Life, have you got the cucumber sandwiches cut for Lady Bracknell?[70]

All this must have rankled with Whistler. Alan Cole notes in his diary[71] that he spent an evening late in March of this year at Whistler's in Tite Street and Whistler was:

Strong on Oscar Wilde taking his notions on Art.

Following the usual description of his clothes, physical appearance and hair, the Newcastle review continues:

But with Emerson ... Oscar believes that a foolish consistency is the hobgoblin of little minds .. .for "to be great is to be misunderstood."[72]

The Value of Art in Modern Life had a varied genesis and on the few occasions Wilde gave it during the first half of 1884 it is quite different to the version he gave after the summer. As the lecture seems to have only been given three times in the first half of the year and the reviews we have are few and each is short, establishing its full content is difficult. However, from the reviews we have, the text of this early version is familiar and we can certainly give an outline of its themes which are, essentially, drawn from the final section of *The House Beautiful* interspersed with some extracts from *Personal Impressions of America*. (A text of the lecture, as given later in 1884 and in 1885, is given in Appendix D.)

Wilde ends his lecturing season with *The Value of Art in Modern Life* at St Jude's Schools, Commercial St, Whitechapel. In a book of 1896[73] this area of London is described — cringingly — as:

... practically in a foreign land, so far as language and race are concerned. The people are neither French nor English, Germans nor Americans, but Jews. In this Whitechapel Ghetto the English visitor almost feels himself one of a subject race in the presence of dominant and overwhelming invaders. Yet the crowds are peaceful and entirely non-aggressive in demeanour. There is no sign of lawlessness, or of molestation of the minority. Indeed, in this respect Whitechapel on Sunday, as on other days, compares most favourably with many parts of Gentile London ... At St. Jude's, in the heart of the Ghetto, the choir sometimes outnumber the congregation; and at Toynbee Hall, close by, where Sunday morning science classes are open for students, some scores of young men are entering with their text-books.

Toynbee Hall and St. Jude's Church, Whitechapel

Wilde's lecture is paraphrased in a review in *The Pall Mall Gazette*[74] as

> Mr. Oscar Wilde preached his gospel in the East-end on Saturday night, and his audience were not only delighted with his humour, but were surprised at the excellent good sense he talked. Mr. Wilde's subject was a plea in favour of "art for schools"

which, in the main, is what *The Value of Art in Modern Life* is. Wilde's opening lines[75] were about the education of children:

> By the present system of education they were merely trying to feed a child upon books and literature long before there was created in the child the power to understand the books

and he continued on familiar ground with his summary of what he felt Victorian education was:

> wearying children with committing to memory the longitude and latitude of countries nobody wants to visit, or long lists of the names and dates of Saxon kings, many of whom he was sure never existed ...

This should be changed:

> For children, he maintained were peculiarly susceptible to

impressions from what is beautiful

and so schools should be teaching them:

> To create and make, and use their hands, the results would be far better. There were plenty of highly-cultivated people in England who could find no better use for their hands than to put them into kid gloves which were far too tight for them ...

This is mainly taken from *The House Beautiful* but then Wilde adds in an anecdote:

> ... one day in coming from Covent Garden market with a bouquet of flowers in his hand, he had to pass some poor children at play in one of the back streets. One of the children seeing the flowers stopped in his play, and exclaimed, "Lor, how rich you are!"

The reviewer demurs:

> His audience might have interpreted the London gamin's remark more literally than did the lecturer, who inferred from it that it indicated a perception of the beautiful.

Wilde was struggling to get his point across to this reporter but he moved on to recommend that every school should have a good workshop and be well designed:

> In which the children of the rich and poor alike should learn some handicraft, some beautiful art, for one or two hours a day ... so beautiful that the punishment for an idle child should be not to be allowed to go to school for a day.

For in this way the student would be taught the beautiful:

> A boy would rather look at a bird or even draw it than throw "his customary stone."

Which would be helped by bringing high quality art into the school:

> the works of art at South Kensington belonging to the nation should be distributed among the schools

thereby inspiring children by surrounding them with beautiful things. These great works of art could be changed every few months. He added that galleries and museums should be opened to the public on Sundays which was well received. He retold a story from *Personal Impressions of America* wherein an American had ordered a copy of the Venus de Milo from the Louvre and on receipt of the cast sued the railway company because it had reached him in such a mutilated condition — without arms — and won his case. Wilde also moved into other areas:

> The lecturer's remarks on household taste and ladies' dress — on crimes in Berlin wool, for instance, or the stolid ugliness of bows — were equally sensible and well put.

which he had touched upon in both *Personal Impressions of America* and *The House Beautiful:* he would cover these topics in more detail during his forthcoming autumn lecture *Dress*. Many Victorian women committed the 'crimes in Berlin wool' when they embroidered 'Home Sweet Home' or similar phrases for display in their homes. Wilde concludes by reusing his favoured quotation from Keats; a phrase they probably would not be embroidering:[76]

> "I have not got the slightest reverence for anything in existence except for the Eternal Being, the memory of great men, and the principle of beauty."

The Value of Modern Life, as delivered in the first half of 1884, is a selection of parts of the lectures Wilde had already given. He was plagiarising his own work, just as he would later do in creating the works we are much more familiar with.

Smoke

WILDE first spoke of the aesthetic benefits of smoke in his lecture *Modern Art Training*, given in June the previous year. He had said that he could not 'praise it on sanitary grounds' but that:

> There was no better answer to those who complained of commerce spoiling art than to turn to Turners pictures … It is better to live in a city of changeable weather than in a city of lovely surroundings.

When he spoke in Sheffield - the city which was internationally famous for both its production of steel and Sheffield plate tableware - on his *Personal Impressions of America,* Wilde took the opportunity to extend his peroration about the clarity of the American climate:[77]

> When referring to the atmosphere of the country, he remarked that he did not believe in the lands of cloudless skies as being the best for producing landscape painters. Bad weather might be personally unpleasant to some people, but it was extremely valuable to the artist. So when in Sheffield, when there was bad weather and terrible fogs, the inhabitants should remember that

however uncomfortable it might make them, they could not help being picturesque in it. When viewed from a distance nothing could be so beautiful as a great commercial town, with its wonderful chimneys, and smoke, and fog, seen far away. He did not, of course, say anything against the Smoke Abatement Act, which he supposed was a public benefit on sanitary grounds. He would merely remind them that on artistic grounds smoke was always beautiful. It was quite impossible for smoke to be anything else. There was a constant change of colour, and nothing could be lovelier. It was perhaps a strange inconsistency in one whose name, he was quite sure, was very clear to many in Sheffield [*applause*] that no voice should be more eloquent or more potent than his (Mr. Ruskin's) in declaiming against the smoke of modern England, and yet that no painter should show the wonderful beauty of smoke so much as Turner, whom he announced as the master.

This naming of the large industrial city in which he was currently lecturing was something Wilde did elsewhere to bring a degree of topicality to his lecture. However, this mention of Ruskin had a special importance for this city as evidenced by the applause: in 1875 Sheffield had been specially chosen by Ruskin for the establishment of the St. George Museum in Walkley[78], south-west Sheffield, high over the beautiful Rivelin Valley. This building had been purchased with the funds of the Guild of St. George, an organisation which Ruskin had founded in 1871 and whose aims were outlined in *Fors Clavigera – Letters to the Workmen and Labourers of Great Britain*[79]. The museum housed Ruskin's teaching collection and he funded an educational programme, under his guidance, to look to 'the liberal education of the artisan'. Ruskin chose Sheffield out of all other industrial cities because he admired the craftsmanship of the metal-workers, and he also loved the position of Sheffield and its proximity to some of the finest mediaeval cathedrals and abbeys which exemplified the Gothic architecture he worshipped. Ruskin himself said that:[80]

> The mountain home of the Museum was originally chosen, not to keep the collection out of smoke, but expressly to beguile the artisan out of it.

In 1877 Edward Carpenter wrote to Walt Whitman:[81]

> Sheffield is finely situated, magnificent hill country all around about, and on the hills for miles and miles (on one side of town) elegant villa residences — and in the valley below one enduring cloud of smoke, and a pale-faced teeming population, and tall chimneys and ash heaps ... and dirty alleys, and courts and

houses half roofless, and a river running black through the midst of them. It is a strange and wonderful sight.

Following this lecture, the next day the Sheffield newspapers[82] criticised Wilde's more impressionistic comments about the value of smoke:

> Mr. Oscar Wilde is good enough to stem the unmitigated abuse which ordinary mortals assail the atmospheric conditions existing in manufacturing towns. In this respect Sheffield has been happier than the Atlantic. That great ocean had the unspeakable misfortune to disappoint Mr. Oscar Wilde. We gather that Sheffield has, on the other hand, had the inestimable privilege of realising his highest expectations.

Then the editor clearly requested that the sarcasm knob should be turned up to eleven:

> We can honestly say for it: that it is a good place for the admirers of smoke. We expected that Mr. Wilde was coming to curse, and lo! He has stayed to bless the very thing that is Sheffield's chief characteristic...he has acquired the knack of finding reason for jollity (we trust Aestheticism will pardon such an unaesthetic word) under the adverse circumstances of others. Mr. Wilde assures the inhabitants of Sheffield that however depressing and unpleasant it may be to dwell in clouds of smoke and seas of fog, they have at least the patriotic satisfaction of knowing that, to outsiders, they cannot help being "picturesque." For our own part we do not feel altogether enthusiastic over the artistic satisfaction of dwelling in smoke, in order to present to chance visitors like Mr. Oscar Wilde the "beautiful" picture of "a great commercial town, with its wonderful chimneys, and smoke, and fog seen far away."

The criticism continues for several sentences with further quotations from Wilde's lecture before:

> ... we have in Sheffield a surfeit of this kind of beauty — we have, in fact, so much smoke that we can't see smoke to judge whether it is beautiful or not. ... Smoke in excess is a distinct abuse of a useful — and we are willing to believe artistically admirable thing.

The newspaper then moved to its final condemnation:

> And we respectfully decline to waive our strong objection to live in unlimited smoke for the special behoof of the lovers of the beautiful.

That *behoof* is wonderful.

Smoke abatement was a major issue, particularly for the enormous manufacturing cities of the North and Midlands. It had been the subject of yet another national exhibition in South Kensington in 1881, which moved to Manchester in 1882. Wilde's balance between the aesthetic benefits and the health and environmental disbenefits of smoke was being criticised. In these lectures he was playing with this idea and, essentially, it is an example of the beauty/utility dichotomy with which he was fascinated. In 1890, Wilde devoted a lengthy section of *The Decay of Lying* to this very matter, drawing upon his impressions here in Sheffield and also on the points he made in his lectures:

> At present, people see fogs, not because there are fogs, but because poets and painters have taught them the mysterious loveliness of such effects. There may have been fogs for centuries in London. I dare say there were. But no one saw them, and so we do not know anything about them. They did not exist till Art had invented them. Now, it must be admitted, fogs are carried to excess. They have become the mere mannerism of a clique, and the exaggerated realism of their method gives dull people bronchitis. Where the cultured catch an effect, the uncultured catch cold.[83]

In May Wilde was assessing the future, knowing well that his marriage at the end of the month would not materially change his finances. He was thinking about lectures for the autumn and on 22 May he wrote to an unknown correspondent:[84]

> I will have two new lectures at least next season – besides those I have delivered … October will do — but my fee is always the same

This letter is likely to have been to Appleton, who was to take over his management from Colonel Morse in the autumn, because it sets out his likely 'offer' and when he would like to start work again.

Thought Reading[85]

JUST before his wedding we get an interesting view of Wilde in a quite different scenario. At that time there were two 'clairvoyants' competing with each other in venues across the world: Irving Bishop and Stuart Cumberland. On the same day Wilde wrote to Appleton about his forthcoming autumn lectures he received an invitation from the *Pall Mall Gazette*:[86]

> Stuart-Cumberland,[87] the 'Thought-reader' is coming to this

office to-morrow (Friday) at 5:30 precisely to display his skill. We are asking a lot of worthies to meet him. Will you join the band?

The band consisted of the editor, W. T. Stead,[88] and about thirty others including Oscar and Willie Wilde,[89] several scientists and Theosophists.[90] All assembled were sceptical of supernatural powers apart from the friends of the Theosophical Society - Madame de Novikoff (close colleague of Madame Blavatsky) and Colonel Olcott, described as an 'Esoteric Buddhist' - who considered that, to them, Cumberland's:[91]

divinations naturally appeared … somewhat insignificant.

Well, they would do when it was reported that:[92]

Colonel Olcott wore on his finger a ring which Mdme. Blavatsky, by her occult power, had caused to grow in the middle of a rosebud, and carried in his pocket a portrait of a seer which the same remarkable woman had willed out of the "astral light" upon a piece of cardboard.

Which sounds a little like a photograph.

All were assembled to witness an experiment by Stuart Cumberland who — rather like the present day Derren Brown — performed miraculous stunts but claimed no mystical powers, just the skills of a conjurer. Unlike his main competitor, Irving Bishop. On the evening[93] he immediately asked Wilde to be his first subject, but, disappointingly, Wilde:

shook his head, and declared he was not a good subject.

I cannot help but conclude that Wilde might just have been worried in case Cumberland made some great revelation, exposing a secret (we could speculate what that may have been), less than a week before his wedding. So another subject had to be chosen and Cumberland performed some small-scale mind-reading tricks with him. After a short rest, Cumberland resumed his demonstration and left the room while a pin was secretly fastened to the lapel of someone's coat. Blindfolded, Cumberland took the volunteer's hand and moved around the room trying to find the pin:

dragging him here, pulling him there, with much vigour.

Unfortunately, Cumberland was struggling and 'probed and poked unavailingly' at an easy chair. A better guide was needed:[94]

"Does anybody else know where the pin is hidden?" the thought-reader inquired.

"I do," said Oscar Wilde.

Clearly, Wilde had by now realised the nature of this exhibition, knew that his secrets were safe and turned out to be a wonderful guide:[95]

> The ponderous aesthete proved to be a much easier subject. ... Mr. Cumberland struck a bee-line and had the pin in no time at all.

Following his exertions, Cumberland:

> was then allowed to take a respite, during which Mr. Oscar Wilde discoursed in his free-and-easy way on art, poetry, and culture.

Wilde suggests the modest decorations in Stead's office were 'unworthy of the darkest ages'. The report continued in a playful manner:

> The poet and apostle has a pleasant way of being disappointed. There was something wrong with the Atlantic, and Niagara was not quite up to the mark. Now he was disappointed with the arrangement of a few simple flowers of the field and a rather striking harmony in curtains which were brought in for the occasion. However, a lecture on art from one so distinguished and so eccentric as Mr. Oscar Wilde is worth hearing. And above all he is a candid critic.

Wilde continued with some of the themes from *The House Beautiful*:

> "Your decorations," he said, "are absurd. There is no system obeyed. One thought, like harmony in music, should pervade the whole. Does it? No. They show no soul. Can you exist without a soul? No soul, no harmony, and no ... "
> "Sunflowers," suggested some one.
> "No. A flower is but an incident."
> In critical vein Mr. Wilde shook his shorn and curling locks, and, fanning himself with an expansive sage green silk pocket handkerchief, proceeded to descant on the maps which hung round the walls.
> "A map should be a work of art, with azure oceans limned on its surface, laden with golden galleys, with poops of beaten gold and purple sails. Let each continent show its rugged mountains, its stretching plains. Look at those seething seas of green hued calico, seas of erysipelas, with big blobs for mainlands and small blobs for islands."
> And thus was abuse showered upon those offending sheets. Mr. Wilde waved his hand with an attitude of despair, and

HARBORNE AND EDGBASTON INSTITUTE,

NOTICE TO MEMBERS.

MR. OSCAR WILDE'S LECTURE.

In consequence of Messrs. Harrison and Harrison's Concert being arranged to be given on TUESDAY NEXT, October 2, the Council of the above Institute begs to intimate that the OPENING LECTURE by Mr. OSCAR WILDE has been POSTPONED until the following Day,

WEDNESDAY, OCTOBER 3.
JOHN LEWIS, Hon. Sec.
7, Waterloo Street.   573

ENTHUSIASTIC RECEPTION LAST NIGHT.

MASONIC HALL, BIRMINGHAM.

TO-NIGHT (THURSDAY), TO-MORROW (FRIDAY), AND
ON SATURDAY EVENING NEXT,
SEPTEMBER 26, 27, 28, AND 29, AT EIGHT O'CLOCK.
DOORS OPEN AT 7.30.

MR. W. IRVING BISHOP,
The First and World-famed
THOUGHT-READER AND EXPLAINER OF SPIRIT
MYSTERIES,

Fresh from his Great London Successes, will give, as above, NEW and STARTLING ILLUSTRATIONS of his MARVELLOUS POWER of

THOUGHT - READING.

FAMOUS SPIRIT MYSTERIES
(Claimed by Spiritualists to be done by the aid of the *Spirits of the Dead*)

REPRODUCED AND EXPLAINED IN FULL VIEW OF THE AUDIENCE.

Tickets: Reserved, 4s. and 2s. 6d.; Area, One Shilling. At Messrs. Rogers and Priestley, Colmore Row.
Manager, Mr. A. GORDON.

Wilde and Irving Bishop in Birmingham

brushing off a fly from his forehead with the sage green pocket-handkerchief, he lowered his slim form gracefully into the bosom of a yielding couch.

Wilde would have been delighted with that 'slim form' but less so with the 'ponderous aesthete'.

Half an hour later, cooled by ices, 'Mr. Cumberland consented to try a much more difficult feat'. This was to find something, whilst blindfolded, outside of the editor's office. Grant Allen,[96] the writer, was the subject chosen, he thought of an object and Cumberland then proceeded to shoot off, out of the door, dragging Allen along:

followed by the more devoted spirits of the assembly … into Northumberland-street, much to the astonishment of the passers-by. Hansoms, foot-passengers, policemen, open-mouthed waiters, stopped to look at the strange procession. The windows of Northumberland-street were shot up with a rattle, maids and matrons in all of them, wondering if the hatless Mr. Oscar Wilde was trying to effect the capture of a new pair of Siamese twins.

This bizarre group stopped at one door, knocked and rang the bell:

> it was timidly opened by a servant who, seeing a blindfolded man followed by a small crowd, promptly shut the door in his face.

The trick had literally hit a closed door and the article then reports that

> The only other person in the street stepped up to Mr. Allen, and whispered to him, "Have you forgotten the house?" "Is this not it?" he replied. "I thought it was the third door down." "No, it is next door."

All this apparently in an inaudible whisper so that Cumberland could not hear but seemingly the reporter could? And who was this mysterious 'only other person in the street'? Straight away they went next door to part of the *Gazette's* offices, upstairs to the first floor, found an ottoman, lifted the lid and brought out 'a hunch of bread' left over from some investigations of eighteen years previous. A more bizarre object one could not wish for:

> This concluded the experiments, much to everyone's satisfaction. Mr. Stuart Cumberland ... will find it difficult to give more conclusive demonstrations of his ability to "read thought" by the delicate muscular action of the hand.

Quite what Wilde made of this whole exhibition is unknown. The final discovery was clumsy and it is difficult to know whether the trick had gone completely wrong and Cumberland required rescuing. Wilde's next big show was to be his wedding; hopefully no rescue would be required there.

The Wedding

OF COURSE, Constance and Oscar's wedding on 29 May received coverage in the press, positive and, inevitably, negative:

> The marriage of Mr Oscar Wilde and Miss Lloyd was celebrated on Thursday, by special license, at half-past three in the afternoon, at St. James's Church, Sussex Gardens, London[97].

So far so good, but then the report continued:

> Some discontent was excited in the neighbourhood before the

commencement of the ceremony at the exclusion from the building, by the bridegroom's orders, of all who had not received cards of invitation. Parishioners complained, and seat-holders loudly protested against a stranger presuming to shut the doors of the church, until, after half an hour of angry remonstrations with the officials by a number of the residents in the immediate vicinity of the church, the order was revoked, and about fifty people, beside the guests, took seats in the pews.

Poor Wilde and his good intentions! I am certain he just wanted some privacy for this important event. It is to be hoped that Constance was unaware of this trouble at the church. One reporter (Nana was her *nom de plume*[98]) did have an invitation:

A simple grey card, whereon is printed in plain black letters

ADMIT

TO

ST. JAMES' CHURCH,

SUSSEX GARDENS,

THURSDAY, MAY 29th, 1884,

AT 2.30 P.M.

is my passport today.

Thereafter, all seemed to go well. Inevitably the bride's dress and the bridesmaids were the focus of reports:[99]

The bride wore white satin and ottoman, striped a very large pattern. The bodice was square cut, and the sleeves, reaching to the elbow, were made with very large puffs set in high on the shoulder. The veil, which was worn hanging at the back of the head, was of white silk gauze, not nearly as becoming as tulle or lace.

But, of course, the groom's appearance attracted comment:[100]

This is a wedding at which more interest is taken in the bridegroom's frock than in the bride's, and ... the Poet of Culture was married in patent leather boots, lavender trousers, black frock coat, buttonhole of lilies, terra-cotta necktie, terra-cotta handkerchief, and new tall hat, which he hands, evidently with some apprehension that he will never see it again, to his brother Willie. ...

I wonder if the 'terra-cotta' items are indeed the often misreported, 'crushed strawberry' silk tie and handkerchief he had been wearing to his lectures throughout the past season. Whistler did not attend but[101] communicated:

> The following telegram from Tite-street was handed in at the church door:- "*From* Whistler, Chelsea, *to* Oscar Wilde St. James's Church, Sussex Gardens: Fear I may not be able to reach you in time for ceremony — don't wait."

But other guests did make it in time: Burne-Jones was there but, in a way which now seems a terrible put-down of one of the greatest Pre-Raphaelite painters, it was reported that other than he, 'no aesthetes' were in the congregation. However other guests[102] included:

> A number of ladies and gentlemen well known in literary and artistic circles were present, friends of the two families.

Those who we know were present in church were Mrs. Bernard Beere,[103] who had known Wilde for some years — she should have been the original *Vera* in 1881 and was to star as Mrs Arbuthnot at the premiere of *A Woman of No Importance* in 1893 — and Charles Brookfield,[104] who was to travesty *Lady Windermere's Fan* in *The Poet and the Puppets*, play Phipps in *An Ideal Husband* in 1895 and then reputedly assisted Queensberry in collecting his damning evidence for the trials. Eventually, the ceremony drew to a close and all eyes were on the bride and groom:[105]

> The bridegroom ... with his own increasing stoutness, and his broad ribbon and seals which were seen suspended from his watch "fob," he might have been suspected of personating the "first gentleman in Europe" himself. As he walked down the aisle with his pretty bride blushing and evidently overcome with emotion, on his arm, he looked proud and pleased, and as they drove away and I saw him give her a husband's kiss, I felt that the day's proceedings were an earnest of a worthier and a happier future for "Oscar the married man."

The use of the word 'earnest' as a noun — a thing regarded as a sign or promise of what is to come — is interesting and apposite. Of course, to us, now, it is a word — together with its homophonic Christian name — which has many implications for Wilde which no newspaper reader of the time could guess at. But it does force us to consider his position as he walked down the aisle 'with his pretty bride blushing on his arm': Oscar Wilde, earnest or not?

Table 3: Lectures January to May 1884

Date	Town	Venue	Time	Lecture
Tues 1 Jan	Belfast	New Theatre Royal	2:30 pm	The House Beautiful
Wed 2 Jan	Belfast	New Theatre Royal	2:30 pm	Personal Impressions of America
Thur 3 Jan	Londonderry	Opera House	night	HB
Fri 4 Jan	Londonderry	Opera House	night	PIA
Mon 7 Jan?	Lecture*			
Tues 8 Jan	Limerick	Theatre Royal	night	HB
Wed 9 Jan	Limerick	Theatre Royal	night	PIA
Thur 10 Jan	Cork	Opera House		HB
Fri 11 Jan	Cork	Opera House		PIA
Mon 14 Jan	Clonmel	Literary Institute		PIA
Tues 15 Jan	Waterford	Town Hall		PIA
Thur 17 Jan	Dundalk	Town Hall	8:00 pm	PIA
Mon 21 Jan	Sheffield	Firth College	8:00 pm	HB
Tues 22 Jan	Sheffield	Firth College	8:00pm	PIA
Wed 23 Jan	Huddersfield	Queen St. Assembly Rooms	night	HB
Thur 24 Jan	Kings Lynn	Music Hall	8:00 pm	PIA
Fri 25 Jan	Lincoln	Masonic Hall	8:00 pm	HB
Sat 26 Jan	Halifax	Dean Clough Institute	evening	HB
Mon 28 Jan	Gainsborough	Temperance Hall	evening	HB
Tues 29 Jan	Harrogate	Town Hall	evening	PIA
Wed 30 Jan	Chesterfield	Stephenson Memorial Hall	evening	PIA
Wed 30 Jan	Chesterfield	Stephenson Memorial Hall	after PIA	Modern Art Training

Thur 31 Jan	York	The Grand Saloon, Fine Art Exhibition	3:00 pm	HB
Thur 31 Jan	York	The Grand Saloon, Fine Art Exhibition	8:00 pm	PIA
Fri 1 Feb	Scarborough	Londesborough Theatre		PIA
Mon 4 Feb	Darlington	Mechanics Hall	evening	HB
Tues 5 Feb	Falkirk	Town Hall		HB
Wed 6 Feb	Edinburgh	Queen Street Hall	night	HB
Thur 7 Feb	Edinburgh	Queen Street Hall		PIA
Mon 11 Feb	Leeds	Albert Hall, Mechanics Institute	3:00 pm	HB
Mon 11 Feb	Leeds	Albert Hall, Mechanics Institute	8:00pm	PIA
Wed 13 Feb	Preston	Assembly Room, New Public Hall	7.45 pm	PIA
Thur 14 Feb	Bradford	Mechanics Institute	night	PIA
Fri 15 Feb	Stockton on Tees	Theatre Royal	8:00 pm	PIA
Sat 16 Feb	Sunderland	Victoria Hall	8:00 pm	HB
Sun 17 Feb	Newcastle upon Tyne	The Circus	6:30 pm	The Value of Art in Modern Life
Mon 18 Feb	Carlisle	County Hall		HB
Tues 19 Feb	Workington	Assembly Rooms		PIA
Wed 20 Feb	Cockermouth	Public Hall	evening	PIA
Thur 21 Feb	Maryport	Athenaeum		HB
Fri 22 Feb	Ulverston	Temperance Hall	night	HB
Sat 23 Feb	Sunderland	Victoria Hall	8:00 pm	PIA
?	North Shields (cancelled)			
Mon 25 Feb	Leek	Temperance Hall	8:00 pm	HB
Mon 3 Mar	Bristol	Victoria Rooms, Clifton	3:00 pm	HB
Mon 3 Mar	Bristol	Victoria Rooms, Clifton	8:00 pm	PIA
Tues 4 Mar	Warminster	Bleek Memorial Hall	evening	HB
Tues 5 Mar	London	Crystal Palace	3:00 pm	PIA

Fri 7 Mar	Leamington	Public Hall		HB
Fri 7 Mar	Leamington	Public Hall		PIA
Sat 8 Mar	Cheltenham	Assembly Rooms	afternoon	HB
Sat 8 Mar	Cheltenham	Assembly Rooms	evening	PIA
Mon 10 Mar	Wolver-hampton	Free Library Lecture Hall		HB
Tues 11 Mar	Walsall	Temperance Hall		HB
Wed 12 Mar	Leicester	Museum Lecture Hall	8:00 pm	HB
Thur 13 Mar	Birmingham	Midland Institute	3:00 pm	HB
Thur 13 Mar	Birmingham	Midland Institute	8:00 pm	PIA
Fri 14 Mar	Northampton	Town Hall		HB
Mon 17 Mar	Colchester	Town Hall	afternoon	HB
Mon 17 Mar	Colchester	Town Hall	evening	PIA
Tues 18 Mar	Ipswich	Town Hall	8:00 pm	PIA
Wed 19 Mar	Great Yarmouth	Royal Aquarium Minor Hall	3:00 pm	HB
Thur 20 Mar	Norwich	Agricultural Hall Assembly Room	evening	HB
Fri 21 Mar	Bury St Edmonds	Athenaeum Hall	night	PIA
Mon 24 Mar	Peterborough	Drill Hall		HB
Tue 25 Mar	Hull	Royal Institution		VAML
Thu 27 Mar	Cardiff	Fine Art Exhibition	4:00 pm	HB
Thu 27 Mar	Cardiff	Fine Art Exhibition	8:00 pm	PIA
Fri 28 Mar	Swansea	Albert Hall	evening	HB
Mon 31 Mar	Newport			
Sat 5 Apr	Southsea	Portland Hall	3:00 pm	HB
Sat 5 Apr	Southsea	Portland Hall	8:00 pm	PIA
Sat 19 Apr	Stoke on Trent	Town Hall	afternoon	An Address on Art
Tues 22 Apr	Southsea	Portland Hall	3:00 pm	HB
Tues 22 Apr	Southsea	Portland Hall	8:00 pm	PIA
Sat 26 Apr	London	St Jude's Schools, Commercial St	8:00 pm	VAML

Key

? either a doubtful date or location

*a possible lecture indicated by the summary accounts

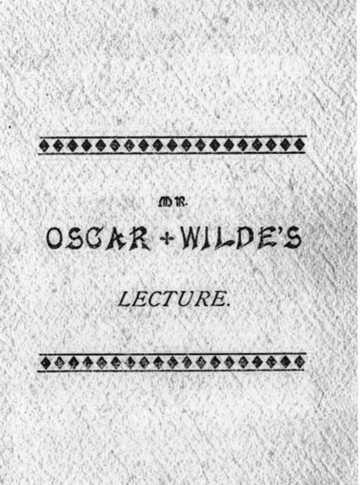

Front of Wilde's flyer for *Personal Impressions of America*
on 10 July 1883

John Ruskin: Wilde disagreed with Ruskin's aesthetics in his lectures.

William Morris: Wilde espoused his theories in *The House Beautiful*

Whistler when Wilde first met him, about 1878

Edward Burne-Jones, about 1882

Wilde in Birmingham, March 1884

Wilde in Birmingham, March 1884

"The Sparks" Studio, MARY ANDERSON.
112 & 114 North Ninth Street,
PHILADELPHIA.

Mary Anderson who turned down *The Duchess of Padua*

Princes' Hall on the right where Wilde gave his first public lecture.

Wandsworth High Street with the Town Hall on the left where
Wilde gave his first lecture after the failure of *Vera*

Cliftonville Hotel, Margate

Ramsgate. The Granville Hotel is the building with five gothic
gabled windows. The tower is the rear of the hotel

The venues where Wilde gave his first two lectures
outside London, in July 1883

Lillie Langtry, about 1883

Southport: the sea front. The Winter Gardens is the iron and
glass building at the far end of the Promenade

Southport Winter Gardens

♠♠♠♠♠♠♠♠♠♠♠♠♠♠♠♠♠♠♠

Mr. Oscar Wilde

Has the honour to announce that he will deliver a

LECTURE,

ENTITLED

"Personal Impressions of America,"

AT

The Winter Gardens,

SOUTHPORT.

At half-past Three o'Clock on the Afternoon of

Wednesday, August 1st, 1883.

Stalls, 4/-　　　　First Seats, 8/-
Second Seats & Balcony, 2/-
Back Seats & Gallery, 1/-
ALL CONTRACTORS TO THE GARDENS, HALF-PRICE.

Doors open at 3.　　　　*Lecture at 3.30.*
Carriages at 5.

Seats booked at the Lord Street Entrance.

♠♠♠♠♠♠♠♠♠♠♠♠♠♠♠♠♠♠♠

◆◆◆◆◆◆◆◆◆◆◆◆◆◆◆◆◆◆

What *The World* says of Mr. OSCAR WILDE'S Lecture,
at Princes' Hall, London, on July 10 :—

"The curiously expectant folk who went out to Princes' Hall 'for
to see' the typical æsthete, were somewhat pleasantly surprised to find a
very sensible and observant young man, who touched on a vast variety
of Transatlantic subjects with decided originality, somewhat audacious
brilliancy, and a good deal of quaintly quiet humour. Mr. Oscar Wilde's
method of lecturing has somewhat puzzled the critics who date from the
era of Albert Smith, and the discourse was a sort of subtle philosophical
all-round chat, sometimes extravagantly coloured, sometimes fanciful,
vague in structure, and full of a strong personal interest and an undercurrent of Irish fun. It was a decidedly new method of approaching
life, and travellers may take an odd hint or two from Oscar's curiously
amusing fashion of making a vivid sketch-book of the men and women,
and mountains and rivers, and theatres, and tea-cups, and magnolias,
and moons, and girls, that he drifted across in his picturesque 'pilgrim's
progress.' I thought the lecture was a little too long, the stories
excellently told, the voice clear and quiet, the paradoxes a little too
subtle for the audience, and the whole thing original, and quaint, and
interesting."

◆◆◆◆◆◆◆◆◆◆◆◆◆◆◆◆◆◆

A. S. Mallett, Printer, Wardour Street, London W

Flyer for Wilde's Southport lecture, August 1883

Marie Prescott who starred in *Vera*

Wilde whilst assisting with rehearsals for *Vera*. New York, August 1883

Wilde in New York, August 1883

Shelbourne Hotel, Dublin where Wilde stayed in November 1883

Kingstown (now Dún Laoghaire) Harbour, Dublin. Carlisle Pier
where the Holyhead ferry arrived is to the right.

Constance Lloyd in about 1883

Wilde in evening dress.
Caricature by 'Ape' (Carlo Pellegrini)
Vanity Fair May, 1884

Tynemouth where Wilde stayed for a weekend, December 1883

Carlisle. The County Hall where Wilde lectured in
February 1884 is centre left

Friar's Crag, Derwentwater visited by Wilde, February 1884

Railway Station, Scarborough, behind is the Pavilion Hotel
where Wilde stayed, February 1884

THE LECTURE (The House Beautiful) is for the most part an exposition of the application of the principles of true artistic decoration to the exterior and interior of the homes of the people, with observations on the choice of colours, styles of furniture, the selection of wall papers, curtains, carpets, and all the interior fittings of homes; and also includes remarks upon dress, personal ornaments, etc.

Mr. Oscar Wilde
Will deliver a
LECTURE,
ENTITLED
"THE HOUSE BEAUTIFUL."
AT
The Royal Institution,
ALBION STREET, HULL,
On Tuesday, October 16th, 1883,
At Eight o'Clock.

The Lecture will contain the principal portion, with additional matter, of that delivered by Mr. Oscar Wilde during his late American tour.

The Proceeds will be given to the Library Fund of the Hull Young People's Christian and Literary Institute.

Admission, 1s.   Reserved Seats (numbered), 2s.

May be obtained at Messrs. Brown & Son's, Savile-street.

THE LECTURE (The House Beautiful) is for the most part an exposition of the application of the principles of true artistic decoration to the exterior and interior of the homes of the people, with remarks upon the choice of colours, styles of furniture, and selection of wall paper, curtains, and carpets, and all interior furnishing. Mr. Wilde will also offer some observations upon style and colour in dress for the house and in the street; on the influence of artistic surroundings upon children; and on the value of handicrafts as the basis of education. The lecture will contain the principal portion of the address delivered by Mr. Wilde during his late American tour, together with much additional matter relative to the present position and future development of art-decoration in this country.

Mr. W. GOMERSAL has the honour to announce that
Mr. Oscar Wilde
WILL DELIVER
A LECTURE
ENTITLED,
The + House + Beautiful
AT THE
THEATRE ROYAL, WORCESTER,
At Eight o'Clock on the Evening of
Tuesday, December 18th, 1883.

Doors open at 7.30.   Lecture at 8.   Carriages at 9

Stalls, 3s.   Upper Circle, 2s.   Pit, 1s.   Gallery, 6d.
Private Boxes, £1 1s. and £1 11s. 6d.

Seats may be booked at Messrs. Deighton's Library, Worcester

Flyers for *The House Beautiful*, 1883

Dorothy Dene: Wilde met her in York, October 1884

Birmingham Midland Institute where Wilde lectured in March 1884

Bradford Mechanics' Institute where Wilde lectured twice in 1884

Wilde in Ryde, 1884, card sent to Philip Griffiths December 1884

Leeds Mechanics' Institute where Wilde lectured four times in 1884

Torquay. The Bath Saloon where Wilde lectured in January 1886 is in the centre of the photograph.

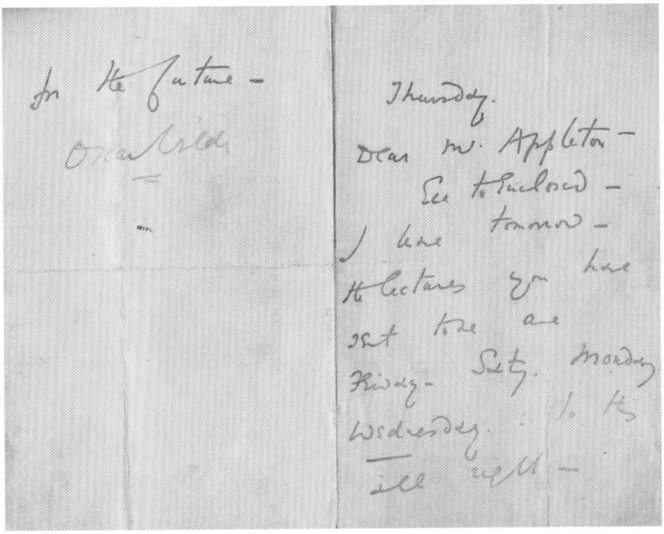

for the future -

Oscar Wilde

Thursday.

Dear Mr. Appleton -

See the enclosed -

I have tomorrow -

the lectures you have

set for me are

Friday - Saty. Monday

Wednesday. [illegible]

ill well -

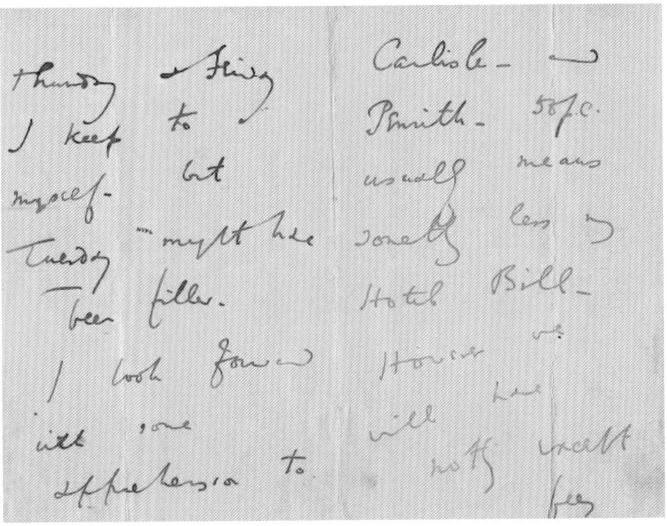

Thursday & Friday

I keep to

myself - but

Tuesday - might have

been filled.

I look forward

with some

apprehension to.

Carlisle -

Penrith - 50 f.c.

usually means

only less my

Hotel Bill -

However we

will have

nothing except

fees

Letter from Wilde complaining to Appleton, January 1885

Letter from Wilde to Appleton, Ulverston, February 1885

Wilde in his fur coat, March 1885
Drawing by Harper Pennington

The Nicholson Institute, Leek where Wilde lectured in March 1885

CHAPTER 4

JULY 1883 to APRIL 1884

A Handful of Notes and Gold

THERE are occasional mentions of Wilde's income from lecturing in *Collected Letters* and in his biographies. Colonel W. F. Morse, his manager for the 1883/84 UK season, wrote[1] that he organised the Princes' Hall lecture of *Personal Impressions of America* and that:

> This introduction of Mr. Wilde to a London audience was deemed sufficient to warrant his presentation throughout the English provinces.

He also commented on the general organisation of the tour:

> The Mechanics' or Literary Institutes of the United Kingdom were usually the agencies by which speakers came into contact with the public ... The lectures of Mr. Wilde took their place on the list, and were a part of the series, except in one or two of the larger cities, where they were managed ... for the joint benefit of the theatre and speaker ... He had no travelling agent or manager except at places where a lecture was arranged for independently of the local managers and associations. As a rule, these were the most successful ones of the season, rarely failing to attract large and appreciative audiences.

Ellmann suggests that Wilde was told he could receive between 10 and 25 guineas for a lecture.[2] In conclusion, Morse wrote that:

> The returns from this series of lectures, while of considerable consequence, were not as large as those in America, for the English scale of compensation to public speakers is not up to the American standard. However, the amount that Mr. Wilde

received was sufficient to provide for his immediate future and to enable him to carry out certain plans that he had formed.

All the indications are that in the early stages the audiences were sufficiently large to make this a decent business proposition which would generate a good income for Wilde and his agents. Wilde must have felt so himself because when he was lecturing in Sheffield in January 1884 he wrote[3] to Lillie Langtry to tell her of his engagement to Constance and he added that he was 'getting quite rich'. Robert Sherard — in the third of his books about Wilde[4] — describes him returning to London from a 'lecture in the provinces' saying that he:

> ... returned to town at intervals, and on more than one occasion pulled out of the pocket of his fur coat a handful of notes and gold which he had earned ... and told me to take what I needed. "It's as much yours as mine ... You know I have no sense of property."

However, approximately a year later in early 1885 things had changed for the worse. There are several letters[5] at this time from a rather angry sounding Wilde complaining to his then manager, Appleton, about the mismanagement of the tour at the time and about the poor remuneration. In one letter, he complains:

> Fifty per cent usually means something less than my hotel bill.

Which must be a reference to a new fee — half the door receipts — Appleton had agreed for the next lectures. In another letter at this time Wilde writes:

> ... after the heavy loss of the last three months ...

Therefore, in 1885, Wilde's income from lecturing was waning.

There were several newspaper stories of the time commenting on Wilde's fees, often with an inevitably sarcastic tone. In Newcastle in October 1883:

> It is a mistake ... to say that Mr. Wilde's lecture fee is only ten guineas. He gets twelve. Aesthetics are dears.[6]

And when he visited again for the hugely successful February 1884[7] lecture:

> Somebody must be making a good thing financially out of these lectures ... if, as is said, Mr Oscar Wilde pocketed £20 for his ...

But the organisers asked to be able to respond to this accusation and the following week a retraction was published:[8]

We mentioned last week that some one must be making a good thing out of the Sunday evening lectures at the Circus in Newcastle. This, it appears, is not the case, for on Sunday evening last the chairman stated that the average attendance was 1,390, and the average takings were £21 14s 9d. The maximum attendance was at Mr Oscar Wilde's lecture, at which it was 3,187, and the takings £37 17s 5d. Prior to that lecture there was a loss of something like £9 6s 1d; but the profit at Mr Wilde's lecture was £18 8s 8d, which turned the loss … into a profit of £8 14s 7d. …

So it was Wilde the major success who came to the financial rescue here with the attendance at his lecture well over twice the average and his receipts far exceeding the others. His fee on this occasion was 50%, or £18 8s 8d. Where figures were published, it looks to have been a similar story elsewhere. In Burnley, Lancashire in December 1884:

THE RECEIPTS AT THE SCIENCE LECTURES. − The receipts this year … speak well for the popularity of the lectures arranged by the directors of the Institute …

and there followed a list with Wilde's lecture topping the receipts at £11 12s 9d.

Fortunately, there is some financial information available, mainly coming from a statement of account for the 1883/84 season of lectures.[9] Unfortunately, this is incomplete and lacks detail for most of the season. From these papers there appear to have been three rates which Wilde received:

a) a flat fee;
b) an agreed share of the gross receipts with the organiser of the lecture paying all costs of the lecture, advertisements, staff, etc;
c) net receipts divided 50:50 between Wilde and his own management where they had made all the arrangements and paid all costs for the lecture.

One example of a shared receipts contract was signed in July 1884 and was for a lecture at the Southport Winter Gardens in September.[10] This Memorandum of Agreement - signed by John Long (*Manager of the Southport Winter Gardens*) and Appleton (*Manager for Mr Oscar Wilde*) - sets out all the details of the contract: location, date, time, seat prices and lecture title (it was to be *Dress*) and is clear about what Long had to provide:

John Long agrees to find Lecture room, usual newspaper advertisements bills & bill posting, money and check takers

MR. OSCAR WILDE'S LECTURES.
SEASON 1883–84.

From

W. F. MORSE,

Manager · Mr. Wilde's Lectures in America and England.

40, Norfolk Street, Strand,
LONDON. W.C.

188

To

Morse's letterhead for Wilde's 1883/84 lecture tour

The terms are:

> Oscar Wilde to take Sixty per cent & the said John Long Forty per cent of the Gross receipts for admission

It says something about Wilde's 'draw' that Long was sufficiently confident of this business opportunity to bear all costs and allow Wilde 60% of the gross receipts before he started to make any money.
The 1883/84 Statements do contain quite detailed accounts for four lectures in three towns where Morse had made all the arrangements and all receipts would be shared equally with Wilde. These details are for two nights in Sheffield (21 and 22 January 1884) and the lectures in Huddersfield (23 January) and Halifax (26 January). It is interesting to have these detailed accounts for lectures so close together (in space and time) and to see exactly what was spent, on what, and what Wilde did earn.

For his two nights lecturing in Sheffield, the costs amounted to £26 10s 7d which included hall hire, hire of attendants, the printing of various items, parcels and telegrams, commission to the ticket sellers and paying someone to paste up the posters. The printed matter for Sheffield amounted to:

>   500 window bills
>   1500 circulars
>   10 large posters
>   2 sets tickets
>   Total: £5/8/1

Which is a phenomenal amount of printing even for two nights' lectures: over 2000 posters and flyers. If Sheffield is a guide, the UK must have been awash with printed materials yet these are extremely rare now. On the other side of the balance sheet are the ticket receipts which are divided into advanced sales and sales on the door on the two nights: advanced sales were higher and the total ticket sales were £42 15s 6d. From this money Wilde was allowed £2 for expenses leaving a clear profit of over £14. With expenses this resulted in the final calculation being:

Amount due Mr Wilde £9 2s 6d

To our modern eyes, a little over £9 profit for two lectures hardly appears to be 'getting quite rich' as he claimed to Lillie Langtry at that very time. It is difficult to translate these amounts into modern money terms but looking at the effects of inflation[11] this £9.125 at 1884 prices becomes equivalent to £850 at 2010 prices. For ease of calculation, the effect of inflation is that current prices (2013) are slightly under 100 times the 1883/84 prices. So Wilde's share of his two Sheffield lectures amounts to about £900 at current prices.

The returns at Huddersfield and Halifax were less good than at Sheffield and were probably why Wilde did not return there. For a single lecture in each town, the individual printing costs were less but together they were roughly equal to Sheffield's two nights (Huddersfield: £3 16s 11d and Halifax: £2 17s 2d.) Similarly, enormous numbers of flyers and posters were printed. However, in Huddersfield the 'very fair attendance'[12] resulted in ticket sales which exceeded the costs by less than £1; in Halifax the net receipts amounted to under £6. In all, for the four lectures, the accounts show that on 4 February Wilde was paid £14 9s 5d which included some cash brought forward from previous lectures. In modern money, the 2013 equivalent amount would be approximately £1400.00 which, for four days' work, I think is not too out of line with what he had told Lillie Langtry.

There are other interesting features of these accounts. One of these is that the very first entry on the first sheet is:

July 10   ½ loss on London Lecture   £1/8/0

There are no further details of the breakdown of this loss but we know there was a good attendance so ticket sales must have been acceptable. It could just have been that the cost of advertising and printing exceeded the receipts: Morse had placed an enormous number of advertisements in the newspapers, presumably to try to ensure a success. On the other hand, however poor this lecture had been in purely financial terms, Wilde had drawn a considerable audience and received an enormous amount of press coverage across the country. On balance, Wilde and Morse must have considered the outcome sufficiently successful to justify a full time lecture tour of the UK, even if there had been a financial loss.

Morse reports[13] that:

> During the season of 1883-84 Mr. Wilde delivered upwards of one hundred and fifty addresses in all parts of the United Kingdom.

The accounts show that all lectures returned a profit other than the Princes' Hall lecture and the lectures in Birmingham and Peterborough, which were both in March 1884 near the end of the season. The Birmingham engagements were for two lectures on one day and one review noted the poor attendance — the 'lecture room was only partly filled'[14] — which would result in these poor receipts.

During the period between the 7 and 31 March, from these accounts, other than the Birmingham and Peterborough losses, Wilde and his managers' share of the receipts ranged between £1 16s 6d at Bury St. Edmunds, to a large £18 8s 6d in Leicester, an amount usually indicating two well attended lectures. The total of 18 lectures during this period, excepting the losses, brought in a total of £161 15s 7d. After expenses and some further minor adjustments for funds for that period, these monies were shared half and half, with Wilde receiving a few pennies over £70.

During the 1883/84 season, in general, Wilde paid his management a commission of 20% (other than where he shared the receipts with them) but he did also pay 10% and 30% on some occasions.

It is difficult from the amounts of income on the statements to assess on what basis Wilde was being paid in all cases. There are the occasional round figures of ten guineas (eg at Ulverston and Leek in February 1884) which would indicate a flat fee. Then there are odd amounts (e.g. Workington £7 18s 6d or Cockermouth £5 16s 8d) which could indicate a sharing of the sale of the tickets, or, on the other hand, it could still indicate a fixed fee but reduced by expenses. Whilst the statements do include a very few references to Wilde's expenses such as cab fares, there is no mention of a hotel bill. This could have been because the local organisers provided his accommodation or that Wilde's management booked him a room in a nearby hotel and it was then left to Wilde to take his share of the receipts at the conclusion of his lecture (the 'handful of notes and gold' in his fur coat pockets, as described by Sherard) and with it pay his hotel bill, hopefully having something left over for himself and his management's commission. By the early months of 1885, as noted above, Wilde was concerned that his fee 'usually means something less than my hotel bill' which could well have been embarrassing.

Overall, from the records of Wilde's 1883/84 lecture tour, he and his management team received approximately £1144 in receipts for under 120 lectures (not including his three losses). This is a large amount of money – well over £110,000 at 2012 prices – and averages at between £9 and £10 per lecture. However, this average disguises wide disparities: in Dublin, whilst he wooed Constance and complaints were made about the cost of the tickets, Wilde's receipts were a massive £41 for each of his two lectures, which is in complete contrast to his lectures in England at the same time which were averaging under £6 and his Bury St Edmunds lecture which grossed him less than £2.

One further benefit of these records is the notes they contain of the number of lectures Wilde gave during his 1883/84 season. The financial information is divided into time periods of a variety of lengths and often the total number of lectures in that period is noted, even if the actual venues are not. From this information I have been able to estimate dates for any lectures which I have not been able to trace up to the end of April 1884 and these are shown in the tables of lectures as 'Lecture'

CHAPTER 5

Autumn to Christmas 1884

Making the House Beautiful

DURING the Wildes' *vacances* in Dieppe, Constance's choice of dress came in for very positive comment in the press:[1]

... the young poet's bride is winning the admiring suffrage of the *habitués* of the "*Plage.*"

The article could not be more complimentary to Constance, reporting that the French ladies:

Recognise the superior right of grace inspired by taste to adorn itself with picturesque becomingness. Mrs. Oscar Wilde, in her large white-plumed hats, her long dusk cloaks of creamy alpaca, richly trimmed with ruches of coffee-coloured lace, in her fresh and somewhat quaintly-made gown of white muslin, usually relieved by touches of golden-coloured ribbon, or with yellow floss silk embroideries, is declared "*charmante,*" and to be dressed with absolute good taste.

This description contrasts with Laura Troubridge's[2] diary entry[3] about when she had invited the Wildes for tea on 8 July, which would have been about two weeks after their return from honeymoon. On this occasion Constance seems to be wearing a very similar outfit to the one she wore to wow the *habitués de la Plage* although it was given a much less *charmante* description:

Mr. and Mrs. Oscar Wilde to tea, she dressed for the part in drimp white muslin, with absolutely *no* bustle, saffron coloured silk swathed about her shoulders, a huge cartwheel Gainsborough hat, white and bright yellow stockings and shoes — she looked too hopeless and we thought her shy and dull — he was amusing of course.

Laura Troubridge's amazement at the lack of bustle shows her to be out of line with not just Wilde's views on women's dress but views which were then gathering prominence through the rational dress movement, driven by concerns over women's health. In fact, Constance was to become an important member, if not one of the leading lights, of the Rational Dress Society and she also became active in the Women's Liberal Federation.[4] At many of the Rational Dress Society public meetings and lectures, which were widely reported, Constance spoke and we receive a perception of her which is much less *shy and dull* and rather different from this diary entry. However, sitting around a tea table when Wilde was in full flow, being *amusing of course* (of course), anyone else might appear rather quiet and withdrawn.

The International Health Exhibition

ANOTHER great exhibition — the International Health Exhibition — was opened on the 8th May 1884 and continued for a period of about six months. This was one of the largest public exhibitions to be held in the country and its aim was to consider seriously the environmental, social and health problems associated with the industrialisation and urbanisation of the UK. It was held in London on a site in South Kensington now occupied by the Science Museum and Imperial College and was visited by four million people in total. It was designed to showcase innovations in sanitation, electric lighting and water supply and it featured electrically illuminated fountains, a replica of an insanitary medieval London street and exhibits of sanitary appliances. The *Illustrated London News* had a slightly negative view of things:[5]

> the mind and eye of the average sightseer do not derive any very ecstatic pleasure from the inspection of models of drain-pipes, sewer-traps, cisterns, pumps, roof-slates, joists, filters and ventilators.

The many volumes of papers of the Exhibition illustrate the range of the discussions which were held and were so topical at the time. All aspects of the health of the nation were under consideration ranging from water supply and sewerage systems, the construction of healthy homes and schools, healthy food production, healthy dress, to the prevention of the spread of disease. This helps to give a context to the matters Wilde was addressing in his lectures and which he was to cover in more detail in his new lecture, *Dress*. These all came under serious academic and popular scrutiny during this Exhibition which included lectures from men such as William Morris and Edward

Godwin who were very influential on Wilde. In particular, Godwin lectured and published a book which Wilde read: *Dress, and its Relation to Health and Climate.*

On the evening of 23 July, a Royal fete was held at the Health Exhibition and it was honoured with the presence of the Prince and Princess of Wales. It was described[6] in the most complimentary terms:

> Nothing more brilliant than the *fête* ... has been witnessed in the metropolis in a long time

and 20,000 or so attended during that evening alone in aid of charities for the London Hospitals. This was a matter the Wildes were interested in even if he was to belittle charities later in life:[7]

> ... in the present state of things in England, the people who do most harm are the people who try to do most good; and at last we have had the spectacle of men who have really studied the problem and know the life — educated men who live in the East End — coming forward and imploring the community to restrain its altruistic impulses of charity, benevolence, and the like. They do so on the ground that such charity degrades and demoralises. They are perfectly right. Charity creates a multitude of sins.

That evening the Exhibition was augmented by:

> a fancy fair. The stalls which were principally for the sale of flowers, ferns, exotics, fruit and light refreshments were attended by a very large number of ladies who had kindly consented to devote their influence and services to the good cause.

The report continues with an enormous list of nobility, rich, fashionable and famous women who helped out during the evening, plus a few men who also contributed. At the inner court of the pavilion:

> Here Miss Fortescue,[8] Mr. Oscar Wilde, Mrs. Wilde, and Mr. Grossmith[9] leant their aid to the sale of a vast variety of floral gifts, including an extensive assortment of sun flowers and lilies

Selling sunflowers and lilies goes to illustrate Wilde's good-natured acceptance of a mild joke at his own expense, even though he had been distancing himself from that old aesthetic persona for some time, rather unsuccessfully. Other memories of his high aesthetic days were represented by his co-stallholders that evening, who must have been

May Fortescue. Drawing by Harry Furniss.

selected for just that reason: May Fortescue — a great beauty of the day — made her debut on the stage in *Patience* in April 1881 and George Grossmith had actually starred in that production as Reginald Bunthorne, the original 'Fleshly Poet', the supposed satire on Wilde. The temptation to reprise their parts by walking with a poppy or a lily in their mediaeval hands must have been resisted. The Royal visitors stopped at some stalls to make purchases and the *Morning Post*[10] could hardly contain itself in its description of this unsurpassed *al fresco* evening in the metropolis:

> The fountains, with their kaleidoscopic changes of colour in rapid and bewildering variety, resembled more a continuous shower of brilliant fireworks than an aqueous display. The myriads of coloured lamps, the glistening lakes, the waterfalls upon which coloured lights were reflected, and the thousands of visitors in evening dress, moving to and fro, all helped to achieve a combination which, in a pictorial sense, left nothing to be desired. No less than six military bands, to say nothing of the

Chinese musicians – who, perhaps, owing to Western prejudices, may be left out of account – performed throughout the evening. The *fête* was not finally over until long after one o'clock this morning

One hopes that the Chinese musicians did not feel too left out, 'owing to Western prejudices'.

Making *The* House Beautiful

BEFORE Wilde returned to the lecture platform, he and Constance had to set up a new home and he knew that whatever he did in decorating it would come under the spotlight: after all, he had been lecturing on *The House Beautiful* for the best part of a year. They took a lease on 16 Tite Street in Chelsea — which was already an artists' enclave — and the press commented upon this location:[11]

> Mr. Oscar Wilde's new home in that quarter of Old Chelsea beloved by Carlyle[12] and Rossetti bids fair to be a practical illustration of the apostle's lecture on "The House Beautiful." There are rumours of an Eastern apartment; and the Cairo galleries at Great Pulteney-street have been laid under contribution for choice examples of the picturesque Musbrebiyeh screen work, the finer specimens of which can now only be obtained with considerable difficulty.

It has been reported that Wilde asked Whistler to design the house for him, but he had refused, kindly suggesting that the proof of the lecturer's theories would be in what he actually accomplished himself. However, following the fiasco after he lectured to art students in June 1883, Wilde probably did not offer that invitation. However, deciding that he did need some practical support in this task, he commissioned the aesthete's architect, Edward Godwin, to take on the work. Godwin was a close friend of Whistler's and Wilde had known him for over seven years. He was a major influence during this period, and not just on Wilde. Max Beerbohm[13] describing an outdoor production of *As You Like It* which Wilde was to review the following year, wrote:[14]

> All Fashion came to marvel and so did all the Aesthetes, in the heart of one of whose leaders, Godwin, that superb architect, the idea was first conceived.

He had already designed two houses on Tite Street, one the White House for Whistler (by this time occupied by Whistler's enemy, 'Arry Quilter[15]) and the other for Frank Miles the artist with whom Wilde

ASSEMBLY ROOMS, BATH.

MR. OLIVER has much pleasure in stating that he
has arranged with

MR. OSCAR WILDE

TO GIVE HIS LECTURE ON

" DRESS,"

IN THE ASSEMBLY ROOMS,

ON THURSDAY EVENING,

OCTOBER 16*th*, 1884.

The great popularity of Mr. OSCAR WILDE as a Lecturer is
sufficiently evinced by the fact that his recent tour extended
without a break from September, 1883, to April of the present
year, during which peri- d he addressed overflowing houses in
every part of the United Kingdom, with the most brilliant
success. His new Lecture on " DRESS " has been pronounced
by the Press to be the hit of the Season.

Admission—Reserved and Numbered Seats, 3s. ; Second
Seats, 2s. ; Back of Room, 1s.

Doors open at 7.30 ; commence at 8.

Plan of Seats at Mr. Oliver's Office, at the Rooms.

Wilde lectures on 'Dress' – the hit of the Season - in Bath

had lived in 1880. Godwin had interests in dress, furniture, theatre production and he designed part of the fashionable Bedford Park development, which exemplified the Queen Anne style Wilde extolled in *The House Beautiful*. So Wilde had the very best of assistance from the polymath Godwin in creating his new home and there is much correspondence in *Collected Letters* from Wilde to Godwin about the works, and the travails, of the renovations at Tite Street.

Lecturing Once More

WILDE'S tour manager from now on was George Appleton who continued to try to make the travelling as efficient as he could: the autumn lecture tour started at Ealing on 1 October and whilst we do see Wilde with dates in the south of England, the lectures group quite well in the Midlands, then Yorkshire and finish before Christmas with Wilde at The Balmoral Hotel, Edinburgh for six nights whilst he lectured in Scotland. The tour continued to be very intensive and a good example of his work rate was on four days in October when Wilde lectured twice on the Monday in Cardiff, twice again on the Tuesday in Bristol, visited the Bristol Industrial Exhibition Wednesday morning before travelling to and lecturing twice in Cheltenham and then lectured once more in Bath on Thursday.

Before their wedding, Wilde had written that for the new autumn season he would have two new lectures at least plus those he had already given. In July it was advertised that:[16]

> MR OSCAR WILDE has returned from his honeymoon, and is looking forward to a season of fresh literary and lecturing activity. He has added three new lectures to his *repertoire* – one on dress, one on the value of art in modern life, and one on Benvenuto Cellini.

During the autumn, Wilde would actually give two new lectures: *Dress* (clearly from the very favourable response to Constance's outfits in Dieppe, he was giving excellent advice, assuming Constance was listening) and a reworked *The Value of Art in Modern Life*. On a very few occasions he also revisited *The House Beautiful*. This was the first but not the last time Wilde promised to lecture on Cellini in the UK, yet I have found no evidence of him ever having done so.

An embryonic version of *The Value of Art in Modern Life* had been given on a very few occasions before the summer but had been recast by Wilde for this season. At first, this lecture was advertised as *Dress: The Value of Art in Modern Life* and was a variation on his lecture *Dress*, which must have been confusing. Later in the season, I assume because of this apparent similarity of the two lecture titles, Wilde dropped the word 'Dress' from its title. Even so, its subject matter overlapped with *Dress* and in a number of cases Wilde mistakenly (or, possibly, not) gave his *Dress* lecture instead of the advertised *The Value of Art in Modern Life* (for example, Stoke, Bristol, Burnley and Nottingham). Nobody noticed, but why and how could they? He had promised new lectures for this season and perhaps, lacking the motivation, this was the only way he could achieve it. This could be Wilde's ultimate plagiarism: two lecture titles but only one lecture.

By the time Wilde began his autumn 1884 lecture tour Constance was pregnant with their first child. A forthcoming family, a house to redecorate with an architect and builders to pay can only have intensified the pressure on Wilde to maximise his income.

BURNLEY MECHANICS' INSTITUTION.

SCIENCE LECTURES FOR THE PEOPLE.

THURSDAY, NOV. 27TH,

" *THE VALUE OF ART IN MODERN LIFE,*"

BY OSCAR WILDE, ESQ.

Doors open at 7-0. Lecture to commence at 8-0,
Admission :—First Seats 1s., Second Seats 6d.,
Third Seats 3d.
Entrance to First Seats—Manchester Road.

C. M. FODEN, Hon. Sec.

Wilde gives a science lecture in Burnley

Dress

AT THE BEGINNING of October in Ealing, west London, Wilde gave his new lecture, *Dress*. On the following day[17] a short and favourable review was published in *The Pall Mall Gazette* under the heading:

MR. OSCAR WILDE ON DRESS.

Wilde's main themes were detailed accurately:

During the past few years a sense of the beautiful appeared to have revived in the country, although this had not yet extended to the matter of dress, there being nothing of the rational or beautiful about it. In order to a reform in this direction what was required was the compulsory teaching of drawing to every child, which would result in a thorough understanding of the grace and beauty of the human form, and the best method of adapting dress thereto.

The great enemy of reform was fashion ... greatly guided by France whose influence had been most pernicious ... dating from 1066

If asked to fix the time when the dress of this country was really lovely he would say the second quarter of the seventeenth century

Mr. Wilde ... spoke highly of the costumes of the Greeks, Assyrians, and Egyptians. The latter particularly observed one very important principle, namely, that of the dress being supported not by the waist but by the shoulder. In modern dress, however, all the weight was on the waist and hip ... this also necessitated the use of the dress improver, which he denounced as extremely ungraceful.

High-heeled boots which threw the whole body forward, he also strenuously condemned, together with tight lacing, which was injurious as well as ungraceful.

The modern tall hat also came in for a share of condemnation, Mr. Wilde expressing a preference for a soft one, but more strongly recommended a hood.

Generally, he expressed himself strongly in favour of such a modification of the Greek costume as would meet the exigencies of our varying climate.

Underclothes should be sufficiently tight, but no so much so as to impede the free use of the limbs. With proper undercloth ... some adaption of the tunic or cloak of the Greeks would be what he would recommend.

He also urged that the basis of dress should be wool, which was the most sanitary of any material, giving the necessary coolness in summer and requisite warmth in winter

Wilde brought his lecture to a conclusion by:

advocating further the use of soft brown leather, such as that of which the doublet of former times was made.

Wilde's promotion of wool shows his conversion to the ideas of Dr. Gustav Jaeger[18] whose philosophy might be supported by Yorkshire industry but not so over the Pennines in the Cottonopolis of Manchester:[19]

Every article of attire is to be of wool. No more fine Irish linen; no more longcloth of calico, or muslin, or cambric. All to be wool, even to the hat, cap, and pocket handkerchief. Of course, as this dress reform comes from Germany it is thought to be inspired by Bismark[20] himself in order to ruin Manchester ... to substitute thereunto the rubbishing German woollen fabrics of which we have already a surfeit ... we hear of one of our great artists being occupied in executing new forms and designs for loose woollen garments which are to throw those of Oscar Wilde completely into the shade.

Jaeger's philosophy of the wearing of wool next to the skin and not using any plant fibres in clothing material was beginning to attract considerable attention and Godwin had echoed these thoughts in his lecture to the International Health Exhibition. Wilde and an enthusiastic George Bernard Shaw[21] became advocates and, later in life, Wilde was quoted[22] as saying:

'Oh, Shaw! That's the man who smokes Jaeger cigarettes!'

The following day the *Pall Mall Gazette* published a letter headed *"MR. OSCAR WILDE ON DRESS REFORM."* written by a Mr Wentworth Huyshe[23]. In this letter Huyshe wished for 'a little space wherein to reply to Mr. Oscar Wilde's ideas upon dress' commenting that few saw a need for reform and those that did 'bring no common sense to bear on the question'. In his letter he ridiculed the idea of modifying ancient Greek dress, suggesting that women would not wear it. As for men, he thought the top hat and trousers did need changing, back to a style of the late eighteenth century. Tailors and hatters ought to lead this change and clothing ought to be appropriate to our climate. If such changes cannot be made we would be better keeping things as they were.

A few days later another letter appeared[24] entitled *"A WOMAN'S RHAPSODY ON DRESS"* introduced with the sentence:

A "Girl Graduate" writes to us as follows on the vexed question raised by Mr. Oscar Wilde.

In this letter the "Girl Graduate" suggests that Wilde is mistaken to criticise high-heeled boots and to favour ancient Greek costume, and the reason he was making these mistakes was that Wilde was not a woman. She writes that only women know that a walk in flat soles and skirts on Park Street 'on a commonplace, muddy, metropolitan day would result in a coating of sticky brown mud' which would require her to have to change clothes the moment she got indoors. That is why women wore high-heeled boots. Corsets and stays allow the weight of clothing to be equalized and distributed. However, if petticoats were abandoned altogether women would be freer (and this was one of the watchwords of the dress reformers -- Freedom):

Let the garb of every man and woman be the unfeigned expression and outcome of individual feeling and thought.

The Girl Graduate concludes that education needs to 'inculcate reverence for individualism' then, maybe, these changes may well take place even if the divided skirt would not be seen. In much of this, the Girl Graduate was completely in step with Wilde's thoughts which he had, and was, elaborating across the country. The divided skirt, though, seems to have been a battleground all of its own with Wilde, in principle, one of its supporters.

All this correspondence provided a golden opportunity for Wilde to respond and to have his views published in the press. This was a chance to build upon his notoriety and have his name associated with something a little more positive than his, to him, now defunct aesthete persona. Frank Harris[25] describes exactly Wilde's attitude to this situation when his name was mentioned in the press: Wilde asked him what he would say to such an article and Harris said he would do nothing. Wilde's attitude was different:

> "You're making a mistake," he said seriously. "If you wish for reputation and fame in this world, and success during your lifetime, you ought to seize every opportunity of advertising yourself ... you must go about repeating how great you are till the dull crowd come to believe it."

> "The prophet must proclaim himself, eh? And declare his own mission?"

> "That's it ... Every time my name is mentioned in a paper, I write at once to admit that I am the Messiah ... The journalist is my 'John the Baptist.' What would you give, when a book of yours comes out, to be able to write a long article drawing attention to it in *The Pall Mall Gazette*? ... I miss no chance"

This was his chance to draw attention himself, this was *The Pall Mall Gazette* and he was not going to let it pass. Although an intervention would not generate any income, Wilde must have seen it as a good opportunity to make some telling, witty points, stoke whatever controversy there was and, perhaps, get an invitation to write on a more permanent basis and be paid for it. In any case, as Wilde knew well, the exposure would generate some free publicity for the lectures. Stead, the editor, had met Wilde in May at the mind reading session in his office and may also have been aware that he had deputised for his brother, Willie, as dramatic critic of *Vanity Fair* during the summer. Therefore he knew that Wilde did have the wit, skill and experience of reviewing for a serious journal. Wilde's response[26] was published under the heading:

MR. OSCAR WILDE ON WOMAN'S DRESS

even though he also deals with men's attire. The full letter is given in *Complete Letters*[27] but it omits the newspaper's short introduction:

> MR. OSCAR WILDE, who asks us to permit him "that most charming of all pleasures, the pleasure of answering one's critics," sends us the following remarks:-

which suggests that a covering letter or note from Wilde containing the phrase in quotation marks may have accompanied the letter/article which followed. It is unfortunate that this no longer exists.

The letter began with a number of responses to the Girl Graduate's letter – virtually all of which were taken directly from the content of his lecture, *Dress*. He began by pointing out that all dress should be hung from the shoulders; agreed that 'some additional height to the shoe was necessary in the street to keep a dress clean from the Stygian mud' but he objected to the height being to the heel only; he waxed extensively on clogs, suggesting that the clog of the time of Henry VI with raised sole and heel was far preferable (later he would make positive comments about clogs as worn in Lancashire) and on the divided skirt he felt it was a step towards perfection. He did agree, though, about its design:

> … I will acknowledge that the fringes, the flounces, and the kilting do certainly defeat the whole object of the dress …

Which was a general point he had made in *Personal Impressions of America* (see Appendix B.) Then, turning to Huyshe's objections, he felt that the unsuitability of Greek dress was one of material only and that wool should be used 'as is supplied by Dr Jaeger', pointing out that his friend and architect, Godwin, had made this suggestion in his lecture at the International Health Exhibition. Wilde stated that the beauty of Greek dress lay in it being suspended from the shoulders. On men's dress, instead of Huyshe's preference for the late eighteenth century, Wilde insisted that the early seventeenth century was the best period because:

> for ease, warmth and comfort this seventeenth-century dress is infinitely superior to anything that came after it

and he hoped for a national revival.

The results of his response were several further letters to *The Pall Mall Gazette*, one again from Huyshe.[28] Wilde must have been very pleased because this resulted in a further reply from him[29] being published. This letter stretched over a full page and a half of the *Gazette*. It was headed:

> *MORE RADICAL IDEAS ON DRESS REFORM.*
> *BY MR. OSCAR WILDE.*

Wilde introduced his subject by pointing out that he had 'been much interested at reading the large amount of correspondence' which showed that the subject of dress reform 'is occupying many wise and charming people' — two of which are praised before he turns his attention back to Huyshe and his further letter: clearly, for Wilde, Huyshe was neither wise nor charming. He wrote in combative form:

> I am not denying the force, or even the popularity, of the "Eave arf a brick" school of criticism, but I acknowledge it does not interest me

before he responded again to Huyshe's arguments about the best historical period for dress. Wilde ridiculed Huyshe's view because he had never worn

> himself the dress which he proposes for general adoption by others (but) I have myself worn this late eighteenth-century dress many times ... and so may claim to have a very positive right to speak on its comfort and suitability

and then he sets out, at length, his three reasons for giving it up. He agrees that it may be 'picturesque' but it is not beautiful, then identifies beauty as 'the perfection of principles' and in the costume of the late eighteenth century 'there are no ideas or principles at all, much less the perfection of either'. Each item of clothing is then demolished, one by one, with great relish, in a lengthy passage before concluding that

> There is not a single rule of right costume which is not violated in it, for it gives us stiffness, tightness and discomfort instead of comfort, freedom and ease.

In contrast to a drawing supplied by Huyshe of what he considered to be 'An Ideal Dress', Wilde supplied a drawing 'by Mr. Godwin from the Duke of Newcastle's delightful book on horsemanship' (one wonders if Wilde was hoping for a reduced bill from Godwin for the Tite Street work with all the puff he was giving him) which is:

> an example of a particular application of principles which are universally right

Huyshe is further criticised for not wishing to import the concept of beauty into dress and to deal only with the practical issues:

> The word practical is nearly always the last refuge of the uncivilised

offers Wilde to the, now, presumably, heavily battle-scarred Huyshe. Wilde then moves on to the issues of beauty and ugliness in dress (his lecture *Dress* is advertised at many venues over the autumn as *Beauty, Taste and Ugliness in Dress*) by pointing out that beauty comes from within and that he has

> no more desire to define ugliness than I have daring to define beauty

AN IDEAL DRESS.   REAL DRESS.

Examples of dress: Huyshe's 'Ideal' and Wilde's 'Real' Dress

which is a return to the theme of his introductory statements in both of his lectures, *Modern Art Training* and *The House Beautiful*. But he then does just that by giving some definitions:

> Beauty is the sign always of the rightness of principles, the mystical seal that is set upon what is perfect, and upon what is perfect only

whereas:

> an ugly thing is merely a thing that is badly made, or a thing that does not suit its purpose; that ugliness is want of fitness; that ugliness is failure; that ugliness is uselessness ...

Wilde's aesthetic philosophy as set out here clearly has a little way to go to reach the position enshrined in the conclusion of his *Preface* to *The Picture of Dorian Gray*:[30]

> We can forgive a man for making a useful thing as long as he does not admire it. The only excuse for making a useless thing is that one admires it intensely.

> All art is quite useless.

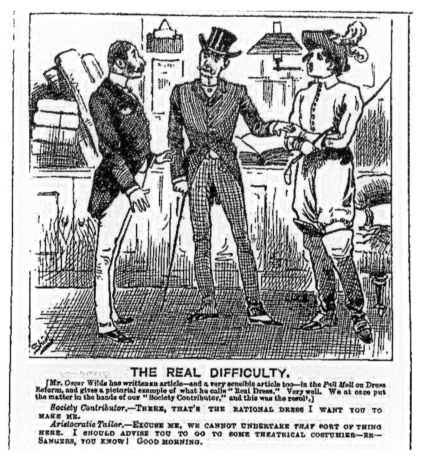

THE REAL DIFFICULTY.

[Mr. Oscar Wilde has written an article—and a very sensible article too—in the *Pall Mall* on Dress Reform, and gives a pictorial example of what he calls "Real Dress." Very well. We at once put the matter in the hands of our "Society Contributor," and this was the result.]

Society Contributor.—THERE, THAT'S THE RATIONAL DRESS I WANT YOU TO MAKE ME.

Aristocratic Tailor.—EXCUSE ME, WE CANNOT UNDERTAKE *THAT* SORT OF THING HERE. I SHOULD ADVISE YOU TO GO TO SOME THEATRICAL COSTUMIER—ER— SANGERS, YOU KNOW! GOOD MORNING.

Cartoon mimicking Wilde's 'Real Dress'

After his highly functional aesthetic stance on beauty, ugliness and dress, Wilde turns to questions raised by other correspondents, the recurrent themes of hanging clothing from the shoulders in particular and then the utility of clogs, which he says 'have raised a great deal of terror' and have been criticised as anachronistic:

Now, whatever is useful cannot be an anachronism. Such a word is applicable only to the revival of some folly; and, besides, in the England of our own day clogs are still worn in many of our manufacturing towns, such as Oldham. I fear that in Oldham they may not be dreams of beauty; in Oldham the art of inlaying them with ivory and with pearl may possibly be unknown; yet in Oldham they serve their purpose.

Quite why Wilde selects Oldham as his exemplar location for clog-wearing and the real-life fusion of beauty and utility, I do not know. But he concludes this section by saying that clogs used to be worn by the upper classes but he has a general objection to adding any height to a shoe. Divided skirts should stop pretending to be skirts and in a final thrust at Huyshe because of a rather rash promise he has made:

> I feel sure ... many graceful and charming girls [will be] ready to adopt a costume founded on these principles, in spite of Mr. Wentworth Huyshe's terrible threat that he will not propose to them as long as they wear it

So ends a lengthy demolition of his critics, support to his supporters and Wilde's opportunity to get a little more publicity for his plea for rational dress. Following his letter-cum-article, there were several other letters in *The Pall Mall Gazette* about dress but Wilde did not ask to be permitted 'the pleasure of answering one's critics,' again.

In launching this short intervention, writing in the press under his own name, Wilde's main objective had been achieved: he had appeared in print, argued with some humour and *élan* for his vision of rational dress and had clearly impressed Stead who then hired him to begin reviewing in early 1885. This began in February with a review of Whistler's *Ten O'clock* Lecture on Art[31] which must have seemed to Stead as a marriage made in heaven (or hell) which I will deal with in the next chapter. Wilde's endeavours in the *Pall Mall Gazette*, as he had hoped, did have the immediate benefit of being useful in drawing further attention to his new lecture, *Dress*: from now on a number of advertisements included the sentence:

> This is the Lecture which has recently excited so much comment in the London Press.

Wilde was a fine judge of the value of self-publicity in manipulating the media of his day.

Wilde lectured in Ryde on the Isle of Wight on 3 October and on the day afterwards it was reported in the local press[32] that:

> Oscar Wilde, who has become very stout, has again turned his attention to matters of dress, and invented a new hat. Herein he follows notable examples.

Here the reporter mentions Beau Brummel, the Prince Regent and Count d'Orsay[33] before continuing:

> Oscar's hat is broad at the base and narrow at the crown ... If the disciple of "culture" will rid us of that hideous, ugly, costly,

and comfortless abomination, the British "top-hat," he will have earned a monument in Westminster Abbey.

(a feat he would not succeed in until the year 2008 and, even then, it would not be for his services in modifying men's hats)

> All Britons groan under the infliction of the national head-gear, and like Britons they grumble and submit. The "top-hat" is clumsy and ungainly in shape, and its flimsy covering ridiculous in the extreme; but it is firmly established, and nothing short of a huge syndicate of swells could banish it.

But this description of the revolutionary hat, although published in Ryde, may just have been a syndicated copy of a similar, mocking London report[34] of about the same time:

> I passed him in the Strand to-day dressed in a more *outré* style than ever. In addition to his close fitting nether garments and a necktie which it would baffle my powers to describe, he wore a hat broad at the base and narrow at the crown. ... The get up was decidedly highwayman like ... but Oscar moved along with a buoyant step and an eye apparently directed to a weather cock on a distant steeple regardless of the laughs and gibes of the giddy and unappreciative multitude, a sublime spectacle of human singularity, and a living protest against conventionality

which, of course, he was. In 1895 he would enshrine the man's hat and dress dilemma in amusingly self-deprecating dialogue:[35]

> LADY MARKBY: a man on the question of dress is always ridiculous, is he not?
>
> MRS. CHEVELEY: Oh, no! I think men are the only authorities on dress.
>
> LADY MARKBY: Really? One wouldn't say so from the sort of hats they wear? Would one?

Wilde lectured twice in York on 9 Oct as part of the Yorkshire Fine Art and Industrial Institution Festival week. This was an annual event following the original festival in 1866 which had raised sufficient funds to build what is now York Art Gallery at Bootham Bar. Wilde's appearances were advertised well in advance as an integral part of the Festival. Throughout the week there was on show a large collection of *Ancient and Modern Pictures* including exhibits from the South Kensington Museum, which Wilde must have been pleased about because he was proposing in his lectures just such a distribution of these art works. Also running at York's Theatre Royal during festival week was the advertised:[36]

The Brilliant Success ! *CALLED BACK* ! by Hugh Conway and Comyns Carr[37]

Presented by: Mr. W. Duck's Provincial Company.

The press described this as *'one of the greatest successes York playgoers have ever seen'*. The actors of particular fame in the cast that week were Dorothy Dene[38] and Fred Terry,[39] both of whom had been well praised for their acting: in fact, the play was frequently interrupted by applause for Dorothy Dene. She was a fascinating character: a very great beauty of the day, she became Sir Frederic Leighton's lover, model and muse, modelling for many of his most famous paintings including 'The Bath of Psyche' and 'Flaming June.' She then became an actress, although she never achieved great success and retired from the stage in 1894. However, her relationship with Leighton and his role in helping her into society and onto the stage places her as the likely model for George Bernard Shaw's Eliza Doolittle in *Pygmalion* (with Leighton as Henry Higgins) which then translated into the famous film *My Fair Lady* with Audrey Hepburn starring in the Dorothy Dene role. Whilst Dene would not act in any of Wilde's plays, in 1892 Fred Terry would act the part of Gerald Arbuthnot on the opening night and London run at The Haymarket Theatre of Wilde's second society comedy, *A Woman of No Importance*.

In researching Wilde's lectures I have looked at hundreds, if not thousands, of newspapers of this period and there were two outstanding plays which toured the country to great acclaim whilst Wilde was lecturing: *Called Back* and *The Silver King* written by Henry Arthur Jones.[40] In fact, at the Theatre Royal in the week preceding *Called Back*, Wilson Barrett's[41] company gave a week's performances of *The Silver King*. Wilde must have envied their authors' success in creating these plays when he, so far, had been so unsuccessful.

Wilde gave his lecture *The Value of Art in Modern Life* in the afternoon[42] to a:

fairly numerous and select assembly — in a morning coat, with light trousers, and a green scarf ... and toyed incessantly with his dog-skin gloves.

As part of his lecture he continued to praise Whistler:

Mr. Whistler possessed every one of the conditions which a true painter – and no painter should be a specialist – ought to have. ... "If," said Mr. Wilde, "you have ... in York any example of Mr. Whistler's pictures, I hope you will have some, in order that you may be able to see the works of a man who represents the highest perfection of modern art, not only in England, but possibly in the world — a man to whom modern painting owes more than it does to any other modern man, and who expresses in his work every single theory of modern art that we might find expressed or symbolised in any modern art movement."

At the end of this afternoon lecture he was handed a letter[43] which should have reached him during the morning. This was from an unknown member of the 'Called Back' company who had requested seats for his afternoon lecture and invited him to the Theatre Royal after their evening's performance. I presume this letter was from the company manager, the rather finely named, Mr W. Duck. Wilde replied:

it would have given me much pleasure to have had some seats reserved for the members of your company — it is always a privilege to number any artists in one's audience: after my evening lecture I will be very glad to visit the theatre.

He adds:

I have heard so much of Miss Dene's genius and beauty that I am extremely anxious to see her.

In the evening he lectured on *Dress* to a 'rather more numerous' audience wearing

evening dress, with Vandyke collar and cuffs, a black stock, but without gloves. Below his vest hung a large bunch of gold seals.

With his letter to the *Pall Mall Gazette* on his mind — his response to Huyshe and the *Gazette's* other correspondents would have to be posted in the next day or two — he stated that:[44]

Dress was most lovely in the second quarter of the 17th Century. With Charles I costume was useful and beautiful. The Restitution of Charles II reintroduced French influence …

which was a terrible thing, all French influence in such matters was bad. Following his lecture, he passed on to the Art Union Drawing where raffle prizes (certain of the pictures on exhibition) were to be drawn,[45] possibly by the celebrity in their midst. After this ceremony, Wilde walked back towards Harker's Hotel where he was staying and visited the Theatre Royal. It was reported[46] that Wilde

had the pleasure of an introduction to the ladies and gentlemen of the 'Called Back' Company.

That evening's performance was advertised as being 'under the Patronage and in the Presence of'[47] four local dignitaries and their wives including F. Lockwood Esq. QC and Mrs. Lockwood,[48] and I would expect that the patrons would have been present when Wilde arrived.

Whilst Wilde was enjoying a modicum of success, Frank Lockwood was definitely on the up. Over the following thirteen years both men were to reach great personal heights and experience considerable changes of fortune. Lockwood had taken silk in 1882 but had failed to become an MP in York in 1883. However, he would succeed and become York's Liberal MP during the General Election of 1885. Nine years after this evening's meeting, Lockwood would become a Freeman of York and Wilde's *A Woman of No Importance* would be playing at The Haymarket Theatre. Ten years' afterwards they would both be close to their individual, personal peaks: Wilde would be writing *The Importance of Being Earnest*; Lockwood would be knighted and become The Solicitor General. And in 1895 they would meet again at the Old Bailey, but as protagonists in the great drama of Wilde's final trial. Lockwood would step in to lead the prosecution: the Freeman of York would be successfully ensuring that Wilde became a Prisoner at Pentonville. Lockwood died in 1897, the year Wilde was released from prison.

Following his evening's entertainment it was back to his hotel and he would be off the following day for the pleasures of the very fashionable nearby spa town of Harrogate.

Birmingham Suburban Institutes' Union – a group of eleven Mechanics' Institutes in and around Birmingham – negotiated a joint group of lectures[49] spread across a period of over two months. Interestingly, the Chairman of the Union at this time was Mr. S Wall Richards who would move to Bournemouth to run a hotel and organise an annual series of entertainments there which included some of Wilde's final lectures between 1886 and 1888. Wilde lectured at the following Birmingham Institutes: Moseley & Kings Heath (21 October), Wedensbury (22 October), Harborne and Edgbaston (4 November), Moseley & Balsall Heath (13 November) and Walsall (26 November). At Moseley & Kings Heath Institute Wilde lectured on *Dress* ('before a large audience'[50]) who applauded his statement that:

> fashion was merely a form of ugliness, so unbearable that we had to alter it every six months.

and they laughed at his quip criticising claims made about fashionable colours, colours being like musical notes:

WALSALL LITERARY INSTITUTE.

PRESIDENT: EARL OF BRADFORD.

Wednesdays.   1884.
Oct. 8.—Inaugural Soirée.
  „ 15.—Pianoforte Recital and Lecture..WALTER MACFARREN, ESQ.
  „ 29.—Recitals.................CLIFFORD HARRISON, ESQ.
Nov. 5.—"Longfellow"...............MISS JENNIE J. YOUNG.
  „ 12.—Concert ....MADAME BEASLEY AND PARTY.
  „ 19.—"Pictures of the Year" (Illustrated Lecture)..........
                                 HENRY BLACKBURN ESQ.
  „ 26.—On "Dress" ....OSCAR WILDE, ESQ.
Dec. 3.—Dramatic Recitals ....THE MISSES WEBLING.
1885.
Jan. 7.—CONVERSAZIONE.
  „ 23.—Lecture....................MRS. FENWICK MILLER.
  „ 30.—Sir JOHN LUBBOCK'S address to the Members of the
           Suburban Institutes Union (Friday).
Wednesdays.
Feb. 4.—Recitals ....J. N. ELLABY, ESQ., B.A.
  „ 11.—Illustrated Lecture
              W. LANT CARPENTER, ESQ., B.A., B.Sc.
  „ 18.—"Charles Kingsley"........OSMUND AIRY, ESQ., M.A.
  „ 25.—Sketching Entertainment ....J. WILLIAMS BENN, ESQ.
March 4.—"Satire, Anecdote, and Caricature," WALTER ROWTON, ESQ.
  „ 11.—Musical Lecture...............REV. WALTER INSULL.
  „ 18.—"The Chemistry of Food" ......PROFESSOR TWEEDIE.
  „ 25.—Astronomical Entertainment......B. J. MALDEN, ESQ.
    Mr. W. HENRY ROBINSON, Hon. Sec.,
                         The Stamp Office, Walsall.

WEDNESBURY INSTITUTE.

PRESIDENT:

THE RIGHT HON. EARL OF SHAFTESBURY, K.G.

CHAIRMAN: JOSEPH SMITH, ESQ.

TREASURER: R. WILLIAMS, ESQ.

Wednesdays.   1884.
Oct. 8.—"Art and Science" ....ALFRED O. CAPPER, ESQ.
  „ 22.—"The House Beautiful" ....OSCAR WILDE, ESQ.
Nov. 5.—Recital....................CLIFFORD HARRISON. ESQ.
  „ 19.—"Egypt and the Soudan" (Illustrated Lecture).........
                   PROFESSOR B. J. MALDEN, F.R.G.S., F.L.S.
Dec. 3.—"Women Warriors"..........MRS. FENWICK MILLER.
  „ 17.—Dramatic Recital......J. N. ELLABY, ESQ., B.A., OXON.
1885.
Jan. 2.—CONVERSAZIONE (Friday).
  „ 21.—"Ballads" (Musical Lecture) { REV. WALTER INSULL,
                                       Dpl. Mus. (Leipzig).
Friday.
Jan. 30.—Sir JOHN LUBBOCK'S Address to the Members of the
           Surburban Institutes Union.
Wednesdays.
Feb. 4.—Dramatic Recital ....The Misses WEBLING.
  „ 18.—Sketching Entertainment—"Faces from the Streets of
           London"................J. WILLIAMS BENN, ESQ.
Mar. 4.—"A Cup of Tea" ....Prof. G. R. TWEEDIE, F.C.S.
  „ 18.—"Three Merry Men" ....WALTER ROWTON, ESQ.
April 1.—"Comic Art"— (Illustrated } T. C. HEPWORTH, ESQ.
           Lecture)................
              Mr. F. W. HACKWOOD, Hon. Sec.,
1131   66, Bridge Street, Wednesbury.

Wilde at the Midland Institutes

What would be said if a musical journal announced that next year B flat would be a fashionable note?

At the Harborne and Edgbaston Institute Wilde again lectured on *Dress* to 'a crowded audience'[51] in what had been previewed as one of 'the most attractive items' in the programme. It may have been on that evening when he first met the 20-year old Philip Griffiths[52] who lived at Harborne. Wilde wrote to him in December[53] sending a signed photograph, one taken in Ryde earlier in the year, and they must have stayed in touch as Griffiths writes again on 8 June 1885,[54] this time from an address in London. Griffiths seems to be an early member of what became a long list of young men to whom Wilde was attracted.

Leeds And Bradford, December 1884

I FIRST read about the lectures Wilde gave in Leeds on 4 December 1884 in Rupert Hart-Davies' *The Letters of Oscar Wilde*[55]. From newspapers of the time I found references to these lectures being Wilde's *'second visit to Leeds'*[56] and a very short note which read that Wilde had lectured:[57]

the previous day to a large audience at the lecture hall of the Mechanics' Institute in Bradford

With these two discoveries of previously unknown lectures my search to locate more began.

It was many years later that I read about a family story told by Beverley Nichols[58] (author, journalist, lover of gardening and cats) concerning his mother, Pauline, and grandmother, Rebecca Shalders, and their meeting with Wilde in West Yorkshire. This version of the story was that during the winter of 1883 (*sic*) Wilde was lecturing in Leeds. Rebecca Shalders lived on the outskirts of Leeds and had gone to hear him lecture on what was a wintry evening and after the lecture she asked the forlorn Wilde if he would like to return to her house to stay the night, an invitation which he accepted. When they finally got back to the Shalders' home, Wilde was introduced to Pauline but refused to 'sing for his supper' because he was too tired, wet and cold. After a large brandy and soda he retired, and as he left them the only thing which Pauline could remember him saying was:

One's only real life, is the life one never leads.

The story continues that Rebecca swore he would have a good breakfast the next day. In the morning, Pauline came down to the 'almost ostentatious' breakfast in the dining room arrayed on silver salvers: kedgeree, sliced ham, pickled cranberries, cold grouse, eggs, bacon and sausages (for us who have been brought up in Yorkshire, this sort of spread for breakfast only manages to be *almost* ostentatious.) Inevitably, in line with the convention, 'Oscar was very late' and was still wearing his fur coat when he appeared. He was offered breakfast from this display but he wanted none of it and walked over to the window, looking out over the icy gardens to the frozen lake. Nichols continues:

> 'I should like some raspberries,' said Oscar.
> 'I beg your pardon, Mr. Wilde?'

> He spoke even more softly, as though, in this incongruous atmosphere, at this unpropitious hour, a prose poem were forming in his wilful brain.

> 'Some *pale yellow* raspberries.'

A slightly different version of this story is given in Bryan Connon's biography of Nichols.[59] A little more detail is given, apparently the story was a well-established family tradition — the family having dined out on a story about breakfast — and the house where the Shalders lived was stated as being *Elmleigh* in Ilkley:

> a vast place with large conservatories filled with semi-tropical trees and plants, with extensive grounds and massive hothouses.

I have seen plans of Elmleigh at this time, it is indeed a large Victorian house with extensive gardens, greenhouses, outhouses and a large fish pond. This version of the story relates that, on their return from the lecture, Rebecca makes a great fuss of Wilde and describes the benefits of growing one's own fruit in hothouses. This further background makes Wilde seem a little less bizarre in his request for a breakfast of '*pale yellow* raspberries' because he had heard much of the homegrown soft fruit. In this version of the story, when he descended for breakfast, he:

> said that it would be perfection if he might have a handful of raspberries, pale yellow raspberries.

This, in December, in Yorkshire, even with hothouses, was an unfulfilled request.

The location of this version is problematic: Ilkley is far from being on the outskirts of Leeds, it is good thirty minutes' drive in a car: it would take considerably longer in a dog cart in a gale and snowstorm. Wilde had to return to Leeds the following morning to catch a train to London and surely would not have gone so far out of his way. However, researching the Shalders family I discovered that the family had moved to Ilkley only in 1887 from their previous home in the up-and-coming Bradford suburb of Manningham. So this clearly provided an answer to these problems: the story's main details remain true, the events took place in December 1884 but the lecture that Rebecca attended was not in Leeds but the well attended lecture on the evening before at the Mechanics' Institute in Bradford, just a mile south of their home at the time. Of course, the vast winter garden with hothouses now disappears and with it my justification for Wilde's hope for a yellow raspberry breakfast.

One element of the story which does have the ring of truth is the saying of Wilde's about 'one's real life' which is a very little known Wildean aphorism and an unusual choice if the story was fabricated. Wilde used minor variations of it two years previously, in *L'Envoi* — his introduction to Rennell Rodd's poems[60] — and in his American lecture: *The English Renaissance of Art*[61]. From *L'Envoi*:

> … for surely here, if anywhere, the real gladness of life might be revealed to one's youth - the gladness that comes, not from the rejection, but from the absorption, of all passion … In some such way as this we could gather up these strewn and scattered petals of song into one perfect rose of life, and yet, perhaps, in so doing, we might be missing the true quality of the poems; *one's real life is so often the life that one does not lead*; and beautiful poems, like threads of beautiful silks, may be woven into many patterns and to suit many designs, all wonderful and all different…

and *The English Renaissance of Art*:

> Art never harms itself by keeping aloof from the social problems of the day: rather, by so doing, it more completely realises for us that which we desire. For to most of us *the real life is the life we do not lead*, and thus, remaining more true to the essence of its own perfection, more jealous of its own unattainable beauty, is less likely to forget form in feeling or to accept the passion of creation as any substitute for the beauty of the created thing.

(The italicised sections are my emphases.) From Pauline Shalders, all we have is the statement, without much in the way of context, whereas in these two published quotations we have it surrounded with Wilde's rephrased Paterian ideals. I can find no reference to Wilde using this phrase about his 'real life' after this time. He was not someone who would let an aphorism go without a very good reason, and the reason I feel he had for not re-using this one is that it was getting a little too close to hinting at his own hidden, but real, life which included friendships with the likes of Philip Griffiths in Birmingham:

> If one tells the truth, sooner or later one is likely to be found out.[62]

Following his breakfast, yellow raspberries or no, Wilde would have travelled to central Bradford to catch a late morning train for the short, cold journey to Leeds. He arrived at the now non-existent Leeds Central Station (its name — Central — was misleading even in 1854 when it opened.) Fortunately, at Leeds, Wilde would have been able to walk from the platform to the Great Northern Railway Station Hotel through a covered passage which protected him from the terrible weather which would result in poor attendances at both his lectures that day.

Wilde had probably been reading *The Times* on the train because it was from the hotel that he wrote to Godwin[63] referring to his letter in the paper that day[64]. In *The Times* there had been significant correspondence about the restoration of Westminster Hall which was being debated in Parliament and causing quite a stir within the architectural profession. Godwin's letter of 4 December attacked a previous correspondent's proposal that, as part of the 'restoration', the hall's ancient roof should be raised several feet by adding to the height of the walls. This type of 'improvement' to ancient buildings was not uncommon at the time. Godwin was one of the voices raised against such mistreatment of this ancient building and Wilde began his letter by congratulating Godwin on this. He told him that he would be back in London the next day and would see him on Saturday morning. Wilde was fretting about the colour scheme for the drawing room ('is it to be vermilion? is it not?'). He then suggests they go to The Lyceum 'and see this thing'. The thing in question was *Romeo and Juliet* with Mary Anderson as Juliet. This had been a controversial portrayal of the part, with critics giving diametrically opposed views of her acting. Wilde had first written to Godwin on 26 October[65] about hoping to see the play but I presume he had been unable to, and still wanted to see her for himself. He then asks about Godwin's interest in a production of his unstaged play, *The Duchess of Padua,* with Kyrle Bellew[66] in the leading role of Guido Ferranti. Unfortunately for Wilde this production would not make it to the stage. Finally in the letter, Wilde asks about the lattice for a window, seemingly implementing his own advice from *The House Beautiful*. However, whereas he suggests the use of lattices to break up the light from what he felt were great, glaring, plate glass windows, in this case it was to screen an unacceptable view:[67]

... as, the window looking on a slum [Paradise Walk], they have entirely covered with a wooden grating on the inside copied from a Cairo pattern ...

At 3 o'clock Wilde lectured in Leeds on *Beauty, Taste and Ugliness in Dress*. Despite the lecture being advertised as:[68]

Pronounced by the London Press "The hit of the season"

there was a meagre audience composed almost entirely of ladies[69] in the Albert Hall. This hall was the large, oval hall in the Leeds Mechanics' Institute (now the Museum) which could seat 3,000 people. It was designed by Cuthbert Broderick and matched the nearby Victoria Hall in his award winning Town Hall. However, his lecture was listened to with great interest and most of the arguments he advanced met with warm approval. Notwithstanding the scanty attendance, at the conclusion of his remarks he was 'heartily applauded'.[70] Following his equally poorly attended evening lecture on the same subject, Joseph Fountain, a local printer and theatrical agent, invited Wilde to the Thursday Smoking Concert at the Leeds Albion Club.[71] Accompanying Wilde that evening was Edward Terry,[72] an old hand comedy actor who starred in musical burlesques and short comedy pieces. Terry was at The Grand Theatre for the week starring in *The Rocket*. The Leeds Albion Club was quite a bohemian and artistic club described as the nineteenth century replica of the Johnsonian Coffee House Club where the conversation was of books and plays, music and art. Its members were mainly actors, artists and musicians from Leeds, numbered amongst them were Wilson Barrett, Atkinson Grimshaw,[73] Phil May,[74] several teachers from the Leeds Academy of Music and many other artists of Leeds. The Smoke Room was a long, well-lit room, with rosy old fashioned armchairs and theatrical pictures and caricatures upon the walls. The Smoking Concerts rarely began before 10 o'clock, after the theatres, and they often continued until the early hours. They were acclaimed as being of the highest standard and both the Albion Club Quartet and Octet of male vocalists were prize-winning singers. Their beautiful part-singing was a great feature of these entertainments, and it was reported that

the beauty of their voices and the delicacy of their phrasing charmed Mr. Oscar Wilde.

After the vocal concert, Wilde

averred that he had recently heard first-class part-singing in Italy and Germany, but that he had heard nothing better than the good old glees as rendered by these four Yorkshire vocalists.

Wilde's only recent visit to the continent was on his honeymoon when he and Constance had visited Paris and Dieppe. This statement is probably an 'exaggeration' by Wilde who may have been thinking of his European visits whilst a student. Or not.

There was no reason for Wilde to leave early: all he had to do in the morning was catch the train back to London. The timetable of the Special Express Trains from Leeds to St. Pancras shows that Wilde had the choice of five in total: the 10.35 would have been attractive being not too early and it arrived in London at a comfortable 3pm.

This research allows us to look at the two days, 3 and 4 December 1884, and know almost everything about how Wilde spent his time and the invitations he received. We also know from the Autumn of 1883 that local dignitaries took him to places of interest in the towns he visited and even gave him presents.[75] I think it is reasonable to conclude that this was far more common than we knew previously and whilst he may have been in unfamiliar situations, he was an attractive guest for socialites, budding aesthetes and artists, and was invited to engagements of all kinds in the towns he visited.

Scotland

JUST before Christmas 1884, Wilde arrived at The Balmoral Hotel, Edinburgh where he stayed whilst he lectured in Falkirk, Glasgow, Edinburgh and elsewhere. From the hotel he wrote to Constance the only letter from him to her which survives.[76] He dates it as Tuesday, which is 16 December, and writes at the top:

Here I stay till Sunday

'Dear and Beloved,' he begins, lamenting their separation:

Here am I, and you at the Antipodes: O execrable facts …

and he finishes by telling her:

I feel incomplete without you. Ever and ever yours

in what reads as a genuine love letter. A few days' later Wilde wrote to Professor J. S. Blackie,[77] professor of Greek at Edinburgh University and an expert on Goethe, asking if he could come and see him

when you have, if you ever have, an idle hour?

Whether Blackie could spare him that idle hour, we do not know.

At some stage of his Edinburgh stay, Wilde's old friend from Magdalen College, David Hunter-Blair,[78] called Dunsky by all his University friends, came to visit.[79] He was now a Benedictine monk in Scotland. They had 'a long chat' and he chaffed Wilde:

But, Oscar, what a humbug you are!

Wilde protested but he continued:

> You don't really believe in this absurd aesthetic gospel of yours

before turning to parts of his prize-winning poem *Ravenna* which he maintained were inaccurate portrayals of what actually happened on that visit to Italy in 1876. Their long chat came to an end:

> We parted friendly after this passage. As I rose to go Oscar suddenly knelt and kissed my hand. "Pray for me, dear old Dunsky," he muttered, and I will swear that there were tears in his eyes. I never saw him again...

Quite what preyed upon Wilde's mind at that moment and brought on this dramatic action, it is impossible to say. Knowing what we do of Wilde's life, it could have been any number of things: his dalliance with but non-conversion to Catholicism, his uncertain future prospects, his financial predicament or his doubts about his marriage and his growing friendships with young men. All of which were aspects of his 'only real life'.

On the 19 December, Wilde writes yet another letter to Godwin[80] about the costs he is incurring at Tite Street as well as the choosing of fabrics for curtains and for covering the settees. He is clearly getting desperate on both grounds because Constance and he intend to move into their house imminently and he asks Godwin to see Constance about the coverings. He finishes his letter:

> I wish you were in Edinboro' with me: it is quite lovely — bits of it. The house *must* be a success: do just add the bloom of colour to it in curtains and cushions.

Wilde finished this leg of his tour on Sunday evening 21 December at the St Andrews Hall, Glasgow which has already been described. He lectured on:

DRESS: Artistic Dress v. Modern Dress.

The Glasgow Herald the next day[81] gave a very short review of the lecture's content:

> Dress was an art ... to dress well one should be a master of colour and form. Fashion rested on folly, and was ephemeral; art rested upon law, and was eternal. The costume of the future would result from a combination of the German principle of science with the Greek principle of beauty.

There were other, fuller reviews in the Glasgow press, but none of them mentioned the subject which was relayed around the country in newspaper articles: a short paragraph on 'Lancashire Mill Girls'.[82]

These articles reported that when speaking on *Dress* in Glasgow, Wilde had said that:

> … a Lancashire mill girl, with a shawl over her shoulders and wearing clogs, knew more about dress than a fashionable London lady recently returned from Paris, because in the former case there was comfort, while in the latter there was discomfort.

This Lancashire mill girl may well have been the very same woman as the Oldham girl who was lauded for wearing clogs back in October. The lecture continued on more familiar ground:

> He was sad to see in the newspapers that such and such a colour was to be the fashion. Colour was viewed by an artist as a piano by a musician. It was a combination of the one and the harmony of the other that made beauty. What would people say if a musical paper stated that B flat was to be the fashionable note next winter?

Wilde relished this generally well-received musical quip.

Reception

WILDE'S reception during this period was mixed: whilst he was still receiving positive reviews of his lectures, the audience numbers were more variable, some being small. Wilde's appearance and clothes continued to fascinate and in Sheffield late in October it was noted:[83]

> Mr. Wilde, who appears to be allowing his curls to grow freely again, was attired very much as on his previous appearance … viz., the conventional evening coat, with black silk vest and ordinary black trousers. Peeping out from his vest was a touch of colour telling of a crimson handkerchief pushed away there, and suspended at the side was a guard with many seals attached. …

And similar observations were made in Bath:[84]

> … all were amused at the witticisms and good-humoured criticisms respecting the absurdities of much of the fashionable dress of to-day. Mr. Wilde himself wore an evening dress, the chief alteration in his personal appearance since his last lecture here, being that he had permitted his hair to grow much longer. It would perhaps help Mr. Wilde, if he be sincere in his desire to reform modern dress, to practice what he preaches more extensively, and show his audience how graceful and

comfortable the doublet, Hessians, &c., that he so much admires, really are. So far he does not seem inclined to go beyond the cloak and the broad brimmed hat.

Two days before this lecture in Bath Wilde was lecturing at the Lesser Victoria Rooms, Clifton, Bristol where Robert Hichens,[85] later to be the author of *The Green Carnation*, first saw him:[86]

> I had once … heard him give an amusing lecture. I could recall the sound of his luscious voice, his ample and suave appearance, his elaborate, condescending manner when before the public, his thick hair parted in the middle, his large shoulders and softly gesturing hands.

At some venues, for example York, there was no explanation offered for the poor attendance but in Leeds and Sheffield reporters suggested that the terrible weather was the reason that so many stayed away. In the case of his Leeds experience, there was some gloating at the poor turnout:[87]

> How are the mighty fallen! The great Mr. Oscar Wilde, once the favourite of Mr. Du Maurier, and the idol of our fickle London Society, has experienced another of the rude reverses of fortune. When he appeared at Leeds at the beginning of the present year to lecture he attracted very considerable audiences — chiefly of ladies — and his visit was entitled to be regarded as a success. But the Albert Hall of that town presented a sorry sight when he once more stood on the platform in that building on Friday (sic) to descant upon dress. Mr. Oscar Wilde would appear to have had his day. It was brilliant enough while it lasted, but it has ended early – as such days too commonly do.

This reporter was clearly in the anti-Wilde brigade and his grudging acceptance of Wilde's previous success in Leeds is heavily qualified by the audience being 'chiefly of ladies', which is clearly considered as being not very good. However, it was not a universal failure: newspaper descriptions ranged from his audiences being so small that he 'presented a sorry sight', to the 'large, unusually large and fashionable and crowded' (Bristol.) In November Wilde was particularly well received at the Birbeck Literary and Scientific Institution in Holborn, London[88] where:

> There was an unusually large attendance of members and their friends, and the lecture was followed with great interest. Mr. Wilde, … was frequently applauded. …

and the autumn tour ended on a decided high note with an enormous audience of 5,000 in Glasgow. That, at least, must have been reassuring to him and Appleton. Whatever the cause of the variation in the size of his audiences, this may well have been one reason for him to seek out other sources of income. But, he had plenty to do before he and Constance could move into their new House Beautiful and it would be Christmas in a few days. I hope he received a suitable Christmas hamper: there was one advertised:[89]

The Aesthete's Guinea Christmas Hamper

One doz. Peacocks' feathers, 1 portable dado, 1 vol. Oscar Wilde's poems, 4 pomegranates, 5 yards white samite (*broad widths*), 6 empty Amphora Wine bottles, 1 packet of views of Bedford Park, 1 bottle tawny hair-dye, and an etching after Cimabue and Botticelli.

Table 4: Lectures September to Christmas 1884

Date	Town	Venue	Time	Lecture
Wed 24 Sep?	Southport	Winter Gardens	3:30 pm	Dress
Wed 1 Oct	Ealing		evening	Dress
Fri 3 Oct	Ryde	Town Hall	evening	Dress
Wed 8 Oct	Chelmsford	Shire Hall	evening	Dress
Thu 9 Oct	York	Great Hall, Fine Art Exhibition	afternoon	The Value of Art in Modern Life
Thu 9 Oct	York	Great Hall, Fine Art Exhibition	evening	Dress
Fri 10 Oct	Harrogate	Town Hall	evening	Dress
Mon 13 Oct	Cardiff	Public Hall	3:00 pm	Dress & VAML
Mon 13 Oct	Cardiff	Public Hall	8:00 pm	Dress & VAML
Tue14 Oct	Clifton, Bristol	Lesser Victoria Rooms	3:00 pm	Dress & VAML
Tue 14 Oct	Clifton, Bristol	Lesser Victoria Rooms	8:00 pm	Dress & VAML
Wed 15 Oct	Cheltenham	Assembly Rooms	3:00 pm	Dress
Wed 15 Oct	Cheltenham	Assembly Rooms	8:00 pm	VAML
Thu 16 Oct	Bath	Assembly Rooms	8:00 pm	Dress
Tue 21 Oct	Moseley	Kings Heath & Moseley Institute	evening	Dress
Wed 22 Oct	Wedensbury	Institute		The House Beautiful
Fri 24 Oct	London	Crystal Palace	3:00 pm	Dress
? Oct	Tunbridge Wells	Pantiles		Dress
Mon 27 Oct	Sheffield	Firth College	8:00 pm	Dress

Thu 30 Oct	Leicester	Museum Buildings	evening	Dress
Tue 4 Nov	Harborne	Harborne & Edgbaston Institute	8:00 pm	Dress
Wed 5 Nov	Stoke on Trent	Town Hall	evening	VAML
Wed 12 Nov	Leamington	Public Hall	afternoon	Dress
Wed 12 Nov	Leamington	Public Hall	evening	Dress
Thu 13 Nov	Moseley	Moseley & Balsall Heath Institute		VAML
Mon 17 Nov	Brighton	Royal Pavilion Music Room	3:30 pm	Dress
Tue 18 Nov	Brighton	Royal Pavilion Music Room	3:30 pm	VAML
Wed 19 Nov	London	Birbeck Literary and Scientific Institution	evening	VAML
Thu 20? Nov	London	Paddington		HB
Fri 21 Nov	London	Crystal Palace	3:00 pm	Dress
Wed 26 Nov	Walsall	Literary Institute		Dress
Thu 27 Nov	Burnley	Mechanics Institute	8:00 pm	VAML
Tue 2 Dec	London	Westbourne Park Institute	8:00 pm	HB
Wed 3 Dec	Bradford	Mechanics Institute	evening	Dress
Thu 4 Dec	Leeds	Albert Hall, Mechanics Institute	3:00 pm	Dress
Thu 4 Dec	Leeds	Albert Hall, Mechanics Institute	8:00 pm	Dress
Tue 9 Dec	Nottingham	Mechanics' Hall	night	VAML
Sat 13 Dec	Stourbridge	Corn Exchange		HB
Tue 15/16? Dec	Sunderland	New Assembly Hall		

Wed 17 Dec	Falkirk	School of Arts		Dress
Fri 19 Dec	Glasgow	St Andrews Hall		
Sat 20 Dec	Edinburgh	Queens St Hall	afternoon	Dress
Sat 20 Dec	Edinburgh	Queens St Hall	evening	VAML
Sun 21 Dec	Glasgow	St Andrews Hall	6:30 pm	Dress

Key

? a doubtful date

CHAPTER 6

1885

There is much to be said in favour of modern journalism [1]

NOTWITHSTANDING a welcoming end to 1884 — lecturing to 5,000 people in Glasgow just before Christmas — during 1885 the number of Wilde's lectures decreased. It is impossible to say why this happened: were Wilde and his business manager, Appleton, responding to a reduction of interest from audiences (clearly not the case in Glasgow but there had been some poor attendances during 1884), was it a conscious decision by Wilde to lighten his workload following the very intense lecturing of the past eighteen months, or was this, following Wilde's forays into journalism, an opportunity to give him time to explore this as a new career? I think it was probably a combination of all three. Perhaps Wilde began to realise that whilst he was newsworthy, his every witticism quoted, his dress commented upon, his wife critiqued and his presence at any event made the event worth reporting, his lectures — as a serious, intense tour, day after day — were becoming of less interest to the public, even though he did generally get very good reviews. Whatever his reasons, he had plenty to think about as the New Year of 1885 dawned, with Constance about three months pregnant, the move into their new Tite Street home taking place and the bills for Godwin and the builder to pay. These bills were to be a major source of irritation for Wilde in the first half of the year: a dispute with the builder over his bill escalated and Godwin became ill. There are many letters to Godwin[2] about these matters which eventually became a court case. Even for a spendthrift such as Wilde, the financial implications of these events must have weighed heavily upon him.

It is also noteworthy that newspaper coverage of Wilde's albeit reduced number of lectures is considerably toned-down and I have found few reviews and even fewer newspaper advertisements from this year. I think that this indicates a more frugal approach by Appleton and Wilde. We have seen the amounts of money that were spent on printing and publicity in 1883/84; newspaper advertisements will have been a major part of their expenditure up until this point and I imagine a decision had been reached that, with a pared-down number of lectures (and therefore a pared-down income), a reduction in expenditure was appropriate. A cheaper option for publicity would be to rely on a small number of posters at the venues and in shop windows with a few flyers, supplemented by any local newspaper reports Appleton could drum up. The combined effect of reduced publicity and a reduced number of lectures was a much reduced number of reviews: what reviews there are often become very short notes lost in the dense Victorian newsprint. Information about Wilde's lectures in 1885, therefore, has become more difficult to find. His reduced number of public appearances following his ubiquity during the previous eighteen months was noted:[3]

> And Mr. Oscar Wilde — where is he? I have no doubt that he is still an ornament of society, and still admired by the ladies as the type of (a certain style of) manly beauty. But one meets him no longer in the pages of *Punch*. His witticisms are no longer recorded in the newspapers. An Oscar Wilde still lives and flourishes; but *the* Oscar Wilde of the great aesthetic revival is to all intents and purposes as dead as Marley in the "Christmas Carol."

So Wilde became newsworthy because he was not in the news.

The Lectures

THE 1885 LECTURES began in gaps between performances of the pantomime, *Jack and the Beanstalk,* at the Gaiety Theatre, Dublin. Wilde continued his lectures on the afternoons of 5 & 6 January with *Dress* and *The Value of Art in Modern Life.* Here, *The Value of Art in Modern Life* was subtitled in the advertisements as: *The Meaning of the Aesthetic Movement* which was the third change to the title of this lecture after it had been first given as a subtitle to *Dress.* A preview of the lectures[4] reported:

> It may be taken as almost a foregone conclusion that he will receive a hearty reception, for whatever opinion may exist as to the special merits of the theories propounded by the "Apostle of Aestheticism," there has never been any difference as to the

wonderful charm which he imparts to his lectures … one may confidently look forward to the presence of a crowded and attentive audience.

Notwithstanding his 'wonderful charm', as well as this advanced and very positive publicity, neither lecture was to draw a large audience. The lecture *Beauty, Taste, and Ugliness in Dress* had an audience which was described as[5] 'hardly satisfactory':

> At most about five hundred persons were present … the audience, though not large, was highly intelligent, critical, and appreciative of the matter and style of the lecturer.

Clearly expectations were high when an appreciative audience of five hundred was almost sneered at. On the next day, for *The Value of Art in Modern Life*, the audience was described[6] as 'very thin'. Even some of that small number were there by mistake: Sherard describes three of them:[7]

> … a gentleman accompanied by two boys came by mistake into the theatre, sat down and listened patiently for some time to Oscar's discourse, and finally got up exclaiming: "What's all this? When's the pantomime going to begin?"

Perhaps it already had.

Both lectures were straight re-runs of the now well-worn versions Wilde had given extensively during the autumn of 1884: he clearly had not done any further work to renew them for the new year, other than to add the subtitle: *The Meaning of the Aesthetic Movement*. However, as regards people's dress and the latest fashions, newspapers were reporting:[8]

> The spring has brought us what are to be the two new colours. … The aesthetic colour is very singular. It is a variation on green … It is a dirty faint colour, rather like unripened hay. Oscar Wilde is said to be largely responsible for it, and to have done his best to have it adopted for evening dresses …

Had they not been listening? Clearly a jibe at Wilde was acceptable even if it demonstrated a lack of attention: had they forgotten the joke about B flat?

Wilde had changed his own dress a little for the New Year. At his first Dublin lecture he was described as wearing:[9]

> A plain black suit without any ornament whatever

Hendon School, Hendon, London, N.W.

SUTTON. — LANGLEY PARK SCHOOL. Situated in the healthiest part of Surrey. Number limited. Every boy under the personal care of the Principal, Mr. A. WILSON DAVIES, formerly Open Scholar of Jesus College, Oxford. TERM begins JANUARY 27.

MISCELLANEOUS.

ARABIAN NIGHTS. — Twenty-five Guineas. Very scarce edition.

ARABIAN NIGHTS.—Very scarce Edition. The 1,001 Nights in 9 volumes, issued by the Vilton Society by subscription. Number printed limited to 500. A copy in perfect condition for disposal; price 25 guineas —Address, A.R.B.N., care of Steel and Jones, Advertising Agents, Spring-gardens, S.W.

MR. OSCAR WILDE will discourse upon "DRESS" at Eight o'clock on Wednesday Next, 21st inst., at the Highbury Athenæum, N. Tickets, 4s., 2s. 6d., and 1s., to be had at the hall or agents.

SOME magnificent thoroughbred ST. BERNARD PUPPIES, by Jumbo, an enormous tawny and white dog, measuring 7 ft. from nose to tail. Price from three guineas each. Can be sent on approval before purchasing.—Hillside, Loudwater, near High Wycombe.

GROSVENOR GALLERY.

WINTER EXHIBITION.

The WINTER EXHIBITION is NOW OPEN from Ten till Six with a
COLLECTION of the WORKS of
THOMAS GAINSBOROUGH, R.A.,
And of DRAWINGS by the
Late RICHARD DOYLE.
Admission, 1s. ; Season Tickets, 5s.

MR. WHISTLER'S "TEN O'CLOCK." —PRINCE'S HALL, PICCADILLY, on the EVENING of February 20th. Tickets at all the Libraries.

STATISTICAL SOCIETY. The THIRD ORDINARY MEETING of the present Session will be held on TUESDAY, the 20th instant, at the ROYAL SCHOOL OF MINES, Jermyn-street, S.W., London, when will be read the Newmarch Memorial Prize Essay (abridged), "On the Extent to which Recent Legislation is in accordance with, or deviates from, the True Principles of Economic Science ; and showing the Permanent Effects which may be expected to arise from such Legislation " by WILLIAM WATT, Esq. The Chair will be taken at 7.45 P.M.

QUEENWOOD COLLEGE, HAMPSHIRE.

Advertisements for lectures by Mr Wilde and Mr Whistler

At his second lecture the reporter extended this rather bare description:[10]

> He was attired in a black frock coat and the same continuations. His white wristbands instead of being turned up as on the last occasion, extended merely half an inch beyond the coat sleeves. He wore a Milton collar and an unobtrusive necktie. His hair was dishevelled in the most careful fashion to give his face the aspect of a Greek poet crowned with bays.

So it was goodbye to Neronian hair and Van Dyke cuffs, hello to a Milton collar and Hellenistic hairstyle. When Wilde lectured at the Highbury Athenæum on 21 January, the reporter agreed with the ordinariness of his suit and referred, yet again, to that old aesthetic persona which he just could not throw off:[11]

> I was much disappointed when the lecturer quietly walked on to the platform in an ordinary dress suit, with no peculiarity whatever about it or him, except a large bunch of seals dangling below his waistcoat, after the manner of our great grandfathers, early in the century. I had quite expected something interesting to look at — say, knee-breeches of velvet. … A plump young gentleman, clad "in rule" down to his patent leathers and up to his white linen collar was not what I went out for to see.

Wilde was obviously fond of his seals on their black moiré silk ribbon: he loved them so much that he would still be wearing them at the first night of *The Importance of Being Earnest*, which was almost exactly ten years ahead.[12]

Wilde lectured at Horncastle, about twenty miles east of Lincoln, on 12 January and also visited his uncle, John Maxwell Wilde,[13] vicar at the nearby West Ashby. He was caught in what he described[14] as a 'Lincolnshire snowstorm' as a result of which he contracted a severe cold. His doctor confined him to his home and forbade him from travelling. Unfortunately, on 15 January, he was expected to appear and speak at a meeting in Leicester to discuss funeral and mourning reform. He wrote to the organiser to give his apologies and set out why he sympathised so strongly with the movement's aims: his letter was read out at the meeting, fully reported[15] and then, inevitably, it received widespread coverage throughout the country. The letter contains some of Wilde's ideas which he was planning to speak about at the meeting and are, in part, relevant to his lectures:

> I consider that white and violet should be recognised as mourning, and not black merely. ... The habit of bringing flowers to the grave is now almost universal, and is a custom beautiful in its symbolism; but I cannot help thinking that the elaborate and expensive designs made by the florist are often far less lovely than a few flowers held loose in the hand.

He said that there was 'one point on which I had hoped to have the privilege of speaking' and it was about his dislike of ugly funeral monuments:

> ... far better models are to be found in the beautiful crosses of Ireland, such as the cross at Monasterboice, or in the delicate bas-reliefs on Greek tombs

which, he felt, were both a 'noble symbol for the guiding of life' rather than just 'an idle panegyric on those who are gone'. He gave examples of the good and the bad, the good being:

> Keats's grave is a hillock of green grass with a plain headstone

Wilde had visited Keats' grave whilst visiting Rome in 1877 and had written an article, 'The Tomb of Keats', which contained a poem in which he describes it:[16]

> No cypress shades his grave, not funeral yew,
> But red-lipped daisies, violets drenched with dew,
> And sleepy poppies, catch the evening rain.

Whilst Keats' grave was beautiful, on the other hand, one of the worst examples was:

> There is in Westminster Abbey a periwigged admiral in a nightgown hurried off to heaven by two howling cherubs, which is one of the best examples I know of ostentatious obscurity.

This fate — 'ostentatious obscurity' — was never going to engulf Wilde. He signed off his letter and cogitated upon his health. During his first trial in April 1895, under strong and, at times, ill-tempered cross-examination, Wilde would be asked if iced champagne was a favourite drink:[17]

> CARSON: Was it a favourite drink — iced champagne?
> WILDE: Yes, strongly against my doctor's orders. *(Laughter)*
> CARSON: Never mind the doctor's orders.
> WILDE: I don't. It has all the more flavour if you discard the doctor's orders. *(More laughter)*

His doctor's orders had kept him from Leicester, but, never minding them now, he travelled north to Newcastle-upon-Tyne where he lectured on *Dress* on Sunday 18 January and on the following day in Sunderland. Wilde clearly enjoyed being in the north-east of England and he lectured many times at towns in this area - from the River Tyne south to the River Tees — which may have been due to the large audiences he tended to draw when there. This was exemplified in Newcastle where, instead of the small audiences of Dublin, he drew a crowd more akin to his Glasgow experience before Christmas. Wilde's lecture was in connection with the Tyneside Sunday Lecture Society which had begun in 1883 with some controversy. The Pall Mall Gazette reported[18] on this 'experiment of wide public interest, as bearing upon the question of the intellectual and moral uses of the Sunday.' The society was established with some famous names installed as vice-Presidents, including Professor Huxley,[19] Sir Frederic Leighton and Professor Max Müller amongst them. The experiment seemed to be a successful one:

> This year the lectures have been given in the Tyne Theatre, a building capable of holding some 3,000 persons, and which, on the occasion of the lectures by Mr. Archibald Forbes[20] and Mr. Oscar Wilde was filled in every part.

The day after Wilde's lecture on *Dress* it was reported[21] that:

Long before the hour announced for the lecture the spacious theatre was filled in every part, many persons being refused admission.

During his lecture, Wilde continued to stress his conversion to the sole use of wool for clothing:[22]

The great mistake that had been made in Europe for the last two centuries was that linen had been used instead of wool.

The interest in Newcastle with Wilde's popularisation of Dr Jaeger's ideas led to the local newspaper informing their readers:[23]

There are probably many persons of the thousands who heard Mr Oscar Wilde's lecture on Sunday night who would like to know where they can obtain the book which he recommended, named "Health Culture." The Dr Jaeger Sanitary Woollen System Company … will send it to any one on receipt of fifteen pence in stamps.

The following day, 'Mr. Oscar Wilde delivered his popular lecture "Dress" to a fairly large audience in Sunderland.'[24].

Whilst the audiences in the north-east of England were larger than those he had drawn in Dublin, the overall picture was not so rosy. During the early months of this year we have a series of informative letters from an irritated Wilde to Appleton[25] about the lectures and Appleton's organisation of them. All are undated but we can now estimate more accurate dates for them. The first letter (noted as 'Thursday') should probably be dated as 22 or 29 January 1885. Clearly things are not going too well because in his letters he mentions that his lecture fee often does not cover his hotel bill. Forthcoming lectures are mentioned in Carlisle and Penrith which are towns in the north-west of England to the immediate north and east of the Lake District. Wilde lectures on *Dress* at the Temperance Hall in Ulverston at the southern edge of the Lake District on 11 February where he had 'a large attendance'[26] and he writes from the County Hotel to complain about Appleton's suggested lecture for Greenock on 13 February: *The Value of Art in Modern Life*. He tells Appleton that he only gives that lecture when he is lecturing on two successive days at the same place: in that situation, he will give *Dress* on the first day and *The Value of Art in Modern Life* on the second. Many lectures in late 1884 and in 1885 do follow this pattern. Wilde lectures at this important and wealthy shipping town on the River Clyde, west of Glasgow, two days after Ulverston and, notwithstanding his complaints, he spoke at the weekly meeting of the local Philosophical

Society on *The Value of Art in Modern Life*. The local newspaper reported[27] that:

> ... there was a large attendance, the lecture hall of the Watt Institution being completely filled

and:

> The lecture was attentively listened to throughout, and highly enjoyed by the large audience. ...His sarcastic humour was at times delightful, and lent a charm to the whole lecture. A vote of thanks to the lecturer closed the proceedings.

Notwithstanding this success, an exasperated Wilde writes to Appleton:

> Nothing puts me out so much as these things which are constantly occurring. ...I am getting sick of the whole thing.

The third of these letters from Wilde begins with:

> I am glad your play was a success

The suggestion is[28] that Appleton's successful play is his comic drama *A Fair Sinner*, which opened on 4 March at the Gaiety Theatre, London. However, *A Fair Sinner* actually had its first performances at the Theatre Royal, Ipswich on 23 January for two nights. Assuming that these were the successful performances allows us to date this letter to earlier in the year, possibly late January, which then makes sense of Wilde's mention of a lecture at Dorchester, which took place on 24 February,[29] and of future lectures in Scotland (Greenock being on 13 February) and Hampstead, which has not been identified. Appleton was very busy in early 1885: he had more than one play running at the time and it can be of little surprise that Wilde had so many gripes about the organisation of his lectures when his tour manager was probably far more interested in making sure his own plays went well than he was in looking after his poor wandering vagabond. The final letter of this group is difficult to date but Wilde begins by writing:

> The lecture cannot be on Cellini — it is on Dress.

This again raises the possibility that some lectures at this time were about Benvenuto Cellini. However, I have found no evidence of this. The only suggestion that he did lecture on Cellini is given in *Personal Impressions of America* where Wilde speaks of his visit to Leadville:

> I read them passages from the autobiography of Benvenuto Cellini telling them that he was a most accomplished rough ...

I explained that he had been dead for some little time which elicited the enquiry "Who shot him?" This gave an insight of the life of the mining people of Leadville: they were quite unable to conceive any method of quitting life other than the one usual in Leadville.

Wilde asks Appleton to send him 'the American and English books of criticisms' and for this reason I estimate that this letter was written towards the end of the tour when these books could be completed, which dates this letter as probably late in April.

In amongst his concerns about the lectures, their organisation and his audiences, Wilde, feeling not too short of funds, visited Sotheby's on 2 March and bought two of Keats' love letters to Fanny Brawne.[30] These were knocked down for £18 and £27 each, much more than his average lecture earnings at the time.

Towards the end of March, Wilde lectured on *Dress* at Leek in Staffordshire in the Large Picture Gallery of the newly opened Nicholson Institute.[31] This Institute was a gift from Mr. Joshua Nicholson[32] and was designed by a local architectural practice – Sugden and Son[33] – in Wilde's favoured Queen Anne style. Leek was famous for its silk production and dyeing techniques and William Morris lived and worked there between 1875 and 1878.[34] He stayed with Thomas Wardle[35] who ran a dyeworks and it was there that Morris learnt all that he could about dyeing and the use of natural dyes. Fascinated by Morris' ideas and designs, Wardle took up the production of Morris' fabrics and collaborated with Morris until his death in 1896. Wilde's own views on wall coverings and fabrics are contained in a letter written in 1885[36] where he states that he prefers a plain wall (which is what he preaches in *The House Beautiful*), but feels that Morris:

> is far more successful with those designs which are meant for textures which hang in folds

It was whilst in Leek that Morris met Larner Sugden[7] – the 'Son' in the architectural practice Sugden and Son – and was inspired by Sugden's ideas about conservation which led him to found the Society for the Protection of Ancient Buildings. This was a very topical subject as urban building projects threatened many ancient buildings and was exemplified by Godwin's interest in the renovation of Westminster Hall at the end of 1884. During his lecture, Wilde mentions the building he is in:[38]

> he spoke of the beauty of the Nicholson Institute, and said that few towns could boast of such an institution

and, turning to Morris:

> paid tribute to Wardle's dyeing and to Leek's special
> contribution to the decorative arts.[39]

Journalism

IN JANUARY, on the advertisements page of the *Pall Mall Gazette*,[40] sandwiched between notices for *The Grosvenor Gallery Winter Exhibition* and *The Statistical Society's Third Ordinary Meeting* was an advertisement for:

> Mr. Whistler's "Ten O'clock" – Prince's Hall, Piccadilly, on the
> evening of February 20th

And on an adjacent column, in between advertisements for a nine volume edition of *The Arabian Nights* and the sale of *Some magnificent thoroughbred ST. BERNARD PUPPIES,* was a notice:

> Mr. Oscar Wilde will discourse upon "DRESS" at Eight o'clock
> on Wednesday Next, 21st inst., at the Highbury Athenæum …

Wilde's first journalistic commission for the *Pall Mall Gazette* was to review Whistler's *Ten O'clock* and it would appear the day after this much-heralded lecture. It got its name from the late and controversial time at which it began, which Whistler had decided was an appropriate time to begin thereby allowing a civilised gentleman the opportunity to enjoy his evening meal without having to rush his postprandial cigar. Therefore Wilde had to attend, write his review that night, or at the very latest complete it early the next day, so that it could appear in the 21 February edition (the *Pall Mall Gazette* was an evening newspaper). Notwithstanding this time pressure, Wilde would have known that it was imperative he produced something very good as a response to this major art event performed by someone who was both a hero to him and an increasingly harsh critic of him. It was a major vote of confidence by Stead in letting Wilde begin with such an important review. However, he was a very shrewd man and through his contact with Wilde must have seen this opportunity — Wilde on Whistler — as a real journalistic coup. He must have been impressed with the results because he gave Wilde's review[41] pride of place, the front page, sharing it with an article about the possibility of a war between Russia and Britain about the Afghan border:

> a war which neither nation desires, and which would in truth
> be a catastrophe for civilization throughout the East.

(*Plus ça change, plus c'est la même chose.*)

Wilde's review is a masterpiece of backhanded compliments and light criticisms: its contents were reported widely and became the subject of comment in the press. Wilde's review rapidly became newsworthy in its own right and as famous as Whistler's lecture. Their names became entwined in the headlines:[42]

MR. WILDE AND MR. WHISTLER

Both this sharing of the headline and the priority given to Wilde's name in it must have grated quite strongly with Whistler: after all, as well as a lecture upon Art, it was a lecture, in part, designed to denigrate Wilde. I do not know whether Whistler knew in advance that Wilde was to review his lecture but after he had read Wilde's views, and the response the review itself received, he must have felt that he had failed badly in his attacks on him. More generally, Whistler's lecture received a mixed reception in the press. One of the more negative reviews which followed Wilde's[43] commented that:

> ... I have no hesitation in stating that the majority of persons who heard Mr. Whistler's lecture on Art came away resentful. There were some who said that they had been done out of ten shillings to listen to a pack of rubbish ... but, whatever Mr. Oscar Wilde may urge, he has not the gifts of a popular lecturer.

Even here in a negative review of Whistler, Wilde is portrayed as Whistler's supporter. On the other hand, *The Times* began an entirely factual report of the lecture[44] with one introductory paragraph which concluded by saying that:

> ... the fashionable audience ... had assembled in the expectation that the eccentric genius of the artist would find them amusement for an hour. Their faith was not misplaced.

Whistler's bad feeling about Wilde can be seen building up during his period of lecturing. Alan S. Cole's diaries[45] pick out some of the underlying themes preying on Whistler's mind leading up to this performance. Almost a year before the *Ten O'clock*, in March 1884, Cole records that Whistler is 'Strong on Oscar Wilde taking his notions on Art' and in October Whistler airs his 'Views on Ruskin & Art' which must have been trenchant. These twin concerns eventually give rise to Whistler working up his ideas about art: he begins the lecture's gestation in October 1884, has a draft ready in December and finalised, with Cole's assistance, in February. Interestingly, following the *Ten O'clock*, Cole goes to *The Times* offices to help with the notice which appeared the following day. It is hard to see what impact he had on this as it amounted to little more than a précis of the lecture's contents. Perhaps he suggested the introductory paragraph's positive tone: 'the eccentric genius of the artist would find them amusement for an hour.'

In the main, Whistler's *Ten O'clock* lecture[46] is an attack on Ruskin. This was personal as well as aesthetic and highlights a long and bitter personal enmity. I will not give a full description and critique of Whistler's *Ten O'clock* here but I will summarise the most relevant parts because they, and Wilde's responses in his reviews, deal not just with the ideas Wilde is promoting in his lectures but with Wilde as a lecturer himself.

From the very beginning of his lecture, Whistler identifies the distance between the artist — who is 'set apart' and who, uniquely, can perceive before he then 'produces that wondrous thing called the masterpiece ' — and the public, who, he claims, have no role in art at all. Throughout, Whistler taunts Ruskin and his followers with sarcastic comments about the moral qualities of Art: he ridicules viewers judging art by asking "What good shall it do?" and how it may 'better their mental or moral state'. He criticises Ruskin and the Pre-Raphaelite's belief in the supremacy of art before Raphael, that certain periods or places were artistic; he criticises the literary approach to the criticism of a painting – what's the storyline? - and the 'Sage of the Universities' (clearly Ruskin as Slade Professor of Fine Art) who has great learning and experience, except in his subject, Art. Whistler concluded this part with:

> We have then but to wait — until, with the mark of the Gods upon him - there comes among us, again, the chosen — who shall continue what has gone before.

As can be seen above, there are long sections of the *Ten O'clock* which make exactly the same points as Wilde has been making in his lectures. The question arises: who is echoing whom? Whistler considered that Wilde had stolen everything from him, and was not slow in letting everyone know. The language they both use is so similar that I am not sure that this is actually and entirely the case. In fact, as stated in Chapter 1, Ross suggests that Whistler took from Wilde some of his phraseology:[47]

> ... Whistler certainly reproduced some of it (*Modern Art Training*) as his own in the *Ten O'clock* lecture

Whistler was a wonderful painter and a sharp, at times unpleasant, wit. But he did not have the brilliant grasp of language or the wide-ranging understanding of the classical debates about aesthetics that Wilde had. Ross who knew them both puts it well:[48]

Wilde was at one time always accused of plagiarising his ideas and his epigrams from Whistler, especially those with which he decorated his lectures, the accusation being brought by Whistler himself and his various disciples. … That Wilde derived a great deal from the older man goes without saying, just as he derived much in a greater degree from Pater, Ruskin, Arnold and Burne-Jones. Yet the tedious attempt to recognise in every jest of his some original by Whistler induces the criticism that it seems a pity the great painter did not get them off on the public before he was forestalled. … As a matter of fact, the genius of the two men was entirely different. Wilde was a humourist and a humanist before everything; and his wittiest jests have neither the relentlessness nor the keenness characterising those of the clever American artist. Again, Whistler could no more have obtained the Berkeley Gold Medal for Greek, nor have written *The Importance of Being Earnest*, nor *The Soul of Man*, than Wilde, even if equipped as a painter, could ever have evinced that superb restraint distinguishing the portraits of 'Miss Alexander,' 'Carlyle,' and other masterpieces.

In all probability, they had spent so much time together that they had borrowed from each other, inadvertently or not. Three examples stand out:

Firstly, Whistler is forceful in identifying all societies as inartistic – 'There never was an Art loving nation' – and Wilde in *Modern Art Training* had said: 'never talk of an artistic people; there never has been such a thing';

Secondly, Whistler has a section which is essentially a prose poem replication of his paintings, which is close not just in sentiment but in vocabulary to the section in *Modern Art Training* where Wilde had spoken of Gower Street as fairyland;

And thirdly, Whistler's constant criticism of Ruskin's moralistic approach to art appreciation is identical to Wilde's views expressed, for example, in *The House Beautiful*.

Then Whistler moves on from his *bête noire*, Ruskin, to criticise another favourite target, Wilde himself, showing that you cannot have too many *bêtes noires* at once:

And now from their midst the Dilettante stalks abroad! – The Amateur is loosed – the voice of the Aesthete is heard in the land – and catastrophe is upon us! …

> Costume is not dress — and the wearers of wardrobes may not
> be doctors of 'taste'! — For by what authority shall these be
> pretty masters! — Look well, and nothing have they invented!
> — nothing put together for comeliness' sake –
>
> Haphazard from their shoulders hang the garments of the
> Hawker — combining in their person, the motley of many
> manners, with the medley of the mummers' closet —

Whistler must have been proud of this alliteration based upon the
letter 'm': his personal attack upon Wilde as aesthete, dilettante, dress
reformer and 'wearer of wardrobes'. But Wilde responded and, from
Whistler's rather strained 'motley of many manners', must have
drawn the inspiration for his own, much better phrased and soon to
become more famous, 'm' based alliterative description of Whistler:

> There he stood: a miniature Mephistopheles mocking the
> majority

This caught the public's eye — and ear — more successfully than
Whistler's digs and newspapers across the country repeated it. Yet
again, with a single bound, Wilde escaped criticism, gained the upper
hand and must have infuriated Whistler. He even attracted attention
to the 'arrows, barbed and brilliant' shot at himself as a dress
reformer: *O mea culpa!* was Wilde's light-hearted response. He then
moves into the main area of his disagreement:

> Of course, with regard to the value of beautiful surroundings I
> differ entirely from Mr Whistler. ... I strongly deny that
> charming people should be condemned to live with magenta
> ottomans and Albert blue curtains in their rooms in order that
> some painter may observe the side lights on the one and the
> values of the other.

Sherard relates that Wilde had a particular horror of magenta:[49]

> With reference to the colour magenta, he declared that the sight
> of it gave him real pain.

Wilde then points out that, rather than Whistler's contention that the
painter was the only judge of a painting,

> only an artist is a judge of art. ...But the poet is the supreme
> artist ...

Wilde's elevation of the poet above the painter is entirely self-seeking
and designed to trump Whistler. The review concludes with further,
wonderfully sly digs at Whistler:

Not merely for its clever satire and amusing jests will it be remembered, but for the pure and perfect beauty of many of its passages — passages delivered with an earnestness which seemed to amaze those who had looked on Mr. Whistler as a master of persiflage only, and had not known him as we do, as a master of painting also.

Moving from Whistler as 'master of persiflage — only' (!) — Wilde rounds off the review with his own view:

For that he is indeed one of the very greatest masters of painting, is my opinion. And I may add that in this opinion Mr Whistler himself entirely concurs.

A tongue-in-cheek appreciation, the general thrust of which Wilde continued to be happy to repeat in his lectures, despite Whistler's personal attacks.

Following Wilde's review, *The World* published a pithy letter from Whistler responding to it and, in a way of publishing in the press that the two of them made their own, also printed Wilde's rejoinder to produce a witty dialogue. Both letters were reprinted in the *Pall Mall Gazette*[50] under the heading:

TENDERNESS IN TITE STREET

Whistler criticises Wilde's choice of painters he had mentioned in the review and responds by saying that Wilde has:

left to 'the Poet' the discovery of *'l'horrible' dans 'le beau'*!

which is a misrepresentation of Wilde's suggestion that even the ugly things of life can be treated beautifully, as he had explained in *Modern Art Training*. Wilde responds that his two chosen artists lectured on art and:

explained themselves away. Be warned in time, James; and remain, as I do, incomprehensible: to be great is to be misunderstood.[51]

Stead must have been delighted with the review and the extensive coverage his newspaper then received, resulting in the controversy which both Whistler and Wilde seemed unwilling to halt. He must have seen considerable mileage in these two great aesthete-critic-wordsmiths continuing their debate, preferably on his own pages. Wilde and Whistler were both eminently news- and quote-worthy and seizing his chance, Stead commissioned a follow-up article from Wilde which appeared a week after his first.[52] Wilde's second review was entitled:

*THE RELATION OF DRESS TO ART. A NOTE IN BLACK AND
WHITE ON MR. WHISTLER'S LECTURE.
BY MR. OSCAR WILDE.*

At the outset, Wilde stakes out the limited area for discussion — the subject of his own lectures: dress and art — and mimics Whistler's own formulation for titling his paintings: although instead of a 'Nocturne' or a 'Symphony' in a colour, we are given a 'Note' in the colours of newsprint. In the first paragraph Wilde quotes from one of Whistler's, and his own, heroes, Baudelaire, translated as:

> Great colourists know the secret of creating colour with a black frock-coat and a white cravat and a grey background.[53]

It is as though he is getting in his retaliation first. Wilde returned to his theme of the value of Whistler's lecture, saying that it was:

> The most valuable, that is, to the painter ...

He emphasises that these lessons were needed by 'the ordinary English painter' and paraphrases *Modern Art Training*:

> the true artist does not wait for life to be made picturesque for him, but sees life under picturesque conditions always.

Wilde then moves on to his *Dress*-based theme that:

> I hardly think that pretty and delightful people will continue to wear a style of dress as ugly as it is useless and as meaningless as it is monstrous, even on the chance of such a master as Mr. Whistler spiritualising them into a symphony or refining them into a mist. For the arts are made for life, and not life for the arts.

Wilde here has a distinctly social, as well as personal, agenda for art and distances himself from Whistler's declared views and, indeed, Pater's. He then restates some of his key themes from *Dress*: dress should be an expression of the loveliness it shields; should not impede motion; should hang from the shoulders and not the waist, thus forming an inverted wine glass effect: then painting could become 'the natural expression of life's beauty'. Whilst he accepts that Art may be about its own perfection, Wilde sees the social benefit of making Beauty:

> the natural and national inheritance of all ... under these more exquisite conditions, what perfect artist born?

This is a riposte to Whistler's stated belief that the painter is born in a sort of miracle beyond social conditions, whereas Wilde saw that:

MORE THAN ONE FAMILIAR FACE WAS THERE.

Wilde (right towards the rear) at the Botanical Fête 30 June 1885.
Whistler is towards the front.

An artist is not an isolated fact. ...

but a product of many forces, some of which are societal.

After these two important reviews, Wilde must have considered
that his re-entry into journalism had gone very favourably: not only
was his first attempt a well-received review of an important artistic
event given front page status but it resulted in the immediate
commission of a follow-up piece. He must have been even happier
when further offers came along: within days he was working for a
new magazine, *The Dramatic Review,* which published his first article,
Shakespeare on Scenery, on 14 March[54]. Wilde developed the theme of
this article — supporting archaeological and costume realism in stage
productions — reusing parts of it for a broader article on staging
Shakespeare, *Shakespeare And Stage Costume*[55] which was published
shortly afterwards. This review was very important and included
issues about dress and costume which were related to his lecture
topics. Both were heavily influenced by the thoughts and practice of

Godwin who was involved in numerous theatrical productions. Godwin was a strong supporter of archaeological realism in theatre and Wilde enthusiastically argued, not just for that view, but that Shakespeare himself had wished for a high level of realism in the production of his plays. This argument is contrary to his very positive comments about the impressionistic Chinese theatre production he had visited in San Francisco three years earlier, views expressed in his first public lecture: *Personal Impressions of America*. This revised, highly realistic view about staging Shakespeare was one which he could not quite leave alone, returning to it again and finally revising it for publication in *Intentions* in 1891 as *The Truth of Masks*. In *Shakespeare and Stage Costume* Wilde restates his views contained in his lectures, sometimes in exactly the same terms:

> For the stage is not merely the meeting place of all the arts, but is also the return of art to life.[56]

which is reminiscent of Wilde's statement in *Dress*:

> that just as drama was the meeting place of life and of poetry, so dress was the meeting place also of life and of the visible arts

In his opening comments to *Dress*, Wilde speaks of the public's improved perception of the beautiful and uses almost exactly the same phrase in *Stage Costume*:[57]

> … in England at any rate, the public has undergone a transformation; there is far more appreciation of beauty now than there was a few years ago

a view he would also repeat in *The Critic as Artist*:[58]

> Ugliness has had its day.

Taking a point from both *Modern Art Training* and his first review of Whistler's *Ten O'clock*, Wilde asserts that Shakespeare:

> … recognises the artistic beauty of ugliness.

His comparison of Greek and English costume could come from *Dress*:[59]

> The Greek dress was the loveliest dress the world has ever seen, and the English dress of the last century one of the most monstrous.

From his important advice on room decoration in *The House Beautiful* he draws this advice for designing a stage as an ensemble:[60]

> For each scene the colour-scheme should be settled as absolutely as for the decoration of a room

And Wilde writes about the use of neutral colours as he had in this lecture:[61]

> ... a time when the beauty of black was understood; but I hardly think that, as regards stagemounting or house decoration, it really is. Its decorative value is, of course, the same as that of white or gold; it can separate and harmonise colours.

He even brought his interest in children's education into the article:

> Indeed if it be really necessary that the School Board children should know all about the Wars of the Roses, they could learn their lessons just as well out of Shakespeare as out of shilling primers, and learn them, I need not say, far more pleasurably.

Finally, Wilde made some more general points on aesthetics which he had elaborated, particularly in *Modern Art Training*:[62]

> ... truth is independent of facts always, inventing or selecting them at pleasure

and, a restatement of the aesthetic creed of 'art for art's sake':[63]

> ... that joy in beauty for beauty's sake without which the great masterpieces of art can never be understood.

To exemplify this developing link between Wilde's lectures, his reviews and his essays, he was commissioned to write a piece for the *New York Daily Tribune* which appeared on 19 April.[64] How this happened we do not know, nor who chose the subject for the article, but it was printed, covering an enormous two full columns, and headed:

THE PHILOSOPHY OF DRESS
BY OSCAR WILDE
Copyright 1885

It is a lengthy but slightly compressed version of his lecture *Dress* with the omission of comments upon men's attire and a few minor additions for his American audience. It gives us the only example we have of a Wilde lecture published in his lifetime under his authorship. Those lectures that have been published have used Wilde's notes as their basis and according to Ross Wilde never contemplated reprinting them.[65] Here, though, is proof that this was not entirely the case. For Wilde these were enduring subjects of interest which, in this particular example, he was happy to work up for publication (it is transcribed in Appendix D.)

As well as lecturing on *Dress*, writing on dress and, apparently, advising Constance on her dress, Wilde did try his hand at designing his own dress. At a private view he was described[66] as wearing:

> … his brown frock coat, designed by himself, his broad-brimmed hat, and his air of sleek self-appreciation.

There was some doubt in the press that brown as a colour for men in the evening would catch on. In terms of his other creative endeavours, he was also beginning to write poetry again and had two poems accepted for publication during the summer: *The Harlot's House* and *Roses and Rue*. He was clearly searching all avenues to express his creativity and for increased income and the press picked up on this. As his lecture tour drew to a close, several newspapers pondered Wilde's future. In early April under the heading:[67]

MR OSCAR WILDE AND THE STAGE

appeared a short note which was repeated elsewhere[68]

> A contemporary announces that Mr Oscar Wilde intends to take to the stage as a profession. It is probable that he will make his debut at York in "Hamlet" about the middle of May. It is announced that he intends visiting Scarborough at the conclusion of his York engagement.

But both the 'contemporary' and the article were wrong: it was improbable that Wilde would ever play Hamlet. What actually happened was that Wilde completed his lecture tour, carried on reviewing and Constance gave birth to their first child, Cyril,[69] on 5 June.

Autumn

THE FIRST lecture of the autumn of which we have a record is at Westminster Town Hall on the evening of the 16 October 1885, Wilde's 31st birthday. Wilde's subject is of interest because it had two titles: *The House Beautiful* is mentioned but so is a new title,[70] *The Mission of Art in the Nineteenth Century*. Wilde must have decided that something new was required for the new season and, after careful consideration, he added *The Mission of Art in the Nineteenth Century* as a subtitle. Both titles continue to be used for Wilde's later lectures in the north-east but thereafter the title of this lecture becomes solely *The Mission of Art in the Nineteenth Century*, without any mention of *The*

House Beautiful. We have been here before: in early 1884, Wilde introduced another new lecture, *The Value of Art in Modern Life,* which began its appearance as a subtitle for his older lecture, *Dress* and, in turn, a year later he subtitled that lecture as *The Meaning of the Aesthetic Movement.*

The Mission of Art in the Nineteenth Century seems to have taken as a starting point the ideas Wilde had been developing about aesthetics and some wider issues about housing and urban planning, possibly inspired by the debates at the International Health Exhibition during the previous year. Two of his comments were seized upon and repeated in the press. The first was his contention that:

> ugliness was first introduced into art when the first bust or portrait of a man was shown.

No reporters agreed with this line at all, the general response being more of the 'portraits are what art is about' variety:[71]

> On the contrary, when the human bust was first introduced into artistic work, art may be said to have come to *a head.*

was one punning opinion. The second of Wilde's observations was that:

> In the silver of the morning and the gold of the evening [posters on a wall] become as fantastic in colouring and as delightful as a Japanese fan

which appears to be an extension of Wilde's previously expressed opinions in *Modern Art Training* that:

> The true artist … took care to see life under pictorial conditions always. … I do not desire that external life should be permanently beautiful but I do know that under certain conditions of light and shade everything would look beautiful.

There are a few other reported observations but altogether these are fragmentary and it is not possible to recreate a lecture from them but I have brought the reports together in Appendix F.

In early November Wilde did a three day stint in the north-east of England with *The House Beautiful, Mission of Art in the 19th Century,* in North Shields, Sunderland and Newcastle-upon-Tyne.[72] Appleton must have been trying some new publicity techniques for the North Shields lecture because it was reported:[73]

> … some boys were walking the streets at North Shields, with boards on their backs, some with the word "Oscar," others with the word, "Wilde." The little army was moving towards the

New Quay, when a cart drove the youths into confusion. On a second start, the "Wilde" boards led the "Oscar" ones, causing the boards to read "Wilde Oscar." Some sailors ... were puzzled, till a mate explained that the words meant "wild ostrages," ... "Oh, aye," said a companion. "an hev seen some on 'em at the Jewlogical Gardens, Lunnen, gannin aboot like gyuses on stilts!"

Unfortunately, whatever the publicity, attendances at the lectures were poor:[74]

the sensational interest that gathered round the name of MR OSCAR WILDE seems to have lessened, in Newcastle, at any rate, if the number of his audience in the Town Hall last night is to be any criterion of his popularity. Yet there are few lecturers whom one can listen to with more pleasure than the 'Prince of Aesthetics' to adopt an expression from the glaring placards announcing his lecture.

And in Sunderland the audience was even poorer:[75]

... Mr. Oscar Wilde, ... has been lecturing in Newcastle and Sunderland this week. Here there was a beggarly array of empty benches, and just imagine the apostle of Aestheticism holding forth for nearly two hours to little over a score of people at Sunderland.

We can only hope that the 'little over' twenty tickets sold in Sunderland was an understatement, but whatever the exact size of this small audience, Wilde's remuneration would not amount to much.

We know that for the three day duration of these lectures, his hotel was the very grand Station Hotel, Newcastle-upon-Tyne because on Sunday, 8 November, he writes from there to Henry Marillier,[76] who is a young man of about twenty. Wilde and Marillier had first met about five years previously but had lost contact. Marillier must have written for the first time on 4 November and there now exist, in total, nine letters from Wilde[77] which are interesting and are suggestive of, at least, a strong intellectual relationship between them. But these letters are useful in this context because of their relevance to Wilde's travels and lectures. They enable us to establish dates for some lectures for which we have no other evidence. (Also, they are very interesting evidence of the speed at which their relationship develops: following Marillier's first letter, Wilde writes on the 5th, must write again on the 6th or 7th, they meet on the 8th in London before Wilde travels to Newcastle, Wilde writes to him again on the 14th, 16th, visits him in Cambridge on the 22nd and writes enthusiastically about his visit on the 27th.)

Two letters on 8 and 12 December place Wilde in Scotland. The first is from The Balmoral Hotel, Edinburgh and four days later he writes to Marillier from the Central Station Hotel in Glasgow.

12 December 1885   Central Station Hotel, Glasgow

Dear Harry, I am away in the region of horrible snow and horrible note paper! Lecturing and wandering — a vagabond with a mission!

This last sentence is so evocative, it provided an excellent title for this book. In between these two letters we know that Wilde lectured on *Dress* to 'a large attendance' at Peterhead,[78] a town north of Aberdeen and some 150 miles north of Edinburgh. This suggests a tour of Scottish venues early in December 1885: the last time he stayed at The Balmoral he gave five lectures in the area.

Wilde gives the last few lectures of 1885 we know of in London: one at the Westbourne Park Institute, Paddington, newly established for adult and technical education; a lecture advertised in the press as *Ladies' Dress* in West Norwood and, in between Christmas and New Year's Eve, Wilde lectured at the London Institution, Finsbury Circus on *Personal Impressions of America.* This is a major departure: he had not given that lecture since April 1884.

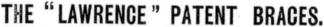

Wilde's testimonial in an advert for braces

On the subject of men's dress, just before Christmas, advertisements appeared[79] for *The "Lawrence" Patent Braces* which included the following endorsement:

TESTIMONIALS

"The *"LAWRENCE"* Patent Braces are made on an exceedingly good principle, and seem to me superior to any other Braces I have seen. I find them most useful and comfortable."

OSCAR WILDE

And on that practical observation upon men's dress by — or, more probably, invented for — Wilde, 1885 draws to a close.

Table 5: Lectures during 1885

DATE	TOWN	VENUE	TIME	LECTURE
Mon 5 Jan	Dublin	Gaiety Theatre	3.00 pm	Dress
Tue 6 Jan	Dublin	Gaiety Theatre	3.00 pm	The Value of Art in Modern Life
Mon 12 Jan	Horncastle		evening	Dress
Thu 15 Jan	Leicester	Temperance Hall		Meeting on Funeral Reform (Wilde writes)
Sun 18 Jan	Newcastle upon Tyne	Tyne Theatre	evening	Dress
Mon 19 Jan	Sunderland	New Assembly Hall	evening	Dress
Wed 21 Jan	London	Highbury Athenaeum	8.00pm	Dress
Fri 23? Jan	Lecture*			
Sat 24? Jan	Lecture*			
Mon 26? Jan	Lecture*			
Wed 28? Jan	Lecture*			
?	Carlisle*			
?	Penrith*			
Wed 11 Feb	Ulverston	Temperance Hall	evening	Dress
Fri 13 Feb	Greenock	Watt Institution	evening	VAML
Sat 14? Feb	Scotland*			
Sun 15? Feb	Scotland*			
Tue 17 Feb	Eton	Albert Institute	evening	Dress
Tue 24 Feb	Dorchester	Town Hall	evening	Dress
Thu 26 Mar	Leek	Nicholson Institute		Dress
? Mar	Hampstead*			

Fri 16 Oct	London	Westminster Town Hall	evening	The House Beautiful, Mission of Art in the 19th Century?
Sun 8 Nov	North Shields	Theatre Royal	7.00 pm	HB, MA19C
Mon 9 Nov	Sunderland	Assembly Hall		HB, MA19C
Tue 10 Nov	Newcastle upon Tyne	Town Hall		MA19C
Tue 24 Nov	Birmingham	Acock's Green Institute		
Tue 8 Dec?	Edinburgh@			
Fri 11 Dec	Peterhead	Large Music Hall	evening	Dress
Sat 12 Dec?	Glasgow@			
winter 85/86	London	Westbourne Park Inst, Porchester Rd		
? Dec	London	West Norwood		Ladies' Dress
Mon 28 Dec	London	London Institution	8.00 pm	Personal Impressions of America

Key

? either a doubtful date or location

*conjectured lectures and dates from letters to Appleton, CL 226, which I posit as possibly 22 January 1885 and CL 252/3.

@conjectured lectures and dates from letters CL 271 & 272. There probably were other lectures in Scotland around these dates.

CHAPTER 7

1886 until 1889

The Final Lectures

1886

I T IS generally accepted that 1886 was a time of significant transition for Wilde. He later claimed[1] that he had his first physical homosexual experience with Robert Ross during 1886 and Frank Harris describes changes in Wilde's behaviour[2] at the time and the rumours which circulated:

> ...as soon as his name came up among men in town, the accusation of abnormal viciousness was either made or hinted. Everyone spoke as if there were no doubt about his tastes, and this in spite of the habitual reticence of Englishmen. ... in the first period of our friendship, I never noticed anything that could give colour even to suspicion of him; but the belief in his abnormal tastes was widespread and dated from his life in Oxford.
>
> From about 1886-7 on, however, there was a notable change in Oscar Wilde's manners and mode of life. He had been married a couple of years... yet instead of settling down he appeared suddenly to have become wilder... I told myself that an assured income and position give confidence; but at bottom a doubt began to form in me. It can't be denied that from 1887-8 on, incidents occurred from time to time which kept the suspicion of him alive, and indeed pointed and strengthened it.

At the very end of 1885 and on 1 January 1886 we find Wilde continuing to write[3] to his young friend Henry Marillier — whom

BOROUGH OF PENZANCE.

TO THE BURGESSES OF THE EAST AND WEST WARDS.

LADIES AND GENTLEMEN,—

It was intended to fully announce Mr. OSCAR WILDE'S visit, for next Monday Evening at Eight, but as it is known from reliable sources that the aristocracy and leading Ratepayers generally have decided to patronise this famous gentleman's Lecture-entertainment, and hear him give his "PERSONAL IMPRESSIONS OF AMERICA," the management is rather at a loss as to how to provide accommodation in St. John's Hall, a more than crowded house being anticipated. It is therefore useless to give further publicity to the coming of the Typical Æsthete other than this, that those who desire best places should reserve their seats at Miss Allsop's, without delay.

The American Tour of Mr. Oscar Wilde covered a period of nearly a year's continuous travel. He visited 34 States and Territories, as well as all parts of the Dominion of Canada, travelling for this purpose upwards of 30,000 miles, and his opportunities for accurate observation of the national and social life of the American people were exceptionally favourable.

Mr. Wilde will offer some observations upon dress for both sexes, with special reference to his own personal attempts to influence American tastes in favour of the adoption of a more graceful style than that which at present prevails.

For general convenience and to prevent a rush and a crush at the Hall next Monday evening, it is desirable that all reserved places be secured beforehand. Unreserved tickets to be had at entrance.

All ratepayers and others are respectfully invited to peruse Institute Syllabus for prices and other details.—Yours obediently,

BARNES RICHARDS,
Hon. Sec. Penzance Institute.

Wilde's Penzance lecture: book early to avoid disappointment

Wilde calls Harry, just as he will do with Lord Henry Wotton in *The Picture of Dorian Gray* — making arrangements to visit him and other young men at a house called Ferishtah on Nightingale Road, Hampton in west London. The date settled upon for the visit was Wednesday 6 January and Wilde suggests:

Let us live like Spartans, but let us talk like Athenians

I am sure that we all wish we could have been a fly on that wall. Following this visit to Hampton, Wilde invited Marillier to Tite Street for lunch and he attended on both Sunday 17 January and on Thursday 21 January, which happened to be days either side of Wilde's lectures in the south-west of England. On the evening of Monday 18 January Wilde lectured in Liskeard, Cornwall — which would have required a very early start from London — on the Tuesday in Plymouth and in Torquay on the Wednesday. In Liskeard and Plymouth his successful lectures were his old favourite, *Dress*. In Liskeard:[4]

The attendance was large, and the lecture throughout was listened to very attentively. It was interesting, and the impression created was favourable.

On the Wednesday afternoon Wilde appeared in Torquay, this time lecturing on *Dress and the Mission of Art in the 19th Century*.[5] This is a new variation of lecture title: the previous autumn Wilde had lectured on *The House Beautiful* which he had then subtitled: *the Mission of Art in the 19th Century*. In Torquay he appeared 'before a large and aristocratic assembly' in slightly different daywear from what he was wearing the previous year:

> ... attired in a double-breasted frock-coat, light tweed trowsers, and a terra-cotta coloured necktie

although we have met the necktie and *'light tweed trowsers'* before. The content of this variant lecture is mostly the same as *Dress* with the addition of some specific suggestions:

> The clothes to be worn by males should be the "Norfolk" jacket and knickerbockers, with the rough stockings and leggings, which the young Englishmen wore when indulging in outdoor sport.

An outfit which Wilde himself wore, as recalled by his son Vyvyan:[6]

> I preferred helping my father to build sand castles ...and when they were finished he would usually pull a few lead soldiers out of his pocket to man the castle walls. I remember him so well, in a Norfolk jacket and knickerbockers, no shoes or stockings and a large gray hat ... We ourselves were dressed in much the same fashion.

The letters to Marillier peter out and the last we have is Wilde's response to a letter he received in Manchester in June[7] complaining that:

> Harry, you must not ask me to read a paper, or say anything. I have too much public work at present and am tired. ...

His phrase 'too much public work' suggests he is still lecturing at this time, although June is much later than his usual tour dates, which had previously finished in April. It also suggests that he is struggling to respond to the demands being put on him: lecturing, seeing plays and reading books then writing the reviews: it must have been very time consuming. On the other hand, he has probably given us a clue to his methodology.[8]

The Coming (?) Dress

The poor reviewers are apparently reduced to be the reporters of the police-court of literature, the chroniclers of the doings of the habitual criminals of art. It is sometimes said of them that they do not read all through the works they are called upon to criticise. They do not. Or at least they should not. ... Nor is it necessary. To know the vintage and quality of a wine one need not drink the whole cask. It must be perfectly easy in half an hour to say whether a book is worth anything or worth nothing. Ten minutes are really sufficient, if one has the instinct for form. Who wants to wade through a dull volume? One tastes it, and that is quite enough — more than enough, I should imagine.

It is quite clear from the number of reviews Wilde is writing and the number of events he attends — many of which receive coverage in the newspapers because of his presence — that time for travelling and lecturing was becoming severely limited and fewer lectures at this time have been uncovered. For the next few years, Wilde's name in the press is overwhelmingly related to an event — a Private View, a celebratory meal, an opening night — rather than a lecture. Or just some gossip, sometimes laced with sarcasm, sometimes more kindly: after all, an authority on dress and house decoration is never off duty:[9]

His advocacy of various fashions and modes of dress is always reasonably accounted for, either on the lines of beauty, comfort, or hygiene. Talking with him the other day ... he said, "I often think of starting a society for the diffusion of cheval glasses amongst the middle classes. One great reason why English women dress so badly is that the majority of them never have a chance of seeing how they look. But few of them have ever seen themselves reflected from head to foot. ...Why do we all perch our mirrors over our fire-places, or on a level with our heads, instead of bringing them down to the floor of a room so as to take in the whole human figure?" I thought these remarks so sound and reasonable, although said partly in fun, that I took them to heart and resolved to have a long panel of good looking-glass fixed in a convenient place. ...

In early October it was announced[10] that:

Mr. Oscar Wilde, the late bard of beauty, is about to start on a lecturing tour. His subjects will be various matters appertaining to aesthetics.

Of course, no reporter worth his salt could afford to mention Wilde's name without some, preferably alliterative, reference to his aesthetic past. Elsewhere, a longer notice appeared[11] and gave a little more detail about those matters 'appertaining to aesthetics':

But perhaps his most pleasing entertainment will be his lecture on Chatterton.[12]

This is news, though, and marks a real departure for Wilde on several fronts: it is a specific rather than general subject, it is literary and it is Wilde's first public foray into his exploration of the inter-relationship between ethics and aesthetics. Thomas Chatterton was a poet and forger of medieval manuscripts whose poverty and suicide at the age of seventeen in 1770 made him a hero to the great Romantic poets who followed. William Wordsworth,[13] in *Resolution and Independence*, described Chatterton as:

> the marvellous Boy,
> The sleepless Soul that perished in his pride.

Samuel Taylor Coleridge[14] wrote *A Monody on Chatterton*; Robert Southey edited his poems; John Keats dedicated probably his most famous poem, *Endymion*, to him and his first dedication, which he later removed, read:

INSCRIBED,

WITH EVERY FEELING OF PRIDE AND REGRET
AND WITH "A BOWED MIND,"

TO THE MEMORY OF

THE MOST ENGLISH OF POETS EXCEPT SHAKSPEARE,(*sic*)

THOMAS CHATTERTON

And, in *Adonais*, Percy Bysshe Shelley's[15] homage to Keats, he ranks Chatterton with other poets who died young:

> When lofty thought
> Lifts a young heart above its mortal lair,
> And love and life contend in it, for what
> Shall be its earthly doom, the dead live there
> And move like winds of light on dark and stormy air.
>
> The inheritors of unfulfilled renown
> Rose from their thrones, built beyond mortal thought,
> Far in the Unapparent. Chatterton
> Rose pale, — his solemn agony had not
> Yet faded from him

More modern writers of the time - Alfred de Vigny,[16] Robert Browning,[17] Dante Gabriel Rossetti and his friend Theodore Watts[18] — had all written about him. *The Death of Chatterton*, an 1856 Pre-Raphaelite painting by Henry Wallis,[19] was the most famous image of Chatterton in the nineteenth century with the young George Meredith[20] modelling the figure of the dead poet. In 1884 Henry Arthur Jones wrote a play about him for Wilson Barrett and Barrett's tour of the USA in the autumn of 1886, which included *Chatterton* in his programme, was much publicised. Miss Gertrude Norman[21] also toured Britain during 1885/86 and, rather interestingly, starred as the tragic poet in a play *The Life & Death of Chatterton*. Certainly, Chatterton was — as Whistler suggested Art was, from the opening of his *Ten O'clock* — 'upon the Town!'

Wilde, though, had been interested in Chatterton for many years, as evidenced by Sherard who describes them[22] together in Paris early in 1883:

> For we interested ourselves in Gerard de Nerval,[23] and the children of sorrow who, like him, trod the path of letters to a very evil goal — Chatterton, Poe,[24] and Baudelaire; and I do not think that a day passed on which we did not speak, and long, of these unhappy poets.

Poe, Baudelaire, de Nerval and Chatterton make an interesting quartet from 1883 but Wilde's specific interest in Chatterton is aroused during 1886 partly through his friendship with Herbert P. Horne[25] to whom he wrote many letters.[26] Horne was an architect who worked with A. H. Mackmurdo[27] and with whom he edited a magazine, the *Century Guild Hobby Horse,* which was seen by some as a supporter of, and an outlet for, Wilde. In December 1885 its first number was reviewed as:[28]

> All we can say at present regarding the *Hobby Horse* is that it is fearfully and wonderfully aesthetic. The type, paper, illustrations, literature – all suggest Mr. Oscar Wilde and the school of which he aspires to be chief.

Which is erroneous regarding Wilde's role in producing the *Hobby Horse* and a little hard on Horne and Mackmurdo. In August Wilde responded positively to Horne's suggestions for the 'renovation' of the Pyle Street School in Bristol where Chatterton had been a pupil and there follow letters between them about the possible design and erection of a plaque to Chatterton. Wilde must have been pressing forward with plans for this memorial because he visited Bristol with Horne and we read letters from him arranging a meeting with other interested parties including Mackmurdo, Theodore Watts and the Rev. Stopford Brooke.[29]

In the *Hobby Horse* of October a note was published saying:[30]

> Mr Oscar Wilde's article on Chatterton has been unavoidably postponed until the January number.

Therefore, in late 1886, we know that Wilde is working in parallel on a lecture and an article about Chatterton, although he was never to publish this article.[31] However, in December the *Pall Mall Gazette* published Wilde's review[32] of a book of essays about poets by Roden

Noel[33] which included one about Chatterton. The rather well clued-up Wilde considers:

> ... the monograph on Chatterton has a good deal of merit, though we must protest very strongly against Mr. Noel's idea that Chatterton must be modernised before he can be appreciated. ... in his desire to emphasise the meaning of Chatterton, he destroys Chatterton's music. ... Nineteenth-century restorations have done quite enough harm to English architecture, without English poetry being treated in the same manner ...

To our knowledge, Wilde's lecture on Chatterton was first given on 24 November at the Birkbeck Literary and Scientific Institution on Chancery Lane, City of London. Afterwards Wilde wrote to Horne:[34]

> I was very nearly coming to fetch you the night of the fog to come and hear my lecture on Chatterton at the Birkbeck, but did not like to take you out on such a dreadful night. To my amazement I found 800 people there! And they seemed really interested in the marvellous boy.

Wilde becomes enamoured of the phrase 'marvellous boy', it is as though he feels that the language of his sexual desires is somehow camouflaged by it being a quotation from Wordsworth. This is a transitional stage for his literary endeavours: Chatterton offers Wilde a real example — and the first with which he will deal with publicly — of an artist whose work and behaviour blurred the distinctions between a work of art and a work of duplicity, even criminality. Wilde delighted in the philosophy and actuality of secrets and lies; it mirrored so closely what his own life was becoming: a family man on the one hand, an increasingly active homosexual on the other. His fascination with subterfuge, with fakes, forgery, criminality and its associated alibis and secrets, increased. These themes are strong in his mature writings: *The Picture of Dorian Gray*, for example, is a novel about sin, crime and secrecy; *The Decay of Lying* is about, well, lying, and his four famous comedy plays — *Lady Windermere's Fan, A Woman of No Importance, An Ideal Husband* and *The Importance of Being Earnest* — all have at their hearts at least secrets, alibis and subterfuge, if not actual criminal activity. *The Importance of Being Earnest*, of course, revolves around two young dandies who lie in order to be somewhere else more pleasant — just as Wilde was beginning to do to Constance. 'Bunburying',[35] his dandy, Algernon Moncrieff, famously calls it, and, a few years later, to paraphrase that play, Wilde would invent an invaluable permanent playwright called Oscar Wilde, in order that he may be able to stay out at a hotel 'working' whenever he chooses.

Other lecture advertisements during this period include one about Mr. S. Wall Richards[36] who had been involved in organising Wilde's lectures in the West Midlands in late 1884. Whilst he is now 'of Bournemouth,' he continues to advertise in the Birmingham newspapers and in November he announces that he:

> ... will be providing entertainments at the Shaftesbury Hall

including an un-named lecture by Wilde during the 1886/87 winter season. Wilde is in good company, other providers of these Bournemouth 'entertainments' include: H. M. Stanley[37] (who had found Dr Livingstone[38] in 1871), Archibald Forbes and Charles Dickens.[39] Wilde does lecture in Bournemouth in January 1887 on *Dress*.

Whistler and Wilde Reprise

W HISTLER'S long-lingering bitterness towards Wilde, bitterness which Wilde had calmly parried and blithely riposted, finally boiled over in November. The opportunity Whistler took was when he wrote to the Committee of the National Art Exhibition and took a swipe[40] at two of his perennial hate figures, Harry Quilter and Wilde:

> Gentlemen,
>
> I am naturally interested in any effort made among Painters to prove that they are alive — but when I find, thrust in the van of your leaders, the body of my dead 'Arry, I know that putrefaction alone can result. When, following 'Arry, there comes on Oscar, you finish in farce. ...
>
> What has Oscar in common with Art? except that he dines at our tables and picks from our platters the plums for the pudding he peddles in the provinces. Oscar — the amiable, irresponsible, esurient Oscar — with no more sense of a picture than of the fit of a coat, has the courage of the opinions ... of others!

Not only did Whistler send this short, insulting letter to the Committee but he copied it to the *World*, where it was published on 17 November, and, just to make sure he did not miss it, he also sent a copy directly to Wilde with the added note:

> Oscar, you must really keep outside 'the radius'!

Even through his bitterness, Whistler concedes that Wilde is amiable (although irresponsible and esurient!) But, importantly in this context, the letter also underlines Whistler's continuing irritation with Wilde's lectures and his peddling in the provinces the ideas he 'picks from our platters.' Wilde responded with a letter[41] to 'Atlas', the editor of the *World:*

> Atlas, this is very sad! With our James 'vulgarity begins at home', and should be allowed to stay there.

In *The Gentle Art of Making Enemies*, Whistler added a rejoinder:[42]

> "A poor thing," Oscar! — "but," for once, I suppose "your own."

Their spat was relayed through the newspapers: the great wits had fallen out. A newspaper reviewing[43] Whistler's new portrait of Lady Colin Campbell[44] — 'a marvellous piece of work' — contained the passing comment:

> He has quarrelled with his bosom friend, Mr. Oscar Wilde, the bard of beauty.

This was the end of a fascinating friendship.

In November Wilde received a letter from a Mr. F. Pilcher, who represented an un-named and currently unknown society, asking if he could lecture to the society on 14 December. Wilde replied[45] that he could and that his fee would be seven guineas. Pilcher must have responded that very day with a reply along the lines of: 'our mutual friend Mr. Edwards[46] of Merton College, Oxford recommended you to us' in the hope of a reduced fee. Edwards happened to be one of the young men from Marillier's house party at Ferishtah at the beginning of the year, when, no matter what else they had got up to, they had talked like Athenians. The next day Wilde wrote to Pilcher again:

> My lecture fee is £10. 10., but I will lecture for you for £5. 5. should that be within the means of your society.

The fee structure seems chaotic at best, oscillating wildly in just two days. Whether the lecture took place is unknown but with a discount to five guineas, I presume it did.

1887

THE QUESTION of Wilde's lecture fee is further complicated in 1887. The first lecture of the year which he gives – 'before a crowded audience' - was for Wall Richards in Bournemouth[47] on *Art in Modern Life, Dress, &c.* By this time Wilde had been lecturing on *Dress* for approximately two and a half years and had converted it into an essay. He was very familiar with his material: the review reports how he gets all the good laughs for his best quips. If he was to tell them how much money was spent on bonnets:

> one half of them would be filled with remorse, and the other half with despair

and even more laughter as he describes these English bonnets:

> Some consisted of a stuffed bird fixed upon a piece of muslin, others of a strip of lace and two beads.

He was happy that the farthingale and crinoline:

> no longer existed; but there still remained that dreadful, that wicked thing called the dress-improver. (Laughter.) He did not think any Greek lady ever wore one. (Laughter.)

But it was not all about the follies of female fashion, he moved on to:

> a few points in the costume of the superior animal, man. (Laughter.)… why the tall glossy silk hat? (Laughter.) What was it? He knew that it was a sign of respectability and orthodoxy on Sundays (Laughter)…

and:

> How about the coat, a garment with a back and no front, the waistcoat, a garment with a front and no back; and the pantaloons? (Laughter.)

Any talk of a gentleman's trousers – a mention of his unmentionables - was guaranteed to either amuse or to outrage. But with Wilde's deft touch he ran no risk of the latter. He then concluded with a slightly amended peroration on ancient Greek values and modern dress:

> He advocated a reasonable, easy-fitting dress more consistent with health and beauty … if people did not return to the Greek ideal of dress, they would at least copy it in its best and most natural characteristics.

Following what must have been a successful lecture, Wall Richards writes to Wilde in June asking him to lecture in Bournemouth again and suggests some topics: Wilde replies that he is too busy to lecture and he has already given lectures in Bournemouth on the suggested topics:

> Otherwise I would only be too glad to speak again under your auspices. Would you kindly tell me what fee I was paid for my lecture this year. Was it £8. 8 or £12. 12?

So, for two lectures only a little over a month apart, Wilde has quoted his own lecture fee as being either five, seven, eight, ten or twelve guineas. The only consistency seems to be that they are all priced in guineas, which was how a Gentleman was paid for his services, as the artist Alan Trevor explained in *The Model Millionaire*:[48]

> "And how much do you get for your picture, Alan?"
> "Oh, for this I get two thousand!"
> "Pounds?"
> "Guineas. Painters, poets, and physicians always get guineas."

As Wilde reduced the number of his lectures, he also became invited to events which were speaking engagements. Whilst these were not lectures, his fame as a public speaker, wit and his ability made him an attractive invitee. In June, for example, he spoke at the annual meeting of the Sunday Society. This organisation promoted the opening of institutions — museums and galleries in the main — on Sundays and Wilde himself had lectured at a number of such events arranged in Newcastle upon Tyne: he had had one of his most successful lectures there in January 1885. The President proposed a motion accepting the annual report and that a petition on this matter should be put to Parliament. Wilde seconded the motion,[49] saying:

> ... in Dublin they were able to have their beautiful picture gallery open on Sundays, and I should be very glad if the great and prosperous City of London followed the example which had been set by the capital of Ireland.

In September, Wilde was invited, presumably as a representative of his mother and of Irish artists, to attend the Southwark Irish Literary Club for a lecture by Justin McCarthy,[50] an Irish MP, on *The Literature of '48*. This was a crowded meeting and his mother was named as one of the few female poets of that time. Following the main lecture Wilde gave a complimentary speech[51] in which he:

> ... mentioned that his mother, Lady Wilde, is about to bring out a volume of Irish legends, and Mr. Wilde availed of the opportunity to say that he would present a copy of the work to every Irish club in London.

In October, almost two years after his positive and witty *Pall Mall Gazette* review of *How to be Happy Though Married*, the author (Edward Hardy), who Wilde famously described as:[52]

> ... the Murray of matrimony and the Baedeker of bliss

invited Wilde to preside at a lecture by him on the subject.[53] This was an amusing evening for all and it would have been interesting to hear Wilde's (public) views on matrimony at this time.

During 1887 Wilde's life was increasingly taken up with writing as a profession. He was selling poems to magazines and writing reviews; the *Pall Mall Gazette* alone published over twenty reviews in this year.[54] He was also very busy writing fiction and arranging the publication of his first short stories: *The Canterville Ghost* appeared in *The Court and Society Review* in two instalments in February and March; *Lord Arthur Savile's Crime* appeared in the same magazine in three instalments in May. In the same month *Lady Alroy* (published in book form as *The Sphinx without a Secret*) appeared in *World* followed by *The Model Millionaire*, both in June.[55]

The year held other, enticing opportunities for Wilde: in March he was offered and accepted the editorship of a magazine, the *Lady's World*, which he would convert into the *Woman's World* and bring out his first number in October. His last two years reviewing must have seemed to have borne fruit at last: a steady income as an editor would be invaluable and it was a job he could enjoy: the post would also bring him a position, too. His letter to Wemyss Reid[56] of the publisher Cassell's in April shows that discussions had begun about this and Wilde was setting out some of his ideas about content. It looks as though Wilde considered that his experience of lecturing on *Dress* was an important consideration for him getting the job because early in his letter Wilde draws attention to this:

> No one appreciates more fully than I do the value and importance of Dress, in its relation to good taste and good health: indeed the subject is one that I have constantly lectured on before Institutes and Societies of various kinds …

From this time much of Wilde's efforts were taken with organising and editing this magazine. He wanted it to be a success and the evidence of the amount of effort he put into this is in the sheer number of letters there are to women of the day requesting articles.[57] He was paid a salary from May and the first number was published to good reviews:[58]

> Mr. Oscar Wilde has triumphed. The first number of the "Woman's World" has already appeared, and has, I believe, been sold out.

With the reviews he was producing of plays, books and exhibitions, the poems, essays and short stories he was writing as well as the magazine he was enthusiastically editing – to begin with, at any rate -

Wilde had little time to spare. He told Appleton as much in September in an undated and previously unpublished letter:[59]

Dear Mr. Appleton,

I fear I will not be able to lecture out of town next season, or much in town either, as I am very busy. I will however lecture at Bournemouth in *April* not October.

Here Wilde does distinguish between lectures in London, which may well continue in a reduced number, presumably because travel time would be minimal, and lectures *out of town* which he expects to cease altogether. From now onwards he would not abandon lecturing but he would be able to pick and choose when and where he did it.

1888

LATE IN JANUARY Wilde 'delivered a discourse' at the Clapham School of Art Prize-giving and Students' soirée.[60] He spoke to the four hundred visitors who were present about 'the advantages of art to a nation' and the subject matter was essentially the closing parts of *The House Beautiful* where he speaks about the use of the arts in education. He says that improvements would be made if:

Greek and Roman history is taught by works of art, pictures and other beautiful objects being exhibited in galleries for the good of all. Great advances in this direction, however, have been made in this country. Valuable pictures are no longer hidden away in private collections, but through loan-exhibitions, and such institutions as Toynbee Hall and the Bethnal Green Museum, [61] are rendered occasionally accessible to the public. Art schools, also, have effected much good, and Mr. Wilde complimented the Head Master, Mr. L.C. Nightingale, on the students' drawings shown that evening.

Wilde did take up Wall Richards' earlier offer of a further lecture and, as he had written to Appleton, he returned to Bournemouth on 7 April as part of another season of well received entertainments at The Shaftesbury Hall. The lecture title this time is given as:

Thomas Chatterton, the boy poet of the 18th Century

Wilde's manuscript entitled *Essay on Chatterton*[62] does exist. It is a major piece of work in an exercise book covering eighty two-page spreads, mainly written on the right-hand pages with occasional notes on the left-hand pages opposite his text. In order to minimise his work, Wilde has taken great chunks of detail from two published biographies[63] and he has actually cut out the chosen pages and pasted them into the exercise book. Many of the handwritten pages contain Wilde's transcript of the other side of these excised pages. All this must have taken considerable time to research and compile even with Wilde's destructive cut-up technique. It contains two references to where certain illustrations should be inserted which indicates that it is an early draft and was intended as an essay for publication. This is almost certainly the delayed 'article on Chatterton' advertised in the October 1886 edition of *The Hobby Horse* which noted that it had 'been unavoidably postponed until the January number'. It is, therefore, by April 1888, about eighteen months old.

However, the first manuscript entry, on the first left hand page, opposite the first page of the essay, consists of a few introductory comments which clearly indicate that Wilde is using these notes for a lecture (because this document is used as Wilde's lecture notes, a full transcription of *Chatterton* is given in Appendix G):

The opening notes of Wilde's 'Essay on Chatterton'

Previous lectures
Romantic movement –
    first in *poetry*
    Chatterton — Coleridge — Keats

The phraseology of the newspaper review of this actual lecture confirms that this first page was drafted specifically for Bournemouth in April 1888:[64]

> Mr. Oscar Wilde, in commencing his address, remarked that on former occasions he had spoken on the art movements of the present century, and to a limited degree, on the art of dress or costume. In the lecture he had the honour to deliver before them that afternoon he wanted to take them back to that marvellous boy in literature who lived in the latter part of the

18th century, who was the direct precursor of Coleridge and Keats, and from whom we might trace all the modern romantic movement in literature.

As we have seen, Wilde very seldom used notes when lecturing, but this subject is a departure from his others and the majority of it is taken up with Chatterton's biography at considerable length. Wilde may well have needed notes to prompt him to recall accurately this mass of detail.

The reference to previous lectures indicates that this is the latest in a series. Wilde had lectured in Bournemouth — in his own estimation, 'to a limited degree' — on *Dress* in January 1887 as part of Wall Richard's previous winter entertainments. The only other lectures in Bournemouth were back in November 1883 when he gave two lectures after he had failed to turn up the previous weekend. The lecture about art movements Wilde mentions was probably not one of these, which suggests another Bournemouth date lecturing on *The Mission of Art in the Nineteenth Century* or *The Value of Art in Modern Life*.

Of this manuscript/cut-up, essay/lecture notes, the key parts are the introductory and concluding passages which are all in manuscript, which illustrate Wilde's thinking about Chatterton and his art. Wilde's introduction is strong:

> The conditions that precede artistic production are so constantly treated as qualities of works of art that one is sometimes tempted to wish that all art were anonymous. For every true artist even the portrait painter or dramatist, be his work absolutely objective in presentation, still reveals himself in his manner. Even abstract forms such as music and colour have much to tell us about the nature of him who fashioned them, and take the place of the biographer. Indeed in some cases it is almost better for us not to search too curiously into the details of the artist's life. The *incompleteness* of Keats' life for instance blinds many of his critics to the *perfection* of his song - and it is well on the whole that we know so little about Shakespeare... Yet there are cases where the nature of the artist is so bound up with the nature of the man, that art criticism must take account of history and physiology in order to understand the work of art.

Over a year previously, in February 1887, Wilde edited this opening for re-use in his review of the poetry of Joseph Skipsey from Newcastle-upon-Tyne:[65]

> The conditions that precede artistic production are so constantly treated as qualities of the work of art itself that one sometimes is tempted to wish that all art were anonymous. Yet there are certain forms of art so individual in their utterance, so purely personal in their expression, that for a full appreciation of their style and manner some knowledge of the artist's life is necessary

This plundering of the essay for the beginning of this review probably indicates that Wilde had decided not to take the essay any further by late 1886 or early 1887.

Towards the end of this lecture the newspaper reports Wilde's handling of the all-important criminal/artist conundrum:

> Discussing the question as to whether we ought to regard Chatterton as a clever forger, — a man who wanted to take people in, — or whether we were to regard him as a great artist, Mr. Wilde said he was convinced that the latter was the right view to take.

The lecture ended with a recitation of Rossetti's sonnet on Chatterton which Wilde had written out longhand. Preceding the sonnet the manuscript has a closing section of over six pages which, unlike the beginning, is much less well developed. Wilde's ideas consist of a series of notes which seem to be exploring the tributaries of a conclusion. As he searches for his theme he begins by dealing with that aesthetical/ethical dilemma:

> Nature of his genius

> was he a mere forger with literary powers or a great artist?

> The latter is the right view. Chatterton may not have had the moral conscience which is Truth to fact but he had the artistic conscience which is truth to Beauty. He had the artist's yearning to represent and if perfect representation seems to him to demand forgery he needs must forge.

This section was obviously emphasised by Wilde in Bournemouth because the newspaper quotes it verbatim. This, though, is a fairly exact annexation of part of Theodore Watts' *Critical Introduction* to the Chatterton chapter of *The English Poets*.[66]

Watts, who added his mother's maiden name 'Dunton' to his surname in 1897, thus inspiring Whistler to telegram:[67]

> Theodore, What's Dunton?

Was a great friend of Rossetti and there is a famous painting of them

Rossetti and Watts at Cheyne Walk

in Rossetti's drawing room at Cheyne Walk from around this time.[68] He is a fascinating man who had taken Swinburne[69] – another of Wilde's heroes - into his household at The Pines, Putney to help him overcome his alcoholism. Watts' authorship of this Chatterton essay in *The English Poets* in 1880 interested and then led to Rossetti's fascination with Chatterton and his eventual creation of the sonnet with which Wilde concluded his lecture. Watts and Wilde already knew each other and Watts was involved in the discussions about the memorial to Chatterton in Bristol.[70] In his introduction to Chatterton, Watts had written:

> Either Chatterton was a born forger, having, as useful additional endowments, Poetry and dramatic imagination almost unmatched among his contemporaries, or he was a born artist, who, before mature vision had come to show him the power and the sacredness of moral conscience in art, was so dominated by the artistic conscience — by the artist's yearning to represent, that, if perfect representation seemed to him to demand forgery, he needs must forge.

Wilde's phraseology in his lecture: 'He had the artist's yearning to represent and if perfect representation seems to him to demand forgery, he needs must forge' is all but identical to the ending of Watts' sentence above. Wilde continues with another direct quotation from Watts about an artist's yearning to create:

there was something in him of "the yearning of great Vishnu to create a world"[71]

before he inserts a personal view:

Yet a destructive note of his own.

Watts' *Critical Introduction* identifies the novel technical aspects of Chatterton's poetry which were taken up by Coleridge – octo-syllabics with anapaestic variations - and he identifies *Christabel* and Keats' *Eve of St. Agnes* as poems which were both influenced by Chatterton. Wilde's notes contain exactly these same technical points and mention *Eve of St. Agnes* and Coleridge's *Kubla Khan*.

There are many overlaps between Watts and Wilde in this manuscript and these are not just Wilde reusing Watts' general ideas but him adopting the same, often quite unusual, phraseology. In Wilde's essay — in draft though it is — he owes a great deal to Watts. He ends his notes with a short quotation from Shelley's *A Defence of Poetry*:

mist of familiarity makes this obscure to us.

There is no grand conclusion written down – it is clearly obscure to Wilde himself - but, according to the review of the Bournemouth lecture, his final comments were a restatement of his opening themes:

… it was not … too much to say that the whole artistic movement of our age was a great deal due to that wonderful boy who died so young by his own hand

before he read Rossetti's sonnet.

The subject of forgery and Wilde's fascination with Shakespeare's Sonnets produced the marvellous *The Portrait of Mr. W. H.* a year later, where Chatterton turns up in the very first paragraph:[72]

I had been dining with Erskine … and we were sitting in the library over our coffee and cigarettes, when the question of literary forgeries happened to turn up in conversation. … I know we had a long discussion about Macpherson, Ireland, and Chatterton, and that with regard to the last I insisted that his so-called forgeries were merely the result of an artistic desire for perfect representation; that we had no right to quarrel with an artist for the conditions under which he chooses to present his work; and that all Art being to a certain degree a mode of acting, an attempt to realise one's own personality on some imaginative plane out of reach of the trammelling accidents and limitations of real life, to censure an artist for a forgery was to confuse an ethical with an aesthetical problem.

The careful editing of Wilde's concluding pages of his essay about Chatterton could create the half paragraph here.

One reason suggested for the abandonment of this essay is that so much of it is, quite literally, taken from published biographies[75] that Wilde felt the task of disguising this would involve too much work. However, Chatterton's life was so short and packed with incident that similar descriptions of it are inevitable and these, albeit extensive, sections could easily have been edited and paraphrased without being recognisable as obvious copies. However, having read the full essay, I consider that it is now far more clear that Wilde's attitude to Chatterton, his poetry and that confusion of an *ethical with an aesthetical problem* relied not so much on his extensive sampling of these biographies but, to a significant extent, on his adoption of the general thrust of argument, and the language, of Watts' *Critical Introduction* to *The English Poets*. He possibly felt that he could get away with this in a lecture – just – especially if it was out of London, but he could not disguise his significant debt to Watts in a published article. However, to remove these sections would undermine the whole point of his essay as well as his own fascination with the subject matter. Whilst, publicly, Wilde had nothing against plagiarism:[76]

> It is only the unimaginative who ever invents. The true artist is known by the use he makes of what he annexes, and he annexes everything

this was an annexation too far and his only course was to abandon it as an article.

But Wilde retained the draft because it remained a valuable prompt for his lectures and some elements of it would be valuable for future use: an explanation of Chatterton's choice of medium for his work:

> Still this forgery came from the desire of artistic self-effacement. He was the pure artist — that it is to say his aim was not to reveal himself but to give pleasure

uses very similar language, if at an earlier stage of development, to the first aphorism of *The Preface* to *The Picture of Dorian Gray*:[75]

> The artist is the creator of beautiful things. To reveal art and conceal the artist is art's aim.

And almost at the end of the essay Wilde underlines Chatterton's role, and, indeed, the artist's role:

> … it is the ideal, not the realistic, artist who expresses his age

which is an idea he explores more fully in *The Decay of Lying*:[76]

> ... the more imitative an art is, the less it represents to us the spirit of its age. ... The more abstract, the more ideal an art is, the more it reveals to us the temper of its age.

Chatterton as the subject of an essay was quietly forgotten. However, Wilde's desire for perfect representation and his fascination with the interlinking of ethics and aesthetics, epitomised by Chatterton, was important to him. Wilde needed another artist/criminal and he found his alternative in Thomas Griffiths Wainewright[77] whom he dealt with in his essay, *Pen, Pencil and Poison*. This was first published as a magazine article in January 1889, about nine months after the Bournemouth lecture on Chatterton, and it eventually became part of *Intentions* in 1891. Wainewright, the eighteenth century aesthete, was, in Wilde's own words:[78]

> ... not merely a poet and a painter, an art-critic, an antiquarian, and a writer of prose, an amateur of beautiful things and a dilettante of things delightful, but also a forger of no mean or ordinary capabilities, and as a subtle and secret poisoner almost without rival in this or any age.

As we can see from this description, Wainewright was a man whose lifestyle and love of the arts made him someone with whom Wilde could identify. Certainly he was more akin to Wilde than 'the marvellous boy' isolated in his medieval room high in a church tower, dirty with soot, scratching away on parchments, concocting his Old English poems.

Wilde must have been writing *The Happy Prince and other Stories*[79] in parallel with his consideration of these aesthetic conundrums because it was published in May 1888, just a month after this lecture: in the famous main story the Prince wants the swallow to help the poor people of the town and his second act is to help someone who resembles Chatterton in his final days in Holborn:

> ... a young man in a garret. He is leaning over a desk covered with papers, and in a tumbler by his side there is a bunch of withered violets ... he is too cold to write any more. There is no fire in the grate, and hunger has made him faint.

1889

IN A FLURRY of literary activity, Wilde published some of his major critical works in 1889: *The Decay of Lying: A Dialogue*[80] and *Pen, Pencil, and Poison: A Study*[81] both appeared in January, as did *London Models*;[82] *The Portrait of Mr. W. H.*[83] came out in July.

In November, Wilde was asked by Henrietta Barnett[84] to lecture at Toynbee Hall, Whitechapel. He declined but wrote:[85]

Some day I will give Toynbee Hall a lecture on Irish Art if I can get someone to help me with a magic lantern — I think that pictures are really necessary to give a proper idea of what one is talking about — but I have never yet had pictures in any lecture

And so, with concerns about new technology and a hope of a lecture on a topic which was close to him, his father and his mother, our knowledge of Wilde's life as a lecturer draws to a close.

Table 6: Lectures in 1886, 1887, 1888 and 1889

DATE	TOWN	VENUE	TIME	LECTURE
1886				
Mon 18 Jan	Liskeard	Literary Institution		Dress
Tue 19 Jan	Plymouth		evening	Dress
Wed 20 Jan	Torquay	Bath Saloon	afternoon	Dress and the Mission of Art in the 19th Century
Mon 25 Jan	Penzance	St John's Hall		D&MA19C
? April	London	Whitechapel		Art In Relation To Dress
before 11 June?	Manchester			
5 Oct				Press statement: about to start a lecture tour
24 Nov	London	Birkbeck Literary & Scientific Institution	Evening	Chatterton
14 Dec	London	A Society		
1887				
Fri 28 Jan	Bournemouth	Shaftesbury Hall	afternoon	Dress
Sat 4 Jun	London	Freemason's Tavern		Seconded motion
Wed 21 Sep	London	Irish Club, Southwark	night	Speech
Thu 26 Oct	London	Kensington Grammar School	evening	Oscar Wilde Presiding
Winter 1887/88?	Bournemouth	Shaftesbury Hall		lecture on art movements

1888

Mon 29 Jan	London	Clapham School evening of Art	Advantages Of Art To A Nation
Sat 7 April	Bournemouth	Shaftesbury Hall afternoon	Thomas Chatterton, The Boy Poet Of The 18th Century

1889

Nov	London	Toynbee Hall	Suggestion of a Lecture on Irish Art

Key

? Indicates an uncertain date

Afterword

THIS investigation of Oscar Wilde and his lectures in the United Kingdom begins in 1883 with a lecture on Art and ends six years later with him considering a lecture on Irish Art.

We know now just how important these years of lecturing were for Wilde. The lectures provided him with funds when he had no other way of earning an income and, in terms of his literary work, for most of 1883 and 1884 Wilde did little else but lecture. During this time he used the impressive Victorian rail network to visit most of the major towns and cities of England, Scotland, Wales and Ireland. The time this absorbed must have been overwhelming but he was considering and lecturing upon some controversial issues of the day: the role of art in society; housing, industry and urbanisation; children's education; public health and rational dress.

In October 1884 Wilde's new lecture on dress drew some criticism and his witty responses in the *Pall Mall Gazette* led the editor to invite him to become a reviewer. He began with a major artistic event, James Whistler's *Ten O'clock* lecture in February 1885. Wilde's very successful performance led to an expansion of offers to review for other newspapers and magazines. Essentially, the lectures paved the way for his journalistic career.

Wilde's income from reviewing at first supplemented and then supplanted his earnings from lecturing. Whilst he still lectured across the UK, this was in a reduced programme which allowed him the time to review on many topics. It also gave him an insight into the world of periodical publication and his fame for his lecture on dress led to an offer to edit the magazine *The Lady's World* in 1887. Wilde renamed the magazine *The Woman's World* and, as the editor, his financial needs could now be at least partially met and with a steady income he could choose his speaking opportunities to suit himself.

The cross fertilisation of the ideas in his lectures, the reviews he was writing and the magazine he was editing was stimulating and Wilde not only broadened his lectures but accelerated his literary output, writing more creatively from early in 1885. Poems, essays, short stories and fairy stories were all published and, before the end of the period covered in this book, Wilde had written and published

The Happy Prince and Other Tales, all the stories which were to be published as *Lord Arthur Savile's Crime and Other Stories* as well as most of his four major critical essays which would become *Intentions.*

The lectures, then, were important in facilitating Wilde's career and bridging the gap between the young aesthete and the writer we recognise today. Throughout this six-year period Wilde was famous but in 1889 we leave him on the very cusp of fortune and, in a further six years, the greatest misfortune of his life.

Index of Places

Places visited by Wilde during his lecture tours

T HIS INDEX lists all the cities, towns and villages in the United Kingdom (as it was during 1883-1889) where Wilde gave a lecture. It also includes places he visited *en route*, places he mentioned or are mentioned in the text.

Introduction to the Appendices

ONLY two of Wilde's UK lectures have been published previously and neither of these was during Wilde's lifetime: *Modern Art Training* (published as *Lecture to Art Students*)[1] and *Personal Impressions of America*.[2] Ross states that the text of *Modern Art Training* is taken from Wilde's original manuscript. Mason does not state the origin of the text of *Impressions of America* but comments in his introduction that it is from:

> Wandsworth Town Hall on Monday, September 24th, when he delivered to an enthusiastic audience a lecture on his "Impressions of America," which is contained in the following pages.

For these two lectures the published versions have been used as the basis for the texts I have compiled here but have been supplemented by newspaper accounts. Also, there are several partial sets of brief notes for *Personal Impressions of America* which I have reviewed. For all the other lectures, only press reports have been available.

Transcribing a lecture from reports is difficult. Robert Ross suggests:[3]

> Of the lectures, I have only included those which exist … in manuscript; the reports of others in contemporary newspapers being untrustworthy.

There is some truth in this as no newspaper could have published an entire verbatim report of any of Wilde's lectures, each of which lasted approximately one and a half hours: no editor would allow such a use of his valuable newspaper space. However, one has only to look at a few reviews to see how the major points were reported and repeated in other reviews. These major points are quite easy to map out from a small number of reviews but in order to give a longer and more comprehensive text of each lecture I have reviewed many hundreds of reports. The methodology I have used to compile these texts is to base them wherever possible on reviews which are lengthy and especially reviews of the identical lecture in the same town when it was covered by several newspapers. During this period it was common for many cities to have several, even many, independent newspapers which would all carry a review. Then I have taken other reviews from different towns at approximately the same time to create a more 'complete' text. I have then considered all other reviews of the period and included any important details not covered adequately in the original reports. I have re-ordered appropriately but minimally to avoid repetition and to make greater sense of the themes Wilde dealt with.

Quite often the reviews have a similarity with some key portions, wherever he was speaking, being repeated word for word. However, reports often mix the order of the key parts of the lecture. I would suggest that this is partially due to reporters giving prominence to parts of the lecture they thought most newsworthy, independently of where it was in the lecture, and also due to the restriction of space which was placed upon them. Sometimes these variations must have been due to Wilde himself who mostly lectured without notes or script of any kind. He spoke from memory and there are key sections and messages he wished to get over and he may have re-arranged the order of these slightly, possibly accidentally, possibly because, at that moment of speaking, he considered the linkages through the different parts of the lecture were better made one way rather than another.

It is, of course, impossible to say that there was any definitive text or that, at any particular lecture, he delivered the lecture in a certain way. However, having read many hundreds of reports, their similarities are striking and it is very clear from them what Wilde's themes were and the language he used to express them.

This is also assisted by reference to his letters on *Dress* in the *Pall Mall Gazette*, his review of Whistler's *Ten O'clock* lecture and other reviews where he reused parts of his lectures. More recently, an article by Wilde in the *New York Daily Tribune*, 19 April 1885 has emerged entitled *The Philosophy of Dress*: the details in this article are very similar and, in major sections, identical to my transcription of Wilde's lecture *Dress*. Having compared these I am confident that my methodology does produce an accurate replication of Wilde's lectures.

Wilde rarely used notes when lecturing. However, for *Impressions of America* he was occasionally reported as using them and there are some extant manuscript sheets of notes:

a. there are six pages of notes on the headed notepaper of the Cliftonville Hotel, Margate made on 26 July 1883 (sold at Sotheby's in 1993) These are very brief and are little more than

headlines which highlight all the main points of the lecture
as given.

b. One page of handwritten notes headed 'men, women, and
children' which deal with girls as 'the prettiest despots in
the world' from close to the end of the lecture.

I have considered these alongside the other sources.

Josephine Guy in her introduction to Volume 4 of the Oxford
Complete Works of Oscar Wilde[4] deals with what she terms a "process of
'editing'" Wilde's text for his essay *Historical Criticism:*

> There are also occasions where Ross 'corrects' Wilde's
> grammar, and substitutes his own phrasing for what he
> presumably judged to be infelicities or solecisms in Wilde's
> phrasing ... not dissimilar to that of Wilde's prison manuscript
> ... (which has) in fact undergone a process of judicious editing

I have faced similar issues with producing these lecture texts from
press reviews and have resisted the temptation to 'improve' them
without a clear material basis for doing so. These texts, then, whilst
collated, are as they were published in newspapers at the time and I
have not ironed out any infelicities (as I may see them) nor tightened
the wording for greater impact.

Finally, having considered all these points and the lectures I
transcribe here, I now consider that a lecture is a verbal and visual
performance. It is far richer than, and likely to vary from, any
supporting notes that Wilde may have used. In many ways, lecture
notes could be considered as merely the skeleton on which the
lecturer builds the body of the lecture. With Wilde I think this was
even more so because he was a born performer. Therefore, it is
possible to argue that press reports, co-ordinated in the numbers and
in the way I have done here, do result in a better description of the
lecture performance than the mere transcription of any of Wilde's
extant lecture notes.

Modern Art Training

Lecture to Art Students

THE TEXT of this lecture is based upon that published by Robert Ross in the *Complete Works* of 1908 under the title *Lecture To Art Students*. In the introduction to this text, Ross stated that it comprised the lecture which was:

> Delivered to the Art students of the Royal Academy at their Club in Golden Square, Westminster, on June 30, 1883. The text is taken from the original manuscript.

W. F. Morse, who managed Wilde's American and first UK lecture tours, commented that:[1]

> He had also a special talk for art schools, delivered first before the students of the Royal Academy, London, upon "Modern Art Training."

On this basis, I have retitled this lecture as *Modern Art Training*.

A reading of the text, especially the last few hundred words, which are very brief and contain quite unconnected phrases, shows the incomplete nature of this manuscript and indicates the possible existence of a more complete draft or, and probably more likely, that Wilde used the notes but extemporised around the framework which they represent. The lecture on 30 June 1883 was not reported very extensively, probably because it was given in a private club to a private audience. However, a number of newspapers did pick up on one small piece of the lecture: where Wilde describes Gower Street and the Thames Embankment in London. In the 1908 text this is dealt with in one sentence:

> In Gower Street at night you may see a letter-box that is picturesque; on the Thames Embankment you may see picturesque policemen

but the newspapers which did review the lecture gave much more extended quotations from this section, with Wilde commenting upon seeing Gower Street when he was coming home from a party at dawn, when its beauty was 'almost fairy-like' and once, on the Thames Embankment in the fog, a policeman became 'an expression of Michael Angelesque grandeur': neither of these statements is in the manuscript we have. I have recreated these statements from several different sources and inserted them.

This lecture was given only a few times: in Chesterfield on 30 January 1884 when, at their request, he addressed the students of the Chesterfield School of Art upon *Modern Art Training* after he had lectured to the general public on *Personal Impressions of America.* Unfortunately, this was not reported. Later, in Stoke on Trent, where Wilde had been asked to give the prizes at a school of art award ceremony, Wilde gave an address on art which, as reported, is an amalgam of this lecture and the concluding section of *The House Beautiful* which deals with art education. This was reported and I have taken several sections from this to add to the original text.

Modern Art Training

I N THE lecture which it is my privilege to deliver before you to-night I do not desire to give you any abstract definition of beauty at all.[2] For we who are working in art cannot accept any theory of beauty in exchange for beauty itself, and, so far from desiring to isolate it in a formula appealing to the intellect, we, on the contrary, seek to materialise it in a form that gives joy to the soul through the senses.[3] We want to create it, not to define it. The definition should follow the work: the work should not adapt itself to the definition.[4]

Nothing, indeed, is more dangerous to the young artist than any conception of ideal beauty: he is constantly led by it either into weak prettiness or lifeless abstraction: whereas to touch the ideal at all you must not strip it of vitality. You must find it in life and re-create it in art.

While, then, on the one hand, I do not desire to give you any philosophy of beauty: for, what I want to-night is to investigate how we can create art, not how we can talk of it; on the other hand, I do not wish to deal with anything like a history of English art. To begin with, such an expression as English art is a meaningless expression. One might just as well talk of English mathematics. Art is the science of beauty, and Mathematics the science of truth: there is no national school of either.[5] Indeed, a national school is a provincial school, merely.

Nor is there any such thing as a school of art even. There are merely artists, that is all. And as regards histories of art, they are quite valueless to you unless you are seeking the ostentatious oblivion of an art professorship.[6] It is of no use to you to know the date of Perugino[7] or the birthplace of Salvator Rosa:[8] all that you should learn about art is to know a good picture when you see it, and a bad picture when you see it.[9] As regards the date of the artist, all good work looks perfectly modern:[10] a piece of Greek sculpture, a portrait of Velasquez[11] — they are always modern, always of our time. And as regards the nationality of the artist, art is not national but universal.

As regards archaeology, then, avoid it altogether: archaeology is merely the science of making excuses for bad art; it is the rock on which many a young artist founders and shipwrecks; it is the abyss from which no artist, old or young, ever returns.[12] Or, if he does return, he is so covered with the dust of ages and the mildew of time, that he is quite unrecognisable as an artist, and has to conceal himself for the rest of his days under the cap of a professor, or as a mere illustrator of ancient history.[13] How worthless archaeology is in art you can estimate by the fact of its being so popular. Popularity is the crown of laurel which the world puts on bad art. Whatever is popular is wrong.[14]

As I am not going to talk to you, then, about the philosophy of the beautiful, or the history of art, you will ask me what I am going to talk about. The subject of my lecture tonight is what makes an artist and what does the artist make; what are the relations of the artist to his surroundings,[15] what is the education the artist should get, and what is the quality of a good work of art.

Now, as regards the relations of the artist to his surroundings, by which I mean the age and country in which he is born. All good art, as I said before, has nothing to do with any particular century; but this universality is the quality of the work of art; the conditions that produce that quality are different. And what, I think, you should do is to realise completely your age in order completely to abstract yourself from it; remembering that if you are an artist at all, you will be not the mouthpiece of a century, but the master of eternity;[16] that all art rests on a principle, and that mere temporal considerations are no principle at all; and that those who advise you to make your art representative of the nineteenth century are advising you to produce an art which your children, when you have them, will think old-fashioned.

But you will tell me this is an inartistic age, and we are an inartistic people, and the artist suffers much in this nineteenth century of ours. Of course he does, I, of all men, am not going to deny that. But remember that there never has been an artistic age, or an artistic people, since the beginning of the world. The artist has always been, and will always be, an exquisite exception. There is no golden age of art; only artists who have produced what is more golden than gold.

What, you will say to me, the Greeks? Were not they an artistic people? Well, the Greeks certainly not, but, perhaps, you mean the Athenians, the citizens of one out of a thousand cities? Do you think that they were an artistic people? Take them even at the time of their highest artistic development, the latter part of the fifth century before Christ, when they had the greatest poets and the greatest artists of the antique world, when the Parthenon rose in loveliness at the bidding of a Phidias,[17] and the philosopher spake of wisdom in the shadow of the painted portico, and tragedy swept in the perfection of pageant and pathos across the marble of the stage. Were they an artistic people then? Not a bit of it. What is an artistic people but a people who love their artists and understand their art? The Athenians could do neither.

How did they treat Phidias? To Phidias we owe the great era, not merely in Greek, but in all art —I mean of the introduction of the use of the living model.

And what would you say if all the English bishops, backed by the English people, came down from Exeter Hall to the Royal Academy one day and took off Sir Frederic Leighton[18] in a prison van to Newgate on the charge of having allowed you to make use of the living model in your designs for sacred pictures? Would you not cry out against the barbarism and the Puritanism of such an idea? Would you not explain to them that the worst way to honour God is to dishonour man who is made in His image, and is the work of His hands; and, that if one wants to paint Christ one must take the most Christlike person one can find, and if one wants to paint the Madonna, the purest girl one knows? Would you not rush off and burn down Newgate, if necessary, and say that such a thing was without parallel in history?

Without parallel? Well, that is exactly what the Athenians did.

In the room of the Parthenon marbles, in the British Museum, you will see a marble shield on the wall. On it there are two figures; one of a man whose face is half hidden, the other of a man with the godlike lineaments of Pericles.[19] For having done this, for having introduced into a bas relief, taken from Greek sacred history, the image of the great statesman who was ruling Athens at the time, Phidias was flung into prison and there, in the common gaol of Athens, died, the supreme artist of the old world.

And do you think that this was an exceptional case? The sign of a Philistine age is the cry of immorality against art,[20] and this cry was raised by the Athenian people against every great poet and thinker of their day - Aeschylus, Euripides, Socrates.[21]   It was the same with Florence in the thirteenth century.   Good handicrafts are due to guilds, not to the people. The moment the guilds lost their power and the people rushed in, beauty and honesty of work died.

And so, never talk of an artistic people; there never has been such a thing.

But, perhaps, you will tell me that the external beauty of the world has almost entirely passed away from us, that the artist dwells no longer in the midst of the lovely surroundings which, in ages past, were the natural inheritance of everyone,[22] and that art is very difficult in this unlovely town of ours, where, as you go to your work in the morning, or return from it at eventide, you have to pass through street after street of the most foolish and stupid architecture that the world has ever seen; architecture, where every lovely Greek form is desecrated and defiled, and every lovely Gothic form defiled and desecrated,[23] reducing three-fourths of the London houses to being, merely, like square boxes of the vilest proportions, as gaunt as they are grimy, and as poor as they are pretentious - the hall door always of the wrong colour, and the windows of the wrong size,[24] and where, even when wearied of the houses you turn to contemplate the street itself, you have nothing to look at but chimney-pot hats,[25] men with sandwich boards, vermilion letterboxes, and do that even at the risk of being run over by an emerald-green omnibus.

Is not art difficult, you will say to me, in such surroundings as these? Of course it is difficult, but then art was never easy; you yourselves would not wish it to be easy; and, besides, nothing is worth doing except what the world says is impossible.

Still, you do not care to be answered merely by a paradox. What are the relations of the artist to the external world, and what is the result of the loss of beautiful surroundings to you, is one of the most important questions of modern art; and there is no point on which Mr. Ruskin so insists as that the decadence of art has come from the decadence of beautiful things; and that when the artist cannot feed his eye on beauty, beauty goes from his work. I remember in one of his lectures, after describing the sordid aspect of a great English city, that art suffered from smoky chimneys, polluted streams, railways, and commerce,[26] and he drew for us a picture of what were the artistic surroundings long ago. Think, he says, in words of perfect and picturesque imagery, whose beauty I can but feebly echo, think of what was the scene which presented itself, in his afternoon walk, to a designer of the Gothic school of Pisa - Nino Pisano[27] or any of his men:[28]

On each side of a bright river he saw rise a line of brighter palaces, arched and pillared, and inlaid with deep red porphyry, and with serpentine; along the quays before their gates were riding troops of knights, noble in face and form, dazzling in crest and shield; horse and man one labyrinth of quaint colour and gleaming light — the purple, and silver, and scarlet fringes flowing over the strong limbs and clashing mail, like sea-waves over rocks at sunset. Opening on each side from the river were gardens, courts, and cloisters; long successions of white pillars among wreaths of vine; leaping of fountains through buds of pomegranate and orange: and still along the garden-paths, and under and through the crimson of the pomegranate shadows, moving slowly, groups of the fairest women that Italy ever saw — fairest, because purest and thoughtfullest; trained in all high knowledge, as in all courteous art - in dance, in song, in sweet wit, in lofty learning, in loftier courage, in loftiest love — able alike to cheer, to enchant, or save, the souls of men. Above all this scenery of perfect human life, rose dome and bell-tower, burning with white alabaster and gold: beyond dome and bell-tower the slopes of mighty hills, hoary with olive; far in the north, above a purple sea of peaks of solemn Apennine, the clear, sharp-cloven Carrara mountains sent up their steadfast flames of marble summit into amber sky; the great sea itself, scorching with expanse of light, stretching from their feet to the Gorgonian isles; and over all these, ever present, near or far - seen through the leaves of vine, or imaged with all its march of clouds in the Arno's stream, or set with its depth of blue close against the golden hair and burning cheek of lady and knight, — that untroubled and sacred sky, which was to all men, in those days of innocent faith, indeed the unquestioned abode of spirits, as the earth was of men; and which opened straight through its gates of cloud and veils of dew into the awfulness of the eternal world; — a heaven in which every cloud that passed was literally the chariot of an angel, and every ray of its Evening and Morning streamed from the throne of God.

What think you of that for a school of design?

And then look at the depressing, monotonous appearance of any modern city, the sombre dress of men and women, the meaningless and barren architecture, the colourless and dreadful surroundings. Without a beautiful national life, not sculpture merely, but all the arts will die.

Well, as regards the religious feeling of the close of the passage, I do not think I need speak about that. Religion springs from religious feeling, art from artistic feeling: you never get one from the other; unless you have the right root you will not get the right flower; and, if a man sees in a cloud the chariot of an angel, he will probably paint it very unlike a cloud.

But, as regards the general idea of the early part of that lovely bit of prose,[29] is it really true that beautiful surroundings are necessary for the artist? I think not; I am sure not. Indeed, to me the most inartistic thing in this age of ours is not the indifference of the public to beautiful things, but the indifference of the artist to the things that are called ugly.[30] For, to the real artist, nothing is beautiful or ugly in itself at all. With the facts of the object he has nothing to do,[31] but with its appearance only, and appearance is a matter of light and shade, of masses, of position, and of value.

Appearance is, in fact, a matter of effect merely, and it is with the effects of nature that you have to deal, not with the real condition of the object. What you, as painters, have to paint is not things as they are but things as they seem to be, not things as they are but things as they are not.[32]

No object is so ugly that, under certain conditions of light and shade, or proximity to other things, it will not look beautiful; no object is so beautiful that, under certain conditions, it will not look ugly. Once in every twenty-four hours everything becomes beautiful.

There is a liking for prettiness prevalent among many modern artists. The commonplace character[33] of so much of our English painting seems to me due to the fact that so many of our young artists look merely at what we may call 'ready-made beauty,' whereas you exist as artists not to copy beauty but to create it in your art, to wait and watch for it in nature.[34]

What would you say of a dramatist who would take nobody but virtuous people as characters in his play?[35] Would you not say he was missing half of life? Well, of the young artist who paints nothing but beautiful things, I say he misses one half of the world.

Do not wait for life to be picturesque, but try and see life under picturesque conditions.[36] These conditions you can create for yourself in your studio, for they are merely conditions of light. In nature, you must wait for them, watch for them, choose them; and, if you wait and watch, come they will.

Even Gower Street, one of the most monotonously dull and colourless of formal London thoroughfares has periods when it is actually beautiful. I remember coming home from a party and passing through it when day was breaking when its aspect was most charming and I was forcibly struck by this fact. In the softening obscurity of the morning mist which had filled it with golden and purple hues, softening its outlines, and giving variety to its shadows, with the sunrays piercing it in long golden shafts, the roofs were shining like molten silver, and the vermilion pillar-post shone like a gem. It was a scene of almost fairy-like beauty. On another occasion I found that the weird effect in a fog on the Thames Embankment[37] which gave even such a very commonplace and unlovely thing as a policeman — with cape and helmet and multiplicity of buttons — which was not, under ordinary circumstances, a thing of beauty or a joy forever,[38] but lit up with dusky light was such an expression of Michael Angelesque[39] grandeur in appearance, that a painter might have sought a better subject a long time before he found it.

I do not desire that external life should be permanently beautiful. Even Venice is not always beautiful, nor France. To paint what you see is a good rule in art, but to see what is worth painting is better. The true artist did not wait until life became picturesque for others. He took care to see life under pictorial conditions always.[40]

Mr. Ruskin[41] had said many dreadful things about the iniquity of smoke, and I am not going to praise it on sanitary grounds.[42] I would only remind you of the beauty Turner[43] saw in those very scenes which Mr. Ruskin so often ran down. There was no better answer to those who complained of commerce spoiling art than to turn to Turner's pictures. It is better to live in a city of changeable weather[44] than in a city of lovely surroundings.

Modern English painting had an extremely hard outline and we might learn something from the Japanese and the way in which Japanese children are taught to draw.

All the world is the property of the artist, and under certain conditions would give him beautiful subjects; and it was to the visible world he should go, and not to literature. We had suffered for the fatal alliance of painting and poetry. We had seen painters pass their lives in illustrating poetry and history, becoming mere adjuncts of literary men.[45] There was plenty of scope for the artist without having recourse to literature for his subjects.

Now, having seen what makes the artist, and what the artist makes, who is the artist? There is a man living amongst us who unites in himself all the qualities of the noblest art, whose work is a joy for all time, who is, himself, a master of all time. That man is Mr. Whistler.[46] He is the greatest artist of the day.[47]

But, you will say, modern dress, that is bad. But if you cannot paint black cloth you could not have painted silken doublet.[48] Ugly dress is better for art, which deals with the facts of vision, not of the object.

All archaeological pictures that make you say 'How curious!', all sentimental pictures that make you say 'How sad!', all historical pictures that make you say 'How interesting!', all pictures that do not immediately give you such artistic joy as to make you say 'How beautiful!', are bad pictures.[49]

We never know what an artist is going to do. Of course not. The artist is not a specialist.[50] All such divisions as animal painters, landscape painters, painters of Scotch cattle in an English mist, painters of English cattle in a Scotch mist,[51] racehorse painters, bull-terrier painters, all are shallow. If a man is an artist he can paint everything.

The object of art is to stir the most divine and remote of the chords which make music in our soul; and colour is, indeed, of itself a mystical presence on things, and tone a kind of sentinel.

Am I pleading, then, for mere technique?[52] No. As long as there are any signs of technique at all, the picture is unfinished. What is finish? A picture is finished when all traces of work, and of the means employed to bring about the result, have disappeared.[53]

In the case of handicraftsmen — the weaver, the potter, the smith[54] — on their work are the traces of their hand. But it is not so with the painter; it is not so with the artist.

Art should have no sentiment about it but its beauty, no technique except what you cannot observe. One should be able to say of a picture not that it is 'well painted,' but that it is 'not painted.'

What is the difference between absolutely decorative art and a painting?[55] Decorative art emphasises its material: imaginative art annihilates it.[56] Tapestry shows its threads as part of its beauty: a picture annihilates its canvas; it shows nothing of it. Porcelain emphasises its glaze: watercolours reject the paper.

What is a picture? Primarily, a picture is a beautifully coloured surface, merely, with no more spiritual message or meaning for you than an exquisite fragment of Venetian glass or a blue tile from the wall of Damascus.[57] A picture has no meaning but its beauty, no message but its joy.[58] That is the first truth about art that you must never lose sight of. It is, primarily, a delight to look at.[59] A picture is a purely decorative thing.[60]

Personal Impressions of America

Introduction

THIS TEXT is how the lecture was delivered in the autumn of 1883. It is based on the 1906 publication *Impressions of America* which suggests the text is as delivered at Wandsworth on 24 September 1883. This is supplemented mainly by two reviews of the first lecture on 10 July (*Freeman's Journal* and *The North-Eastern Daily Gazette*) plus reviews of the lectures at Bath in September, Brighton and Dublin in November 1883.

Personal Impressions of America

I FEAR I cannot picture America as altogether an Elysium. Perhaps, from the ordinary standpoint, I know but little about the country. I am afraid that this lecture will contain very little useful information. I cannot give its latitude or longitude;[1] I cannot tell you what its exports or its imports might be; I cannot compute the value of its dry goods,[2] and I have no very close acquaintance with its politics. These are matters which may not interest you, and they certainly are not interesting to me. I merely want the opportunity to express certain things about America which struck me while in that country.

The steamer on which I had been conveyed anchored outside New York on a wild, stormy night. Yet there suddenly leaped on board from a small steamer what I could only suppose to be the literary pirates of America coming to seize the first manuscript on board. These turned out to be the first interviewers. They at once came to me and asked me my opinion concerning America. At that time all that I had seen was a small gas-lamp and I was naturally, favourably and deeply impressed, and I gave, on the whole, a very flattering account of my experiences of America as far as it had gone. Now that I have seen it, it is more difficult.

The first thing that struck me on landing in America was that if the Americans are not the most well-dressed people in the world, and I am afraid they are not, they are the most comfortably dressed. I was struck with the prosperity that is seen everywhere. When one thinks that even in London, a great imperial city like that, our civilisation is so much purple surrounded by rags; within a few minutes' walk of any rich street in London one comes across alleys filled with people in rags and poverty and misery, it is something to come to a country where there are no rags, where there is no poverty, where there seems to be very little misery indeed. No rags at all: men are comfortably though not elegantly dressed. A great many badly fitting coats, of course, but nobody without a coat; very few patent leather boots but no boots with holes in; millions of men seen there with chimney-pot hats[3] of the most dreadful proportions, as here, but there are very few hatless men; men wear the shocking swallow-tail coat, but few are to be seen with no coat at all.

The second thing that struck me is that Americans are always in a hurry. There was an absence of romantic unpunctuality in America, everybody seems in a hurry to catch a train, it was a sort of national amusement. This is a state of things which is not favourable to poetry or romance. Had Romeo or Juliet been in a constant state of anxiety about trains, or had their minds been agitated by the question of return-tickets, Shakespeare could not have given us those lovely balcony scenes which are so full of poetry and pathos.

Everybody in New York seemed busy, and America is the noisiest country that the world can ever have seen — or listened to. One is woken up in the morning, not by the singing of the lark but by the steam whistle shrieking in 'consecutive fifths' and instead of falling asleep to the note of the nightingale, one had the scream of the locomotive under one's window.

It is surprising that the sound practical sense of the Americans does not reduce this intolerable noise. I fail to see why these whistles could not be set to very beautiful notes of music. It might not be possible to treat the hearers to a symphony of Beethoven's played by them — I have to acknowledge that would be *too* elaborate — but at least the whistle might play some form of musical sound somewhat less harrowing. All Art depends upon exquisite and delicate sensibility, and such continual turmoil must ultimately be destructive of the musical faculty.[4.]

There is not so much beauty to be found in American cities as in York or Oxford,[5] full of beautiful architecture where there are lovely relics of a beautiful age. You would find great howling cities like Birmingham and like Manchester, very rich and full of commerce, and one who stopped to admire the architectural beauty of any building would be disappointed. But still there is beauty to be seen in them now and then, but only where the American has not attempted to create it. Where the Americans have attempted to produce beauty they have signally failed and had produced great, noisy, modern towns with huge hotels, and mammoth mansions of millionaires.

A remarkable characteristic of the Americans is the manner in which they have applied science to modern life. This is apparent in the most cursory stroll through New York. In England an inventor is regarded almost as a crazy man, and in too many instances invention ends in disappointment and poverty. In all applications of modern science to machinery the Americans were wonderfully successful. In their great riches, in the gigantic machinery, everywhere great bridges, in the perfectly beautiful uses of the electric light, there was no country in the world in which they were so well able to apply a great invention. Commonplace as their modern cities looked at daytime it was very different when night-time came on. Indeed the sun both in America and in England was a great Philistine, always in a hurry and exposing anything in the most ruthless manner; whereas when the night came on the whole aspect of the city changed. Madison Square, in New York, lit by a great mast from which the electric light hung in lanterns, was one of the most beautiful sights one could see. It was in these things one could see the real beauty of America, and not quite so much in buildings where one sought for beauty.

In America an inventor is honoured, help is forthcoming, and the exercise of ingenuity, the application of science to the work of man,[6] is, there, the shortest road to wealth. There is no country in the world where machinery is so lovely as in America.

In Chicago there stands a curious monstrosity in the shape of a Gothic castle, seemingly built entirely of pepper boxes, and provided with all kinds of contrivances for emptying lead on the enemy. Enclosed in this castle were the waterworks of Chicago. I have always wished to believe that the line of strength and the line of beauty[7] are one. That wish was realised when I contemplated American machinery. It was not until I had seen the water-works at Chicago that I realised the wonders of machinery;[8] the rise and fall of the steel rods, the symmetrical motion of the great wheels is the most beautifully rhythmic thing I have ever seen.[9]

As regards nature, it is difficult to describe, with its variations from the tropical heat of Florida to the chilly cold of New York. Pennsylvania, with its rocky gorges and woodland scenery, reminded me of Switzerland, the prairie reminded me of a piece of brown blotting paper. Still there were some qualities about American scenery different from our own: one is impressed in America, but not favourably impressed, by the inordinate size of everything. The country seems to try to bully one into a belief in its power by its impressive bigness. It behaves like a big boy at a private school. Everything was twice as large and twice as far off as it should be. The atmosphere was so abnormally clear that they had no vistas at all, and everything looked like a gigantic foreground. So clear, in fact, was the atmosphere that, looking down the street, I could see to read the names on a brass door plate two and a half miles away. I assure you it is impossible to exaggerate this. I am constantly trying to but never succeed.

Consequently, until I went to America, I never knew how to appreciate English mists and fogs. We in England grow disgusted with fogs and mist and drizzle, and the discomforts of wet days. I can assure you that the consolation is that all great landscape painters came from countries where fogs and mists and other disagreeables abounded: the great schools of landscape painting had always come from countries like Holland or France or Great Britain. America had never yet produced a landscape painter; and even in the autumn, when the gold and crimson and forest and hill beautified the scene, the conditions did not seem to be favourable for pictorial art – it might be suitable for decorative art, but it was not what the landscape painter wanted. So in future when fogs are sufficiently thick to be cut with a hatchet we must be thankful with the consciousness that they are artistically delightful.[10]

The Falls of Niagara, like the Atlantic, were at first sight extremely disappointing: most people must be disappointed with Niagara. Every American bride is taken there, and the sight of the stupendous waterfall must be one of the earliest, if not the keenest, disappointments in American married life. The neighbourhood seemed full of melancholy tourists trying to imagine a sublimity of feeling which the guide books assured them could be secured free of charge. One sees it under bad conditions, very far away, the point of view not showing the splendour of the water. To appreciate it really, one has to see it from underneath the fall, but to do so involves a degradation of the aesthetic feelings, and the donning of that most abominable of all abominations, yellow oilskins which are as ugly as a mackintosh - and I hope none of you ever wears one of those. It is a consolation to know, however, that one of the most charming women of modern times, an artist such as Madame Sarah Bernhardt,[11] has not only worn that yellow, ugly dress, but has been photographed in it with Niagara as a sort of unpretentious background; and so I consented to adopt it myself. I have to acknowledge that I was well repaid, because I saw one of the most splendid sights that anyone could see, anywhere in the world.

In America travelling was almost entirely done in trains. There was very little riding and no coaching at all. When one was lucky enough, as one usually was, to get into a Pullman car, there one remained in perfect luxury to the end of one's journey. In the ordinary car, however, one had as much privacy as if one sat in an armchair in the centre of Piccadilly. I found but poor consolation for this journey in the fact that the boys who infest the cars and sell everything that one can eat — or should not eat — were selling editions of my poems vilely printed on a kind of grey blotting paper, with all the stops left out for the low price of ten cents, or five pence. Calling these boys on one side I told them that though poets like to be popular they desire to be paid, and selling editions of my poems without giving me a profit is dealing a blow at literature which must have a disastrous effect on poetical aspirants. The invariable reply that they made was that they themselves made a profit out of the transaction, that was all they cared about, and that settled the question. I concluded that any attempts to touch the conscience of Americans result in failure, particularly in the case of little boys who sell pirated editions of one's works. One little boy I remember particularly was engaged in selling what the American nation was particularly fond of: peanuts. He offered me some, but I strongly rejected them. "You might," he pleaded, "buy some peanuts; I never sold peanuts to a poet yet."

Perhaps the most beautiful part of America is the West, where one saw what a civilisation the Americans had made by themselves and for themselves. They, of all nations, had a country so vast as to be able to colonise within their own borders and this was one of the secrets of their great cosmopolitan character. The habit which the cities of the East of America had of sending colonies into the Western States was one of the reasons why that country had yet got a sense of the unity, why all its parts responded to the same cause of national feeling, why they all read the same literature. In order to reach the west, however, it involves a journey by rail of six days, racing along tied to an ugly tin-kettle of a steam engine. One had to cross the alkali plains, which were so ridiculously vast that Nature, when it came to decorate them, seemed to have become alarmed and given up in despair. There were no trees or flowers – nothing of any colour – nothing of any shape. With the pitiless steel-grey sky overhead it was an expanse of monotony so vast that the train passing over it seemed immobile. For days we travelled, stopping occasionally at a small station, where what, by some curious process of reasoning, was called a meal was served. Here there could be seen the civilised Indian and the uncivilised Indian: the latter was delightfully picturesque with beautifully wrought moccasins and leggings, with a robe over his shoulders, feathers in his hat and carried a tomahawk; but the latter became very ugly in a frock coat which was never made for him and a straw hat which did not fit him. The uncivilised was really charming – the civilised had nothing to recommend him. I had the opportunity of conversing with many Indians through the medium of an interpreter, and their language reminded me of German metaphysics in that it was very fine so long as it was unintelligible. When it was interpreted I generally found it to convey a request for half a dollar or some tobacco.

It is a popular superstition that in America a visitor is invariably addressed as 'Stranger', made familiar to English people by the works of Bret Harte.[12] I was never once addressed as 'Stranger.' On approaching the borders of Texas I was called 'Captain'; when I got to the centre of Texas I was addressed as 'Colonel,' and, on arriving at the borders of Mexico, as 'General.' I was also addressed by the impressive title of 'Professor.' But on the whole, however, 'Sir,' the old English method of addressing people is the most common. It is, perhaps, worthwhile to note that what many people call Americanisms are really old English expressions which have lingered in our colonies while they have been lost in our own country. They used 'Sir' exactly as one read it in Boswell's *Life of Johnson*.[13] Many people imagine that the term 'I guess,' which is so common in America, is purely an American expression, but it was used by John Locke in his work on 'The Understanding,'[14] just as we now use 'I think.'

It is in the colonies, and not in the mother country, that the old life of the country really exists. If one wants to realise what English Puritanism is, not at its worst, when it is very bad, but at its best, and then it is not very good, I do not think one can find much of it in England, but much can be found about Boston and Massachusetts. In New England, Puritanism existed in a disregard of all the graces of life, and sermons were preached which one would have expected to hear in the time of Cromwell. Even the nasalism of the modern American had been retained from the Puritan Fathers. We have got rid of Puritanism. America still preserves it, to be, I hope, a short-lived curiosity.

California is the very garden of the Pacific Ocean, as beautiful as the Riviera in spring, especially San Francisco, with its wonderful surroundings and its lovely gardens built upon what a few years ago were merely desolate sandhills. San Francisco is a really beautiful city with its Golden Gates[15] and I was further enlightened on the enterprise of the Americans. There I found a remarkable instance of their passion for advertising, for on the back of a seal, basking on the point of the 'Seal Rock,' I saw an advertisement for some famous tooth powder.

But in this monarch American town is China Town, peopled by Chinese labourers who came over to California to lay the railways and work in the mines, but they brought with them the traditions of beauty which China had given them. These strange, melancholy Orientals, with their pallid faces and exquisite hands, were discontented with the American notions of beauty and therefore they built for themselves a little town of their own which they decorated in a thoroughly artistic manner. It is the most artistic town I have ever come across and one passed at night-time suddenly into a little city with little winding streets which were lit, not by gas, but by painted paper lanterns, the beautiful lattice-work of the projecting windows reaching sometimes across these little winding thoroughfares through which there was a constant procession of Chinese. One walked through the streets like one in a dream who was always meeting the same person. Many people would call these Chinese people common, and they are certainly very poor, but they were a most artistic people, and what was most pleasing about the Chinese was that everything they did and touched was beautiful. And whatever was beautiful they used. Unlike the people of England, who hoarded their beautiful art works in cabinets, these Chinese have determined that they will have nothing about them that is not beautiful for general use.[16] In the Chinese restaurant, where these navvies meet to have supper in the evening, I found them drinking tea out of china cups as delicate as the petals of a white rose,[17] whereas at the gaudy hotels I was supplied with a delft cup an inch and a half thick. When the Chinese bill was presented it was made out on rice paper, the account being done in Indian ink as fantastically as if an artist had been etching little birds on a fan. Their poetry was far too delightful to be locked up in books which perhaps people would not read, so the poet wrote his sonnets upon fans and pocket handkerchiefs, and sometimes embroidered them upon beautiful dresses, and in that way Chinese poems were much better known to the Chinese than European poems were known to Europeans.

Their theatre was the most imaginative and artistic theatre in the whole world. Their theory of art was very different to ours. We say let the stage hold the mirror to nature, let it give us some picture of life. The Chinese say, 'No, bring us into a world entirely unlike anything we have ever seen.' They object to realism, and build up an entirely fantastic world not dependent on gorgeous scenery and splendid decorations, the actors having their art permanently and entirely in the imagination.[18] I remember on one occasion seeing a young actor preparing for his part. He was first fanned by his servant, then he got his cup of tea, then he sent for a beautiful background in the shape of a yellow satin umbrella, and lastly took two long rods of bamboo with little lamps at the ends, and two masked servants held them up one on each side of his face in order that the audience might feel delighted at his wonderful natural facial expression. That was really imaginative acting: with these preparations the actor felt he could produce the right artistic impression on the audience. Sometimes a play went on for days. When I arrived at San Francisco they were acting the third act of some great tragedy. I have no doubt that they had reached by this time the one hundred and forty-third act. The Chinese, too, did not express their appreciation of an actor by greeting him with torrents of applause, but by greeting him with torrents of tea, every one having with them a little delicate set of tea things ready for that purpose. The Chinese newspapers, in noticing the *début* of a great actor, did not mention the rounds of applause with which he was greeted but the number of cups of tea which the audience had consumed.

I next visited Utah which was a curious place full of strange fantastic things. I must confess to having been a little disappointed by Salt Lake City's prosperity. It is a struggling industrial town, but not quite so fine as I expected. What struck me was the unusually large number of beautiful children playing in its streets. Salt Lake City contains only three buildings of note erected by the Mormons: the Tabernacle, the Amelia Palace, and the co-operative stores. The chief of these being the Tabernacle, which is in the shape of an ordinary tea kettle with the decorations of an ordinary gaol, and is very much admired by the Mormon people. I asked whether the theatre was large enough to lecture in. The answer was 'Oh, yes; it will hold nine families.' It is decorated by the only native artist, and he has treated religious subjects in the naive spirit of the early Florentine painters, in sepia on whitewashed walls, representing people of our own day in the dress of the period side by side with people of Biblical history who are clothed in some romantic costume. This wonderful design and these marvellous decorations were mysteriously communicated to Brigham Young.[19] It is satisfactory to know that no architect of modern times had anything to do with them. Of a series of frescos, much spoken of by the Mormons, I saw one which represented Brigham Young receiving the book of the Mormon law from the prophet. It represented a very portly gentleman with a tall hat and frock coast and umbrella, walking in a sort of valley of geological horrors. On the top of one of the mountains was an old gentleman rather lightly attired, brandishing what seemed to be the local guide book, and really with no more dignity than one might imagine an old gentleman to have who had lost his bathing box by the seaside.

I found the Mormon President extremely charming, a highly educated gentleman, living in a beautiful house which belonged originally to the favourite wife of Brigham Young, a lady named Amelia,[20] very pretty and brilliant. The building next in importance is called the Amelia Palace, in her honour. When Brigham Young died the present president of the Mormons stood up in the Tabernacle and said that it had been revealed to him that he was to have the Amelia Palace, and that on this subject there were to be no more revelations of any kind! The lady now resides elsewhere. As a rule, however, the whole of a Mormon household lived under one roof, the only difference being that each wife has a right to a separate hall door, and so, as one drives through Salt Lake City, most of the houses were nothing but hall doors. Each wife, again, insisted on painting her hall door a different colour from everybody else's. On the whole the influence of polygamy on architecture could hardly be said to be refining. Their great commercial building — the co-operative stores — with a strong conception of how religion should enter into everyday life, had nothing remarkable about it except the dreadful character of its name, which was the 'Zion Co-operative Hallelujah Stores.' I could not discover any difference between this store and any other store, except that the 'Gentiles,' as those who are not Mormons are called, are consistently overcharged for any article they buy there.

The Mormons were very courteous and industrious, mainly very happy, the children beautiful, but the people themselves certainly not beautiful.

From Salt Lake City one travels over the great plains of Colorado to Denver, where I lectured, which was now very prosperous, though a few years ago it was hardly known. It was astonishing how quickly a city sprang up in America, and how as soon as a man made money he devoted his energy and much of his means to making his own city beautiful. Their opera house was one of the most beautiful in America, and it was built quite recently by the governor, who, not long ago, was a poor man.

From there I next travelled up the Rocky Mountains which rose with characteristic abruptness right out of the vast plain and are one of the most splendid natural objects in America. But one of the great features of America is the advertiser who defaced even the most beautiful parts of the Rocky Mountains with their advertisements, generally for some horrible medicine. The mountains were interesting because it was supposed to be the neighbourhood inhabited by the roughest specimens of American life and that desperado life described by Bret Harte and others. So infinitesimal did I find the knowledge of Art, west of the Rocky Mountains, that an art patron — one who in his day had been a miner — actually sued the railroad company for damages because the plaster cast of Venus of Milo, which he had imported from Paris, had been delivered minus the arms. And, what is more surprising still, he gained his case and the damages.

The scenery of the Rocky Mountains was absolutely beautiful and on the top of which is Leadville, inhabited entirely by miners, the roughest and richest city in America. There the calm stillness of the moonlit nights is only disturbed by the singing of the nightingales and the popping of revolvers. Every man's dress was picturesquely ornamented with knives and pistols, and where the miners were in the course of their perambulations they were in the habit of firing round the corner of a street just to let one know they were coming. I was told that if I went there they would be sure to shoot me or my travelling manager. I wrote and told them that nothing that they could do to my travelling manager would intimidate me. I was received by a quiet, well-armed mob, altogether the best-dressed people I had seen in America amongst the men. They wore broad-brimmed hats which would protect them from sun and rain, cloaks which were picturesque and always graceful, and knickerbockers and high boots.[21] I made them promise before I left that they would not change their dress even if they became millionaires.

It was quite a mistake, however, to suppose that Western people should be called roughs. They are miners, men working in metals. I am afraid that the people of Leadville imagined that art was so bound up with respectability that there was no room for them on the scroll of artists. So I lectured to them on the Ethics of Art[22] as I felt bound to explain to them that between art and respectability there was really no connection at all. I read them passages from the autobiography of Benvenuto Cellini[23] telling them that he was a most accomplished rough; how he came to Rome, killed a man in a brawl, was ordered to exile by the Pope, begged and obtained an interview with the Pontiff, and, showing him a beautiful bar of silver, was at once forgiven. These and other incidents in the life of Cellini seemed to delight the people of Leadville. They believed in the words of the poet that Cellini 'was a bully boy' and I was reproved by my hearers for not having brought him with me. I explained that he had been dead for some little time which elicited the enquiry 'Who shot him?' This gave an insight of the life of the mining people of Leadville: they were quite unable to conceive any method of quitting life other than the one usual in Leadville. They afterwards took me to a dancing saloon at the end of which was a piano and the typical pianist playing, where I saw the only rational method of art criticism I have ever come across. On the wall, right over the piano, was printed a notice:

PLEASE DO NOT SHOOT
THE PIANIST.
HE IS DOING HIS BEST.

There, one felt one had come across a wonderful height of musical culture. The slightest false note, the slightest false emphasis even, and the life of the artist is forfeited, I think, quite justly. I think death should be the penalty for bad art, and I told them how much I wished that we had in England a rigorous system, for so many Royal Academicians, and other bad artists, would be swept out of the way. The mortality among pianists in that place is marvellous and these statistics were so much beyond the ordinary average that the city used to find a difficulty in getting musicians.

Then they asked me to supper in a silver mine, and having accepted, I had to descend the mine in a rickety bucket in which it was impossible to be graceful. Having got into the heart of the mountain I had supper. The menu was decidedly curious, and perhaps characteristic: the first course being whisky, the second whisky and the third whisky, all the courses were whisky. They appeared to have no idea of any other kind of supper and I enjoyed the novelty, and the evening was one of the most pleasant I have ever had in my life.

I went to the Theatre to lecture and I was informed that just before I went there two men had been seized for committing a murder, and in that theatre they had been brought on to the stage at eight o'clock in the evening, and then and there tried and executed before a crowded audience. But I found these miners very charming and not at all rough.

On leaving Leadville next morning I set out for Kansas. In the month of June I went south, journeying to the heart of Mexico, very much threatened by yellow fever, but having survived journalism one could always survive yellow fever. Nothing impressed me so much there as the care which the people bestowed upon the graves of their dead.

No people seemed as indifferent to the pomp of ceremony and official dress as the Americans. They did not care, perhaps, to realise life by what they looked at, but sometimes in New Orleans one came across the old love of pageantry which manifested itself in ceremonies of all kinds. There I saw many relics of old life and old forms of thought which the colony had preserved though the mother colony had cast them off. There were remains of the old monarchical grandeur, and French was spoken not as it now was in Paris but as at the time of Rabelais.[24]

I also found Mr. Jefferson Davies[25] living quietly and simply amidst a most lovely plantation of magnolia trees, and had an opportunity of seeing there some traces of the dignity of the South in antique times. Here the refined and beautiful aristocratic life of the old southern planter was a thing of the past. Nature there, however, was still beautiful with its vast forests of magnolias, with their blossoms of ivory, which at night filled the streets with perfume. It was here that now and then one came across, and was able to study, bits of antique life of the past, including that of Louis Quatorze and Louis Seize.

Among the more elderly inhabitants of the South I found a melancholy tendency to date every event of importance by the late war and I never knew what ravages war could bring about until I saw Charleston. In Galveston on the Gulf of Mexico I joined some gentlemen in their favourite pastime of bathing at night in the Gulf. When the moon was gilding the bay with silvery streaks, I turned to a gentleman who was standing next to me and said:

'How beautiful the moon is to-night,'

'Yes,' was his reply, 'but you should have seen it before the war.'

One thing that struck me with regard to the young generations of Americans was that they seemed to have no memories, and generally referred to the late civil war with the same unconcern as if it was as ancient as the wars of the Greeks and Romans. I would not say they had no memory; but certainly they did not allow themselves to be trammelled by the memories of the past: the younger generation of the South was being brought up to love the Union. There seemed to be no trace of bitterness whatever. Generals and others who had borne a part in the war, and to whom I had spoken, showed no bitterness, but merely said to me:

'We have fought a fight and lost it, and now we wish to make our State as fine without slavery as it was before.'

As I toured through the South I came into contact with Negroes, whose lazy and cheerful contentment charmed me much.

If I was going to settle in America I would choose Virginia, the pleasing country life of which was its chief characteristic, and in which it so resembled England.

All the cities that have beautiful names derive them from the Spanish or the French or the Indian. The English people give intensely ugly names to places. One place had such an ugly name that I refused to lecture there unless its name was altered. The inhabitants declined to make the alteration, preferring the old name to my lecture. American towns are usually named after the most prominent resident. In this town the most prominent man was named Griggs, and it was called Griggsville — a combination which for vulgarity could not be surpassed. The introduction of the French word *ville*, with the Anglo-Saxon *Griggs*, was enough to drive any professor of philology into the grave. Supposing I had founded a school of Art there: fancy 'Early

Griggsville.' Imagine a School of Art teaching 'Griggsville Renaissance.'

Now, you would ask me something about the men, women and children one sees in America. Well, there do not seem to be so many children in America as there are in England, nor did they look so healthy and joyous as English children. American youths are pale and precocious, or sallow and supercilious, but were wonderfully clever, and immensely amusing. For health and beauty they were behind English children, which I think was because they live in big cities and have no outdoor games, which were very little practised. Many of the universities and schools were without gymnasiums. They had not the same love of games and outdoor work as the English people.

But American girls are pretty and charming: little oases of pretty unreasonableness in a vast desert of practical common-sense. The American girl was the prettiest despot in the world: she left school at about fourteen or fifteen wonderfully bright, able to talk on every subject whether she knew anything about it or not, with lovely hands and feet, and the prettiest boots in the world. But what was most delightful to me was the open, free friendship that was allowed to exist between young girls and young men of the same age. It was a pleasant, intellectual friendship. Every American girl is entitled to have twelve young men devoted to her. They remain her slaves and she rules them with charming nonchalance. As for slang I did not hear much of it, though a young lady who had changed her clothes after an afternoon dance did say that 'after the heel kick she shifted her day goods.'

There was no country in which women could travel with such ease as in America. In doing so she was not exposed to the slightest insult or annoyance. There, also, the intellectual side of a woman's nature was fully appreciated, and no country had ever offered women such a career as America; and in no country had the career of women as fitly justified the opportunity and privileges given to them. The chief difference which I observed between our life and American life was that women in America held a far higher position in public life and in the possibility of an unmarried woman earning her own livelihood.[26] As regards their beauty there were distinct types: in the north the girls were bright and clever, with wonderfully beautiful eyes and lovely hair, carelessly *spirituelle* and in many cases amusing. In the south they were more languid, much more beautiful.

The young women dressed extremely well, if you took the French milliner as the standard. I do not. I contend that the milliner should not dress the nation, but the artist: the secret of good dressing was to know the proportions of the human figure, a matter which very few milliners really studied. They ignored all the beautiful curves of the body, and were responsible for much of the tight lacing which produced such deplorable results among the sex. Small hands and feet were never beautiful because they were small. I maintain that beauty did not consist merely in smallness, it was to be found in the curves and relative proportion of the human body.[27] Milliners believe that the more you cut up a simple fabric the more beautiful it was, good material frequently being obscured by numerous bows and ribbons. Better, I hold, that a dress should be sent home incomplete, and that it should be left to the lady to decide what flower, lace or ribbon should be used to give the note of tone and colour.[28] We find, then, that milliners have to regulate our fashions, and what is the fashion as we understand it? Why, it is one form of ugliness which grows so intolerably ugly that it has to be changed every six months.[29]

The men are entirely given to business; they have, as they say, their brains in front of their heads. There were no idle men in America. Idleness was not with them what it was with us, one of the fine arts. They are also exceedingly acceptive of new ideas. Their education is practical and of a shorter duration than in England and they marry earlier. They go into business very much earlier, by twenty-one an American had probably made three or four successful bankruptcies and become a millionaire. One career they went into extensively was journalism. The basis of American education was the newspaper, which permeated the life of the States to such an extent that the American baby, as soon as he could read and write, thought nothing of editing a family newspaper. It seems strange to English people the intrusion of journalists into private life. I was asked by an interviewer at Chicago for some details of my private life, but I told him I had not got one – it was stopped at the Customs House in New York. Their humour was, I think, a sort of philosophy, like that of Rabelais. I learned from the newspaper interviewers what the people of America thought about art, and what particular points of art I ought to discuss in my lectures. One very satisfactory thing in American journalism was that it contained no reference to Greek mythology: editors were able to discuss the price of wool without entering into the history of Jason and the Golden Fleece.

We base the education of children entirely on books, but we must give a child a mind before we can instruct the mind. Children have a natural antipathy to books and handicraft should be the basis of education.[30] Boys and girls should be taught to use their hands to make something, and they would be less apt to destroy and be mischievous.

The arts the Americans loved most were music and the stage. These were democratic arts capable of giving the greatest pleasure. In

London, at too many theatres, the glare of the decorations robbed the stage. It was not so in America. The Madison Square Theatre was the most perfect I have ever seen. It had a lovely curtain, and there was a ventilator under every seat so well contrived that it was possible to freeze a hostile critic in a few minutes. Of their actors the Americans admired the comedian rather than the tragedian. I particularly admired Joseph Jefferson,[31] Lawrence Barrett,[32] Clara Morris[33] who I found most interesting, Mary Anderson[34] who was an actress of extraordinary beauty, Mrs. Drew[35] who was the American Mrs. Stirling,[36] and Miss Marie Prescott[37] who was an actress who one day will be called great.[38] American theatrical audiences, when they did not take to a play, quietly quitted the building and left the actors alone in their glory. This plan I think better than the English one of exhibiting hostility.[39]

I conclude by saying that much more important than what I have seen was what I had learnt in America. In going to America one learns that poverty is not a necessary accompaniment to civilisation. There at any rate is a country that has no trappings, no pageants and no gorgeous ceremonies. I saw only two processions during my whole visit, one was the Fire Brigade preceded by the Police and the other was the Police preceded by the Fire Brigade.

Every man when he gets to the age of twenty-one is allowed a vote, and thereby immediately acquires his political education. The Americans are the best politically educated people in the world.

What was really the greatness of America? Well, the greatness had nothing to do with science or Niagara, or anything of that kind. The people were brought up in a country where no-one is debarred from reaching the highest possible office without regard to birth or parentage. They could point to such men as Abraham Lincoln,[40] one of the best and purest-minded men the world has ever seen, men who sprang from the people. This gave them a splendid ambition in life, one of America's chief characteristics.

It is well worth one's while to go to a country which can teach us the beauty of the word 'Freedom' and the value of the thing 'Liberty'.

APPENDIX C

The House Beautiful

THIS TEXT represents this lecture as delivered by Wilde in early 1884. Looking at reviews it is clear that over Christmas 1883 Wilde had revised his text and ideas a little. The pre-Christmas 1883 lectures were significantly variable which leads me to conclude that some issues became more important for him at that time and eventually formed the framework for the final, post-Christmas version.

In early 1884 the reviews of his lectures in February and March have a similarity with some key portions, wherever he was speaking, being reported word for word.

Most of the lecture — before and after Christmas 1883 — is new notwithstanding the advertised claim that it contained 'the greater portions of the lecture given in America'. It did include portions of this and certain sections are repeated in very similar ways, using similar language, but the majority of the lecture had been revised for the UK tour.

The text I give here is a concatenation of lectures given in February and March of 1884. The main reviews I have relied upon are from Ulverston in the Lake District (lecture given on 22 February 1884) and Northampton (lecture 14 March 1884.) I have also reviewed the report published in the Appendix of Sherard's *The Life of Oscar Wilde*.

The House Beautiful

The true principles of decorative art, as applied to the exterior and interior decoration of the homes of the people.

I DO not desire to give any abstract definition of the word beauty, even if I was able, because I think we can get on very well without philosophy of that kind[1] if we only learnt how to surround ourselves and our children with beautiful things.[2] And when I say that everything in our houses should be beautiful, please believe me that I do not preach to you any mere poet's dream. There was a time in this lovely little island of ours when everything that was made by the hand of man was beautiful, from the stately house of the prelate with its gorgeous tapestry and its rich moulding, down to the simple house of the honest yeoman with its pleasantly decorated plaster set between the broad oak beams that held up the roof, and inside the brightly painted and prettily carved oak chest. I cannot for a moment believe that the spirit which once touched everything into loveliness was dead amongst us. I rather fancy that those who have cared to watch the artistic revolution of the last six or seven years have seen that the desire for beauty had been there already, and that all one could hope to do was merely to point out how that desire for beauty could be best fanned, brought to the most perfect completion and bear its right blossom and fruit.

And if I was asked what was the basis of any artistic revolution, I would answer that the possibility of our having art in England as art should be, the natural and national inheritance of all, better than luxury and more permanent than fashion,[3] depended absolutely and entirely on the value and the honour we give to handicraft. Until people realise that to make the very simplest little bit of ornamentation — the little leaf that ran round the rim of a cup or a plate, the design for a wallpaper or a carpet — to do work that well, there must go with the greatest delicacy of hand the greatest refinement of imagination: an eye that could see beauty in the world about it, and a capacity to transmit that beauty to others.[4] I could not, I believe, get these things done amongst the very worst of us, but only by the very best, and until people recognise that there was no nobler profession for any young man or young woman, provided that they had the refined qualities that art demanded, than any one of these simple handicrafts, however common we might think them now, though we might have art as the luxury and the passion of the few, we should never really have it permanently and strongly rooted amongst us.

Sometimes I have been met by objections that while we all of us would desire to have every beautiful thing about us, still there were practical difficulties. That if we had very delicate things in daily use they would be quite certain to be broken either by ourselves or by others, and that at the end of six months one would be found sitting amidst the picturesque ruins of one's devotion to art.

When I was in America I saw such a clear instance of the contrary, if I needed one, that I can hardly forbear from taking the opportunity of quoting it. In the city of San Francisco[5] there was a small quarter that was built by the Chinese navvies who came over to lay down railway lines and to dig the mines of California, to do what was called the common work of the west, and very common people, I am sorry to say, the Californians insisted on thinking them. And yet these men had come from a race that had so valued beauty, and they themselves in childhood had been brought up in the midst of surroundings so exquisite, that everything that they used was beautiful, and every beautiful thing that they had, they used. In the common little restaurant, for instance, in the little tavern where the Chinese navvy would go to have his supper after his work on the railway, or in the mine, I would see them drink their tea out of delicate little porcelain cups as dainty as the petal of a white rose. And in the hotel where I was, I always had my tea in the morning in a delft[6] cup about an inch and a half thick. If these men, so wrongly called common men, could use these delicate things, if the hand that could wield the axe and shovel in the daytime was yet so trained from childhood to the handling of beautiful textures, and to freely use porcelain so thin that in this country only the finger of a girl might touch it, then a great English-speaking race like the Americans need not always have such gross things in their habitations. And, perhaps in houses nearer home, there might be far more delicate things in daily use than in many cases were found at present. The reason, no doubt, that so many lovely things in all our houses were broken by rough handling came entirely from the fact that by the great heaviness and grossness of much that we used in Europe we had really destroyed the exquisite qualities of the sense of touch. In the Orient, where there was every beautiful textile and delicate thing, the sense of touch was far beyond what it was in Europe.

In any views I might give you with regard to the decoration of houses I do not desire to narrow you down to any particular style to which I might be sympathetic. It was right that you should recognise how absolutely various taste was, but let you be sure it was always taste and not the want of it. Aestheticism and the philosophy of aesthetics was not a style or a particular colour but purely a principle, the principle of beauty that underlaid everything, the faculty of observing it first, creating it afterwards and creating a national artistic temperament.[7]

People must not merely know what they liked, it was better they knew what to like. All that one could try to do was to see whether there might not be certain general rules underlying the principles of art that we might lay down as our foundation, and then build whatever fairy palaces of beauty one wished to rear upon it. The first rule I have heard given by Mr. William Morris[8] — who had given some very sensible rules to people who were going to furnish their houses and whose name as a poet and handicraftsman was familiar to many — was not to have in one's house anything but what one either knew to be useful, or thought to be beautiful.[9] If that rule were carried out by us, if you did not get a great deal of splendid art in return, you would get rid of a good deal of the bad ornamentation that even found its way, in some mysterious manner, into the houses of really charming and delightful people: the coarsely moulded china figures, bad imitations of Dresden, glaring ormolu ornaments, wax flowers and the wax peach — if it still lingered anywhere — would no longer repose under the glass shade, and possibly some limit might be put even to the crimes that have been committed in the name of Berlin wool.[10] At any rate, an end might be put to the endless array of antimacassars[11] which really reduced some rooms to the level of a sort of eternal washing day.

Mr. Morris's second rule was not to have in one's house anything but what one felt must have been a joy to the man who made it, and was a joy to the man who used it.[12] A noble rule, because it struck at the whole meaning, and motive, of decoration and all ornament, which was that noble-minded men and women, having felt the beauty of the world around us, must needs convey to others by the work of their hands the joy and delight which that beauty had given them.[13] If people in choosing their pottery, or furniture, or decorations, stopped to think whether what they were choosing was the expression of joy and pleasure, or was merely the work of over-worked artisans, of people who had no joy or pleasure in their lives, the end aimed at would be attained.

To these two rules might be added a third, which was not to have any imitation of one material with another,[14] not to paint one wood like another more costly, or to paint wood or iron like stone. Mr. Ruskin,[15] who laid a great deal of stress on the ethical side of art, had declared that it was extremely immoral for anyone to pretend that his hall was yellow Siena marble when it was obviously papered, and that it reduced the owner of the house to the permanent telling of falsehoods to everybody who happened to call on him, and that inclined to a kind of depravity. I am not sure that I take exactly such a view; in fact I do not. It was perhaps better to leave these fine moral words aside, and rather to remember that the morality of art was merely its beauty and its immorality was its ugliness, and I feel that we could dismiss the matter on this artistic ground without entering into the question as to whether an ugly object meant anything very grave as regarded the character of the master of the house.[16]

With regard to architecture, there were in England two spirits influencing it.[17] One was the national feeling of freedom and beauty: the Gothic spirit.[18] The other was the foreign, misunderstood Greek spirit: the spirit of monotony, of tyranny, and of restraint. The right spirit to believe in was the Gothic, though I believe many people were alarmed when it was suggested to build in that style, thinking it involved a deal of elaborate carving. Mr. Ruskin stated that architecture did not begin to be architecture until they had carving or moulding of some kind. It seems to me that a building was beautiful first through its mass, proportions, and secondly through its colour. With regard to colour, I would suggest the use of red brick, or, where stone had to be utilised, the placing of red tiles or pale sea green slates as a relief to the grey tone of the building. Red brick is the most desirable material for making houses beautiful on the exterior, and my inclination is for what is commonly known as the Queen Anne style,[19] although it was by no means specially connected with the name or reign of that sovereign.

Coming to the hall door, I think the woodwork should not be painted to resemble a wood it was not. It should show as much as possible the character of the wood of which it was made, or it might be painted with a light shade of green. The knocker on the door was by no means a common thing and I have seen some specimens in a museum at Derby[20] which were most artistic. I think a pleasant, bright brass knocker was always better than the heavy cast iron, black leaded monstrosity which was so prevalent. For flooring in the hall, I do not like linoleum or floorcloth, but would recommend tiles or a stone or imitation stone pavement. The Italians had a decorative way by which they made beautiful the stone floors or marble walls of their corridors. It consisted in sizing lines with a sharp instrument in a pattern and filling these lines with coloured matter. I prefer to distemper or wainscot the walls in the hall and do not support the practice of hanging pictures there. Good pictures should not be hung in the hall, good pictures should only be hung in places where people had leisure and quiet to enjoy works of art, and not in a place where there was constant running in and out.[21] And bad pictures should be hung - nowhere. One of the great secrets in connection with the hanging of pictures was to keep everything flat, not to have the pictures with the frames hanging out, which interfered with the flat appearance of the wall.

I would ask you to remember that there was nothing in your houses so common that art might not make it beautiful. The old spirit of art was really the right one. They used to say 'Let us make the useful things of life beautiful, the common things of life so beautiful that nothing shall ever be called common again.' The nineteenth century began in an entirely different way. They said 'Let everything that we use and touch and handle be as ugly in form, as coarse in texture, and as glaring in colour as it can possibly be.'

As regarded rooms, assuming you had the modern whitewashed square box so often left in our hands by the builder, and you had to decorate it, what was the first thing to think about? The first thing one should be absolutely certain about in decorating a room was the scheme of colour.[22] Many modern rooms were a mere chaos of loveliness without the presiding spirit of art or any real meaning or motive. Every bit of furniture in one's room should have its definite value in colour, in proportion and in form, and should be vital to the decoration of the room.[23] Just as a note or chord on the piano in the symphony of music, so one should not be able to remove anything without harming the beauty of the room. If one had a scheme of colour, perfect, definite, and fixed in one's mind, one would find one could use far fewer ornaments than many people did at present, and that a few things well chosen and of the proper colour would have a far finer effect than a mere crowd of things brought promiscuously together.

I hope I will not be asked what was the 'artistic' colour: a question I am constantly being asked. Remember that all colours were equally beautiful; they lay before the decorative artist exactly as the notes of a piano lay before the musician. One was not lovelier or uglier than another, but certain combinations of colour were fine. Few things strike me as being so absurd as announcements, which I am constantly reading in the newspapers, that such and such a colour was going to be very fashionable next season. That merely meant that society had to turn extremely short-sighted or blind with regard to all the other beautiful colours. Suppose that one read in a musical magazine that next season B flat was going to be a very fashionable note. All would recognise how extremely foolish that suggestion was. To say that a certain colour was to become fashionable was quite as ridiculous.[24]

An artistically decorated room was not a gloomy one, which, I am sorry to say, was the idea many people had. An artistically furnished room should give one the impression of great freshness and beauty of colour along with repose.[25] In room decoration, therefore, the walls should be treated as the background and a neutral tint should be chosen, such as russet or sage green,[26] but, however small it were, there should always be one piece of pure colour for the eye to rest upon. A silk curtain was about the best object for that purpose. Glare on the one hand and dinginess on the other were the two rocks to be avoided but it was only by a proper knowledge and use of the neutrals that we would ever attain to real decorative art. Compare the colour schemes of Europe, in the fine coloured windows of our cathedrals and churches, by means of the primary colours being used in small masses set in a neutral background, and of the East. I would say that the former displayed most of pure colour but the best effects were produced in Eastern countries by prevailing neutral tints, as, for instance, in a Persian carpet.[27] This was an example of my ideal, one of the best examples of decorative art that could be seen. The general effect was that of great brightness and joyousness of colour, but the primary hues were used only here and there in bright masses like jewels. The real secret of all decorative art lay in the proper use of the neutrals: black and white, or gold or grey. I would emphasise the importance of the use of gold in decoration, as imparting tone and colour. Perfect specimens of decorative art were St. Mark's at Venice and the Alhambra in Spain which is a splendid example of the artistic use of gold.[28]

Our builders had of late turned rooms into conservatories by putting in large windows with huge panes of plate-glass which admitted, not light, but glare, which had the same relative importance to light as noise had to music. Besides, they only encourage us in that bad habit of looking into the streets to see what our neighbours are doing,[29] and they also encourage our neighbours in the still worse habit of looking in at our windows to see what we are doing. They gave one the impression that one was living in a great glass case. The result of which was that we required the assistance of the upholsterer to tone it down. The upholsterer came and placed a huge pole like the mast of a ship across the top of the window, terminated at each end with huge representations of the pineapple, which nobody ever admired. From that, by rings far larger than they need be, he hung a curtain much too long, falling on the floor, collecting all the dust of the room, and requiring to be tucked up with a goodly display of ropes, Titanic tassels and other wicked things. The curtains were usually decorated with patterns running from top to bottom, whereas, if the lines of decoration were crosswise, the folds of the curtain, combined with light and shade, would produce an endless variety of graceful curves.

I would recommend smaller panes as much better than the plate-glass ones, and the far more frequent use of stained glass. I do not mean by stained glass those dreadfully preposterous chromo-lithographs which Germany in general and Munich in particular[30] insisted on sending over to England. The staining of glass had nothing to do with making a picture, but really with making light beautiful by passing through coloured surfaces.[31] The panes need not always be square and I would recommend the adoption of the lattice-work windows of the East.[32] The back of the window shutters might be artistically painted, so that when closed they would constitute a rich alcove of decoration.

Turning to the subject of carpets, I consider that they ought never to cover the whole of the room because it looked heavy and they collect the dust. Oriental carpets with a border are recommended.

I feel most modern rooms were far too high or looked too high. To determine whether a room was in good proportion, you should stand in the middle of it, and if, without raising your eyes, you could see where the cornice met the frieze, the room was in good proportion. I entirely dissent from the scientific opinion that we must have lofty rooms because the heated atmosphere produced by gas must ascend to the top of the room to not asphyxiate the inhabitants below. A well ventilated and low room was surely, I would maintain, far healthier than a lofty room which contained a certain amount of overheated or bad air. This is caused by lighting the room with large flaring gasoliers with four jets and bowls hanging from that exaggerated plaster vegetable which grew in the middle of so many ceilings. If one insisted on lighting his room like that, his arrangements were certainly simplified very much. At the end of six months it did not make the slightest matter what you had in your room. The ceiling was soiled and all colour was tarnished: probably few things were so perfectly ruinous to colour and delicacy of texture as gas, of the quality one usually got containing so much sulphur. I cannot see why the largest sitting room could not be perfectly well lighted by candles or oil lamps. The light of a lamp was soft, extremely beautiful, and pleasant to read by, and never vitiated the air or harmed your colour, this fact being one of the many cases in which one found the principles of beauty and those of utility[33] to be the same.

If the room were too high its height could be apparently diminished by broad horizontal lines — not dividing it into two equal halves — and there might be a frieze above, and a dado below, but not all three unless the wall was very high. I think the best dados were of wood. If a room was too wide a good wall paper of a broad decorative pattern would diminish the width; while if a contrary effect was desired, plain colour would give a certain sense of space. Remember, that in most cases the wall was a background, and I favour the Japanese style of decorating, not the covering of the whole surface with ornamentation but the paper, or distemper, should be of a very low note of colour, the highest colours being reserved for your beautiful porcelains, delicate embroideries and such like ornaments, placed just in the right spots. Many good artists now designed beautiful wallpapers.

I do find objectionable the dreary whiteness of the modern ceiling and I advocate the decoration of ceilings by means of raised surfaces. In this way the space might be broken into pleasant light and shade, while the old raftered ceilings gave plenty of scope for harmonious panelling. And there are beautiful designs in wrought plaster.

I would point out that, as it was inadmissible to give away or sell anything that was not perfectly beautiful, it became a problem what to do with an ugly thing. But suppose a man became possessed of a dreary white marble chimney piece with machine-made curves, what was he to do with it? It would be clearly immoral to sell it, for they should never ask money for what was ugly, and it would be equally immoral to give it away, for they should never wish any of their friends to possess what was ugly. They might, however, paint such a chimney piece or adopt the Italian method of incised lines with coloured cement in the interstices. Or it could be disguised with a valance or embroidered curtains. As regards the fireplace the more tile, brick and brass work the better. Have the floor of red brick, the sides of tiles, not with any elaborate figure pattern. I approve of a brass or copper fender, in preference to the black-leaded cast iron or the polished steel one. The more copper or brass near the fire the better, as that reflected every flicker of the burning embers. But consider those coal-scuttles of the period consisting of a fluted cylinder, with a papier-mâché top, containing a picture by Landseer or Tintern Abbey by moonlight, with a mother-of-pearl moon.[34] Or similar themes upon coal scuttles which you do not want. A plain brass or copper one which will reflect the ruddy glow was sufficiently beautiful.

In decorating, carry one thing in the room almost up to the ceiling – a door with a fine lintel, or a good corner cupboard or screens which take away the uselessness of the corners of a room. The mantelpiece naturally commends itself as the thing to treat in this way: it might be carried up to the ceiling, with delicate shelves of wood on each side of the over-mantel and the panels filled in with decoration, where might be stored Venetian glass or delicate ornamentation.[35] In the centre of the mantelpiece might be a pretty circular mirror, or an oblong or square one, with bevelled edges. I would leave it entirely to Mr. Ruskin to tell the effect large mirrors had in encouraging people to be always looking at themselves in the glass, and I merely concern myself with the artistic side of the matter. Large mirrors reflect the ugliest part of the room, the ceiling. A large mirror suddenly created a large gap in a wall; one fantastic hole was created by reflection, and every one of one's straight lines was to a certain extent duplicated, every one of one's best colours to a certain degree tarnished. Sometimes a very large mirror over the mantelpiece could be faced by another equally large mirror on the opposite wall, producing a series of cross reflections or vistas. This was so entirely subversive of beauty of decoration that I regard it as one of the many unpunished crimes of the nineteenth century.

Some chairs used at the present day are heavy and gross and seem to have been made in a warlike age when people thought it might be of advantage to have furniture so solid as to be useful as a weapon of defence. Something lighter and more graceful was required. Furniture should be well made and comfortable, fitting in with the lines of the human body and not too over-ornamented. On the choice of furniture, a maxim of mine is that it should be made by people of refinement, for people of refinement, and would grow more beautiful as it grew older. The Gothic style was only suitable for ponderous articles, such as chests or sideboards. There was very little beautiful about the modern gilt or imitations of the Louis Quatorze style. I would point out that gilt furniture deteriorated with age and I would advocate work of some modern makers, but would not praise any one designer indiscriminately. But I think the furniture of, amongst others, chairs by Chippendale,[36], the Brothers Adam,[37] Sheraton,[38] and Hepplewhite[39] satisfied the conditions I have laid down and are preferable to the modern arm-chair.

As to pictures, I would point out that as really good pictures are so expensive, the £50 so frequently devoted to decorating a house would be much better laid out in purchasing many other delicate objects. If we have good pictures all the decorations will be subordinate to them. Good pictures were worth all the wallpapers in the world but were very rare, and a bad picture is a worthless possession. There are, however, other decorations than pictures and for less than the price of a picture a room can be made beautiful with Venetian glass, rich silk embroideries, lovely porcelain, or pretty brass *repoussé* work which were finer than mediocre pictures and they would not cost nearly so much money. I must admit a partiality for old wood engravings with a strong fine line and also for good etchings. In framing engravings, I would condemn white mounts as being as bad as white ceilings. While photographs were well enough in portfolios, I do not approve of the hanging up of photographic pictures, most of which are solar libels on nature or the great masters, although Velasquez's[40] works principally lend themselves to the photographer's art. With regard to photographs of one's relations, of course, if one's relations were very decorative one would hang their photographs on the wall. Supposing that dreadful instance might happen in which a relation was not decorative - and we do not have the choosing of them - and you had to make a Stoical and Roman choice between the dictates of domestic affection and the principles of decorative art, I hope that decorative art would be allowed to have the first and not the second place.

I dislike intensely the glossy, over varnished, ugly aspect of the modern grand piano but I would urge you that a well decorated piano was a necessity.

If we are to surround ourselves and our children with beauty as the basis of the artistic movement, I consider that that we have made a very great mistake in education. We have founded it entirely upon books, entirely upon literature, long before we have created in the child the power of enjoying literature or of understanding books at all.

Which of us was there who could not remember in our boyhood the many weary and dreary hours that he had passed among books; books, I dare say, good enough in their way but not by any means good enough for us in our way, and a child learnt very little from them.

But out in the open air a child learnt a good deal of what he should learn. There was a great deal to be learnt from watching a man working at something useful, as, for instance, a potter at his wheel, a smith at his anvil, or a carpenter in his shop.[41] But from books, not much. If, instead of merely giving them knowledge of that kind, we would teach them the use of their hands, teach them the simple handicrafts, those beautiful decorative arts, such as carpentry, wood carving in the flat, the use of the potter's wheel, the decoration of pottery, weaving, dyeing, working in metal, beating out sheets of brass into raised *repoussé* work, we would, I am quite certain, be making children far happier in school than they were at present. And whenever a child was perfectly happy that child was perfectly good. What a source of knowledge and delight in after life would be given them?

If you went into a school and asked children what they knew, well it was quite wonderful what a modern child of the nineteenth century really did know.[42] They knew the population of Madagascar: how many black people and how many white people there were, as if it were a matter of the remotest importance how many people there were in Madagascar or what colour they chose to be. Then a child knew the names of all the kings of the Saxon heptarchy, that was to say, they were thoroughly well up in the private lives of people who never existed. Thus most of us passed our boyhood in the accumulation of facts so absolutely uninteresting that on growing to man's estate we had the infinite pleasure in forgetting them immediately. Let them be sure before they directly appealed to the mind or soul by books that there was a mind to appeal to, and how could they better do so than by teaching a child design?

If instead of teaching little boys and girls the latitude and longitude of countries that nobody wanted to go to, which was what people called geography,[43] and that criminal calendar of Europe that they termed history, if artistic education began at the earliest period of a child's life, how changed things would be.[44] I think children of refined people would of necessity be interested in how those things that made lovely their fathers' houses were made. As regarding the artistic power of children of course I am merely alluding to the very simple decorative art in handicraft. I do not suppose that every child could be an artist. There was not the slightest chance of that: the artist had a very rare and exquisite conception.

I would even take that problem of the nineteenth century, the noisy boy who would not read his books but spent his time in throwing stones at his neighbours' large plate glass windows — well I might forgive him for that — or at little birds — which I would not forgive — well, I would even take him. You might ask me whether I think that boy was of an artistic nature. I do not think children would be cruel to animals or throw stones if they were taught designing and handicraft. If taught handicraft they would then learn to admire all bright-eyed and furry things that live in woods and fields. I think that boy was in possession of one important truth about life, and that was that one's hands were given to one in order to be used. We had ignored in our educational system the value of the human hand. England, speaking broadly, was divided into two great communities: one of them could work with their hands, it was true, but in many cases their hearts and their heads had been starved of what should rightly be theirs; and then, on the other side, we had a large mass of people who had both hearts and heads of the very best but could find no better use for their hands than putting them into kid gloves that were far too tight for them. By isolating what were called the higher and more educated classes from handicrafts we had robbed them of great knowledge, and we brought great discredit on these beautiful decorative arts by banishing them from the lives of those classes, and art had thus become of less value to us because it was unaccompanied with the joy of the knowledge of beautiful work of any kind.

I think every child has a keen sense of colour, a keen delight in all imaginative work, and a pleasure and a joy at looking at lovely things. We know, for instance, in literature, how perfectly faultless the taste of a child was. No child, if left to itself, would ever read a Parliamentary Blue Book, or a leading article in The Times, or a scientific primer. A child, if it was a boy, would read a book of adventure that was pure romance, if a girl would read a fairy tale that was purely imagination. The child lived quite naturally and freely under the regime of the imagination, having really the right artistic attitude towards life, and understanding the meaning of this attitude, that was, whatever is beautiful must be true, and whatever is beautiful must be good.[45] Every child seemed perfectly prepared to accept these two formulae of life. But afterwards, all that joy and delight of the imagination seemed somewhat to be killed out of the child by our modern system and, particularly, as regarded the feeling of children towards beauty.

Had we been remiss in a good deal of the decoration of our schools? It was quite true that great improvements had been made in schools of late, but as a rule, I think the improvement has been confined purely to external work. External work, of course, was very gratifying to the ratepayers but hardly effective was the work inside. Even if you did pass under your Gothic portico to enter the school, you passed through a gloomy corridor, and in the school were whitewashed walls, looking cheerless in the daylight, walls against which some little boy with a perfectly misplaced idea of decorative art was quite certain to have flung his ink bottle. Trained in a sort of eternity of grime and amid ugly surroundings, which of us could learn anything? The school should be the most beautiful place in every town or village, should be so beautiful that the punishment for an idle little boy should be that he should not be allowed to go to school the next day. It would be to the child a pleasure house, not a house in which we succeeded in giving our children headaches, calling this education, but under the fourth standard.

There are many treasures of art to be found in the South Kensington Museum[46] and other places and I advocate the lending of such pictures and works of art to the schools throughout the country, to be left there till the children got tired of them. The exhibition should be a constant succession of such beautiful artistic productions. This would be of much greater service than they were under the present regulations, for I know of nothing so depressing as a thoroughly well-arranged museum with everything in its glass case. The education in art and design that children would thus get, would be far more practical than a good deal of the knowledge they got at present.

If you taught the child design you opened its eyes, first to the wonder and beauty of the world about it: the pageant of the clouds in the morning and in the evening, the flight of birds, the moon, the sea, the waving grass, and so on. When his eyes were opened to these beauties and, then, when the child felt that beauty so strongly that he must needs communicate to others the delight and joy that beauty had given him, surely then was the time to show him how there was no mechanical instrument ever invented in the whole world which, for perfect delicacy or exquisiteness, for power and for adaptability, could match the human hand. And yet while that was so, so many people went through life without any knowledge at all of the marvellous artistic power that there was in the hand. But, with a knowledge imparted to children of every one of these little decorative arts, out of the few children that really had the inventive and creative faculty might come a race of handicraftsmen whose work would be so beautiful that there would be no flower of our meadows that would not weave its tendrils round our pillows, no little leaf in our woodlands that would not lend itself to design, no single spray of wild rose or briar that would not live for ever over carven doorway or on painted chest.

The mission of art was very simple.[47] It had no elaborate philosophy about it. It merely claimed to bring into the life of every one of us a little joy, to touch the fleeting hours of day and make them gracious.[48]

And if men ask me what creed one could get in this mysterious passion for beauty and love of art, I do not know what better answer one could give than what was said by an English poet of this century who loved beauty more purely and passionately than any since Shakespeare: John Keats. Somebody writing to Keats asked him to have reverence for some tradition or prejudice of his day, and Keats wrote back and said "I have not got the slightest reverence for anything in existence except for the Eternal Being, the memory of great men, and the principle of beauty."[49]

Dress &
The Philosophy of Dress

Introduction

THIS APPENDIX gives a text of this lecture as it was delivered late in 1884 and early in 1885. It is based upon reviews in Ulverston and Brighton with additions from many other locations. I have also reviewed the report published in the Appendix of Sherard's *The Life of Oscar Wilde*.

Late in the writing of this book, an article by Wilde came to light entitled *The Philosophy of Dress* published on 19 April 1885 in the *New York Daily Tribune*. I include this article here as it is essentially an abridged, written version of his lecture. I have also compared it with my transcription of Wilde's lecture and feel its similarity — even the identical wording in lengthy parts — bears out my methodology in producing these texts of Wilde's lectures.

Dress

DURING the past few years a sense of the beautiful appeared to have revived in the country. There has been developed an artistic taste and a revival of artistic feeling that was without parallel in the history of any art of this century. It was impossible to go into a friend's house without being struck by the great change that had taken place in this respect. There was a far greater feeling for colour, a far greater feeling for the delicacy of form, and a sense that art can touch the very commonest things of a house with a certain grace and loveliness.[1] The horsehair sofa[2] no longer glared at one from the window; the wax peach had ceased to ripen under its glass case, whilst some limits had been placed upon antimacassars.[3] However, no matter how beautiful a house might be, it should be only a background for the men and women who dwell in it. The beauty of the house was abnormal so long as there was a large side left untouched by this artistic sense: I mean the apparel, the costume, of men and women, which has been neglected, there being nothing of the rational or beautiful about it. Whenever art had been a living and actual reality to a nation, the costume of the people had been the first thing to assert it. In the times when noble architecture and beautiful decoration prevailed in England, they would find that the costume of the people of England was beautiful also, for the same principle which showed itself in the stately palace or the cathedral was expressed also in the way in which the people cut and wore their dress.

Dress was not merely one of the arts, but it was one of the fine arts. When I call it an art, I do not exaggerate its importance. To dress well, one should be a master of colour and of form. Nay more: there was something in dress which gave it a position which I do not say is unique but still one that gave it a very high place indeed in the hierarchy of the other arts. I mean this: that just as drama was the meeting place of life and of poetry, so dress was the meeting place also of life and of the visible arts.[4] Dress, in the first place, should be expressive of the grace, beauty and proportions of that which it covered. It should suit and yield to its every motion and not, as it so often happened, be merely a highly decorated prison that confined and limited the freedom of the body under it. The beauty of dress depended on it expressing properly the human form.[5] What one was called upon to dress, to attire, to make beautiful, was not a mere senseless thing, not a milliner's dummy, or a tailor's block and the chief objection to ladies' dress of the present age was that it was ill in accord with the natural beauty, and grace and mobility, of the human form.

The first necessity to try and produce any greater artistic feeling about dress was by the compulsory teaching of drawing to every child[6] quite as early as they were taught to write. A desire to draw is natural; no little boy or girl fails to cover its lesson book with pictures of its parents or friends, or of the house over the way, or the animals in the field. Writing, on the contrary, is an acquired art, and there is no reason why children should not be taught drawing as they are taught writing. They might commence by drawing plane figures - squares or cubes - proceeding afterwards to the study of the human figure, in the first place from the casts of the ancient Greek statues. This would result in a thorough understanding of the body and the best method of adopting dress thereto. They would then soon learn that the waist, for instance, was a very delicate and beautiful curve from one part of the body to the other, and not, as the milliner fondly imagined, an abrupt right angle suddenly occurring in the centre of the person.

Size — bigness or littleness — was of course, a mere accident of existence[7] and it was not a quality of beauty. A foot was not by any means beautiful simply because it was small, any more than it would be if it were large. A foot was beautiful when it gives the idea of being the firm basis on which the body rests and was in direct proportion to the rest of the figure. So it was in the case of the hand, which is not beautiful because it was small, but when its curves and those of the wrist are graceful and unbroken. I do not know where these erroneous ideas had been gathered. The poets, who are generally blamed for everything, are probably responsible for the idea that a small waist is necessarily beautiful. Chaucer[8] and Dunbar[9] are amongst the guilty; one talks of a lady whose waist was 'as small as a willow-wand.' Or maybe we had fiction to thank for it: I invariably find if I take up a modern novel that the heroine has an exceedingly small foot, and an exceedingly small hand. If they went to China, they found both the smallest foot and the smallest hand, and consequently the most ugly. Stature, again, was a question of proportion. The proper adjustment of line and of proportion was the first thing one had to see to in dress, every principle that applied to decoration applied to dress also.

All art was the expression of certain laws and principles, which remained the same whether one was building a cathedral or making a gown, though the application might be different. The child that has learned to draw will know that the effect of horizontal lines on dress upon the figure is to reduce its apparent height, whilst that of vertical lines is to increase the height. The same principle, as is well known, holds in the case of a house. If a ceiling be too high, a fault very common in our modern houses, it is easy to reduce its seeming height by running any broad band, such as a dado, horizontally around the room. If, on the contrary, the ceiling is too low, as occasionally occurs in very old houses, it was always easy to give height and proportion to the wall by means of a vertical line from the ceiling to the floor, either in panel or in pillar.[10]

My first contention in regard to modern dress was that it disregarded all artistic rules with regard to the adoption of patterns. If a lady be too tall, a broad belt or sash lessens her apparent height; whilst if she happens to be small the lines of her dress should be as much as possible vertical. A person looking at the fashion plates of the period of the first French Empire[11] will be struck by the apparent height of the beautiful ladies of the time. The cause is that by wearing the waist of their dresses — or a sash — higher than usual, thus shortening the waist, they could apparently increase their height by the effect of lengthening the skirts and making them fall in a series of vertical folds. As to oblique lines in a dress, they always gave great dignity and grace to the figure, as might be seen by the Grecian works of Art.

Any horizontal line in dress at once diminished the height so that it was a mistake for ladies of short stature to wear low dresses giving a horizontal line at the shoulders. I would point out that it was not suitable for persons of little stature to wear a lofty head-dress. People imagined that they gave themselves height by wearing a lofty head-dress, or bonnet with lofty plumes. This was quite a mistake. In the Court of Marie Antoinette,[12] who had exceedingly charming ideas of taste, the ladies wore head-dresses three or four feet high, and imagined that they gave dignity to their appearance. All these ladies, charming all of them, looked small because of the enormous head-dress. When anyone looks at another, the highest point which should strike one should be the eyes and forehead, and this was entirely prevented by the towering head-dress which meant that they put the face out of its proper position and diminished the real height of the figure. Anyone who imagined herself too small, instead of wearing a lofty head-dress, should have a strongly-defined series of vertical lines in their costume, giving elegance, grace and real height to the figure. Tall people should wear horizontal lines and, if ladies, they might wear broad puff sleeves of the seventeenth century.

With regard to colour, I insist that in a room — unless it was wanted to be a museum — it is essential to adhere to some harmonious scheme of colour.[13] The same holds true of dress. I do not wish to give any arithmetical basis for a question of art, but as a general rule I am of the opinion that simplicity — one colour — was best for short people and lent a certain additional dignity to the height. If one was taller, two colours, perhaps at most three colours, unless very exquisitely harmonised, were as many as could be safely employed, for it should be understood that any contrasting colour concentrated attention on a mere detail. Vivid colours — a bit of scarlet where it should not be in ribbons or feathers in the head-dress — are dangerous also, because they interfere with the attention and attract undue observation, detracting from the face which should be the highest note the eye should strike.

Then, as regards the kind of colour, I am quite sure you will not ask me a question that elsewhere I have often been asked — what was the artistic colour? Remember that all colours were equally beautiful and these lay before the decorative artist exactly as his piano lay before the musician. One note was not lovelier than another, nor one colour even more beautiful than its neighbour, but certain combinations of colour were good, certain notes of harmony were good also. It was with the combination that the artist or the musician had to do. But as regarded the actual colours themselves, one should never have any preference for one over the other. Nothing distresses me more than to see a paragraph in which it was stated that such and such a colour was going to be very fashionable next season, and I hold that it would not be more ridiculous to read in a musical magazine that B flat was going to be a very fashionable note next season.[14]

Then there was the question of pattern. Patterns were pretty, but great care was required as to the size of the checks. They should not be too definite, to begin with. If one wore a very strongly marked check, the slightest inequality in the figure, as between the two shoulders, became at once very apparent; and the eye was distracted from the dignity of the proportions. Then the pattern should not be too large. Quite recently at a tailor's in Regent Street in London I was looking for some stamped grey velvet or grey plush suitable for making a cloak of. In every shop I visited, I was shown the most enormous patterns, something far too big for an ordinary wallpaper, or for ordinary curtains; something that would require a good sized public building to show it off to any advantage. I entreated the shopmen to show me some pattern that was in some definite and rational relation and proportion with the figure of somebody who was not over ten or twelve feet high. But the shopmen said they were extremely sorry, they were quite unable to do so, as the smaller patterns were no longer being woven; in fact, these large patterns were 'the fashion.'

When a man mentioned the word fashion, he mentioned the greatest enemy to Art in this as in all other centuries. It is a giant that puts men in chains. Art seeks to give expression to individuality, fashion insists upon every man doing as every other man. Fashion rested upon folly, and art upon law. Fashion was perfectly ephemeral, art was eternal. After all, what was a fashion?[15] A fashion was merely a form of ugliness, so absolutely unbearable that they had to alter it every six months.[16] At present the great enemy of reform was the tyrant fashion, and in this respect we had been greatly guided by France. The history of costume in England, wherever it was monstrous, extravagant and ridiculous, was due either to a French invasion or a marriage with a French Princess: every time, in fact, English dress had been good the French had always spoilt it. The French influence had been most pernicious, dating from the time when William the Conqueror landed in England. In the eleventh century he found the people wearing a dress both beautiful and simple: the Saxon lady was extremely well dressed in her tunic and gown, fairly closely fitting, sleeves long, with slits in the end to push through the hand, which then had no glove, for gloves were not invented, just a cloak, cape and hood. There was nothing to object to in that dress, it was perfectly simple and served its purpose. The ladies of his court, however, introduced the exaggerated styles which superseded those of the inhabitants of this country. There came everything that was monstrous, the sleeves were lengthened till they were useless and trailed on the ground, the dress had a monstrous train which swept the street, and the material was tortured under the tailors' scissors. From the French we had got the enormous ruff to begin with. The ruff could be made very beautiful – a slight ruff like that worn by Mary Stuart,[17] not the huge ruff extending beyond the shoulders – then the awful farthingale (as shown in some of Holbein's pictures of Queen Elizabeth[18]) were all from the French. In this matter France had abrogated to herself a position and exercised an influence which they by no means deserved. France had not the slightest right to dress any other nation but itself: France had no artistic history.

In my opinion, if the English dressed according to their own principles they would dress in a more sensible and beautiful manner. Were it rational or beautiful, or both, they would not alter it: they would be only too glad to have those two, rather rare, qualifications. Whenever a dress had been beautiful or rational, it had lasted a long time: much longer than people fancied, much longer than I had fancied myself. In the Egyptian department of the British Museum I have seen a dress that had lasted for certainly 2,000 years and the Greek dress had lasted certainly for 900 if not for 1,000 years. Here and there new dyes would be brought from the vat, new textures brought from the loom, but still the lines of dress remained unchanged.

And even if one was not ready to accept a purely artistic reason in this connection, I am quite ready to rest it on what would be called a purely practical basis: a question, say, of economy. The amount of money spent every year in this country upon dress was something perfectly fabulous. If I told you the sum of money spent every year in bonnets alone, I am quite sure half of you would be filled with remorse, and the other half with desperation. I will not name the exact sum, but it was something really quite out of proportion to what it should be. It is for this reason: modern dress in England was not distinguished by any great extravagance or splendour of material, time was when cloth of gold, rich brocades and the like were not infrequent in the streets of old English towns. But in modern days the materials were more or less simple: they were not always well treated, but still they were simple, and lasted for a certain time. The simplicity of modem dress, so far as colour and material went, certainly did not account for this immense expense. The reason was surely this: the constant change of dress, and change of type of dress, that fashion seemed to demand. The economy would, indeed, be great if dress could be rendered permanent.

I have been told - and am quite ready to believe it - that if a very charming person had spent all her pocket money in buying the latest Paris bonnet, and worn it to the rage and confusion of the neighbourhood for a fortnight, after that time her dearest friend was quite certain to call upon her to mention, incidentally, that *that* particular bonnet had gone completely out of fashion, that no one dreamt of wearing *that* colour or *that* particular shape, now. So, consequently, a new bonnet had at once to be bought, more expense entered into, whereas if they rested dress on a question of law — artistic and scientific — there would be no anxiety at all for this change. What was beautiful looked always 'the thing,' always new, never became old-fashioned, they did not get weary of it. On a pure question of economy, they would find a great national gain in trying to get rid of this constant tyranny of fashion.

If you were to ask me what style I proposed, I would say I propose no style at all in the sense of an historical style: archaeology had nothing to do with art. No attempt should be made to imitate ancient costume because it was ancient, no idea of turning life into a Fancy Dress Ball.[19] But still, if, amongst the great nations of the past they found certain lines of dress carried out, they might, as a matter of convenience, appeal to those nations simply to show that the laws were practical. It was not too much to say that there was no nation of antiquity from whom one might not learn something. I would say that in England, as in every other country, the national costume was permanent until the end of the sixteenth century. But if asked to fix the time when the dress of this country was really lovely, I would say it was in the second quarter of the seventeenth century. During the reign of Charles I[20] the costume of this country was both useful and beautiful. The Restoration of Charles II,[21] however, resulted in the reintroduction of the French influence, and the beautiful and artistic dress decayed.

Contrasting the dress of the present day with that of the ancient Egyptians, I would say that the latter had one great recommendation: that it was suspended from the shoulder always, and never from the waist, and so did not distort the human figure, as was the tendency of modern dress. The shoulder was the proper place from which to suspend anything. A weight ceased to be cumbersome when the shoulders carried it: Nature herself pointed that out to us as the place from which apparel should be hung. All ugly and uncomfortable dress was due to the fashion that had been prevalent for some hundreds of years in Europe, of suspending the lower garments from the waist instead of from the shoulders. By suspending the clothing from the waist, where Nature provided no means of support, an artificial ledge had to be made by means of a corset and this gave rise to some support being required for heavy clothing. If they looked over any history of costume, they would find that whenever dress seemed particularly uncomfortable and ugly it came from the introduction of a bad fashion which did not see that from the shoulders, and from the shoulders only, should all garments be hung. Take the sixteenth century: in England it opened extremely well. It was quite true there was a certain extravagance in texture that perhaps was too costly. About the middle of the century this unfortunate fashion of hanging the lower garments from the waist was introduced. At once, in order to support the great weight of the lower garments, and to keep them really in their places - to prevent them from falling off - came the introduction of the farthingale. The farthingale was a huge structure, made sometimes with ribs of iron or steel, sometimes with wicker-work, like a very large clothes-basket attached to the waist in order to support the great weight of the lower garments and extending out an immense width on each side of the person. So in the reign of Elizabeth in England, a lady in full dress took up quite as much room as they would now give to a very good-sized political meeting. That was a selfish custom, nobody had a right to monopolise so much room, and the custom should not be encouraged. This was not all, for with it came the tight corset of Catherine de Medici,[22] to compress or absolutely crush the waist into smaller proportions. She was accused of many crimes, but I am not sure that the invention of this corset was not the worst. It was a huge structure, made of iron or steel, done in open work; it had a back and front, like the breast-plate of a modern young Guardsman, and it had to be padlocked with a key under the right arm, just like a big American trunk. It was extremely difficult to get into it, and extremely difficult to get out of it. It could hardly be accepted as any beautiful addition to costume. In the last century, we had the hoop that was ridiculed by Hogarth[23] in his pictures and in old English comedy, and in this century we had the crinoline up to some years ago.

You will tell me that English ladies had long ago given up the farthingale, the hoop, and the crinoline. That was so, and I think they should be very pleased and gratified that they had. But still, did there not linger even to the present amongst us, that dreadful, that wicked thing, called the dress-improver?[24] I am quite sure that none of you present ever dreamt of wearing them but there were some who were not so wise, and to these I would like to point out that its effect is to cut across the curve of the body, just as it becomes beautiful, and so entirely spoilt the whole grace of the figure. Very often a modern dress began extremely well, that was, the upper part of the dress from the shoulders to the waist followed out the lines of the figure more or less completely; but suddenly when these lines arrived at the waist, they were abruptly cut off. Now, neither in decoration nor in dress should any line ever abruptly come to an end. A line, of course, might alter its direction — take the case of Moorish ornament — but still it should never be exactly cut off. Then again, a dress should be a complete harmony from the neck to the feet, where, as the lower part of the dress was much heavier, instead of delicate lines they had harsh curves and harsher angles. The dress became bell shaped, and it was this want of harmony between the two parts of a dress that diminished the stature, and was in itself, artistically, a source of discord. If the garment was suspended from the shoulder it would present no anxiety: there would be no need for tight lacing, for any artificial means - crinoline, dress-improver, or the like - to support the weight of the garments. There would be far more freedom, far more ease, and consequently far more grace.

An ideal dress was that of the Athenian woman in the days of Athenian glory, when Athens was pre-eminent in her arts and her philosophy.[25] They borrowed from the Orient, from which all things have come, including a softer variety of woollen cloth, similar to cashmere. The Assyrians, with the Oriental fondness for bright colours, dyed their dress in vivid shades. The Greeks, with more artistic feeling, discarded the colours and the horizontal lines of the Assyrian girdle, which they diminished to two small cords that serve to relieve the vertical lines of the robe by retaining oblique folds in position. The Greeks wore absolutely the most beautiful dress the world had ever seen.[26] The reason was simply this: the Greeks knew that all beauty was organic, that was to say, beauty came from within, not without, from the perfection of its own being, and not from any added prettinesses. It can be seen how Greek dress gave freedom of action and lent itself to the grace and beauty of the form, and showed the beauty of the curves into which the light material employed naturally fell. The Greek lady, either for her own or for her husband's sake, was extremely economical. Modern dress was perhaps really weakened by the enormous amount of work that was involved in making it. Ready-made ornaments, bows where there should be no bows, and flounces where there should be no flounces, were unnecessary.[27] Paris was constantly designing something monstrous, and unfortunately fashionable people tried to squeeze themselves in some way into these dresses, whereas they should be designed entirely with reference to our figures.

A great change in dress had come from the giving up of the hood and cloak as part of everybody's general attire. A cloak with a hood not intended merely for an ornament was a very ancient and most admirable garment. It was decidedly English in ancient times and can be seen in old sculptures. The hood should be made to protect the head from rain – that was its use.

On the other hand, the Greek lady suffered under many disadvantages: she had never seen the modern bonnet. Can I remind you that in Athens there were no milliners and consequently no milliners' bills, and, having spoken in favour of the hood worn by the Athenian ladies, I must condemn the bonnets of the present day as wholly unsuited to the climate, and as useless as a means of protection to the face. I could imagine a Greek lady saying to an English lady, 'Why is it that with your climate so treacherous, rainy, and stormy, your head covering is made of texture so easily spoilt — is made of material so ephemeral, so absolutely flimsy?' What would she have said if she had seen in the north of England a very elaborate bonnet consisting of a stuffed bird alighting on a piece of tulle or a rose made out of muslin reposing on a bank of golden bees? It scarcely struck one as being sensible. I have lately seen a very large picture of such a bonnet and at the bottom of the page there was this note:

With this kind of bonnet the mouth is worn slightly open.

That was surely the *ne plus ultra* of folly.

The tight-fitting half veil worn by ladies was ugly and useless. If it was to be worn at all, it should be worn as it was by Turkish ladies, over the lower face and mouth. Then, for absolute ugliness nothing could exceed the spotted veil and I would remind you all that the spots on a veil seriously injured the eyes, and that I cannot help thinking how dreadful life must seem to ladies who looked at it through a veil dotted with black spots: the world seen through such a medium was not half so beautiful as it would otherwise appear.

Greek sandals allowed the foot to remain perfectly flat and the figure to stand erect, where the modern high-heeled shoes were derived from a two-prop clog - one under the foot and the other under the heel - which was in use in this country in the time of Henry II.[28] In modern times we only retained the prop under the heel. Without at all proposing clogs as being in any way absolutely necessary things, [29] I certainly would say that it was better to walk upon two props than to totter upon one, and better to have one's foot almost flat than at an extremely harsh angle. I consider that, by throwing the body forward, they did not, as some imagined, add to the height, whilst they deprived the wearer of all graceful motion.

Passing on to the divided skirt — I do not know if there was one present — but I could not say that in its present form I admired it. With its flounces, frills, and heavy kilting, it was too cumbrous and heavy to secure the freedom of action and the cleanliness from the soil it was designed to give. It seems the divided skirt was very anxious to look like anything but what it really was. But I think it well to consider whether its principle was not good under certain conditions: for instance long walking on a country road. I think the principle of it was good, but the skirt must be stripped of its frills and kiltings: in my opinion an adaptation of the Turkish knickerbockers — loose around the limbs and confined at the ankle — would also be fit in England.

In the matter of jewellery ornamentation, I prefer the artistic appreciation of the Greeks over the inartistic decoration prevalent in this country. Englishmen seemed to buy jewellery by its weight: we might just as well buy a statue by the ton, or a picture at so much per square yard. English jewellery was far too heavy and too expensive; whereas Greek jewellery, which I commend, was not only thinner, but was more economic.

In summing up, I would argue that that ladies' dress of today was wanting in grace and freedom and was too costly, and, without maintaining that the Greek dress could be used in our northern climate, I hold that all dress should be modelled upon the lines, or principles of beauty, it embodied. There was no good to be got from imitating anything or anybody, however, but the principles, the laws of Greek dress, might be perfectly well realised in the modern shaped gown with regular sleeves. The other point observable in the costume I have described is that it was undivided and unseamed. The beauty of the dress was entirely dependent upon the manner in which it was worn.

There was only one difficulty of any importance that had been suggested to me: it was said that the climate in Northern Europe was so cold that many garments, one over the other, were obliged to be worn. Therefore, it was impossible for dress in England to at all follow out, with any success, the lines of the figure, and it was necessary that modern dress must look, in a certain degree, heavy on account of our climate. That objection was founded on the idea that the warmth, the comfort of apparel, depended on the number of garments worn. Underclothes should be sufficiently tight, but not so much as to impede the free use of the limbs. With proper undercloth, some adaption of the tunic or cloak of the Greeks would be what I would recommend. The actual warmth depended entirely on the material of which these garments were made. The great mistake that had been made in Europe for the last two centuries was that linen had been used instead of wool, which is superior to any other as a dress material. For our changeable climate I advocate woollen garments, so made as to reveal the beauty of the human form. Wool was a non-conductor, and this implied a great deal, giving the necessary coolness in the violent heat of summer and the required warmth in the cold of winter, and was the most sanitary of any material. I have heard it said that wool was a coarse texture but it was the finest and most delicate texture in the world: the woollen stuffs of Kashmir were finer than the finest silk. The use of wool as the basis of materials for dress was greatly recommended by eminent physicians, for example by Dr. Gustav Jaeger of Stuttgart,[30] who had pointed out that wool could be made to an astonishing fineness. By combining the German principle of science with the Greek principle of beauty, would come the costume of the future for this country.

Turning to men's dress, which was not of so much consequence – but we must wear something – no fashion was too ugly, too monstrous, too bizarre that men have not welcomed it with alacrity and worn it with delight. I am afraid more ridiculous fashions had prevailed than had ever been seen in the dress of a woman. Even the dress of the present day was not so sensible as people represented it to be. The tall hat was an illustration. Why the glossy silk cylinder on the head?[31] A monstrously ugly object which had somehow come to be regarded as a symbol of the immense respectability of the owner upon week days and absolute authority upon Sundays.[32] Englishmen carried them in all parts of the world as an emblem of English liberty and the apex of London civilization. Why, I ask, did man wear this immense cylinder upon his head? It was perfectly unsuitable to our variable climate, and in the first shower was reduced to ruin. It might, it was true, be ironed in private, but its youth was gone forever. The law for whatever one wore on the head, hands or feet should simply be that it should be made of a soft material and it should take its shape more from the way one wore it than from any stereotyped design. Lastly, it should not be easily spoilt. As a substitute, I would recommend a hat of soft material, with a large brim that could be used to protect the face, or doubled back if not required: it afforded protection from the sun and the wind which was a reason for its adoption. The large felt hats seen in Vandyke's[33] portraits were comfortable and graceful. I would ask for the hat of the future to be made of soft material, with not too high a crown and if the material were to be extended, it might be on the brim.

I would point out how graceful and comfortable the cloak worn in the time of Charles I was, how it could be thrown on one side when the weather was warm, and wrapped around the body when cold: how graceful the folds of such a garment were, compared with the hideous incongruity of modern garments. There was the coat and waistcoat - the former a garment with a back but no front, and the latter a garment with a front but no back. I propose that it was better to amalgamate the two into one in the doublet: have the coat so made that it should fold over the chest with a double thickness and thus protect the vital parts. The Inverness cape[34] is more commodious than the overcoat.

I also approve of the soft, high leather Hessian boots worn in the seventeenth century which had a great deal to be said for them for wearing in muddy streets, instead of the present, inconvenient trousers.

I think we would be all perfectly contented if the dresses in towns and in society were as beautiful as the dress of the young men of England when they were playing tennis, shooting, fishing, or enjoying any outdoor sports. It was curious that there should be this beautiful rational dress in the country. If a dress was really properly constructed with reference to utility, beauty was added. After all was said, who were really the well-dressed people in England? Generally, the well-dressed people were those whom we were in the habit of calling the lower orders. They were people like the Lincolnshire ploughboy in his smock-frock, which was the doublet worn in the fourteenth century by the king and his nobles. The French workman's blouse was the short tunic of the same century worn by kings and princes. A Lancashire mill girl, with a shawl over her shoulders and wearing clogs, knew more about dress than a fashionable London lady recently returned from Paris, because in the former case there was comfort, while in the latter there was discomfort.[35] I must acknowledge that all ugliness of dress had come entirely from those who were called the upper classes. It had come entirely from Courts, at all events from people who had nothing to do and had done it, whereas beauty of dress would always be found in the dress of people with something to do and who knew how to do it.

Among peasants and fisher folk generally - men and women – we never found ugly dress. They thought of what was suitable and useful and what corresponded to their needs, and so they obtained what was really beautiful. I do not propose we should imitate any other class of people: half of the beauty of the fisher people's dress was spoiled when wrought into fashionable dress and worn in the streets of a town, but it was a shame to us that we had not been able to make our own dress in town as good, simple, and beautiful as the dress of the people like ploughboys and fisher folk.[36]

Of the nineteenth century, all the beautiful things had been made when something useful was attempted, and all the ugly things when something beautiful was tried.[37] Ugliness was simply a want of fitness and greater usefulness and beauty in dress could not fail to add to our happiness.

We need to recreate in all dress a general sense of the value of individualism. Each one should try to stamp their individuality upon their dress. The real liberty they wanted was not so much that of the masses of people, but that liberty to the individual which would allow freedom for everyone to dress as they chose.[38]

In conclusion, Art would gain immensely by an improvement in dress. Art was now an affair of the studio, but the proper places for its study were the streets of our towns and cities.[39] Our modern dress did not at all express dignity, and that instead of our having to go to picture galleries and the like in search of beauty, we ought to find in life itself an infinite possibility of beauty, so that an ordinary afternoon walk from town to country and back to the street would really teach us as much as a picture gallery, and perhaps more.[40]

I would urge that all dress should be made subservient to the principles of health, comfort and Art. Were we able to find the principles of art in fashion, how much better able we should be to realise what made the Greek ideal: a perfectly healthy and beautiful mind in a body that was clothed in a healthy and in a beautiful manner.

THE PHILOSOPHY OF DRESS

BY OSCAR WILDE.

Copyright 1885.

THERE has been within the last few years, both in America and in England, a marked development of artistic taste. It is impossible to go into the houses of any of our friends without seeing at once that a great change has taken place. There is a far greater feeling for color, a far greater feeling for the delicacy of form, as well as a sense that art can touch the commonest things of the household into a certain grace and a certain loveliness. But there is also a whole side of human life which has been left almost entirely untouched. I mean of course the dress of men and of women. . .

I have been sometimes accused of setting too high tan (sic) importance on dress. To this I answer that dress in itself is a thing to me absolutely unimportant. In fact the more complete a dress looks on the dummy-figure of the milliner's shop, the less suitable is it for being worn. The gorgeous costumes of M. Worth's *atelier*[1] seems to me like those Capo di Monte[2] cups, which are all curves and coral-handles, and covered over with a Pantheon of gods and goddesses in high excitement and higher relief; that is to say, they are curious things to look at, but entirely unfit for use. The French milliners consider that women are created specially for them by Providence, in order to display their elaborate and expensive wares. I hold that dress is made for the service of Humanity. They think that Beauty is a matter of frills and farbelows. I care nothing at all for frills, and I don't know what farbelows are, but I care a great deal for the wonder and grace of the human Form, and I hold that the very first canon of art is that Beauty is always organic, and comes from within, and not from without, comes from the perfection of its own being and not from any added prettiness. And that consequently the beauty of a dress depends entirely and absolutely on the loveliness it shields, and on the freedom and motion that it does not impede. From this it follows that there can be no beauty of national costume until there is a national knowledge of the proportions of the human form. To Greek and Roman such knowledge came naturally from the gymnasium and the palaestra, from the dance in the meadow and the race by the stream. We must acquire it in the employment of art in education. And knowledge of this kind I propose would soon become the inheritance of all, if each child were taught to draw as early as it is taught to write. ...

And if a child does study the human figure it will learn a great many valuable laws of dress. It will learn, for instance, that a waist is a very beautiful and delicate curve, the more delicate, the more beautiful, and not, as the milliner fondly imagines, an abrupt right angle suddenly occurring in the middle of the person. He will learn again that size has nothing to do with beauty. This, I dare say, seems a very obvious proposition. So it is. All truths are perfectly obvious once one sees them. The only thing is to see them. Size is a mere accident of existence, it is not a quality of Beauty ever. A great cathedral is beautiful, but so is the bird that flies round its pinnacle, and the butterfly that settles on its shaft. A foot is not necessarily beautiful because it is small. The smallest feet in the world are those of the Chinese ladies, and they are the ugliest also. It is curious that so many people, while they are quite ready to recognize, in looking at an ordinary drawing-room, that the horizontal line of frieze and dado diminishes the height of the room, and the vertical lines of pillar or panel increase it, yet should not see that the same laws apply to dress also. Indeed in modern costume the horizontal line is used far too often, the vertical line far too rarely, and the oblique line scarcely at all. The waist, for instance, is as a rule placed too low down. A long waist implies a short skirt, which is always ungraceful as it conveys an effect of short limbs, whereas a high waist gives an opportunity of a fine series of vertical lines falling in the folds of the dress down to the feet, and giving a sense of tallness and grace. Broad puffed sleeves, again, by intensifying the horizontal line across the shoulders, may be worn by those that are tall and slight, as they diminish any excessive height and give proportion; by those who are small they should be avoided. And the oblique line, which one gets by a cloak failing from the shoulders across the body, or by a gown looped up at the side, is suitable to almost all figures. It is a line which corresponds to the direction of motion, and conveys an impression of dignity as well as of freedom. There are of course many other applications of these lines. I have mentioned merely one or two in order to remind people how identical the laws of architecture and of dress really are, and how much depends on line and proportion. Indeed the test of a good costume is its silhouette, how, in fact, it would look in sculpture. But besides line there is also color. In decorating a room, unless one wants the room to be either chaos or a museum, one must be quite certain of one's color-scheme. So also in dress. The harmony of color must be clearly settled. If one is small the simplicity of one color has many advantages. If one is taller two colors or three may be used. I do not wish to give a purely arithmetical basis for an aesthetic question, but perhaps three shades of color are the limit. At any rate it should be remembered that in looking at any beautifully dressed person, the eye should be attracted by the loveliness of line and proportion, and the dress should appear a complete harmony from the head to the feet; and that the sudden appearance of any violent contrasting color, in bow or riband, distracts the eye from the dignity of the *ensemble,* and concentrates it on a mere detail. Then as regards the kind of colors, I should like to state once for all that there is no such thing as a specially artistic color. All good colors are equally beautiful; it is only in the question of their combination that art comes in. And one should have no more preference for one color over another than one has for one note on the piano over its neighbor. Nor are there any sad colors. There are bad colors, such as Albert blue, and magenta, and arsenic green, and the colors of aniline dyes generally, but a good color always gives one pleasure. And the tertiary and secondary colors are for general use the safest, as they do not show wear easily, and besides give one a sense of repose and quiet. A dress should not be like a steam-whistle, for all that M. Worth may say.

Then as regards pattern. It should not be too definite. A strongly marked check, for instance, has many disadvantages. To begin with, it makes the slightest inequality in the figure, such as between the two shoulders, very apparent; then it is difficult to join the pattern accurately at the seam; and lastly, it distracts the eye away from the proportions of the figure, and gives the mere details an abnormal importance.

Then, again, the pattern should not be too big. I mention this, because I happened lately in London to be looking for some stamped gray plush or velvet, suitable for making a cloak of. Every shop that I

went into the man showed me the most enormous patterns, things far
too big for an ordinary wall paper, far too big for ordinary curtains,
things, in fact, that would require a large public building to show
them off to any advantage. I entreated the shopman to show me a
pattern that would be in some rational and relative proportion to the
figure of somebody who was not over ten or twelve feet in height. He
replied that he was extremely sorry but that it was impossible; the
smaller patterns were no longer being woven, in fact the big patterns
were the fashion. Now when he said the word fashion, he mentioned
what is the great enemy of art in this century, as in all centuries.
Fashion rests upon folly, Art rests upon law. Fashion is ephemeral.
Art is eternal. Indeed what is fashion really? A fashion is merely a
form of ugliness so absolutely unbearable that we have to alter it
every six months! It is quite clear that were it beautiful and rational
we would not alter anything that combined these two rare qualities.
And wherever dress has been so, it has remained unchanged in law
and principle for many hundred years. And if any of my practical
friends in the States refuse to recognize the value of the permanence
of artistic laws, I am quite ready to rest the point entirely on an
economic basis. The amount of money that is spent every year in
America on dress is something almost fabulous. I have no desire to
weary my readers with statistics, but if I were to state the sum that is
spent yearly on bonnets alone, I am sure that one-half of the
community would be filled with remorse and the other half with
despair! So I will content myself with saying that it is something quite
out of pro-portion to the splendor of modern dress, and that its reason
must be looked for, not in the magnificence of the apparel, but rather
in that unhealthy necessity for change which Fashion imposes on its
beautiful and misguided votaries.

I am told, and I am afraid that I believe it, that if a person has
recklessly invested in what is called "the latest Paris bonnet," and
worn it to the rage and jealousy of the neighborhood for a fortnight,
her dearest friend is quite certain to call upon her, and to mention
incidentally that that particular kind of bonnet has gone entirely out
of fashion. Consequently a new bonnet has at once to be bought, that
Fifth-ave. may be appeased, and more expense entered into. Whereas
were the laws of dress founded on art instead of on fashion, there
would be no necessity for this constant evolution of horror from
horror. What is beautiful looks always new and always delightful, and
can no more become old-fashioned than a flower can. Fashion, again,
is reckless of the individuality of her worshippers, cares nothing
whether they be tall or short, fair or dark, stately or slight, but bids
them all be attired exactly in the same way, until she can invent some
new wickedness. Whereas Art permits, nay even ordains to each, that

perfect liberty which comes from obedience to law, and which is something far better for humanity than the tyranny of tight lacing or the anarchy of aniline dyes.

And now as regards the cut of the dress.

The first and last rule is this, that each separate article of apparel is to be suspended from the shoulders always, and never from the waist. Nature, it should be noted, gives one no opportunity at all of suspending anything from the waist's delicate curve. Consequently by means of a tight corset a regular artificial ledge has to be produced, from which the lower garment may he securely hung. Where there are petticoats, there must be corsets. Annihilate the former and the latter disappear. And I have no hesitation in saying that whenever in history we find that dress has become absolutely monstrous and ugly, it has been partly of course through the mistaken idea that dress has an independent existence of its own, but partly also through the fashion of hanging the lower garments from the waist. In the sixteenth century, for instance, to give the necessary compression, Catharine de Medicis (*sic*), High-Priestess of poison and petticoats, invented a corset which may be regarded as the climax of a career of crime. It was made of steel, had a front and a back to it like the cuirass of a fire-brigade man, and was secured under the left arm by a hasp and pin, like a Saratoga trunk. Its object was to diminish the circumference of the waist to a circle of thirteen inches, which was the fashionable size without which a lady was not allowed to appear at court; and its influence on the health and beauty of the age may be estimated by the fact that the normal waist of a well-grown woman is an oval of twenty- six to twenty-eight inches certainly. As one bad habit always breeds another, in order to support the weight of the petticoats the fardingale (*sic*) was invented also. This was a huge structure, sometimes of wicker-work like a large clothes basket, sometimes of steel ribs, and extended on each side to such an extent that in the reign of Elizabeth an English lady in full dress took up quite as much room as we would give now to a very good sized political meeting. I need hardly point out what a selfish fashion this was, considering the limited surface of the globe. Then in the last century there was the hoop, and in this the crinoline. But, I will be told, ladies have long ago given up crinoline, hoop and fardingale. That is so. And I am sure we all feel very grateful to them. I certainly do. Still, does there not linger, even now, amongst us that dreadful, that wicked thing called the Dress-Improver? Is not that vilest of all diminutives, the crinolette, still to be seen? I am quite sure that none of my readers ever dream of wearing anything of the kind. But there may be others who are not so wise, and I wish it could be conveyed to them, delicately and courteously, that the hour-glass is not the ideal of Form. Often a modern dress begins extremely well. From the neck to the waist the lines of the dress itself follow out with more or less completeness the lines of the figure; but the lower part of the costume become bell-shaped and heavy, and breaks out into a series of harsh angles and coarse curves. Whereas if from the shoulders, and the shoulders only, each separate article were hung, there would be then no necessity for any artificial supports of the kind I have alluded to, and tight lacing could be done away with. If some support is considered necessary, as it often is, a broad woollen band, or band of elastic webbing, held up by shoulder straps, will be found quite sufficient.

So much on the cut of the dress, now for its decoration.

The French milliner passes a lurid and lucrative existence in sewing on bows where there should be no bows, and flounces where there should be no flounces. But, alas! his industry is in vain. For all ready-made ornamentation merely makes a dress ugly to look at and cumbersome to wear. The beauty of dress, as the beauty of life, comes always from freedom. At every moment a dress should respond to the play of the girl who wears it, and exquisitely echo the melody of each movement and each gesture's grace. Its loveliness is to be sought for in the delicate play of light and line in dainty rippling folds, and not in the useless ugliness and ugly uselessness of a stiff and stereotyped decoration. It is true that in many of the latest Paris dresses which I have seen there seems to be some recognition of the value of folds. But unfortunately the folds are all artificially made and sewn down, and so their charm is entirely destroyed. For a fold in a dress is not a fact, an item to be entered in a bill, but a certain effect of light and shade which is only exquisite because it is evanescent. Indeed one might just as well paint a shadow on a dress as sew a fold down on one. And the chief reason that a modern dress wears such a short time is that it cannot be smoothed out, as a dress should be, when it is laid aside in the wardrobe. In fact in a fashionable dress there is far too much "shaping"; the very wealthy of course will not care, but it is worth while to remind those who are not millionaires that the more seams the more shabbiness. A well-made dress should last almost as long as a shawl, and if it is well made it does. And what I mean by a well-made dress is a simple dress that hangs from the shoulders, that takes its shape from the figure and its folds from the movements of the girl who wears it, and what I mean by a badly made dress is an elaborate structure of heterogeneous materials, which having been first cut to pieces with the shears, and then sewn together by the machine, are ultimately so covered with frills and bows and flounces as to become execrable to look at, expensive to pay for, and absolutely useless to wear.

Well, these are the principles of Dress. And probably it will be said that all these principles might be carried out to perfection, and yet no definite style be the result. Quite so. With a definite style, in the sense of a historical style, we have nothing whatsoever to do. There must be no attempt to revive an ancient mode of apparel simply because it is ancient, or to turn life into that chaos of costume, the Fancy Dress Ball. We start, not from History, but from the proportions of the human form. Our aim is not archaeological accuracy, but the highest possible amount of freedom with the most equable distribution of warmth. And the question of warmth brings me to my last point. It has sometimes been said to me, not by the Philistine merely but by artistic people who are really interested in the possibility of a beautiful dress, that the cold climate of Northern countries necessitates our wearing so many garments, one over the other, that it is quite impossible for dress to follow out or express the lines of the figure at all. This objection, however. which at first sight may seem to be a reasonable one, is in reality founded on a wrong idea, on the idea in fact, that the warmth of apparel depends on the number of garments worn. Now the weight of apparel depends very much on the number of garments worn, but the warmth or (*sic*) apparel depends entirely on the material of which those garments are made. And one of the chief errors in modern costume comes from the particular material which is always selected as the basis for dress. We have always used linen, whereas the proper material is wool.

Wool, to begin with, is a non-conductor of heat. That means that in the summer the violent heat of the sun does not enter and scorch the body, and that the body in winter remains at its normal natural temperature, and does not waste its vital warmth on the air. Those of my readers who play lawn tennis and like out-door sports know that, if they wear a complete flannel suit, they are perfectly cool on the hottest day, and perfectly warm when the day is cold. All that I claim is that the same laws which are clearly recognized on the tennis ground, flannel being a woollen texture, should be recognized also as being equally suitable for the dress of people who live in towns, and whose lives are often necessarily sedentary. There are many other qualities in wool, such as its being an absorber and distributor of moisture, with regard to which I would like to refer my readers to a little hand-book on "Health Culture," by Dr. Jaeger, the Professor of Physiology at Stuttgart. Dr. Jaeger does not enter into the question of form or beauty, at least when he does he hardly seems to me very successful, but on the sanitary values of different textures and colors he speaks of course with authority, and from a combination of the principles of science with the laws of art will come, I feel sure, the costume of the future. For if wool is selected as the basis and chief material of dress, far fewer garments may be worn than at present, with the result of immensely increased warmth and much greater lightness and comfort. Wool also has the advantage of being almost the most delicate texture woven. Silk is often coarse compared to it, being at once harder and colder. A large Cashmere shawl of pure wool can be drawn through a tiny ring, indeed by this method do the shawl-sellers of the Eastern bazaar show to one the fineness of their goods. Wool, again, shows no creases. I should he sorry to see such a lovely texture as satin disappear from modern dress, but every lady who wears anything of the kind knows but too well how easily it crumples; besides it is better to wear a soft than a hard material, for in the latter there is always a danger of harsh and coarse lines, whereas in the former you get the most exquisite delicacy of fold.

We find, then, that on the question of material Science and Art are one. And as regards the milliners' method of dress I would like to make one last observation. Their whole system is not merely ugly but useless. It is of no avail that a stately lady pinches in her waist in order to look slight. For size is a question of proportion. And an unnaturally small waist merely makes the shoulders look abnormally broad and heavy. The high heel, again, by placing the foot at a sharp angle bends the figure forward, and thus so far from giving any additional height, robs it of at least an inch and a half. People who can't stand straight must not imagine that they look tall. Nor does the wearing of a lofty headdress improve the matter. Its effect is merely to make the head disproportionately large. A dwarf three feet high with a hat of six cubits on his head will look a dwarf three feet high to the end. Indeed height is to be measured more by the position of the eyes and the shoulders than by anything else. And particular care should be taken not to make the head too large. Its perfect proportion is one-eighth of the whole figure. ...

But I know that, irrespective of Congress, the women of America can carry any reform they like. And I feel certain that they will not continue much longer to encourage a style of dress which is founded on the idea that the human figure is deformed and requires the devices of the milliner to be made presentable. For have they not the most delicate and dainty hands and feet in the world? Have they not complexions like ivory stained with a rose-leaf? Are they not always in office in their own country, and do they not spread havoc through Europe? *Appella, non ad Caesarem, sed ad Caesaris uxorem.*[43]

OSCAR WILDE

The Value of Art in Modern Life

Introduction

THIS APPENDIX gives the text of this lecture as delivered in 1885. It is based upon the Dublin reviews (*Freeman's Journal and Daily Commercial Advertiser* Wednesday, January 7, 1885) with additions from Brighton, Edinburgh and Stoke. I have also reviewed the report published in the Appendix of Sherard's *The Life of Oscar Wilde*.

The Value of Art in Modern Life

I DO not desire to give any abstract definition of the word beauty, even if I was able, because I think we can get on very well without philosophy of that kind.[1] We only need to learn how to surround ourselves and our children with beautiful things.[2] I want to point out what were some of the tendencies of art, and what were some of the qualities you should look for in any beautiful thing.

I rather fancy that those who have cared to watch the artistic revolution of the last few years in this country and elsewhere will have seen that there had been a strong development of artistic feeling and artistic beauty in the internal arrangements and furnishing of our houses, not alone of the wealthy but of all classes. There was a better perception of form and colour, and a greater sense of harmony ran through every room.[3] Certain old ornaments had disappeared. The wax peach no longer ceased to ripen under its glass shade; the horse-hair sofa no longer glared at one from the window and other cumbrous and useless furniture had been more and more laid aside. Even some limits had been placed upon antimacassars.[4] There was a sense that art could touch the very commonest things of life with beauty, and quicken them into loveliness. There was nothing so common that art could not make a treasure.

[Several venues — e.g. Stoke, Bristol, Burnley, Nottingham — then continued: 'But whilst there was this improvement in the household, the costume of the people remained entirely unchanged …' and Wilde then gave the complete lecture on *Dress*…]

I will endeavour to show the scientific basis of that movement. Modern science taught that every organism, whether plant or animal, sought its proper environment. There was no reason why mankind should not seek for theirs. Plato in his *Republic*[5] taught that children should be brought up in the midst of all fair sights and sounds, so that the soul might be brought naturally into harmony with all that was beautiful and good, and made to reject all that was evil and ugly.[6] In this way we would put ourselves in tune with art. The idea was to make the soul and body in perfect harmony with the external world and my aim is to show that the power of adequately appreciating objects of beauty, whether in Nature or in Art,[7] constituted the chief of human pleasures. Formerly, abstract definitions of the beautiful were aimed at, but the artistic temperament was better developed by beautiful surroundings,[8] which teach by giving a perception of every type of beauty.

I am not sure that the real meaning of art was understood. Beauty was organic, that was, it came from within, not from without, not from added prettiness,[9] but from the perfection of its own being. Most people imagined that it was in some way synonymous with ornamentation, but ornamentation was merely a branch of art. True ornamentation consisted in the purgation of all superfluities.[10] Art was primarily a question of construction, next, of adaptability to a purpose, and lastly, of proportion. A thing might be a perfect work of art without being ornamental at all, and some of the most beautiful things were entirely without ornament. Within the last few years ornamentation had become an enemy of art. A mistake made in schools was in not distinguishing from the ornament and the thing to be ornamented. The best kind of ornament was that suggested by the method of construction or by the material used.

In the house one should always begin by having useful things beautiful.[11] But I have found that all ugly things were made by those who strove to make something beautiful, and all the beautiful things by those who strove to make something useful. An example of this, which I would condemn, was that the exquisite symmetry and proportions of articles sent out from our modern potteries should so often be spoiled by over ornamentation: soup plates with sunsets, covered with meaningless landscapes or sprawling flowers.[12] I strongly deprecate having articles supplied with inappropriate embellishments, and for that reason I would condemn the practice of ornamenting coal scuttles with landscapes[13] and the elegantly decorated wheelbarrow or trowel, as usually presented to persons in performing the inauguration of certain public ceremonies, as monstrosities. Another thing which hindered artistic development was the wrong use of materials. You can see looking glasses framed in plush and painted with flowers. Plush was chiefly good for the delicate folds that it afforded, and the merit of a looking-glass was that it reflected its object. Both these effects were lost in such frames, yet the manufacturers said the public would not buy the things unless they were covered with ornament.

It was very rarely that anyone could decorate a thing well which they had not themselves made, and I would point out how in the East, unlike the system adopted here, the two operations were combined in the one workman. Bad ornamentation had arisen from the separation of the function of the artist and the workman. Ornament should never for a moment disturb outline and proportion, nor should it add to the apparent weight of anything.

What is, exactly, the value of nature and works of nature as regards art?[14] The highest artistic works are not those which absolutely imitated nature. Nature was beautiful in its exquisite details and in the pageantry of its changing moods. Nature was its own ideal but she was to the artist the purely rough material.[15] As regarded art, nature was not the ideal for the artist, for the moment he tried to imitate it he must fall short of perfection:[16] the artist should rather take suggestions from nature. All bad art arose from nature being taken as the ideal for art: nature was the rough material from which art selected.[17] Look at the examples of old Celtic art, and at Persian, Hindu, and other Oriental arts in their general characteristics. In old Celtic art there was no imitation of a single object in nature. The prohibition in the Koran of the imitation of natural objects led to an exceedingly fine school of Mahommedan decorative art. These all dealt in exquisite lines, beautiful proportions, and lovely masses of colour.[18]

Therefore, Art was not a mere imitation of natural objects which, however cleverly done, might be of very little value so far as art was concerned. With regard to art schools, the pupil might draw accurately a bird on the wing, or a flower on the spray, and yet be perfectly incapable of applying the ornament of decoration and making it something which served the principle of art. Art training must be founded on the principles which underlie decoration, and on making natural objects fit into that decoration.[19] Decorative art, like music, depended absolutely on certain laws: on laws of alternation, symmetry, and series, corresponding more or less to melody in music, on laws of repetition and mass corresponding to harmony. Until the student had completely mastered every one of the laws of decoration, whatever his imitative powers in drawing or in painting might be, they were of very little value.

With regard to materials, when wood was used, curves should be avoided. The curved furniture of the Louis Quatorze[20] period was invariably gilt, so as to look like metal. In modern English furniture they saw the mahogany writhing into all sorts of shapes, giving a sense of insecurity and heaviness.

But should not art be national? I feel obliged to say no. Art was entirely universal, and to talk of national art was as foolish as to speak of national mathematics. Mathematics was the science of truth, and art was the science of the beautiful.[21] Both were founded on natural laws of universal application. There was a certain side of nationality which might have its place in art, I mean in the selection of the particular details which might exemplify the rule of decorative ornament. The Greeks made a certain use of the honeysuckle in the ornamentation of their buildings but now, provided the principles of decoration were adhered to, any other flower would do as well.

In furnishing one's house one should begin by having useful things, and then, if means permitted, lovely, ideal things for the delight they gave to look at them. As a rule, however, in the modern room they would sometimes find a preponderance of things that were of no use whatsoever, but simply encumbrances, and very rarely added to the beauty of the apartment.[22] You should not furnish your houses as if you wanted to please a professor of history.

If I was asked for a definition of what a really beautiful thing was, I am sure that my answer would be: such an object as would harmonise with all other beautiful objects, no matter of what century or nation. These objects would be in agreement because they expressed the same laws. Between examples of ancient Irish art and examples from the Alhambra, or from Oriental mosques of the Byzantine period, there would, therefore, be no discord.[23] One could select from all these, and the best furnished house would be the one which could not be absolutely localised as regarded forms of art. Everything should be in proportion as to colour and form, and a mere spirit of archaeology should not prevail.[24]

Why was this movement called "aesthetic?"[25] There was a deeper sense in that word than the merely beautiful. In past ages decorative art was symbolic and expressive of ideas, as instanced in ancient Greece. Afterwards art developed from the simply expressive to the simply impressive, and consequently became aesthetic.[26] In the period of the Renaissance Italian decorative art took the same direction. Symbolism had a tendency to putrefaction and to the stoppage of growth: on the other hand, when the aesthetic impulse came into play, there was a constant growth and admission of new fight. When art was healthy it was constantly changing in its details. We should try to get rid of the symbolic meaning in art and have the pure thing which gave joy and delight. To us in the nineteenth century the aesthetic side of art had more application than the symbolic. Anciently symbolism was a means of conveying ideas in morals, religion, and philosophy; but since printing the enormous increase of books had almost put an end to that function, and ornamentation now mainly appealed to the eye and thereby a greater amount of beauty was attained.

I might be thought to be limiting the sphere of art, but modern painters were too much in the habit of taking subjects from history and literature,[27] and of resorting to symbolism. Before this era, painting was more used as a means of intellectual expression, for the purpose of telling some story. But in this direction I would point out that the painter was unable to compare with the writer in telling a story or pointing a moral.[28] From this I would argue that it should be the aim of the painter to deal with what the writer was less able to deal with, to take the picturesque side of life and reproduce bits of life and scenery under certain conditions of loveliness. In the Royal Academy the majority of the pictures were illustrations of English history or subjects of domestic pathos or domestic sentiment. But I feel that there was no need for the painter to illustrate literary works in this manner: his subject ought merely to be what was given to him by his eye, but not by casting his eye over a dictionary.[29]

We should be careful to go to art, the highest kind of beauty, in order that we might derive from it the highest kind of joy.[30]

Decorative art was to be distinguished from imaginative art. Decorative art emphasised its material and made it more beautiful than before. Imaginative art annihilated its material: they did not regard the canvas of a picture or the stone of a piece of sculpture.[31] Again, they could place a piece of decorative art where they liked, but they could not do so with a picture. They had to hang the picture where they could see it under certain conditions of light and shade.[32] Decorative art depended largely on traditions, whereas the art of the picture or the statue was purely individual. Decorative art was purely impressive, like music. They did not ask what a piece of music meant, but how it affected them.[33] But imaginative art expressed not merely the facts of nature but the wonderful power of the hand and eye of the artist.

The training and culture of the eye, upon which modern painting greatly depended, was usually overlooked. In the great masters' pictures for the past two or three hundred years they were not struck with the picture being cleverly painted, but thought how wonderful it was there should have been a man who looked at life with such marvellous eyes. You will have heard of the lady who once went to Turner's[34] studio and, looking at his sunset sketches, said:

> "They are charming, Mr. Turner. I have never seen a sunset of that kind."
> "Ah, madam," said the artist, "don't you wish you could?"

I regret that in many modern schools of art young students were taught a sort of cleverness that could be achieved by mere manual dexterity and precision. But so far as the art that could be obtained in this way was concerned, I think that most people were on the same level. It was rather the eye that should be trained to see the beautiful.[35] The artist was not distinguished from his compeers by any cleverness in drawing or technique. What chiefly constituted the artist was his power of vision, by his power of looking on life and seeing in it new and delightful conditions and by his ability to reproduce it under specially picturesque conditions.[36]

An increased sense of technical excellence was to be greeted with feelings of mingled pleasure and hope by all interested in modern art. Art should be easy, natural and graceful, as the blossom of the rose tree, but that must, of course, be preceded by a great amount of technical work. Art should be healthy and joyous. Health was the right use of the material according to the virtue and essence which that material possessed. There should be no direct difference between the subject and its treatment, but in the higher art, as in music, they should blend. No work was finished until all signs of the means by which it had been produced had entirely disappeared.[37]

I think that in art schools here there was too much use of hard outline and that students commenced their studies with a hard pointed pencil. This was his ruin from an artistic point of view, as it destroyed his power of giving that exquisite delicacy of outline and softness, such, for instance, as characterised Japanese work. The Japanese artists did better by teaching their students to use a soft brush, and also by making them paint from the shoulder without any rest for the wrist.

In landscape painting[38] the true artist regarded the landscape as the composer or the musician did the whole range of keys on his instrument. He knew they were equally beautiful, that certain combinations of notes would harmonise[39], and that certain selections would make up his composition. It was the power of selection and rejection which formed the musician as it formed the artist. Looking at the landscape he would not aim to give every detail in it: he would pass over things which others would notice in order to emphasise the beauty of the few things he noticed himself. A great landscape painter was remarkable by what he left out as well as put in.[40]

But, besides the beauty of fact, there was with them the beauty of effect.[41] The Dutch school of artists were the first to discover that ugly objects might be made beautiful.[42] In the case of many modern young painters, there was to be observed a sort of wilful blindness to the marvellous power that light and shade had of transfiguring the very ugliest and commonplacest of things. Velasquez[43] was remarkable, not for the beauty of his works, but for being capable of producing by far the finest portraits that had ever been painted in the history of the world, though they were not those of beautiful people.

There was no object in life so hideous that it might not become beautiful under certain atmospheric or other conditions of light and shade.[44] What the artist should do was to watch for the moment when indifferent objects became thus transformed, had an artistic moment that turned it into a form of beauty, which it was for the artist to crystallize and make eternal.[45]

[In Edinburgh, December 1884, it was reported that Wilde gave: 'a long disquisition on Corot and the Impressionist school of painters, condemning realism strongly'. Unfortunately, no other details were given.][46]

Many an excellent artist has been ruined by the assumption on the part of the public that his style was confined to that of the particular picture with which he happened to achieve success. At a London exhibition a young artist gained great *éclat* by a picture in which he introduced in the foreground three silver birch trees. For a while afterwards the public would have nothing but silver birch trees. The artist wisely remonstrated against this, and painted a picture with trees of a different kind, which he exhibited, and was informed by a dealer that a gentleman was ready to pay him his own price for it if only he would put in the foreground three silver birches.

I consider the growing specialism of the present day is detrimental to the progress of Art. There was a tendency in young painters to narrow themselves down to pure specialism: one man would perhaps paint Scotch cattle in an English mist all his lifetime, whilst his neighbour would possibly devote his professional abilities throughout his career to the painting of English cattle in a Scotch mist.[47] This was a mistake. The great artists had no signs of specialism: they could paint anything they saw.[48] Of this specialism which was doing so much harm in this country, they would find no traces in the works of Mr. Whistler[49] — whose works were much misunderstood — no traces of narrowness of vision. Mr. Whistler possessed every one of the conditions which a true painter ought to have. He is the painter who had most completely separated himself from any literary feeling, one whose pictures I would praise as little points of modern life caught under new and exquisite conditions.[50]

I would compare the beauty of these paintings with some of Robert Browning's poems[51] and to the symphony and, like music, their form, expression, and subject must be regarded not separately but in their entirety.[52] Mr. Whistler had rejected all literary titles for his pictures: indeed, none of his works bore any name but that which signified their tone, and colour, and method of treatment. This, of course, was what painting ought to be, no man ought to show that he was merely the illustrator of history. Even the accusations made by some persons against Mr. Whistler's pictures, that they "looked just as well upside down," only meant, in my opinion, that the simple splendour of their effect was the same whichever way one looked at them.[53]

I ask you, have you any example of Mr. Whistler's pictures? I hope you will have some — in order that you may be able to see the works of a man who represents the highest perfection of modern art, not only in England, but possibly in the world — a man to whom modern painting owes more than it does to any other man, and who expresses in his work every single theory of modern art that we might find expressed or symbolised in any modern art movement.[54]

The practice of decorative art ennobled labour, and contained within itself an enormous store of economic wealth, owing to the extent to which the value of material was enhanced by the work of the artist. It was always possible for a nation, by artistic power, to give to the commonest material vastly increased value.

[In Dublin Wilde continued: 'There was no reason why we in Ireland should not do this. There was in all the Celtic races this power of decoration. Whether you viewed the remains of ancient art in the Royal Irish Academy or in the museums of northern Europe, you would be struck by the far greater sense of beauty evinced in the early Celtic work[55] than in old English art, which was deficient in delicacy and sense of proportion. And there was no reason why you should not show that those perceptions of the beautiful, and capacities of delicate handling as to hue and colour, were not dead.']

In modern writing many claims were made for art to be a teacher. I regard Mr. Ruskin[56] as one of the greatest men that England had produced in any century. He was the master of the secret of noble living as well as of the wisdom of many spiritual things, but I could not say that I was able to agree with him in his art criticism,[57] because he was always symbolical, and estimated a picture by the number of noble and moral ideas that he found contained in it.

But the universality of art was as a method of making the world more intelligible and lovely to us.[58] I would especially point out that the purpose of the painter was to give us eyes and show us that under certain conditions modern life may become lovely. True art dealt with the effect of loveliness, and not with the mere facts of ordinary life.[59] The channels by which all fine, imaginative work could reach or touch the soul were questions purely of the vision of the artist, the loveliness of his colour, his use of light and shade, and the whole harmony of his composition.[60]

The Mission of Art in the Nineteenth Century

*T*HE *Mission of Art in the Nineteenth Century* as a lecture is first recorded in the UK in the autumn of 1885, as a subtitle for Wilde's older lecture, *The House Beautiful*. Thereafter, *The House Beautiful* is dropped from the title. In the closing section of *The House Beautiful* Wilde had said:

> The mission of art was very simple. It had no elaborate philosophy about it. It merely claimed to bring into the life of every one of us a little joy, to touch the fleeting hours of day and make them gracious.[1]

Surprisingly, then, in January 1886 in the south-west of England, *The Mission of Art in the Nineteenth Century* occurs but now as a subtitle for what had become Wilde's famous lecture, *Dress*.

It is not, though, the first reference to this lecture. In Wilde's piece for the *Century Guild Hobby Horse*, in July 1886, he wrote:[2]

> During my tour in America I happened one evening to find myself in Louisville, Kentucky. The subject I had selected to speak on was the *Mission of Art in the Nineteenth Century*, and in the course of my lecture I had occasion to quote Keats's *Sonnet on Blue* as an example of the poet's delicate sense of colour-harmonies.

Interestingly, the website of the 1882 American lecture tour[3] shows this lecture to have been *The English Renaissance of Art* which does have several references to Keats and his importance for art in England.

The reviews of this lecture in the UK are so fragmentary that I give here just those references rather than any attempt to recreate an entire lecture.

The Pall Mall Gazette Saturday, 17 October, 1885

MR. OSCAR WILDE'S reputation would be gone if it became known that he had ever uttered a single speech without a word of nonsense in it. Hence his assertion that "ugliness was first introduced into art when the first bust or portrait of a man was shown" may be regarded simply as a saving clause, a sort of trade mark, like the clown's "Here we are again!" Otherwise his little speech at the Westminster Town Hall last night was full of good sense. His vindication of the aspects of beauty in commonplace city life — even in a hoarding of picture posters – came in aptly, though to most people it is something of a truism. More novel though not less true is his protest against the growing practice of building houses higher than the street they are in is wide. "Northumberland-avenue,"[4] he said, "was being rapidly destroyed, the abnormal height robbing the architecture of the play of sunlight, which was one of the chief beauties of any fine building." From a sanitary as well as an æsthetic point of view this principle deserves to be kept in mind. The Roman proverb that where the sun does not enter the doctor does, holds good elsewhere than in Rome. The cavernous *calli* and *strade* of Genoa and Naples pay for their picturesqueness in their cholera returns, and as constructions like Northumberland-avenue become common, they, and especially the back streets around them, may possibly develop the tendency to cholera without the picturesqueness.

Illustrated Police News Saturday, 31 October 1885

MR. OSCAR WILDE is a gentleman blessed with a much stronger imagination than the rest of his fellow-creatures, but we must confess that we are astonished to find that even he can see beauty in posting bills.[5] He is reported to have said that "in the silver of the morning and the gold of the evening," even these hideous monuments of our modern rage for advertising sometimes "becomes as fantastic in colouring and as delightful as a Japanese fan." If Mr. Oscar Wilde will go to Sheffield once again we feel sure they can gratify him to his heart's delight. No town in the provinces could show such a hideous variety of the bill-sticking art as that which may be seen from New Pinstone-street. Even the metropolis itself would have a difficulty in finding such a concentrated display of paper and paste. It may show lack of imagination on our part, but we certainly cannot find one redeeming feature in the flaming posters, and should be devoutly thankful if the Government would follow the example of the Belgian rulers, and impose a tax upon them.

Tyneside Echo **Wednesday, 11 November 1885**

MR OSCAR WILDE the son of the 'Speranza' of young Ireland fame is great on aesthetic definition. In the course of an interesting if not particularly novel lecture in Newcastle last night he spoke of the definition of beauty given by Michaelangelo 'the purgation of all superfluities.'[6] This the lecturer explained - and many needed an explanation - meant that the thing of beauty had been stripped of all parts which were not required of its perfection and had still not been deprived of any necessary point! Exactly...

APPENDIX G

Chatterton
Essay and Lecture

THE TRANSCRIPT which follows these introductory remarks is taken from the *Essay on Chatterton* held in the William Andrews Clark Memorial Library at University of California, Los Angeles[1]. I am grateful to Merlin Holland for his permission to publish this material and for the help of staff at the library, at Cengage, Gale Group and at the British Library. It is an important and intriguing piece of work and is published here because, although it began as an essay for the *Century Guild Hobby Horse*, it was then abandoned as an essay and used by Wilde as a supporting text for his lecture *Chatterton*.

A few notes on how the text is presented:

All ordinary text reproduces the pages Wilde has cut out of two biographies of Chatterton:
Chatterton: A Biographical Study by Daniel Wilson
Chatterton: A Story of the Year 1770 by David Masson.

All bold text is Wilde's own manuscript.

All bold italic text is Wilde's manuscript copy of text from the biographies.

[illegible] indicates a doubtful word or phrase; sometimes I make a suggestion.

A Transcription of Wilde's Essay on Chatterton

Previous lectures

Romantic movement –
    first in <u>poetry</u>
    Chatterton – Coleridge – Keats[2]

<u>**Language**</u> **– expression. Instrument of technical process precedes arts.**

<u>**Emerson**</u>   **A man is only half himself, The other half is his <u>expression</u>.**
he reveres men of genius because they are more himself than he is.[3]

Son of a poor widow – a boy – who began to write at 12 — and died at 17 — matured genius.

And greet with smiles the young-eyed Poesy
All deftly masked as hoar antiquity[4]

[5]<u>Chatterton.</u>

The conditions that precede artistic production are so constantly treated as qualities of works of art that one is sometimes tempted to wish that all art were anonymous.[6] For every true artist even the portrait painter or dramatist, be his work absolutely objective in presentation, still reveals himself in his manner. Even abstract forms such as music and colour have much to tell us about the nature of him who fashioned them, and take the place of the biographer. Indeed in some cases it is almost better for us not to search too curiously into the details of the artists life. The <u>incompleteness</u> of Keats' life for instance blinds many of his critics to the <u>perfection</u> of his song — and it is well on the whole that we know so little about Shakespeare.

  Mr. Mathew Arnold[7] has so well expressed in verse what I am trying to convey in prose that I venture to quote from his sonnet to Shakespeare:[8]

Others abide our question. Thou art free.
We ask and ask — Thou smilest and art still,
Out-topping knowledge. For the loftiest hill,
Who to the stars uncrowns his majesty,
Planting his steadfast footsteps in the sea,
Making the heaven of heavens his dwelling-place,
Spares but the cloudy border of his base
To the foil'd searching of mortality;

And thou, who didst the stars and sunbeams know,
Self-school'd, self-scann'd, self-honour'd, self-secure,
Didst tread on earth unguess'd at. — Better so!

All pains the immortal spirit must endure,
All weakness which impairs, all griefs which bow,
Find their sole speech in that victorious brow.

Yet there are cases where the nature of the artist is so bound up with the nature of the man, that art criticism must take account of history and physiology in order to understand the work of art. And this is specially so in the case of Chatterton — without a full comprehension of his life the secret of his literature is not revealed. And so in going over the details of the life of this marvellous boy[9] I do so not to mar the perfect joy and loveliness of his song by any overemphasis of the tragedy of his death, but simply to enable us to understand the curious form he used, and to appreciate an art that to many may seem an anachronism.

Bristol   city built by merchants — Cathedral.

Thomas Chatterton, the father of the Romantic movement in literature, the precursor of Blake,[10] Coleridge and Keats, the greatest poet of his time, was born on the 20th November 1752 in the house adjoining the Pyle Street School in Bristol. The house is still standing. A posthumous child – his father having died three months previously. His father not the sexton — though that office for some centuries had been hereditary in his family.

Character of his father[11] - a subchorister in the cathedral — fond of music and wrote glees — fond of poetry — of magic — deeply read in Cornelius Agrippa[12] — an antiquarian — collector Roman coins. Dissipater and reckless Bohemian - *an old relative said of him*

he talked little, was very absent in company, and used often to walk by the river side, talking to himself, and flourishing his arms about

His mother[13] gentle and kindly — married at 18. Was just of age at birth of her son — described by an old servant of her daughter *as* "attering"[14] *a word used in the north of Scotland as equivalent to fretful.*
Eccentricity of the father became genius in the son, from his mother he inherited his nervous temperament

Not a precocious child

  "dull in learning, not knowing many letters at four years old"

At five he was sent back from the Pyle Street School as an incorrigible dunce – To *Cromek*,[15] *a London engraver, we owe the preservation of many details about him — especially for the information derived from Mrs. Edkins.*

She appears to have resided with Mrs. Chatterton, assisting her as a sempstress, and thus enjoyed the most favourable opportunities for studying the disposition and habits of the boy. She was present at his birth, and was wont to speak of him tenderly as her foster-child. "Many," says she, "were the uneasinesses that his singularities cost his mother; and until he was six years and a half old, they thought he was an absolute fool." But this hasty conclusion seems to have been mainly based on his distaste for the rudimentary studies of a child's schooling. One of his sister's earliest remembrances of him was his "thirst for preeminence. Before he was five years old he would always preside over his playmates as their master, and they his hired servants." His foster-mother also states: he was so ingenious when a child, that if anything got out of order he was always set to mend it, and generally succeeded, to the admiration of his mother; when older, his ingenuity in the mechanic arts was surprising, and he used to observe that a man might do anything he chose. His mother, however, considered him in general as stupid, because, when quite a child, he would sit alone crying for hours, nobody knew what for. Once when he was in one of his silent moods, she said, "When will this stupidity cease?" and Mrs. Edkins added to rouse him, "I wish your father was alive, he would manage you;" at which, starting, he replied, "I wish he was!" uttering a deep sigh, and spoke no more for a long time.

These strange musings, which ere long were the precursors of his poetical activity, were incomprehensible to those among whom he moved, and only excited suspicion, or doubt of his sanity. His mother said, "He had cost her many uneasy hours, from the apprehension she entertained of his going mad; as he was accustomed to remain fixed for above an hour at a time quite motionless, and then he would snatch up a pen and write incessantly." What he did write, after such prolonged reveries, does not seem to have excited any curiosity.

Plato[16]

The secret of the seemingly dull nature of this boy is that he was influence by externals. Things of sense became fraught with a spiritual meaning for him. His love of colour induced him to learn to read. The illumination of an old French M.S.S. of Music fascinates him — also a black letter Bible — born in a classical age cradled in mediaevalisms — From this began to [improve?] *"At eight years of*

age so eager for books that he read from the moment he waked which was early until he went to bed, if they would let him.

His delight was to lock himself up in his little attic, with his books, papers, and drawing materials. He appears to have had an intuitive taste for drawing, as for so much else that was strange for his years; and there also, before long, he is found with his parchments, great piece of ochre in a brown pan, pounce bags full of charcoal dust, which he had from a Miss Sanger, a neighbour; also a bottle of black-lead powder, which they once took to clean the stove with, and made him very angry." So at length his mother carried off the key, lest he should hurt his health in this dusty old garret, from whence, after long abstinence, he was wont to emerge, begrimed with the traces of his antiquarian handicraft. Thus excluded from his favourite haunt, "he would come to Mrs. Edkins and kiss her cheek, and coax her to get it for him, using the most persuasive expressions to effect his end."

Appearance[17]

Two great influences of his childhood — St. Mary Redcliffe and the Canynge M.S.S.

St Mary Redcliffe one of the loveliest specimens of parochial architecture in England; and its elevated site on the "cliff" greatly adds to the effect of a building which has excited the admiration of successive generations. William of Worcester, Camden, Fuller,[18] and many another worthy of later centuries, have lavished their praises on its stately tower, richly groined and many-windowed avenues of nave, choir, transepts, and Lady Chapel. But when the child-poet yielded to its aesthetic influences, the taste for such memorials of ancient piety was at its lowest ebb. But the imaginative boy anticipated this medieval passion, and lived apart in an olden world of ideal perfection. "This wonder of mansyons," he exclaims, in one of his early utterances from behind the antique mask which he so speedily assumed, "was ybuildenne bie the nowe Mastre Canynge,[19] of whych need no oder to bie said botte see ytte and bee astonyed. Ytte was desyned bie Johne a Shaillinger, a Bristowe manne borne; who yn the sayde chyrche wyll shewe hys Reede for aye: each one pyllare stondynge as a letterre in hys blase."

This idea of fame reaching far into the coming time was strong within him even as a child; and it grew and took its strange shape as he made himself familiar with the ancient dwellers in Redcliffe Church: pondering over the beautiful altar-tomb of William Canynge and his wife Joan, or studying the quaint sculpture of the nameless occupant of an adjoining tomb, where the reputed purse-bearer of the old merchant and church-builder lies, with an angel supporting his head, and at his feet his dog with a huge bone in its paws. Near by a plain slab, decorated only with a large knife and strainer, records in antique characters a prayer for the soul of one faithful servitor, supposed to have been his cook; another slab, with incised cross, is dedicated to his reputed brewer; while on an adjoining altar-tomb reposes a nameless ecclesiastic commonly regarded as the same "riche merchant of Bristowe," in his later character as Dean of Westbury.

Thus on every hand the boy found that old generation reposing there in dignified contrast to the men of his own day. Nor was he wholly limited to Canynge and his times. Under the great window of the north transept lies the effigy of a mailed knight, cross-legged after the fashion of an old crusader: supposed to represent Robert de Berkeley, Lord of Bedminster and Redcliffe, whose armorial bearings, along with those of the Beauchamps, Montacutes, and other benefactors of the church, are sculptured on bosses in the north aisle of the nave. Other benefactors are commemorated in like heraldic fashion, in sculpture or painted glass; and in earlier times the windows were rich with the blazonry of the Cradocks, Sturtons, Says, Fitzwarrens, Rivers, and others, who claimed a share in the exequies and requiems for founders and benefactors. Everywhere walls and floor were enriched, as they still are, with graven brasses of ancient knights and dames, chief justices, and civic dignitaries, of the times of the Roses; judges and magnates of the Tudors and Stuarts; and on one of the pillars, the armour and banners of Admiral Sir William Penn, father of the more celebrated founder and legislator of Pennsylvania.

Such were the chosen associates of Chatterton's boyhood, in whose company many a pleasant hour was dreamt away, until that old past, with its knights, priests, and merchant princes, became for him the world of realities in which alone he willingly dwelt.

> So the foundations of his mind were laid.[20]
> In such communion, not from terror free,
> While yet a child, and long before his time,
> Had he perceived the presence and the power
> Of greatness; and deep feelings had impressed
> Great objects on his mind, with portraiture
> And colour so distinct, that on his mind
> They lay like substances, and almost seemed
> To haunt the bodily sense.

Of the church itself Chatterton wrote many lovely lines of which these are probably the best[21]

Thou seest this mastery of a human hand,
The pride of Bristowe and the western land;
Yet are the builder's virtues much more great,
Greater than can by Rowley's pen be scann'd.
Thou seest the saints and kings in stony state,
That seem with breath and human souls dispand;
As 'pared to us enseem these men of slate,
Such is great Canynge's mind when 'pared to God elate.

St. Mary Redcliffe forms, accordingly, the centre around which revolve all the quaint, fanciful, and richly poetic phases of the Rowley fiction. The hold it retained on his imagination repeatedly manifests itself even in his latest London correspondence; as in his letter to Cary, "Step into Redcliffe Church," he exclaims, "look at the noble arches, observe the symmetry, the regularity of the whole; how amazing must that idea be which can comprehend at once all that magnificence of architecture. Do not examine one particular beauty, or dwell upon it minutely; take the astonishing whole into your empty pericranium, and then think what the architect of that pile was in building, Allen is in music." When he wrote this he seemed to be absorbed in the excitement of London, and the politics of the day. But the moment his thoughts reverted to Bristol and its church, the old feelings revived. It was the cradle of his inspiration, and the cynosure of all his latest fancies. Within its charmed precincts he passed at will into another life, and his antique dreams became credible and true. In all his guisings and literary masquerades, the same antique realism predominates. He lives in the middle of that fifteenth century in which lived William Canynge as merchant, mayor, church-builder, priest, and dean; and revels in fancy amid the noble doings of this hero of his romantic dream. With this key to the plot, the Rowley manuscripts acquire a consistent unity, imperfect as they are.

And what are the Rowley manuscripts —

Over the north porch of St. Mary Redcliffe — rebuilt on the site of an earlier structure, and traditionally affirmed to have been completed at the cost of William Canynge, merchant, and mayor of Bristol in the reigns of Henry VI. and Edward IV[22] — there is a chamber, designated in ancient deeds the Treasury House, in which lay, deposited in six or seven oaken chests, the charters and titledeeds of the church, including documents of a still earlier date than the present noble edifice. Among those was one large, iron-bound coffer secured with six locks, designated in a deed of the fifteenth century, "William Canynge's chest in the treasury-house of the church of the Blessed Mary of Redcliffe." Such receptacles for the safekeeping of the holy vessels, vestments, charters, and service-books, are still common in old churches, and are frequently ornamented with iron scroll-work, or wrought in carved panelling. But Master Canynge's coffer was long guarded with peculiar jealousy, as in the days when it held the treasures of the old merchant. Two of its six keys were entrusted to the vicar and procurator of the church, two to the mayor, and one to each of the churchwardens: whereby it is no marvel that by and by they could nowhere be found. An impatient vestry wanted access to certain deeds; and so, about the year 1730 the locks, not only of Mr. Canynge's coffer, but of all the chests, were forced, the deeds relating to the church property removed, and the remaining papers and parchments exposed to neglect, because the vestry attorney could not read them, and they seemed valueless as title-deeds of any church estates.

The actual worth of the ancient documents to the ignorant custodians to whom they were now abandoned, was simply the material on which they were engrossed. The muniment room was accessible to the sexton and his family, and its contents were turned to account as mere waste paper. Some of the old documents were even employed to wipe the church candlesticks, and many more were carried off for equally vile uses. But the most unscrupulous plunderer was the old sexton's heir, Thomas Chatterton, father of the poet, who found he could turn them to account in various ways in the parish Free School. From time to time, accordingly, bundles of the parchments were removed; until at length, summoning to his aid a posse of the schoolboys, he carried off a large basketful, and deposited the spoils in a cupboard of the school-room for common use.

Primers and copy-books were thenceforth furnished with wrappers that would now be worth more than any volume they could cover. Twenty Bibles presented to the boys by the Vicar of St. Mary Redcliffe prior to 1744, were covered with the old parchments; and when the death of the schoolmaster necessitated his widow's removal from Pyle Street, in 1752, there still remained so large a stock that she emptied the school-room cupboard "partly into a large deal box where her husband used to keep his clothes, and into a square box of a smaller size." The ample receptacles indicate the abundance of the antique store, after all the depredations it had suffered at the hands of her husband and his pupils. It is inconceivable, indeed, that the boxloads still remaining were all parchments. The greater part were probably the ordinary parish registers, accounts, &c., usually found in such repositories: but still including curious, and probably valuable deeds.

Old parchments were thus more abundant in the poor widow's house than ordinary paper: "some being turned into thread-papers, some into patterns, some into dolls" and applied to other equally mean uses. In all probability, Chatterton's first efforts with the pencil and pen were scrawled on the margins of deeds in imitation of characters engrossed in the time of the Plantagenets, or when Occleve and Lydgate[23] were feebly re-echoing Chaucer's[24] rhythm. Thus the child, who acquired his first knowledge of letters from the illuminated capitals of an ancient music-book, and learned their use in the pages of an old black-letter Bible, was familiar from infancy with medieval palaeography and the aspect of antique parchments.

The antique poems had no doubt made some progress, and the romance begot in the strange reveries of the young dreamer was assuming shape and consistency, before an actual Thomas Rowley, priest and poet of the olden time, was called into being as their assigned author. The Rowley romance had been realized in the purlieus of St Mary Redcliffe, by the child-poet, in very early years. But, to his simple unimaginative mother, his reveries were suggestive rather of defective intellect than poetic inspiration. Hence he learned to conceal his poetical recreations as reprehensible, if not altogether criminal indulgences. With a strength of filial attachment which never failed him, he nevertheless cherished his most familiar thoughts in his own breast: until we have to note among his many characteristics, a **singular secretiveness and love of mystery**

Admitted into Colston's Hospital on 3rd of August 1760 — sort of Blue coat school — cf. Charles Lamb[25] & Coleridge — at first delighted — *thinking he would there get all the learning he wanted — but soon seemed hurt — as he said,*

> *he could not learn so much at school as he could at home*

Consciousness of aims and powers beyond those of the other boys was even now manifesting itself.

As a mere child he had shown a thirst for pre-eminence; claimed to take the lead among his playmates and already indulged in dreams of future fame. While still very young, a manufacturer of earthenware undertook to present Mrs. Chatterton's children with specimens of his art, and asked the boy what device he would have upon his. "Paint me," he replied, "an angel, with wings and a trumpet, to trumpet my name over the world."

It is not to be wondered that to such a child, Colston's Hospital should prove distasteful. Instead of wandering at pleasure about St. Mary Redcliffe, or musing over its monuments till he dreamt of himself as the monk-poet of the days when it was in building, he had to submit to the actual durance of a modern Bluecoat monk. The absence of all means of retirement must have been no less irksome to him than the inadequacy of the instruction received. This may well account for his sister's remark, that he became gloomy from the time he began to learn. All his bright anticipations of getting the knowledge he craved had vanished; and he instinctively longed to return to his own little study, and his solitary musings in Redcliffe Church.

But no impediments could shut out the eager youth from the acquisition of knowledge. By his tenth year he was perusing all the books accessible to him; and expending the little pocket-money his mother allowed him in hiring others from a lending library. Then, too, brief hours of release from the noisy playground and the unattractive studies of the school recurred at frequent intervals. Each Saturday brought about its precious half-holiday; and, like its great London prototype, the Bristol Bluecoat School held the saints' days of the Anglican Calendar in becoming reverence. On those welcome occasions the boys were emancipated from the hospital bounds from noon till eight in the evening; and then Chatterton hastened home to the happy solitude of the attic he had appropriated as his study under his mother's roof. Each Saturday, says Mrs. Edkins, he was always at home, returning punctually a few minutes after the clock struck twelve, to get to his little room and shut himself up. There were deposited his own little stock of books, parchments, and all the materials already in use by him in the first efforts of his antique muse. His scheme of a series of poems to be produced under the guise of an ancient poet-monk was already in embryo; and he would lock himself in his favourite retreat, and frequently remain there without food the whole day: till his mother became alarmed for his health; and wonder grew into doubt and suspicion at his strange proceedings, the apparatus, the parchments, both plain and written, "and the begrimed figure he always presented when he came down at tea-time, his face exhibiting many stains of black and yellow. All these circumstances began to alarm them; and," as Mrs. Edkins relates, "when she could get into his room, she would be very inquisitive, and peep about at everything. Once he put his foot on a parchment on the floor to prevent her from taking it up, saying, 'you are too curious and clear-sighted, I wish you would bide out of the room; it is my room.' To this she replied it was only a general lumber-room, and that she wanted some parchments, some of his old Rowley's, to make thread-papers of;" - for already he had familiarised those at home with his imaginary monk - "but he was offended, and would not permit her to touch any of them, not even those that were not written on. But at last, with a voice of entreaty, he said, 'Pray don't touch anything here,' and seemed very anxious to get her away."

At other times, it was only by entreaty, or threats to force the door, that he could be induced to unlock it; and then, as Mrs. Edkins described it, he sat surrounded by the strange materials of his antique art: his ochre, charcoal, pen and pencils, the little square deal table covered with letters, papers, and parchments in utmost confusion, and all round the room a complete litter of parchments. His hands and face betrayed, as usual, the nature of his work. But it has been too hastily assumed that the boy was systematically engaged in the conversion of modern parchments into spurious antiques. His antique poems became, ere long, voluminous enough; but as to the spurious parchments, all ever produced could have been manufactured in a few days. But he was a self-taught draughtsman; delighted in realizing to the eye his fancies of the long-vanished architecture of the Bristowe, of Ælla, Canynge, and Rowley: as in the elaborate elevations of the Bristowe Castle of A.D. 1138, gravely reproduced, with accompanying ground-plans, in Barrett's "History," as "engraved from drawings on vellum, preserved to this day." Such drawings are spoken of as numerous. His uncle Phillips had some; Barrett and Catcott obtained others. His relative Mr. Stephens, Mr. Palmer, Mr. Richard Smith and others, had many of his heraldic drawings; and Mrs. Edkins, in describing to Mr. George Cumberland "the old deeds that came from the muniment room, which were used indiscriminately for any purpose," adds, "there were many of them covered with strange figures of men's heads, &c., on the backs" which she supposes were his drawing. It may be assumed, therefore, that the half-holidays of the Bluecoat boy were more frequently spent in gratifying his artistic and antiquarian tastes — in recreating, in such visible form, his conceptions of the past — than in manufacturing professed originals of his Rowley poems. Such spurious antiques belong altogether to a later period, after the poems themselves had been produced, and the originals were called for by Barrett and others.

In every step of Chatterton's brief career we meet with surmises and suspicions of his contemporaries, dealt with at a subsequent period as facts. Towards the close of his residence in Colston's Hospital, where we know some of his Rowley poems were written, he was observed to seclude himself more than ever in his little study. When Mrs. Edkins narrated this to Mr. Cumberland long afterwards, she entertained no doubt that he was then assiduously labouring at the Rowley manuscripts. But this was an afterthought. So little did even the mother and other nearest relations comprehend the strange boy, that when he was nearly fourteen years of age they became apprehensive "lest he should be doing something improper, knowing his want of money and ambition to appear like others;" but the only idea they could conjure up to account for his recluse habits was, "that these colours were to colour himself, and that, perhaps, he would join some gipsies one day or other, as he seemed so discontented with his station in life."

Sometimes, however, especially in the earlier period of his residence in the Bluecoat School, he would spend his holidays in his mother's company, writing "on the seat of the schoolroom window, which was high, and to accomplish which he was obliged to stand on a chair. If any of his mother's pupils interrupted him, he would get down from it in a great rage, and strike them to make them quiet. Occasionally his mother would take the children into an upper room when he was thus engaged, that he might not be disturbed." It was not therefore from an unsocial disposition, or any undue secretiveness, but from the natural craving of the young poet for silence in his hours of inspiration that he *learned to court the privacy of his little study -*

Began to write poetry when only 10 years old – His first poem religious – Christ's Coming – published in Felix Farley's[26] Journal *"He had been gloomy," his sister remarked, "from the time he had begun to learn but was more cheerful after he began to write poetry - "* **then we find him coming forward as the champion of Mediaevalism – and satirising the churchwardens for desecrating the graveyards.**

Chatterton now gave full play to his intellectual powers. His reading was pursued with unwearied zeal; and the usher reported that he made rapid progress in arithmetic. Between his eleventh and twelfth years, as his sister reports, "he wrote a catalogue of the books he had read, to the number of seventy. History and divinity were the chief subjects;" and these, as his schoolmates informed her, he retired to read at the hours allotted for play. Ere long, also, the elder poets were lovingly studied. Chaucer was his special favourite. The motto to his "Epistle to Mastre Canynge" is taken from Barbour's[27] "Bruce" his MSS in the British Museum include an extract from "Piers Ploughman," though elsewhere he ascribes its authorship to Chaucer. His own writings furnish evidence of his familiarity with Shakespeare, Milton, Dryden, Prior, Cowley, and Gray; Pope and Thomson were studied with care; and Churchill[28] became his favourite model as a satirist. It was probably for modem authors such as those that he resorted to the circulating library; while private collections chiefly supplied the rarer folios and quartos of Hall, Hollingshed, Camden, Stowe, Weever,[29] and the like historical, heraldic, and antiquarian works, which furnished delightful occupation for the play-hour.

We hear of him reciting poems to his friends on the school steps, and satirising the masters in verse. Though to one master he was particularly attached – <u>Phillips</u>[30] **– a poet of a minor order.** *Before he was twelve years old he has conceived the idea of a series of antique poems, ascribed to the imaginary Thomas Rowley, a monk of the 15th century.* **Thistlethwaite, a school fellow, tells us the following story** *"Going down Horse Street near the school, one day during the summer of 1764, I accidentally met with Chatterton. Entering into conversation with him,* he informed me that he was in possession of certain old MSS which had been deposited in a chest in Redcliffe Church, and that he had lent some or one of them to Phillips. Within a day or two after this, I saw Phillips, and repeated to him the information I had received from Chatterton. Phillips produced a MS on parchment or vellum, which I am confident was 'Elinoure and Juga' a kind of pastoral eclogue, afterwards published in the *Town and Country Magazine.*

Different manuscript copies exist of some of Chatterton's larger antique poems, showing that they were carefully elaborated, and underwent repeated revisions ere he recognised them as complete; but this eclogue, or rather ballad, is only known as it appeared in the Town and Country Magazine for May 1769, under the title "Elinoure and Juga: written three hundred years ago by T. Rowley, secular priest."

Two tearful maidens, the nut-brown Elinoure and fair Juga, sit by the banks of the river Rudborne, near St. Albans, bewailing the perils of their absent knights, both of whom prove to have fallen, fighting for the White Rose, in the old wars of York and Lancaster.

JUGA.

Sisters in sorrow, on this daisied bank,
Where melancholy broods, we will lament;
Bewet with morning dew and even dank;
Like levind oaks in each the other bent;
Or like forletten halls of merriment.
Whose ghastly mitches hold the train of fright.
Where lethal ravens bark, and owlets wake the night.

EUNOURE.

No more the miskynette shall wake the morn,
The minstrel dance, good cheer, and morris play;
No more the ambling palfry and the horn
Shall from the lessel rouse the fox away;

I'll seek the forest all the live-long day;
All night among the graved church-glebe will go,
And to the passing sprites lecture my tale of woe.

Many such poems he no doubt read to his schoolfriends, but his first real attempt at deception was the great De Bergham Pedigree.

Mr. Henry Burgum[31], *a Bristol worthy* and pewterer by trade, had a shop on the road between the school and Chatterton's home. He was a man who had tried to educate himself late in life, was fond of music. *One Saturday half holiday in the spring of 1767, Chatterton paid a visit to the shop of* this worthy pewterer and informed him *that he had discovered among the ancient parchments of Redcliffe Church an heraldic blazon of the De Bergham arms, and a pedigree which proved his descent from some of the noblest families in England.* **Bergum was filled with delight and** craved sight of the wondrous pedigree; and within a few days was presented with the De Bergham quarterings blazoned on an old piece of parchment about eight inches square, and a first instalment of the pedigree itself, in Chatterton's own handwriting, copied into a book in which he had already transcribed portions of antique verse with this title: "Poems by Thomas Rowley, Priest of St John's, in the City of Bristol, containing The Tournament, an Interlude, and a piece by Canynge, called the Gouler's Requiem." From this pedigree it appeared that Mr. Burgum's ancestor, Simon de Seyncte Lyze, alias Senliz, came into England with the Conqueror, married Matilda, daughter of Waltheof, Earl of Northumberland, and in 1075, after the execution of the Earl for high treason, obtained a deed of gift of Bergham Castle, with the title of Earl of Northampton. The document in which this, and much else of the like kind, was set forth, bore this heading in large text: "Account of the family of the De Berghams, from the Norman Conquest to this time; collected from original Records, Tournament Rolls, and the Heralds of March and Garter's Records, by Thomas Chatterton." The arms alone claimed to be of ancient authority. Nevertheless the sources of the family pedigree are of the most indisputable character. Marginal references abound, with such authorities as the "Roll of Battle Abbey", "Ex stemma fam. Sir Johan de Leveches," "De Lee," &c.; Stowe, Ashmole, Collins, Dugdale, Rouge Dragon, Garter, Norroy, and, better than all, "Rowley's MSS."

By a brilliant if somewhat daring act of imagination

Chatterton had contrived to fit into the De Bergham pedigree a learned record of one of the pewterer's ancestors, who in the 24th year of the reign of Henry VI obtained a patent for the use of alchemy, whereby this philosophic metallurgist was to transmute the inferior metals into gold or silver. There was a delicate flattery in this discovery, that working in the baser metals was an honourable art pertaining to the Burgums as a hereditary chartered right. Immediately following this comes another paragraph, no less apt and curious. Thomas de Asheton, the old alchemist, left issue four sons, of whom, according to the De Bergham pedigree, the second was "Edward Asheton, of Chatterton in the right of his wife, the daughter and heir of Radcliffe de Chatterton of Chatterton, the heir-general of many families." The name is sufficiently suggestive now, though Mr, Burgum doubtless passed it over without thought of its bearing any reference to his humble protégé. RADCLIFFE DE CHATTERTON! There is a volume of poetical romance crowded into the very name. It is an epitome of the whole biography of the inspired charity boy.

The delight of the glorified pewterer on the acquisition of his patent of nobility may be imagined. His aspiring partner had already achieved notoriety by more than one notable deed, duly set forth ere long in Chatterton's satirical effusions; but here was he, without effort of his own, exalted to an equality with the proudest peer of the realm. The first act of the ennobled tradesman was to present the discoverer of his pedigree with five shillings. The sum, though but poor largess from the hands of a De Bergham of Norman lineage, was probably a greater amount than the young herald had ever before possessed; and its acceptance cost him no scruples, either then or afterwards. It figures at a later date, among other counts in the satirical indictment against Burgum and others, appended to his Will, where he exclaims:

> "Burgum, I thank thee, thou hast let me see
> That Bristol has impressed her stamp on thee;
> Thy generous spirit emulates the Mayor's;
> Thy generous spirit with my Bristol pairs,
> Gods! what would Burgum give to get a name
> And snatch his blundering dialect from shame!
> What would he give to hand his memory down
> To time's remotest boundary? A crown!"

But this was an after-thought, if not a mere piece of satirical exaggeration, when he had exchanged the Bluecoat school for an attorney's office; and experience had given him further insight into the value of money. At the time it was given, Burgum's crown-piece amply rewarded the genealogist, for what I conceive to have been no more, at first, than a roguish experiment on the credulity of the pewterer. [Note: section crossed out by Wilde] surmounted, for a crest, by what its inheritor describes as a queer-looking flower, tinted **gules, with a Scroll over it, labelled The Rose of Virginity!**

For heraldry Chatterton had a great passion — The one decorative art where tradition is unbroken was full of wonder for him — architecture, music, painting, sculpture — antiquarian like Scott,[32] like Scott could make the dry bones live — *Among the M.S.S. at the British Museum is an elaborate piece of Blazonry with nine shields* — intended as an imaginary genealogy of the Chattertons.

It was with Chatterton's heraldry, as with his antique prose and verse: a vein of earnestness is inextricably blended with what, in other respects, appears as palpable fraud. We are reminded of the boy and the visionary dreamer, in the midst of his most elaborate fictions, till it becomes a puzzle to determine how much of self deception and of actual belief were blended with the humour of the jest.

Bristol Patrons.
  George Catcott
  Doctor Barrett – surgeon & antiquarian

1767 **went to Canynge's office**
1st July — Mr Lambert — very unhappy

Opening of Bridge
Gross Forgery

 The Rowley Romance.
Great recreation of the past. An [elaborate?] historical novel - objective power.

Thomas Rowley, a native of Somersetshire, and a zealous Yorkist, of the times when the Red and the White Roses were the badges of party strife in England, was priest of St. John's, in the city of Bristol, in the year 1465. From early years he had borne the most intimate relations with the Canynges' family. He and William, the second son of John Canynge, a youth of cunning wit, as we learn from the "Lyfe of W. Canynge," one of the Chatterton MSS., [**were educated by**] the Carmelite brothers, in the old priory which once occupied the site of Colston's School. In fact, they were Bristol Bluecoat boys of the good old times. "Here," says Rowley," began the kindness of our lives; our minds and kinds were alike, and we were always together." William's father loved him not as he did his brother Robert, because, while the latter was a man after his own heart, — greedy of gain and sparing of alms, — William was courteous and liberal in word and deed. But both father and brother died the same year, leaving William to inherit their great wealth; and about the same time his old school-mate, Thomas Rowley, took holy orders, and was made his chaplain and confessor. A brief extract from the good priest's account of his friend and benefactor will serve to illustrate the quaint graphic style of the narrative: "Master Roberte, by Master William's desyre, bequeathed me one hundred marks; I went to thank Master William for his mickle courtesie, and to make tender of myselfe to him. 'Fadre,' quod he, 'I have a crotchett in my brayne that will need your aide.' 'Master William,' said I, 'if you command me I will go to Roome for you.' 'Not so farr distant,' said he; 'I ken you for a mickle learned priest; if you will leave the parysh of our Ladie, and travel for mee, it shall be mickle to your profits.' I gave my hands, and he told mee I must goe to all the abbies and pryorys, and gather together auncient drawyngs, if of anie account, at any price. Consented I to the same, and pursuant sett out the Mundaie following for the Minster of our Ladie and Saint Goodwyne, where a drawing of a steeple, contryvd for the belles when runge to swaie out of the syde into the ayre, had I thence. It was done by Syr Symon de Mambrie, who, in the troublesome rayne of Kyng Stephen, devoted himselfe, and was shorne."

In like fashion the good priest continues to collect valuable drawings and manuscripts for Master Canynge, and to partake liberally of his bounty. But the death of **the latter's** tenderly loved wife, Johanna, in child-bearing, leaves him widowed and childless; and he thenceforth devotes himself to the patronage of art, letters, and all good works. Then did his nobleness show forth to the world.

The Sir William Canynge of the Rowley Romance is himself a man of letters, an artist, and even at times a poet: devoted to all liberal tastes, and especially to architecture; and he gathers around him a group of kindred spirits. There is his friend, Carpenter, Bishop of Worcester, not incapable of penning a stanza at times: as appears from an inscription affixed to the cover of an old mass book, which Chatterton was able to recover for Mr. Barrett with Rowley's aid. Maystre John a Iscam, Canon of St. Augustine's Abbey, — himself a poet, — also bears his part, on more than one occasion, in the dramatic performances at the Rudde House; and wins the special commendation of Maistre Canynge, in the character of "Celmonde," when Rowley acts "Ælla" in his own "Tragycal Enterlude." In a letter of Rowley to his brother-poet, he thus jestingly invites him to become verse-monger to a niggard patron of the muse: "I haveth metten wythe a syllie knyghte of twayne hondreth poundes bie the yeere. 'God's nayles,' quod hee, 'leave oute mie scarlette and ermyne doublette, I know nete I love better than vearses. I woulde bestowe rentalls of golde for rolles of hem.'

Sir Thybbot Gorges, a neighbouring knight of ancient family, contributes to the "Tragycal Enterlude" one of the minstrels' songs, as his quota of verse; enacts the character of "Hurra" the Dane, among the Rudde House amateurs; and pledges, in surety of a liberal benefaction towards the rebuilding of Redcliffe Church, certain jewels of great value. The group is completed by Sir Allan de Vere, Mastre Edwarde Canynge, and others: knights, aldermen, and minstrels; among whom we may specially picture to ourselves John a Dalbenie — a citizen fond of wordy strife, and prone to mar the pleasant gatherings at the Rudde House by intruding politics into that haunt of the Muses — who is twitted by the host in this epigrammatic fashion:

Johne makes a jarre boute Lancaster and Yorke;
Bee stille gode manne, and learne to mynde thie worke.

The old merchant prince of Bristowe, the centre of this group, formed in the estimation of Dean Milles — most enthusiastic among the early champions of the ancient Rowley — a parallel to Maecenas with his three friends, Virgil, Horace, and Varus.[33] To him Rowley sends his verses from time to time, ever sure of some liberal acknowledgment in return. At times the real author expressed under this guise his own estimate of some of those wondrous creations of his muse, given away, or requited by the niggard dole of Catcott or Barrett; for his chief antique productions figure in Rowley's narrative with their becoming reward. "I sent him," writes the good priest, "my verses touching his church, for which he did send me mickle good things;" and again: "I gave Master Cannings my Bristow tragedy, for which he gave me in hands twentie pounds, and did praise it more than I did think myself did deserve; for I can say in troth I was never proud of my verses since I did read Master Chaucer; and now haveing nought to do, and not wyling to be ydle, I went to the minster of our Ladie and Saint Goodwin, and there did purchase the Saxon manuscripts, and sett myself diligently to translate and worde it in English metre, which in one year I performed, and styled it the Battle of Hastyngs. Master William did bargyin for one manuscript, and John Pelham, an esquire, of Ashley, for another. Master William did praise it muckle greatly, but advised me to tender it to no man, beying the menn whose name were therein mentioned would be offended. He gave me 20 markes, and I did goe to Ashley, to Master Pelham, to be payd of him for the other one I left with him. But his ladie being of the family of the Fiscamps, of whom some things are said, he told me he had burnt it, and would have me burnt too, if I did not avaunt. Dureing this dinn his wife did come out, and made a dinn, to speake by a figure, would have over sounded. the bells of our Ladie of the Cliffe; I was fain content to get away in a safe skin."

antique or modern rival :

"Oh thou, or what remains of thee,
Ælla, the darling of futurity,

Let this, my song, bold as thy courage be,
As everlasting to posterity!

"When Dacia's sons, whose hair of blood-red hue.
Like kingcups bursting with the morning dew,
Arranged in drear array.
Upon the lethal day
Spread far and wide on Watchet's shore:
Then didst thou furious stand.
And by thy valiant hand
Besprenged all the meads with gore.

"Drawn by thine anlace fell,
Down to the depths of hell
Thousands of Dacians went
Bristowans, men of might,
Ydared the bloody fight.
And acted deeds full quaint.

"Oh thou, where'er — thy bones at rest —
Thy sprite to haunt delighteth best;
Whether upon the blood-embrued plain.
Or where thou kenst from far
The dismal cry of war.
Or seest some mountain made of corse of slain;
Or seest the hatched steed
Yprancing on the mead.
And neigh to be among the pointed spears;

Or in black armour stalk around
Embattled Bristowe, once thy ground,
And glow ardiirousi on the castle-stairs;
Or fiery round the minstre glare:
Let Bristowe still be made thy care.
Guard it from foemen and consuming fire;
Let Avon's stream encire it round,
Ne let a flame enharm the ground,
Till in one flame all the whole world expire."

This episode of a poetical challenge and rejoinder between the Laureate of Henry VI and the imaginary Rowley is completed by a transcript of commendatory verses, by Lydgate, in which, after glancing at the great poets of elder times, he concludes by saying that now "in these mokie days" Chaucer lives over again in every line that Rowley writes.

The fragmentary Tragedy of Godwin also is supposed to have been acted by Canynge and Rowley at the Rudde house and all the Chatterton antique poems are connected with the Rowley circle.

The wonderful song to Ælla, Lorde of the Castle of Bristowe is Rowley's own composition, sent to Lydgate the Laureate of Henry VI in answer to a friendly challenge. So marvellous is this Ode that one cannot pass it without quotation. Contains this fine Ode to Liberty, one of the noblest of our martial lyrics:

"When Freedom, drest in blood-stained vest,
To every knight her war-song sung,
Upon her head wild weeds were spread,
A gory anlace by her hung.
She danced on the heath;
She heard the voice of Death;
Pale-eyed Affright, his heart of silver hue,
In vain assailed her bosom to acale.
She heard unflemed the shrieking voice of woe.
And sadness, in the owlet, shake the dale.
She shook her burled spear;
On high she jeste her shield;
Her foemen all appear
And flie along the field.
Power with his heafod straught into the skies,
His spear a sunbeam and his shield a star; "

The Battle of Hastings, as I before noticed, was supposed to [Note omitted: be] *the work of Turgot, a Saxon monk of the 10th century,* and to have been translated by Rowley. How charming are these two stanzas from it.

"White as the chalky cliffs of Britain's isle,
Red as the highest coloured Gallic wine,
Gay as all nature at the morning smile :
Those hues with pleasaunce on her lips combine,
Her lips more red than summer evening skyne,
Or Phoebus rising in a frosty morn;
Her breast more white than snow in fields that lyen,
Or lily lambs that never have been shorn :
Swelling like bubbles in a boiling well
Or new-burst brooklets gently whispering in the dell.

Brown as the filbert dropping from the shell,
Brown as the nappy ale at Hocktide game,
So brown the crooked rings that featly fell
Over the neck of the all-beauteous dame.

Grey as the mom before the ruddy flame
Of Phoebus' charriot rolling thro' the sky;
Grey as the steel-hom'd goats Conyan made tame:
So grey appear'd her featly sparkling eye;
Those eyne that did oft mickle pleased look
On Adhelm, valiant man, the virtues' doomsday book."

and this charming ballad is from the poem of Sir Tybbot (sic)
Gorges

superb ballad on the death of Sir Charles Baldwin —

The feathered songster Chanticleere
Had wound his bugle horn,
And low the early villagers
The coming of the morn –

King Edward saw the ruddy streaks
Of light eclipse the grey,
And hear the raven's croaking throat
Proclaim the fated day.

Many other charming stories of Canynge are written in the
Rowley M.S.S. such as his *account of his masonic lodge opened on the*
vigil of Epiphany 1432 with its address on the value of the fine arts in
their application to trade to a chapter composed of 27 Friars 16
gentlemen and three brother aldermen in which this sly touch of
humour betrays the modern Rowley's hand: "I did speak of the use of
the Arts to improve the trade. The Friars did enlarge, the gentlemen
attend, and the Council men fell asleep!"
The collection of letters closes with a panegyric of Canynge by
Rowley: "As a learned wisacre he excelled in all things. As a poet and
a painter he was great. With him I lived at Westbury six years before
he died, and be now hasting to the grave myself." *So ends this*
marvellous romance which Chatterton not only wrote but lived. It is
his own story - but he had not yet found his Canynge.

His attempts to gain a publisher as a patron.

His first attempt was when Dodsley[34] the publisher of the Pall
Mall, the author of some literary trifles and the founder of the
Annual Register. One morning in December 1768 *the worthy*
publisher finds among his letters one from Bristol addressed in a
small neat hand and worded as follows:

Bristol. Dec. 21. 1768.

Sir,

     I take this method to inform you that I can procure copies of several ancient poems; and an interlude, perhaps the oldest dramatic work extant; wrote by one Rowley, a priest of Bristol, who lived in the reigns of Henry the VI. and Edward IV.

 If these pieces will be of service to you, at your command copies shall be sent to you by your most obedient servant

                    D. B.

Please to direct for D. B. to be left with Mr. Thomas Chatterton Redcliffe Hill. Bristol

Dodsley presumably answered this for among his papers was found this other letter from Chatterton

                           Bristol, Feb. 15, 1769.

Sir, — Having intelligence that the tragedy of Ælla was in being, after a long and laborious search I was so happy as to attain a sight of it. I endeavoured to obtain a copy of it to send you; but the present possessor absolutely denies to give me one, unless I give him one guinea for a consideration. As I am unable to procure such a sum, I made a search for another copy, but unsuccessfully. Unwilling such a beauteous piece should be lost, I have made bold to apply to you. Several gentlemen of learning who have seen it join with me in praising it. I am far from having any mercenary views for myself in the affair; and, was I able, would print it at my own risk. It is a perfect tragedy — the plot clear; the language spirited; and the songs (interspersed in it) flowing, poetical, and elegantly simple; the similes judiciously applied and, though wrote in the age of Henry VI., not inferior to many of the present age. If I can procure a copy, with or without the gratification, it shall be immediately sent to you. The motive that actuates me to do this is to convince the world that the monks (of whom some have so despicable an opinion) were not such blockheads as generally thought, and that good poetry might be wrote in the dark days of superstition, as well as in these more enlightened ages. An immediate answer will oblige. I shall not receive your favour as for myself, but as your agent.

I am, sir, your most obedient servant,

                         "Thomas Chatterton.

P.S. — My reason for concealing my name was lest my master (who is now out of town) should see my letters, and think I neglected his business. Direct for me on Redcliffe Hill.

(Here followed an extract from the tragedy, as a specimen of the style.)

The whole contains about one thousand lines. If it should not suit yon, I should be obliged to you if you would calculate the expenses of printing it, as I will endeavour to publish it by subscription on my own account.

To MR. JAMES DODSLEY, Bookseller, Pall Mall, London.

This attempt to extract a guinea from the publisher failed. Mr. Dodsley did not think the speculation worth risking a guinea on; and "Ælla, a Tragycal Enterlude, or Discoorseynge Tragedie, wrotten by Thomas Rowllie; plaiedd before Mastre Canynge, atte hys Howse, nempte tke Rodde Lodge " remained useless among Chatterton's papers.

Chatterton however was undaunted. [The next patron he?] tried was Mr. Horace Walpole.[35]

The son of a great Minister of the First and Second Georges. Walpole was destined to be a man of letters — Had a dream of mediaevialism — *converting Strawberry Hill into a pseudo Gothic Palace,* **and had published in 1764 his Castle of Otranto — supposed to be a translation by William Marshall of an real Italian story. To him accordingly Chatterton addresses the following note:**

Bristol. March 25. Corn St

Sir,

— Being versed a little in antiquities, I have met with several curious manuscripts, amongst which the following may be of service to you in any future edition of your truly entertaining anecdotes of painting. In correcting the mistakes (if any) in the notes, you will greatly oblige your most humble servant,

Thomas Chatterton

Appended to this letter [was enclosed a manuscript of?] the Rise of Painting in England - as well as some *specimens of Rowley Poetry -* **Walpole was altogether taken in and writes the following letter:**

Arlington St., March 28, 1769.

Sir, — I cannot but think myself singularly obliged by a gentleman with whom I have not the pleasure of being acquainted, when I read your very curious and kind letter, which I have this minute received. I give you a thousand thanks for it, and for the very obliging offer you make of communicating your manuscript to me. What you have already sent me is valuable, and full of information; but, instead of correcting you, Sir, you are far more able to correct me I have not the happiness of understanding the Saxon language, and, without your learned notes, should not have been able to comprehend Rowley's text.

As a second edition of my Anecdotes was published last year, I must not flatter myself that a third will be wanted soon; but I shall be happy to lay up any notices you will be so good as to extract for me, and send me at your leisure; for, as it is uncertain when I may use them, I would by no means borrow or detain your MSS.

Give me leave to ask you where Rowley's poems are to be found. I should not be sorry to print them, or at least a specimen of them, if they have never been printed.

The Abbot John's verses that you have given me are wonderful for their harmony and spirit, though there are some words that I do not understand. You do not point out exactly the time when he lived, which I wish to know, as I suppose it was long before John van Eyck's discovery of oil-painting; if so, it confirms what I have guessed, and hinted in my Anecdotes, that oil-painting was known here much earlier than that discovery or revival.

I will not trouble you with more questions now, Sir; but flatter myself, from the urbanity and politeness you have already shown me, that you will give me leave to consult you. 1 hope, too, you will forgive the simplicity of my direction, as you have favoured me with none other.

I am, Sir, your much obliged and obedient servant,

Horace Walpole,

P.S. — Be so good as to direct to Mr. Walpole, Arlington Street.

Chatterton writes and frankly tells Walpole *that he was the son of a poor widow* **and a** *clerk to an attorney* **- but that he desired to take up literature – he sends some specimens of the great treasures of old poetry found in his native town.**

Walpole's tone at once changed. He wrote back to Chatterton that [he advised him?] against taking up literature, and that he had submitted the Rowley poems to some of his friends who were doubtful of their authenticity.

Chatterton replied in a bitter letter – [He justified?] his [claim?] of the genuineness of his Rowley M.S.S. but [proceeded?] to say:

> *though I am but sixteen years of age I have lived long enough to see that Poverty attends literature. I am obliged to you, Sir, for your advice and will go a little beyond it by destroying all my useless lumber of literature and never using my pen again but in Law.*

His great hope had failed him.

A week later he applied for the return of his papers — **Walpole paid no attention and went off to Paris. On his return he found on his table what seemed to him a "singularly impertinent letter" but what seems to us rather spirited and manly:**

> Sir, — I cannot reconcile your behaviour with the notions I once entertained of you. I think myself injured, sir; and did you not know my circumstances, you would not dare to treat me thus.
> I have sent twice for a copy of the manuscripts; — no answer from you. An explanation or excuse for your silence would oblige
>
> Thomas Chatterton.
>
> July 24th

Walpole accordingly returned the M.S.S. Chatterton's dream of a real Canynge was over.

Coleridge:
O ye who honour the Name of man rejoice that this Walpole is called a Lord[36]

Spoke casually to one of his friends —

The effect on Chatterton — Satire - political letters.

Moody, and subject to fits of despair. Contemplated suicide and drew up this extraordinary document now in the Bristol Museum:

> This is the last Will and Testament of me, Thomas Chatterton, of the City of Bristol: being sound in body, or it is the fault of my last surgeon. The soundness of my mind the Coroner and Jury are to be judges of; desiring them to take notice, that the most perfect masters of human nature in Bristol distinguish me by the title of the Mad Genius; therefore if I do a mad action, it is conformable to every action of my life, which all savoured of insanity.
>
> Item. If after my death, which will happen to-morrow night before eight o'clock, being the Feast of the Resurrection, the

Coroner and Jury bring it in lunacy, I will and direct, that Paul Farr, Esq. and Mr. John Flower, at their joint expense, cause my body to be interred in the tomb of my fathers, and raise the monument over my body to the height of four feet five inches, placing the present flat stone on the top, and adding six tablets.

Then follow the inscriptions, in French, Latin, and English, in memory of real and imaginary ancestors, occupying three of the tablets. The fourth reads:

To the Memory of Thomas Chatterton. Reader, judge not; if thou art a Christian, believe that he shall be judged by a superior power. To that power only is he now answerable.

The fifth and sixth tablets are devoted to his favourite heraldic achievements; and then it thus proceeds:

And I will and direct, that if the Coroner's inquest bring it in felo-de-se, the said monument shall be, notwithstanding, erected. And if the said Paul Farr and John Flower have souls so Bristolish as to refuse this my Bequest, they will transmit a copy of my Will to the Society for supporting the Bill of Rights, whom I hereby empower to build the same monument according to the aforesaid directions. And if they, the said Paul Farr and John Flower, should build the said monument, I will and direct that the second edition of my Kew Gardens shall be dedicated to them in the following Dedication: — To Paul Farr and John Flower, Esqs. this book is most humbly dedicated by the Author's Ghost.

Item - I give and bequeath all my vigour and fire of youth to Mr. George Catcott, being sensible he is most in want of it,

Item - From the same charitable motive, I give and bequeath unto the Reverend Mr. Camplin, .senior, all my humility. To Mr. Burgum all my prosody and grammar, likewise one moiety of my modesty; the other moiety to any young lady who can prove without blushing that she wants that valuable commodity. To Bristol all my spirit and disinterestedness: parcels of goods unknown on her quay since the days of Canyng and Rowley. I leave also all my religion to Dr. Cutts Barton, Dean of Bristol, hereby empowering the subsacrist to strike him on the head when he goes to sleep in church. My powers of utterance I give to the Reverend Mr. Broughton, hoping he will employ them to a better purpose than reading lectures on the immortality of the soul. I leave the Reverend Mr. Catcott some little of my freethinking, that he may put on the spectacles of Reason, and see how vilely he is duped in believing the Scriptures literally. I wish he and his brother would know how far I am their real enemy; but I have an unlucky way of railing, and when the strong fit of satire is upon me, spare neither friend nor foe. This is my excuse forwhat I have said of them elsewhere. I leave Mr. Clayfield the sincerest thanks my gratitude can give; and I will and direct that whatever any person may think the pleasure of reading my works worth, they immediately pay their own valuation to him, since it is then become a lawful debt to me, and to him as my executor in this case.

I leave my moderation to the politicians on both sides the question. I leave my generosity to our present Right Worshipful Mayor Thomas Harris, Esq. I give my abstinence to the Company at the Sheriffs annual feast, in general, more particularly to the Alderman.

Item - I give and bequeath to Mr. Mat. Mease a mourning ring with this motto, "Alas poor Chatterton !" provided he pays for it himself. Item. I leave the young ladies all the letters they have had from me, assuring them they need be under no apprehensioin from the appearance of my Ghost, for I die for none of them. Item ' I leave all my debts, in the whole not Five pounds, to the payment of the charitable and generous Chamber of Bristol, on penalty, if refused, to hinder every member from ever eating a good dinner, by appearing in the form of a Bailiff. If, in defiance of this terrible spectre, they obstinately persist in refusing to discharge my debts, let my two creditors apply to the supporters of the Bill of Rights.

Item - I leave my mother and sister to the protection of my friends, if I have any.

Executed in the presence of Omniscience, this 14th of April, 1770.

THOMAS CHATTERTON.

To this is added the endorsement:

all this wrote between 11 and 2 o'c Saturday in the utmost distress of mind,
   April 14th

There is also with it an apostrophe to Catcott:

Thy friendship never could be dear to me,
Since all I am is opposite to thee,
If ever obligated to thy purse,
Rowley discharges all my first, chief Curse.
For had I never known the antique lore,
I ne'er had ventured from my peaceful shore,
To be the wreck of promises and hopes,
A boy of Learning, and a Bard of Tropes,
But happy in my humble sphere had moved,
Untroubled, unrespected, unbeloved.

About the same time in another letter he writes: "*I abominate the Muses and their works – They are the nurses of poverty and insanity*"

These lines on suicide also show his despair, though dated 1769.

Since we can die but once, what matters it
If rope, or garter, poison, pistol, sword.
Slow-wasting sickness, or the sudden burst
Of valve-arterial in the noble parts.
Curtail the miseries of human life ?
Tho' varied is the cause, the effect's the same;
All to one common dissolution tends.

And his friends became alarmed. Mr Lambert found on his desk in a letter addressed to Mr Clayfield threatening suicide — and forwarded it to Mr Bennett who at once sent for Chatterton and remonstrated with him — The next day he received the following letter:

Sir, — Upon recollection I don't know how Mr. Clayfield could come by his letter ; as I intended to have given him a letter, but did not. In regard to my motives for the supposed rashness, I shall observe that I keep no worse company than myself. I never drink to excess ; and have, without vanity, too much sense to be attached to the mercenary retailers of iniquity. No! it is my pride, my damn'd, native, unconquerable pride, that plunges me into distraction. You must know that 19-20ths of my composition is pride. I must either live a slave, a servant; have no will of my own, no sentiments of my own which I may freely declare as such ; or die!

— perplexing alternative. But it distracts me to think of it. I will endeavour to learn humility, but it cannot be here. What it "will cost me on the trial Heaven knows!

I am, your much obliged, unhappy, humble Servant,

T. C.

In a short time his Indentures were cancelled and he started for London never to see Bristol again. His first letter is full of enthusiasm - he writes,

London April 26 1770

[Note: this letter is pasted into the book but then crossed out by Wilde.]

Lodging with a plasterer in Shoreditch of the name of Walmsley, with whom resides an aged relative a Mrs Ballance.

Sir Herbert Crofts[37] **visits:**

The man and woman where he first lodged are still (1780) living in the same house. He is a plasterer. They, and their nephew and niece (the latter about as old as Chatterton would be now, the former three years younger), and Mrs. Ballance — who lodged in the house and desired them to let Chatterton, her relation, live there also — have been seen. The little collected from them you shall have in their own words ...

Mrs. Ballance says he was as proud as Lucifer. He very soon quarrelled with her for calling him 'Cousin Tommy' and asked her if she ever heard of a poet's being called Tommy; but she assured him that she knew nothing of poets, and only wished he would not set up for a gentleman. Upon her recommending it to him to get into some office, when he had been in town two or three weeks, he stormed about the room like a madman, and frightened her not a little by telling her that he hoped, with the blessing of God, very soon to be sent prisoner to the Tower, which would make his fortune. He would often look steadfastly in a person's face, without speaking, or seeming to see the person, for a quarter of an hour or more, till it was quite frightful; during all which, time (she supposes from what she has since heard) his thoughts were gone about something else. ... He frequently declared that he should settle the nation before he had done: but how could she think that her poor cousin Tommy was so great a man as she now finds he was? His mother should have written word of his greatness, and then, to be sure, she would have humoured the gentleman accordingly.

Mr. Walmsley observed little in him, but that there was something manly and pleasing about him, and that he did not dislike the wenches.

Mrs. Walmsley's account is, that she never saw any harm of him — that he never mislisted her, but was always very civil whenever they met in the house by accident; that he would never suffer the room in which *he used to read and write to be swept, because, he said, poets hated brooms. That she told him she did not know anything poet-folks were good for, but to sit in a dirty cap and gown in a garret and at last to be starved – that during the nine weeks he was at her house he never stayed out after the family hours except once when he did not come home all night, and had she heard been poeting a song about the streets.*

The niece says, for her part, she always took him more for a mad boy than anything else, he would have such flights and vagaries - that but for his face and her knowledge of his age she should never have thought him a boy he was so manly, and so much himself. That he never touched meat, and drank only water, and seemed to live on the air. That he was good-tempered and agreeable, but sadly proud and haughty – nothing was too good for him, nor was anything to be too good for his grandmother, mother, and sister, hereafter. That he used to sit up almost all night, reading and writing - and that her brother said he was afraid to lie with him - for, to be sure, he was a spirit, and never slept. For he never came to bed till it was morning, and then for what he saw never closed his eyes.

The Nephew (Chatterton's bed-fellow during the first six weeks he lodged there) says that, notwithstanding his pride and haughtiness, it was impossible to help liking him; that he lived chiefly upon a bit of bread, or a tart, and some water — that Chatterton, to his knowledge, never slept while they lay together; that he never came to bed till very late, sometimes three or four o'clock, and was always awake when he (the nephew) waked, and got up at the same time, about five or six; that almost every morning the floor was covered with pieces of paper not so big as sixpences, into which he had torn what he had been writing before he came to bed.

In the letter to his mother he had penned he was going to *call on Dodsley, Edmunds, Hamilton and Fell.* **Of Dodsley we have already spoken – Edmunds was Editor of Middlesex Journal – Hamilton of Town and Country Magazine and Fell of the Freeholder's Mag., an ardent Wilkite. At first Chatterton jubilant. "I am familiar with the Chapter Coffee House" he writes "and know all the geniuses there – Wilkes"[38] he tells her "wishes to know him." He gets to know Beckford[39] — goes to theatres Garrick[40] acting Hamlet — addressing Cato**

<u>sketch of English [Psalter?] here</u>

Brooke Street, Mrs. Angell, a sackmaker, – Sir Herbert Croft was never able to see her, but he found a neighbour *of hers – Mrs Wolfe, a barber's wife, who spoke of Chatterton's proud and haughty spirit, adding that he appeared to her and to Mrs. Angell as if born for something great.* There was also one Cross an apothecary who had a great liking for Chatterton *and found his conversation, as he told Warton, very captivating, a little infidelity excepted.*

When Beckford died he was perfectly frantic and out of his mind and said he was ruined:

Lost by his death	1.11.6
Gained by writing on him	5.5.0
am glad he is dead by	3.13.6

Gets despondent in July.

Ballad of Charity – rejected by the Town and Country Magazine.

<u>Read</u>[41]

On 15th August writes desponding letter to his mother – and tells strange story of his falling into a grave in a churchyard. *A friend who was with him helped him out, and laughing, congratulated him on the resurrection of genius – Chatterton replied with a sad smile, "my dear friend, I feel the sting of a speedy desolation — I have been at war with the grave for some time, and find it is not so easy to vanquish as I imagined — we can find an asylum from every creditor but that"* -

Barrett refuses certificate.

Finally, Friday 24th Aug., Mrs. Wolfe tells us that *Mrs. Angell told her that "as she knew he had not eaten anything for 2 or 3 days." She begged he would take some dinner with her, but he was offended at her expressions which seemed to hint he was in want and assured her (though his looks showed him to be 3 parts starved) that he was not hungry.* On Saturday 25th August found dead. The room *covered with scraps of paper.*

No notice at the time – in December Cary's Elegy in Town & Country Mag.[42]

April 23 1771. First Academy Dinner.

Goldsmith[43] tells about poems and said he believed in them. S. Jonson[44] laughs at him. Walpole hearing of Chatterton's death. <u>1776</u> Jonson and Boswell[45] visit Bristol. see Catcott see opp

[Note: the following paragraph is on the opposite page:]

Boswell has preserved a lively account of the interview of Catcott with Dr. Johnson, when the latter visited Bristol in 1776. "On Monday, April 29th," writes Boswell, "he and I made an excursion to Bristol, where I was entertained with seeing him inquire, upon the spot, into the authenticity of Rowley's poetry. George Catcott, the pewterer, attended us at our inn, and with a triumphant air of lively simplicity, called out, ' I'll make Dr. Johnson a convert.' Dr. Johnson, at his desire, read aloud some of Chatterton's fabricated verses, while Catcott stood at the back of his chair, moving himself like a pendulum, and beating time with his feet, and now and then looking into Dr. Johnson's face, wondering that he was not yet convinced. Honest Catcott seemed to pay no attention whatever to any objections, but insisted, as an end of all controversy, that we should go with him to the tower of St Mary Redcliffe, and view with our own eyes the ancient chest in which the manuscripts were found. To this Dr. Johnson good-naturedly agreed ; and, though troubled with a shortness of breathing, laboured up a long flight of steps, till we came to the place where the wondrous chest stood. 'There,' said Catcott, with a bouncing, confident credulity, 'there is the very chest itself.' After this ocular demonstration there was no more to be said."

1777. Tyrwhitt[46]
1782. Mills[47]

Controversy

Nature of his genius

Was he a mere forger with literary powers or a great artist?

The latter is the right view. Chatterton may not have had the moral conscience which is Truth to fact but he had the artistic conscience which is truth to Beauty. He had the artists yearning to represent and if perfect representation seems to him to demand forgery he needs must forge[48]**. Still this forgery came from the desire of artistic self effacement. He was the pure artist — that it is to say his aim was not to reveal himself but to give pleasure**[49] **— an artist of the type of Shakespeare and Homer**[50] **as opposed to Shelley**[51] **or Petrarch**[52] **or Wordsworth. He was essentially a dramatist and claimed for the artist freedom of mood. He saw the realm of the imagination differed from the realm of fact.** [53]
There was something in him of "the yearning of great Vishnu to create a world."?[54]
He loved to let his intellect play – to separate the artist from the man. This explains his extraordinary versatility, he could write

polished lines like Pope, satire like Churchill, Philippics like Junius,[55] fiction like Smollett.[56]
 Gray, Collins,[57] Macpherson, Ossian[58]
    Yet a destructive note of his own.
    Also his statements that *"He is a poor author who cannot write on both sides"*. And this curious note found in his papers:

> *"In a dispute concerning the character of David, it was argued that he must be a holy man from the strain of piety that breathes through his whole works. Being of a contrary opinion and knowing that a great genius can affect anything, endeavoured in the forgoing poems to represent an enthusiastic Methodist"*

What Coleridge classed as a new principle in poetry – the anapaestic variations in correspondence with some transition in the nature of the imagery or passion – was in reality Chatterton's – Influence of Chatterton seen in Coleridge's Kubla Khan and hinted in Keats' Eve of St Agnes.[59]

Feeling
    Music and poetry are the romantic arts - Poetry has both - colour and new melody — also

1 mediaevalism
2 love of nature

① variety of life — sympathy with passion — sensuous imagery — is images as opposed to ideas

continuity of English poetry: Chaucer – Spenser[60]— Chatterton Coleridge — Keats —Tennyson[61] — Morris[62]

② nature - quote

What do we learn?
Can only be understood by being [unintelligible].
Not "criticism of life"[63] - but it is the ideal, not the realistic, artist who expresses his age.[64]

    Mist of familiarity makes this obscure to us.[65]
    Shelley

Picture of Rossetti in the House[66]

> *With Shakespeare's manhood at a boy's wild heart*[67]
> *Through Hamlet's doubt to Shakespeare near allied*
> *And kin to Milton through his Satan's pride*
> *At Death's sole door he stooped, and craved a dart*

And to the dear new bower of England's art
Even to that shrine Time else had deified
The unuttered heart that soared against his side
Drove the fell point and smote life's seals apart

Thy nested homeloves, noble Chatterton
The angel trodden stair thy soul could trace
Up Redcliffe's spire, and in the world's armed space
Thy gallant swordplay: These to many a one
Are Dear[68] for ever - as thy grave unknown,
And love-dream of thine unrecorded <u>face</u>.

Abbreviations

CL	*The Complete Letters of Oscar Wilde,* edited by Merlin Holland & Rupert Hart-Davis, Fourth Estate 2000
Criticism	*The Complete Works of Oscar Wilde,* General Editor: Ian Small, OUP, Josephine Guy, Volume 4 Criticism: *Historical Criticism, Intentions, The Soul of Man*
CW	*The Complete Works of Oscar Wilde,* Introduced by Vyvyan Holland, Collins 1973; referred to in the text as 'abridged work title',
Ellmann	*Oscar Wilde,* Richard Ellmann, Hamish Hamilton 1987
Friendship	*Oscar Wilde The Story of an Unhappy Friendship,* Robert Harborough Sherard, Greening 1909
Harris	*Oscar Wilde His Life and Confessions,* Frank Harris, Panther 1965
Journalism	*Selected Journalism,* edited by Anya Clayworth, Oxford University Press 2004
Life	*The Life of Oscar Wilde,* Robert Harborough Sherard, Werner Laurie 1906
Marius	*Marius the Epicurean,* Walter Horatio Pater, Macmillan 1924
Mason	*Bibliography of Oscar Wilde,* Stuart Mason, Werner Laurie 1914
Peacock	*Irish Peacock & Scarlet Marquess,* Merlin Holland, Fourth Estate 2003
Real	*The Real Oscar Wilde,* Robert Harborough Sherard, Werner Laurie 1917
Renaissance	*Studies in the History of the Renaissance,* Walter Horatio Pater, Macmillan, 1873, reprinted, edited Matthew Beaumont, Oxford University Press 2010
Ross	*The Complete Works of Oscar Wilde,* edited by Robert Ross in 14 volumes, Methuen, Charles Carrington 1908 referred to in the text as: 'the volume name'
Trials	*The Trials of Oscar Wilde,* edited H. Montgomery Hyde, Hodge 1948
Whistler	*The Gentle Art of Making Enemies,* James McNeill Whistler, Heinemann 1953

Bibliography

BIOGRAPHIES OF WILDE

Croft-Cooke, Rupert, *The Unrecorded Life of Oscar Wilde*, W H Allen 1972

Ellmann, Richard, *Oscar Wilde*, Hamish Hamilton, 1987

Gagnier, Regenia, *Idylls of the Marketplace Oscar Wilde and the Victorian Public*, Scolar Press 1986

Gide, Andre, *Oscar Wilde*, William Kimber 1951

Harris, Frank, *Oscar Wilde His Life and Confessions*, Panther, 1965

Holland, Merlin, *The Wilde Album*, Fourth Estate 1997

Holland, Merlin, *Irish Peacock & Scarlet Marquess*, Fourth Estate, 2003

Holland, Vyvyan, *Son of Oscar Wilde*, Rupert Hart-Davis 1954

Hyde, H. Montgomery, *Oscar Wilde a Biography*, Harford Productions 1975

Hyde, H. Montgomery editor, *The Trials of Oscar Wilde*, William Hodge and Company 1948

Knox, Melissa, *Oscar Wilde a Long and Lovely Suicide*, Yale University Press 1994

McKenna, Neil, *The Secret Life of Oscar Wilde*, Century 2003

O'Brien, Kevin, *Oscar Wilde in Canada An Apostle for the Arts*, Personal Library 1982

Pearson, Hesketh, *The Life of Oscar Wilde*, Methuen & Co. Ltd., 1952

Schmidgall, Gary, *The Stranger Wilde Interpreting Oscar*, Abacus 1994

Schroeder, Horst, *Additions and Corrections to Richard Ellmann's Oscar Wilde*, Braunschweig 2002

Sherard, Robert Harborough, *The Life of Oscar Wilde* Werner Laurie, 1906

Sherard, Robert Harborough, *Oscar Wilde The Story of an Unhappy Friendship* Greening, 1909

Sherard, Robert Harborough, *The Real Oscar Wilde* Werner Laurie, 1917

Woodcock, George, *Oscar Wilde The Double Image*, Black Rose Books 1989

WORKS BY WILDE

Ross, Robert editor, *The Complete Works of Oscar Wilde*, Methuen, Charles Carrington, in 14 volumes 1908

Ross, Robert editor, *The Complete Works of Oscar Wilde*, Methuen, Charles Carrington, John Lane in 20 volumes 1909

The Works of Oscar Wilde, His Life With a critical estimate of his writings, T. T. Brainard 1909

Holland, Vyvyan Introduction, *The Complete Works of Oscar Wilde*, Collins, 1973

Murray, Isobel, *The Oxford Authors Oscar Wilde*, Oxford University Press 1989

Mason, Stuart, *Impressions of America*, Keystone Press 1906

Clayworth, Anya editor, *Selected Journalism*, Oxford University Press 2004

Jackson, Russell and Small, Ian General Editors, *The Complete Works of Oscar Wilde*, Oxford University Press, Volume I, 2000; Volume 2, 2005; Volume 3, 2005.

Guy, Josephine; Small, Ian General Editor, *The Complete Works of Oscar Wilde, Volume 4, Criticism: Historical Criticism, Intentions, The Soul of Man*, Oxford University Press 2007

Schroeder, Horst, Various articles on the above *The Complete Works of Oscar Wilde, Volume 4, Criticism* published in *The Wildean*, numbers 34, 35, 36, 37, 38, 39 and 42 between January 2009 and January 2013.

Hart-Davis, Rupert Editor, *The Letters of Oscar Wilde*, Rupert Hart-Davis 1962

Hart-Davis, Rupert Editor, *More Letters of Oscar Wilde*, Oxford University Press 1987

Holland, Merlin; Hart-Davis, Rupert, Editors, *The Complete Letters of Oscar Wilde* Fourth Estate, 2000

GENERAL WORKS ABOUT WILDE

Beckson, Karl, *The Oscar Wilde Encyclopedia*, AMS Press 1998

Brown, Sally, *Oscar Wilde*, The British Library 2000

Callow, Simon, *Oscar Wilde and his Circle*, NPG 2000

Chamberlin, J. Edward, *Ripe was the Drowsy Hour The Age of Oscar Wilde*, A Continuum Book, 1977

Connon, Bryan, *Beverley Nichols: A Life*, Timber Press 2000

Ellmann, Richard, *Oscar Wilde A Collection of Critical Essays*, Prentice Hall International 1986

Gere, Charlotte with Hoskins, Lesley, *The House Beautiful Oscar Wilde and the Aesthetic Interior*, Lund Humphries 2000

Hichens, Robert, *The Green Carnation*, The Unicorn Press 1949

Mason, Stuart, *Bibliography of Oscar Wilde*, Werner Laurie 1914

Mikhail, E. H., *Oscar Wilde, Interviews and Recollections*, Macmillan 1979

Raby, Peter Editor *The Cambridge Companion to Oscar Wilde*, Cambridge University Press 1997

Roditi, Edouard, *Oscar Wilde*, New Directions Books 1947

von Eckhardt,Wolf; Gilman,Sander L.; Chamberlin, J. Edward, *Oscar Wilde's London*, Michael O'Mara Books Limited 1987

Oscar Wilde, Sotheby's Catalogue London 29 October 2004

Wilde Querying Spaces, Fales Library 1995

WORKS ABOUT THE LATE NINETEENTH CENTURY AND ART

Barnes, Janet, *Ruskin in Sheffield*, Sheffield Arts and Museums Department 1985

Calloway, Stephen and Orr, Lynn Federle Editors, *The Cult of Beauty The Aesthetic Movement 1860-1900*, V&A Publishing 2011

Dakers, Caroline, *The Holland Park Circle Artists and Victorian Society*, Yale University Press 1999

Gaunt, William, *The Aesthetic Adventure*, Jonathan Cape 1945

Hope-Nicholson, Jaqueline Editor, *Life Amongst the Troubridges by Laura Troubridge Journals of a Young Victorian 1873-1884*, Tite Street Press 1999.

Lancaster, Marie-Jacqueline Editor, *Letters of Engagement 1884-1888 The Love Letters of Adrian Hope and Laura Troubridge*, Tite Street Press 2002

Le Gallienne, Richard, *The Romantic '90s*, Putnam & Company 1951

Masson, David, *Chatterton: A Story of the Year 1770*, Macmillan 1874

Pennell, E. R., and J., *The Life of James McNeill Whistler*, Heinemann 1908

Soros, Susan Weber Editor, *E. W. Godwin Aesthetic Movement Architect and Designer*, Yale University Press 1999

Stanford, Derek Editor, *Writing of the 'Nineties from Wilde to Beerbohm*, Dent 1971

Warner, Eric & Hough, Graham, *Strangeness and Beauty An Anthology of Aesthetic Criticism 1840-1910*, Cambridge University Press 1983

Wilson, Sir Daniel, *Chatterton: A Biographical Study*, Macmillan 1869

Closer to Home The Restoration of Leighton House and Catalogue of the Reopening Displays 2010, Leighton House Museum 2010

Welcome to Leighton House Museum, Leighton House Museum 2010

WRITERS OF THE LATE NINETEENTH CENTURY

Pater, Walter Horatio, *Studies in the History of the Renaissance*, Macmillan, 1873 reprinted, edited Beaumont, Matthew, Oxford University Press, 2010

Pater, Walter Horatio, *The Renaissance Studies in Art and Poetry The 1893 Text*, edited Hill, Donald L., University of California Press 1980

Pater, Walter Horatio, *The Renaissance Studies in Art and Poetry*, Fontana 1961

Pater, Walter Horatio, *Marius the Epicurean*, Macmillan, 1924

Pater, Walter Horatio, *Appreciations*, Macmillan

Watts, W. Theodore, 'Poetry', *Encyclopædia Britannica* (9th edition), 1885

Watts, W. Theodore, Critical Introduction to *Chatterton* in *The English Poets, Selections with Critical Introductions*, Volume 3, editor T. H. Ward, Macmillan 1880

Watts-Dunton, W. Theodore, *The Renascence of Wonder*, Dutton 1914

Whistler, James McNeill, *The Gentle Art of Making Enemies*, Heinemann, 1953

Baudelaire: Selected Writings on Art and Artists, Translated P. E. Charvet, Penguin Books 1972

Notes

INTRODUCTION

1. *De Profundis, CW*, p 922
   Chapter 1

2. Ruskin, John (1819–1900) art and social critic

3. Pater, Walter Horatio (1839–1894) author, academic and aesthete

4. Whistler, James Abbott McNeill (1834–1903) painter and printmaker

5. Ellmann, p 125

6. Godwin, Edward William (1833–1886) architect, aesthete and designer

7. Rodd, James Rennell, first Baron Rennell (1858–1941) diplomat and classical scholar. Wilde would write the preface for his volume of poems, *Rose Leaf and Apple Leaf*, but without Rodd's approval, which led to a falling out between them.

8. *Portrait Of The Artist, The Life Of James McNeill Whistler*, E. K. and J. Pennell, vol 2, pp 11-14

9. Quilter, Harry (1851–1907) art critic

10. Miles, George Francis (1852–1891) painter

11. Story, Thomas Waldo (1855–1915) English/American sculptor and art critic
    Story, Julian (1857-1919) American Painter

12. Sickert, Walter Richard (1860–1942) English painter

13. Pennington, Robert Goodloe Harper (1855-1920) American Painter

14. Rossetti, Dante Gabriel (1828–1882) painter and poet

15. Burnand, Sir Francis Cowley (1836–1917) playwright and editor of *Punch*

16. Du Maurier, George Louis Palmella Busson (1834–1896) illustrator, cartoonist, and novelist

17. Theatrical partnership of the librettist W. S. Gilbert (1836-1911) and the composer Arthur Sullivan (1842–1900)

18. Ellmann p 130

19. Carte, Richard D'Oyly (1844–1901) theatre impresario

CHAPTER 1
THE LECTURES BEGIN

1. *Nottingham Evening Post*, Thursday 28 December 1882

2. *Bury and Norwich Post*, Tuesday 16 January 1883

3. *Aberdeen Journal*, Monday 8 January 1883

4. *Sheffield Independent*, Saturday 13 January 1883

5. Mason p 249

6. Prescott, Marie (1850-93) actor of great beauty and wit

7. *The Liverpool Mercury*, Thursday March 15 1883. *Daily Chronicle* noted in *The Woman's Union Journal*, July 1 1883

8. *Don't Shoot Me I'm Only the Piano Player*, 1973

9. Anderson, Mary (1859–1940) actor

10. Sherard, Robert Harborough (1861-1943) English writer and journalist

11. *Real* p 282

12. At this time the United Kingdom included the whole of Ireland. (*Britannica* 1905)

13. *The Works Of Oscar Wilde - His Life.* The C T Brainard Publishing Co. Edition De Luxe 1909. Chapter VI. Lectures In Great Britain. By W. F. Morse. p 159

14. Vezin, Hermann (1829-1910) American actor, teacher of elocution and writer

15. *Real* pp 289-291

16. Wilde (*née* Elgee) Jane Francesca Agnes, Lady Wilde [Speranza] (1821–1896) writer and Irish nationalist

17. 5 June at the home of a Mr & Mrs Bishop. *The Morning Post*, Thursday, June 7 1883.

18. Ruskin to Mrs Francis Alexander 7 October 1882, The Works of John Ruskin Library Edition Volume 32, p xxi-xxii

19. Leighton, Frederic, Baron Leighton (1830–1896) painter

20. Burne-Jones, Sir Edward Coley, first baronet (1833–1898) painter and Georgiana Burne-Jones (*née* Georgiana Macdonald) Lady Burne-Jones (1840–1920) wife and biographer of EB-J

21. Temple, William Francis Cowper-, Baron Mount-Temple (1811–1888) politician – his wife was Temple, Georgina Cowper (*née* Georgina Tollemache) Lady Mount-Temple (1821?–1901) religious enthusiast

22. Appleton, George Webb (1845–1909) author and playwright

23. *CL* 212, 213

24, Robertson, Eric Forbes- (1865–1935) British figure and landscape painter

25. Ross, Robert Baldwin (1869–1918) Wilde's friend, lover, literary executor, writer and gallery owner

26. *Essays and Lectures*, Ross, Methuen 1913, p x

27. *Miscellanies*, Ross p 309

28. *Renaissance* p 3. Incidentally, a little further on, Pater makes another statement Wilde will echo in *Earnest*: 'And he who experiences these impressions strongly … has no need to trouble himself with the abstract question what beauty is in itself, or what its exact relation to truth or experience, — *metaphysical questions, as unprofitable as metaphysical questions elsewhere.'_* [my emphasis] which prefigures Gwendolen's criticism of metaphysical speculation which she considers to have: '… very little reference at all to the actual facts of real life, as we know them.' in Act I of *Earnest CW* p 330.

29. *The Renaissance, Studies in Art and Poetry*, The 1893 Text, Walter Pater, edited Donald L. Hill, University of California Press, 1980, p 186

30. *De Profundis CW* p 917/8

31 Arnold, Matthew (1822–1888) poet, critic and inspector of schools. *On Translating Homer* 1862, and *The Function of Criticism at the Present Time,* 1864

32. Pericles (c. 495-429 BC) Greek statesman, general of Athens during the city's Golden Age

33. Phidias (c. 480-430 BC) Greek sculptor, painter and architect, commonly regarded as one of the greatest of all sculptors of Classical Greece

34. Aeschylus, Euripides, Socrates: two of ancient Greece's great

tragedians and Socrates the philosopher who was sentenced to death.

35. *Art & Morality*, Stuart Mason, Palmer 1912, and *CL* pp 428-450

36. Pisano, Nino (1349 – 1368) Italian sculptor
The Two Paths, Lecture III, Ruskin 1859 p123

37. *The Evening News*, Monday July 2 1883 & *The Globe*, Monday July 2 1883

38. *Moonshine*, Saturday July 14 1883

39. Turner, Joseph Mallord William (1775–1851) landscape painter

40. See Chapter 3, esp. PIA, Sheffield January 1884.

41. *CW* pp 970-992; 1009-1059

42. *Poison CW* p 997, *Critic CW* p 1028 & *CW* p 1030 … the primary aim of the critic is to see the object as in itself it really is not. …

43. *Lying CW* p 988

44. *Critic CW* p 1051

45. *Critic CW* p 1030

46. *Critic CW* p 1051

47. *Lying CW* p 987

48. unknown newspaper, 4 July 1883

49. *Portrait Of The Artist. The Life of James McNeill Whistler*. Heinemann 1908. E. K. and J. Pennell, vol 2, p 16

50. Ellmann, p 225

51. *Essays and Lectures*, Ross, Methuen 1913, p x

52. *Aberdeen Weekly Journal*, Wednesday June 27 1883

53. *Lady's Pictorial* ref. *Derby Mercury*, Wednesday June 13 1883

54. *Real* p 200

55. *The North-Eastern Daily Gazette*, Wednesday, July 11, 1883

56. *Leicester Chronicle and the Leicestershire Mercury*, Saturday,

July 21, 1883

57. The title Prince Regent is most commonly associated with George IV, who held the style HRH The Prince Regent during the incapacity, because of mental illness, of his father, George III between 1811 and 1820.

58. *The Preston Guardian etc*, Saturday, June 2, 1883

59. Nero (Nero Claudius Caesar Augustus Germanicus 37-68) Roman Emperor 54 to 68

60. *CL* p211

61. *Liverpool Mercury etc*, Thursday July 12 1883

62. *The Bury and Norwich Post etc*, Tuesday July 17 1883

63. *Freeman's Journal and Daily Commercial Advertiser*, Wednesday, July 11, 1883

64. *CL* pp213, 214

65. *The World*, July 18 1883

66. *Daily Telegraph*, 12 July 1883

67. *On Murder Considered as one of the Fine Arts*, De Quincy, 1827

68. *Dorian Gray*, *CW* p 47

69. *The World*, July 18 1883

70. *The Queen*, July 14 1883

71. *The World*, July 18 1883

72. *The Morning Post*, Thursday, July 12, 1883

73. *The Tatler. Bell's Life in London and Sporting Chronicle*, Saturday, July 14, 1883

74. *The Pall Mall Gazette*, Wednesday, July 11, 1883

75. *Glasgow Herald*, Friday, July 13, 1883

76. *Freeman's Journal and Daily Commercial Advertiser*, Wednesday, July 11, 1883

77. *Freeman's Journal and Daily Commercial Advertiser*, Wednesday, July 11, 1883

78. *Soul of Man, CW*, p 1089

79. *Soul of Man, CW*, p 1102

80. *The Brighton Guardian* Wednesday, 7 November 1883

81. *The Bristol Mercury and Daily Post*, Thursday, July 12, 1883

82. Bernhardt, Sarah Henriette Rosine (1844–1923) actor

83 *The Bristol Mercury and Daily Post*, Thursday, July 12, 1883

84. *Freeman's Journal and Daily Commercial Advertiser*, Wednesday, July 11, 1883

85. Morris, William (1834–1896) designer, author and visionary socialist

86. *Freeman's Journal and Daily Commercial Advertiser*, Wednesday, July 11, 1883

87. *Journalism* p 44 & note p 183. The two essays were *Shakespeare on Scenery* and *Shakespeare and Stage Costume.*

88. *Masks, CW* p 1060

89. *Masks, CW* p 1078

90. *The Bath Chronicle,* 4 October 1883

91. *Freeman's Journal and Daily Commercial Advertiser*, Wednesday, July 11, 1883

92. Davis, Jefferson Finis (1808-1889) American statesman serving as President of the Confederate States of America for its entire history, from 1861 to 1865.

93. *Freeman's Journal and Daily Commercial Advertiser*, Wednesday, July 11, 1883

94. *The Standard,* Wednesday, July 11, 1883

95. *Journalism,* p 91

96. *Freeman's Journal and Daily Commercial Advertiser*, Wednesday, July 11, 1883

97. *Freeman's Journal and Daily Commercial Advertiser*, Wednesday, July 11, 1883

98. *The West Middlesex Advertiser, etc,* Saturday 14 July 1883

99. *The Era,* Saturday, July 14, 1883

100. *Daily Gazette for Middlesbrough,* Wednesday 11 July 1883

101. *The West Middlesex Advertiser, etc.,* Saturday 14 July 1883

102. *The Standard,* Wednesday, July 11, 1883

103. *The Works Of Oscar Wilde - His Life.* The C T Brainard Publishing Co. Edition De Luxe 1909. Chapter VI. *Lectures In Great Britain.* By W. F. Morse. p162

104. Pugin, Edward Welby (1834–1875) architect

105. Smithers, Leonard Charles (1861–1907) publisher and bookseller *CL* pp 1031/32

106. *Keable's Gazette,* Saturday July 21 1883

107. *The Southport Advisor etc,* Saturday July 28 1883

108. Langtry, Lillie (1853-1929) (née Emilie Charlotte Le Breton) British music hall singer and stage actress

109. *Liverpool Mercury etc,* Thursday, August 2, 1883

110. Don Mead, Personal Impressions of America — Oscar Wilde in Southport, *The Wildean* 16, Jan 2000

111. *Southport Guardian,* 4 August 1883

112. *Southport Visiter,* 2 August 1883

CHAPTER 2
ENGAGEMENT

1. *The Era,* Saturday, September 8, 1883

2. *The Era,* Saturday, September 8, 1883

3. *The Illustrated Police News,* Saturday, September 22 1883

4. *Freeman's Journal,* Saturday, 15 September 1883 & *Western Mail,* Monday, September 17 1883

5. *Birmingham Daily Post,* Saturday, September 29, 1883

6. Irving, Sir Henry (real name John Henry Brodribb) (1838–1905) actor

7. *Daily News*, Monday, October 29, 1883

8. *The Era*, Saturday, September 22, 1883

9. Ellmann p 229

10. *Soul of Man, CW*, p 1098

11. Paxton, Sir Joseph (1803–1865) landscape gardener and architect

12. Lloyd, Constance Mary (1858–1898)

13. Ellmann pp 229/30

14. *CL* pp 221/2

15. Harris, James Thomas (known as Frank) (1856?–1931) journalist and storyteller

16. Harris pp 59-61

17. *Birmingham Daily Post*, Wednesday, December 19, 1883

18. *Earnest CW* p 332

19. Ellmann p 220

20. *CL* pp 224-226 and 240-2

21. *The Sheffield & Rotherham Independent*, Wednesday, January 16, 1884

22. The sub-title of 'Patience' was 'Bunthorne's Bride'.

23. *Aberdeen Weekly Journal*, Thursday, December 20, 1883

24. Baudelaire, Charles Pierre (1821-1867) French poet and critic

25. Gautier, Pierre Jules Théophile (1811-1872) French poet, novelist, journalist, art and literary critic

26. *Real*, p 286

27. Which means going without a meal.

28. Cascara Sagrada means 'sacred bark' in Spanish. It was long used as a laxative by Native American groups of the northwest Pacific coast.

29. *Punch* 10 November 1883

30. *CL* p 220 and notes 3 & 4

31. This telegram was published in Hesketh Pearson, *The Man Whistler*, London, 1952, p.119 & Hesketh Pearson *The Life of Oscar Wilde*, 1952, p96

32. *The Irish Times*, Thursday November 22 1883

33. *Derby Mercury*, Wednesday, October 24 1883

34. 'A Few Maxims' …, *CW* p 1204

35. Carson, Edward Henry, Baron Carson (1854–1935) politician and lawyer

36. *Peacock*, p 64 also *Trials,* 1948, p 120

37. Browning, Oscar (1837–1923) teacher and historian

38. *The Derby Mercury*, Wednesday October 31 1883

39. *The North-Eastern Daily Gazette,* Friday November 16 1883

40 *Northern Echo*, Friday November 30 1883

41. *The Fifeshire Journal*, October 25 1883

42. *The North-Eastern Daily Gazette,* Friday November 30 1883

43. *Irish Times*, Friday 23 November 1883

44. Yeats, William Butler (1865–1939) poet

45. Ellmann p 230

46. *The City Lantern and Free Lance*, October 11 1883

47 *Life* p 225 & *Real* p 296

48. *Hull News*, Saturday 20 October 1883

49. *The Derbyshire Times*, Saturday November 3 1883

50. *Ayr Advertiser*, Thursday 6th December 1883

51. *Nottinghamshire Guardian*, Friday December 21 1883

52. Le Gallienne, Richard (1866-1947) English author and poet

53. *Birkenhead & Cheshire Advertiser*, Saturday, December 15 1883 and *The Romantic '90s*, Richard Le

Gallienne, 1951, pp 140-2

54. *The Irish Times*, Friday 23 November 1883

55. *The Chester Chronicle*, Saturday November 24 1883

56. *Northern Echo*, Friday November 30 1883

57. *CL* pp 219 and 223

58. Bemrose, William (1831–1908) writer on wood-carving and ceramics

59. *The Derby Mercury*, Wednesday, December 19, 1883

60. Gladstone, William Ewart (1809–1898) prime minister and author

61. *Shields Daily Gazette*, Thursday 29 November 1883

62. It was by the discovery of Wilde's lecture in Middlesbrough that we now know that on the weekend of the 1 and 2 December Wilde was with friends – the Thursfields and Herberts – at the lovely seaside town of Tynemouth. The Middlesbrough lecture allowed the correct dating of a letter in *CL* (page 244) where lectures in Newcastle and Middlesbrough are mentioned. From the lecture list we now know that this letter should be dated 26 November 1883, over a year earlier than the estimated date of 8 January 1885. The Herbert family were from Gateshead, just across the River Tyne from Newcastle. Both Wilde and Constance were friendly with one of the daughters, Emily (1851-1949) who lived with her husband, James Thursfield (1840-1923) a naval historian, in Chelsea. She had married James in 1880 and he had been a tutor of Wilde's at Oxford. Some of Emily's sisters then lived at Tynemouth.

63. *Funny Folks*, Saturday, November 17 1883

64. *CL* p 220

65. *Hull News*, Saturday 20 October 1883

66. *Aberdeen Weekly Journal*, Saturday, October 20, 1883

67. *The Dundee Courier and Argus*, Saturday October 20 1883

68. *Dundee Advertiser*, Saturday October 20 1883

69. *Border Advertiser*, 31 October 1883

70. *The North-Eastern Daily Gazette*, Friday November 30 1883

71. *The Chester Chronicle*, Saturday November 24 1883

72. *Phrases CW* p 1205

73. *Birkenhead & Cheshire Advertiser*, Saturday, December 15 1883

74. *Hull News*, Saturday 20 October 1883

75. Sarony, Napoleon (1821-1896) American photographer. He had taken an extensive series of photographs of Wilde when he arrived in New York in 1882.

76. *Ayr Advertiser*, Thursday December 6 1883

77. *Earnest CW* p 360

78. *Aberdeen Weekly Journal*, Friday, October 19, 1883

79. *Cheshire Observer*, Saturday, November 24, 1883

80. *Shrewsbury Journal* 28 November 1883

81. *North East Daily Gazette* Friday November 30 1883

82. *The Romantic '90s*, R Le Gallienne, Putnam & Company 1951 p 141

83. *Chester Chronicle* Saturday 24 Nov 1883

84. *The Brighton Herald*, Saturday November 3 1883

85. *Northern Echo*, Friday, November 30, 1883

86. *Earnest CW* p 362

87. *Phrases CW* p 1206

88. *Ayr Advertiser*, Thursday December 6 1883

89. *Ayr Observer*, Friday December 7 1883

90. *The City Lantern and Free Lance,* October 11 1883

91. *Irish Times*, Friday November 23 1883

92. *Berrow's Worcester Journal*, Saturday, December 22, 1883

93. *Irish Times*, Friday November 23 1883

94. *Hastings Observer*, 3 November 1883

95. *Worcester Daily Times*, Wednesday 19 December 1883

96. *North Eastern Daily Gazette*, Friday 30 November 1883

97. *Shrewsbury Chronicle* 30 November 83

98. *Nottinghamshire Guardian*, Friday, December 21, 1883

99. Harris p 63

100. *The Model Millionaire, CW* p 219. Hughie Erskine is on his way there when he meets the eponymous model at his friend's studio and the professional model also makes his rounds there (*Miscellanies*, Ross, p 70)

101. *Cheshire Observer*, Saturday, November 24, 1883

102. *The Derby Mercury*, Wednesday October 24 1883

103. Millais, Sir John Everett, first baronet (1829–1896) painter

104. Alma-Tadema, Sir Lawrence (1836–1912) painter

105. see: http://www.asia.si.edu/

106. *CL* p 195

107. *Closer to Home*, Leighton House Museum, 2010 p 6

108. *Welcome to Leighton House Museum*, Leighton House Museum, p 2. For general and detailed descriptions see also: *Closer to Home*, Leighton House Museum, 2010

Mashrabiya is the Arabic term given to a type of projecting oriel window enclosed with carved wood latticework ...

often lined with stained glass. Wilde used lattice at one window in Tite Street which overlooked houses at the rear.

109. Crane, Walter (1845–1915) illustrator, designer and painter

110. De Morgan, William Frend (1839–1917) potter and novelist

111. *Renaissance* p 4, *Poison CW* p 996

112. *The Brighton Herald*, Saturday November 3 1883

113. *The Brighton Gazette*, Thursday November 1 1883

114. *The Telegram*, October 5 1883

115. *The Dorset County Chronicle etc*, October 4 1883

116. *Aberdeen Weekly Journal*, Saturday, October 20, 1883

117. *The Derby Mercury*, Wednesday, October 31, 1883

118. *The Newcastle Courant etc* Friday, November 30, 1883

119. *The Telegram*, October 5 1883

120. William Morris, *The Beauty of Life* (lecture) 1880. Believe me, if we want art to begin at home, as it must, we must clear our houses of troublesome superfluities that are for ever in our way ... if you want a golden rule that will fit everybody, this is it: 'HAVE NOTHING IN YOUR HOUSES THAT YOU DO NOT KNOW TO BE USEFUL OR BELIEVE TO BE BEAUTIFUL.'

121. William Morris, *The Beauty of Life* (lecture) 1880. ... and show us the victorious days when millions of those who now sit in darkness will be enlightened by an ART MADE BY THE PEOPLE AND FOR THE PEOPLE, A JOY TO THE MAKER AND THE USER.

122. *Birmingham Daily Post*, Saturday, December 15, 1883

123. *Aberdeen Weekly Journal* Saturday, October 20, 1883

124. *Berrow's Worcester Journal*, Saturday, December 22, 1883

125. *The Derby Mercury*, Wednesday, October 31, 1883
126. *Friendship*, p 25/6
127. *The Newcastle Courant* etc, Friday, November 30, 1883
128. *Aberdeen Weekly Journal*, Saturday, October 20, 1883
129. *Aberdeen Weekly Journal*, Saturday, October 20, 1883
130. *Worcestershire Advertiser*, Saturday December 23 1883
131. *CL* pp 258-260
132. *Dorian Gray, CW* p 46
133. Ellmann, p 546
134. *Nottinghamshire Guardian* Friday, December 21, 1883
135. *The Derby Mercury*, October 31 1883
136. *Cheshire Observer*, Saturday, November 24, 1883
137. *Renaissance* p 121
138. Keats, John (1795–1821) poet
139. Letter to Reynolds, 9 April 1818
140. *CL* p 225 footnote 1

CHAPTER 3
MARRIAGE

1. *The Pall Mall Gazette*, Monday, January 21, 1884
   The Sheffield & Rotherham Independent, Saturday, January 26, 1884
2. Sarony, Oscar Wilde No. 18
3. *The Newcastle Courant etc,* Friday, January 11, 1884
4. *The Dundee Courier & Argus and Northern Warder*, Friday, February 15, 1884
5. *CL* pp 224 – 227. The two letters to George Appleton about arrangements for future lectures (*CL* pp 226/7) are probably incorrectly dated and should be early 1885.
6. *Huddersfield Daily Examiner*, Thursday 24 January 1884
7. *The Preston Guardian etc,* Saturday, February 2, 1884

8. *The Preston Guardian etc,* Saturday, February 2, 1884
9. *The Hampshire Telegraph etc,* Saturday April 26 1884
10. *The Belfast News-Letter,* Thursday January 3 1884
11. *The North-Eastern Daily Gazette,* Wednesday, January 23, 1884
12. *Birmingham Daily Post,* Thursday, January 31, 1884
13. Rignold (Rignall) George Richard (1839–1912) actor and theatre manager born in Leicester who toured the USA and Australia, finally settling there.
14. *The York Herald*, Wednesday, February 13, 1884
15. *Western Mail*, Friday, March 28, 1884
16. *West Cumberland Times*, Saturday February 9 1884
17. *Vanity Fair*, 24 May 1884
18. Pellegrini, Carlo (Ape) (1839–1889) caricaturist. He had lived in the same Charles Street rooms before Wilde moved in.
19. Wilde, Sir William Robert Wills (1815–1876) surgeon
20. *Cumberland and Westmorland Advertiser,* Tuesday February 26 1884
21. The 1896 *Black's Guide to the English Lakes* calls Mr. Jenkinson 'the *doyen* of modern Lake Guides'.
22. Southey, Robert (1774 – 1843) English poet of the Romantic school and Poet Laureate from 1813 to his death in 1843. Southey's wife, Edith Fricker, whom he married at St. Mary Redcliffe, Bristol – the church from which Thomas Chatterton took his inspiration - in 1795 was the sister of Coleridge's wife, Sara Fricker. The Southeys set up home at Greta Hall, Keswick. Also living at Greta Hall with Southey and supported by him were Sara Coleridge and her

three children following their abandonment by Coleridge, and the widow of fellow poet Robert Lovell and her son. *Lodor* is a famous waterfall and onomatopoeic poem by Southey.

23. Rawnsley, Hardwicke Drummond (1851 – 1920) In 1883, having secured the support of Sir Robert Hunter, solicitor to the Commons Preservation Society, the social reformer Octavia Hill, and Ruskin, under whose influence Rawnsley had come while at Oxford, Rawnsley successfully led a campaign to prevent the construction of railways to carry slate from the quarries above Buttermere. This success led to the formation of the Lake District Defence Society whose members included Robert Browning, Ruskin and Alfred, Lord Tennyson, with whom Rawnsley had a family connection. He originated the idea of a National Trust that could buy and preserve places of natural beauty and historic interest for the nation. The Trust became a reality in 1895; its co-founders were Rawnsley, Octavia Hill and Sir Robert Hunter. Until his death, Rawnsley worked as Honorary Secretary to the Trust.

24. *Freeman's Journal and Daily Commercial Advertiser*, Friday, January 4, 1884

25. *Friendship*, facing page 184

26. Gide, André Paul Guillaume (1869-1951) French author and winner of the Nobel Prize in 1947

27. *The Wilde Album*, Merlin Holland, 1997 pp106/7 shows two but incorrectly dates the photographs as November 1884. One other has recently been discovered and is used here on the dust wrapper and as the frontispiece.

28. *The Belfast News-Letter*, Wednesday, January 2, 1884

29. *Sheffield and Rotherham Independent*, Tuesday January 22 1884

30. *Leeds Mercury*, Tuesday February 12 1884

31. *The Bristol Mercury etc*, Tuesday March 4 1884

32. MacDermott, Gilbert Hastings (1845 –1901) one of the biggest stars of the Victorian music hall. He performed under the name of 'The Great MacDermott', and was well-known for his rousing rendition of a war song: the song's chorus of "We don't want to fight but by jingo if we do, We've got the ships, we've got the men, and got the money too!" introduced the word jingoism into the English language.

33. 'Arry appeared in the pages of *Punch* in verse letters and cartoons and was the 'cheeky-cockney' invention of the editor, E. J. Milliken (1839-97.) *The 'Arry Ballads: An Annotated Collection of the Verse Letters by Punch Editor E.J. Milliken*, Editor Patricia Marks, McFarland 2006, p 4

34. *Husband CW* p 517

35. *The Preston Guardian etc*, Saturday, February 16 1884

36. *Earnest, CW* p 345

37. *Western Mail*, Friday March 28 1884

38. *Bradford Daily Telegraph*, Saturday, February 16 1884

39. *The Sheffield & Rotherham Independent*, Friday, February 1, 1884

40. *Leeds Mercury*, Tuesday February 12 1884

41. *Saint Oscar*, Terry Eagleton, 1989

42. *Leeds Mercury*, Tuesday February 12 1884

43. *De Profundis, CW* pp 905 & 913

44. *Leeds Mercury*, Tuesday February 12 1884

45. *The Huddersfield Chronicle and West Yorkshire Advertiser*, Saturday, January 26, 1884

46. *The Belfast News-Letter*, Wednesday, January 2, 1884

47. *Northern Echo*, Tuesday, February 5, 1884

48. *The North-Eastern Daily Gazette*, Saturday February 16 1884

49. *The Sheffield & Rotherham Independent*, Friday, February 1, 1884

50. *The Scarborough Gazette*, Thursday February 7 1884

51. *York Herald*, Friday February 1 1884

52. *The Hampshire Telegraph etc*, Saturday April 26 1884

53. *The Belfast News-Letter*, Wednesday, January 2, 1884

54. *Northampton Herald*, Saturday 22 March 1884

55. *The Bristol Mercury and Daily Post*, Saturday, March 1, 1884

56. *The Bristol Mercury and Daily Post*, Tuesday, March 4, 1884

57. *The Bristol Mercury and Daily Post*, Tuesday, March 4, 1884

58. *The Bristol Mercury and Daily Post*, Wednesday, March 26, 1884

59. *Western Mail*, Friday, March 28, 1884

60. *Birmingham Daily Post*, Friday, March 14, 1884

61. Chamberlain, John Henry (1831 – 1883) nineteenth century English architect who mainly worked in and around Birmingham where he was a major figure in civic life. Working predominantly in the Victorian Gothic style, he was one of the earliest and foremost exponents of the ideas of Ruskin.

62. Kenrick, William (1831–1919) partner Kenrick's tinned hollowware company, West Bromwich. In 1862 he married Mary Chamberlain, the elder sister of Joseph Chamberlain, with whom William became a close political ally. William's sister Harriet was the first wife of Joseph Chamberlain, and his cousin Florence Kenrick the second wife.

63. See V&A website: http://www. collections. vam.ac.uk/ item/ O10987/room-panelled-room-from-the-grove/

64. *Birmingham Daily Post*, Tuesday October 23 1883

65. Gosse, Sir Edmund William (1849–1928) writer

66. Müller, Friedrich Max (1823–1900) Sanskritist and philologist

67. *Birmingham Daily Post*, Wednesday, October 24, 1883

68. *Birmingham Daily Post*, Friday, March 14, 1884

69. *The Newcastle Courant etc*, Friday, February 15, 1884

70. *Earnest, CW* p 321

71. see *The Correspondence of James McNeill Whistler* at University of Glasgow at http://www. whistler.arts.gla.ac.uk/ Cole diaries: March 26th 1884.

72. See also Wilde's response to Whistler in 1885, *CL* p 250: 'Be warned in time, James, and remain, as I do, incomprehensible: to be great is to be misunderstood' and: *Critic, CW* pp 1015/6 '... I am but too conscious of the fact that we are born in an age when only the dull are treated seriously, and I live in terror of not being misunderstood.'

73. *Whitechapel - East London Sketches of Christian work and workers*, Henry Walker. Pub. the Religious Tract Society, 1896. This book also quotes: 'It was in 1867 that Denison, an Oxford student who had been profoundly impressed with the

gulf existing between the rich and the poor in London, took lodgings near the London Hospital, and tried to share his life with the poor of the district. His example was contagious, and by the year 1874 it had become the custom for a few Oxford graduates to spend part of their vacation in the neighbourhood of St. Jude's, Whitechapel, and to join in some of the work of the parish. Among them was Arnold Toynbee. The intensity which Denison and Toynbee threw into their teaching and example made a great impression on public opinion, and the settlement at Toynbee Hall took an organised and permanent form in the year 1884. From that date up to the present time its scope and aims have been ethical, social, and educational … its object is to 'provide education and the means of recreation and enjoyment for the people of the poorer districts of London.' Toynbee Hall 'has become a name under which a society holds together, formed of members of all classes, creeds, and opinions, with the aim of trying to press into East London the best gifts of the age.'

74. *Pall Mall Gazette*, Monday April 28 1884

75. *The Newcastle Courant etc,* Friday, February 22, 1884

76. John Keats, letter to Reynolds April 9th 1818: 'I have not the slightest feeling of humility towards the public, or to anything in existence but the Eternal Being, the principle of Beauty, and the memory of great men . ...' Wilde was very fond of this quotation, using it in *The English Renaissance of Art* and wanting to use it in *Poems*. However, after America, he

omitted the reference to 'the public.'

77. *The Sheffield & Rotherham Independent*, Friday, February 1, 1884

78. *Ruskin in Sheffield*; Janet Barnes; Collection of the Guild of St. George, Sheffield, 1985. Ruskin's proposal to establish similar museums all over the country did not materialise. The Ruskin Collection, known officially as the Collection of the Guild of St George is maintained and displayed by Museums Sheffield and is on permanent exhibition at the Millennium Gallery, Sheffield.

79. The letters of *Fors Clavigera* were written on a variety of topics that Ruskin believed would help to communicate his moral and social vision. He was principally concerned to develop a vision of moral value in sincere labour. It was in *Fors Clavigera* that Ruskin published his attack on the paintings of Whistler, which had been exhibited at the Grosvenor Gallery in 1876.

80. Letter from Ruskin to *The Times*. *Works* vol XXX p 317

81. *Ruskin in Sheffield*; Janet Barnes; Collection of the Guild of St, George, Sheffield, 1985 p 7

82. *The Sheffield & Rotherham Independent*, Thursday, January 24, 1884

83. *Lying*, CW pp 986/7

84. Bonhams 12 Jun 2012, *Books, Maps, Manuscripts and Historical Photographs*, Auction 20137

85. For more information see *The Wildean*, No. 42, January 2013: 'Oscar Wilde and the Mystics', Geoff Dibb

86. Lord Milner, *Pall Mall Gazette* to Wilde May 22 1884. *Stetson Catalogue* 1920.

87. Cumberland, Stuart (1857-1922) (born Charles Garner) conjurer,

open faker of magical phenomena.

88. Stead, William Thomas (1849–1912) newspaper editor and spiritualist

89. Wilde, William Charles Kingsbury (1852–1899) journalist

90. In 1875 Helena Blavatsky, Henry Steel Olcott, and William Quan Judge co-founded The Theosophical Society. Blavatsky combined Eastern religious traditions with Western esoteric teachings to create a synthesis she called the 'Perennial Religion'.

91. *The Pall Mall Gazette*, Saturday, May 24, 1884

92. *The Pall Mall Gazette*, Saturday, May 24, 1884

93. *Pall Mall Gazette*, Saturday, May 24, 1884

94. *Nottinghamshire Guardian*, Saturday 12 November 1887

95. *Daily News*, Wednesday, June 4, 1884

96. Allen, (Charles) Grant Blairfindie (1848–1899) science writer and novelist

97. *The North-Eastern Daily Gazette*, Wednesday, May 30, 1884

98. *The Sporting Times*, Saturday, May 31, 1884

99. *The North-Eastern Daily Gazette*, Wednesday, May 30, 1884

100. *The Sporting Times*, Saturday, May 31 1884

101. *Hampshire Telegraph and Sussex Chronicle etc*, Saturday, June 7, 1884

102. *The North-Eastern Daily Gazette*, Wednesday, May 30, 1884

103. Beere, Mrs. Bernard (Fanny Mary) (1856-1915) English actor

104. Brookfield, Charles Hallam Elton (1857–1913) actor and playwright

105. *The Bristol Mercury and Daily Post*, Saturday, June 7, 1884.

George IV was called 'the first gentleman in Europe,' because he was handsome, and had fine manners.

CHAPTER 4
A HANDFUL OF
NOTES AND GOLD

1. *The Works Of Oscar Wilde - His Life.* The C T Brainard Publishing Co. Edition De Luxe 1909. Chapter VI. Lectures In Great Britain. By W. F. Morse. p 159

2. *Ellmann* p 224

3. *CL* pp 224/5

4. *Friendship* pp 88/9

5. *CL* pp 252/253 & 226/227. The first letter pattern of lectures does not fit into February 1884 but does into January 1885. The second because of the Ulverston and Greenock lectures should be February 1885. See also Chapter 6.

6. *The North-Eastern Daily Gazette* Saturday, October 13, 1883

7. *Newcastle Courant*, Friday 22 February 1884

8. *Newcastle Courant* Friday 29 February 1884

9. *Wilde (Oscar) and his Literary Circle Collection of Papers* http://www.oac.cdlib.org/ findaid/ark:/13030/tf338nb1zb *Statements of receipts for Wilde's English lecture tour.* 1883-1884, 5 leaves. 8 x 5 in. & *Ledgers of accounts for English lecture tour.* Wilde, Oscar, 1854-1900. 1884 February 28 MS 7 leaves. 12-1/2 x 8 in. [Bound in grey boards]

10. It is not known whether this lecture actually took place on the date in the agreement.

11. For RPI etc, see: http://safalra.com/other/ historical-uk-inflation-price-conversion/

12. *The Huddersfield Daily Chronicle*, Thursday, January 24, 1884

13. see note 1 above

14. *Birmingham Daily Post*, Friday, March 14, 1884

CHAPTER 5
MAKING
THE HOUSE BEAUTIFUL

1. *The Derby Mercury*, Wednesday, September 3, 1884

2. Troubridge, Laura (married: Hope) (1863-1929) illustrator and writer

3. *Life amongst the Troubridges*, ed Jacqueline Hope-Nicholson, Tite Street Press 1999 p 169

   Also see: Ellmann p 244 which slightly misquotes this entry from the diary (changing 'drimp' to 'limp': he may be correct, there is no such English word as drimp; but also omitting 'absolutely' when describing her lack of bustle.)

4. E.g. *Northern Echo*, Friday May 24 1889

5. www.makingthemodernworld/. org.uk/stories/the_industrial_town/ 06.ST.02/?scene=6&tv=true

6. *The Ladies' Treasury: A Household Magazine*, September 1, 1884

7. *Soul of Man, CW* p 1079

8. Fortescue, May (1862-1950) singer, actor and a protégé of playwright W. S. Gilbert.

9. Grossmith, George (1847–1912) entertainer and author

10. *The Morning Post*, Thursday, July 24, 1884

11. *Manchester Courier and Lancashire General Advertiser*, Wednesday 30 July 1884

12. Carlyle, Thomas (1795–1881) author and historian

13. Beerbohm, Sir Henry Maximilian (Max) (1872-1956) caricaturist and writer

14. 1880, Max Beerbohm

15. Quilter, Harry (1851–1907) art critic

16. *Yorkshire Gazette*, Saturday 12 July 1884

17. *The Pall Mall Gazette*, Thursday, October 2, 1884

18. Jaeger, Gustav (1832-1917) German naturalist and hygienist: the system of clothing associated with his name originates from *Die Normalkleidung als Gesundheitsschutz* ('Standardized Apparel For Health Protection', 1880) where he advocated the wearing of rough fabrics such as wool "close to the skin", objecting especially to the use of any kind of plant fibre. The teachings of Jaeger inspired the creation of the Jaeger clothing brand.

19. *Birmingham Daily Post*, Friday 17 October 1884

20. Otto von Bismarck (1815-1898) German statesman

21. Shaw, George Bernard (1856–1950) playwright and socialist

22. quoted by Richard Le Gallienne: *The Romantic Nineties*, Putnam 1951 p.81.

23. *The Pall Mall Gazette*, Friday, October 3, 1884

    Huyshe, Wentworth (1847-1934) was a journalist with a passion for medieval times.

24. *The Pall Mall Gazette*, Tuesday, October 7, 1884

25. Harris pp 69/70

26. *The Pall Mall Gazette*, Tuesday, October 14, 1884

27. *CL* p233

28. *The Pall Mall Gazette*, Saturday, October 18, 1884

29. *The Pall Mall Gazette*, Tuesday, November 11, 1884. This is not in *Complete Letters* but I feel deserves to be, it being a response to correspondence and has Wilde's name at the bottom of the article, making it more of a letter than his October missive. It is printed, though, in *Miscellanies*, Ross, pp 52-62.

30. *CW* p 17

31. *The Pall Mall Gazette*, February 19, 1885

32. *Isle of Wight Observer*, Saturday, October 04, 1884 & *Isle of Wight Observer*, Saturday, October 11, 1884. Plus: Daniel Novak 'A Wilde Ryde' *Wildean* 12, Jan 1998

33. Brummell, George Bryan "Beau" (1778-1840) English dandy, arbiter of men's fashion in Regency England & Alfred d'Orsay, known as the Count d'Orsay (Alfred Guillaume Gabriel) (1801-1852) French dandy, and man of fashion

34. *The Dundee Courier & Argus and Northern Warder*, Tuesday, September 9, 1884

35. *Husband, CW* p 517

36. *The Evening Press*, Thursday October 9 1884

37. Conway, Hugh (pen name of Frederick John Fargus) (1847-1885) English novelist and playwright & Carr, Joseph William Comyns (1849-1916) English art critic and playwright

38. Dene, Dorothy (born Ada Alice Pullen) (1859-1899) actor, muse and artist's model for the painter Lord Leighton

39. Terry, Fred (1863–1933) actor

40. Jones, Henry Arthur (1851–1929) playwright

41. Barrett, Wilson (real name William Henry Barrett) (1846–1904) actor and playwright

42. *The York Herald*, Friday, October 10, 1884

43. *CL* p 232

44. *The York Herald*, Friday, October 10, 1884

45. *The York Herald*, Saturday, October 11, 1884

46. *The York Herald*, Saturday, October 11, 1884

47. *The Evening Press*, Thursday October 9 1884

48. Lockwood, Sir Frank (1846–1897) lawyer and politician

married Julia Rosetta Salis-Schwabe in 1874

49. *Birmingham Daily Post,* Saturday, September 20, 1884

50. *Birmingham Daily Post*, Wednesday, 22 October 1884

51. *Birmingham Daily Post*, Wednesday 5 November 1884, preview *The Owl*, Wednesday October 8 1884

52. Philip Manlow Griffiths was the son of Thomas Griffiths, a wealthy Birmingham businessman who manufactured 'holloware', a term that refers to table service items such as sugar bowls, creamers, soup tureens and other metal items.

53. *CL* p 239 and Don Mead, *The Wildean* 4, 1994, on Griffiths letters at a Christies sale.

54. *CL* p 263

55. now *CL* p 241

56. *Leeds Mercury*, Friday 5 December 1884

57. *The Yorkshire Post*, 4 December 1884

58. Nichols, (John) Beverley (1898–1983) writer.

    Oscar Wilde Interviews and Recollections, E H Mikhail, Barnes & Noble, 1979 pp 122-3

59. *Beverley Nichols: A Life,* Bryan Connon, 1991 pp 20/1 (and is also retold in *The Maker of the Omnibus*, Jack Hodges, 1992)

60. *L'Envoi An Introduction to Rose Leaf and Apple Leaf* by Rennell Rodd, J. M. Stoddart, Philadelphia, 1882. *Miscellanies*, Ross, p 38

61. 'The English Renaissance of Art', *Miscellanies*, Ross, p 256

62. 'Phrases And Philosophies For The Use Of The Young', *Chameleon,* December 1894, *CW* p 1205

63. *CL* p 241

64. *The Times*, Thursday, December 4 1884

65. *CL* p 236

66. Bellew, Harold Kyrle Money (1850-1911) British stage and silent film actor

67. Adrian Hope's description, letter to Laura Troubridge, Sunday 15 March 1885; *Letters of Engagement 1884-1888*, ed Marie-Jaqueline Lancaster, Tite Street Press, 2002, pp 102-4

68. *The Leeds Mercury*, Thursday, December 4, 1884

69. *The Leeds Mercury*, Friday, December 5, 1884

70. *Leeds Saturday Journal*, 6 December 1884

71. *The Yorkshireman, A Magazine of Literary and Football Gossip*, Saturday December 13, 1884

72. Terry, Edward O'Connor (1844–1912) actor and theatre proprietor

73. Grimshaw, (John) Atkinson (1836– 1893) landscape painter

74. May, Philip William (1864–1903) illustrator

75. eg *CL* pp 239, 232, 223 see also Chapter 3.

76. *CL* pp 240-2

77. Blackie, John Stuart (1809–1895) classical and Scottish Gaelic scholar *CL* p 242. As Wilde says he is in 'Edinboro' for 3 days this must be dated 19 December 1884.

78. Hunter-Blair, Sir David, 5th Bt (1853-1939) Monk of the Order of St Benedict and Abbot of Dunfermline

79. *In Victorian Days*, London 1938, David Hunter Blair, pp 115-143

80. *CL* pp 242-3

81. *Glasgow Herald*, Monday, December 22, 1884

82. *The Lancaster Gazette and General Advertiser etc*, Saturday, December 27, 1884

83. *Sheffield Daily Telegraph*, Tuesday 28 October 1884

84. *Bath Chronicle and Weekly Gazette*, Thursday 23 October1884

85. Hichens, Robert Smythe (1864–1950) writer

86. *The Green Carnation*, Robert Hichens, The Unicorn Press 1949, p vi

87. *The Illustrated Police News etc*, Saturday, December 13, 1884

88. *The Morning Post*, Thursday, November 20, 1884

89. *Funny Folks*, Saturday, December 27, 1884

CHAPTER 6.
THERE IS MUCH TO BE SAID IN
FAVOUR OF MODERN
JOURNALISM

1. *Critic, CW* p 1048

2. *CL* pp 252 – 263

3. *The Leeds Mercury* Saturday 14 March 1885

4. *Freeman's Journal etc*, Monday 5 Jan 1885

5. *Freeman's Journal etc*, Tuesday 6 Jan 1885

6. *Freeman's Journal etc*, Wednesday 7 Jan 1885

7. *Life* p 236

8. *The Lancaster Gazette*, Wednesday March 18 1885

9. *Freeman's Journal etc*, Wednesday, January 7, 1885

10. *The Belfast News-Letter*, Wednesday, January 7, 1885

11. *Hampshire Telegraph and Sussex Chronicle etc*, Saturday, January 31, 1885

12. *The Secret Life of Oscar Wilde*, McKenna, Century 2003, p 333

13. Wilde, John Maxwell (1806-1885) vicar, Wilde's father's older brother.

14. *CL* p246/7

15. *Leicester Chronicle and the Leicestershire Mercury*, Saturday,

January 17, 1885

16. 'The Tomb of Keats', 1877, Ross, *Miscellanies*, p4

17. *Peacock*, p 170 & variation in *Trials*, p 144

18. *Pall Mall Gazette*, Thursday 5 February 1885

19. Huxley, Thomas Henry (1825–1895) biologist

20. Forbes, Archibald (1838–1900) journalist and lecturer with whom Wilde fell out in the USA in 1882

21. *The North-Eastern Daily Gazette* Monday, January 19, 1885

22. *Newcastle Weekly Chronicle*, 24 January 1885

23. *Newcastle Courant*, Friday 23 January 1885

24. *The North-Eastern Daily Gazette*, Tuesday January 28 1885

25. There are four in total, two which have been dated as being from February 1884 (*CL* pp 226/7) and two from 1885 (on pp 252/3). The first letter (Wilde noted it as a Thursday) mentions a series of forthcoming days when he is lecturing: February 1884 does not have this pattern of lectures. More likely is either 22 or 29 January 1885. The second letter must be from Ulverston in February 1885 preceding his lecture in Greenock. See also Chapter 4 which deals with these letters.

26. *Barrow Herald,* 17 February 1885

27. *The Greenock Telegraph and Clyde Shipping Gazette*, 14 February 1885

28. Merlin Holland's suggestion is that Appleton's successful play is the comic drama *A Fair Sinner*, which opened at the Gaiety Theatre on 4 March, so the letter must have been written after this date. Appleton was very busy at this time having his comedy drama *Zana!* commence touring on 16 March which had been heavily advertised for over a month. However, the Ipswich *Fair Sinner* dates look to be the best candidates.

29. *Western Gazette* Friday, 27 February 1885

30. Brawne (married: Lindon) Frances (1800–1865) fiancée of John Keats *Liverpool Mercury*, Thursday, March 5, 1885

31. *Leek Times*, 28 March 1885

32. Nicholson, Joshua (1812–1885) silk manufacturer

33. Sugden, William (1820-1892) architect

34. There are a number of legacies of William Morris' time in Leek, one being the interest he took in the Leek School of Embroidery which was founded by Mrs Wardle in the 1880s. He offered to design a rug for her woolwork and sent items to a textile museum that she created. Another monument to Morris in the town was the establishment of the William Morris Labour Church designed by Larner Sugden shortly after his death. Much of the work in the Church was carried out from designs by Walter Crane who signed Morris's obituary in the *Leek Times*: it had red painted walls with stencilled tracery; woodwork painted green and the curtains were blue velvet of one of Morris's designs.

Morris' interest in Leek was the consequence of an interest in returning to the colours in dyes derived from natural materials. He came to the town several times from February 1875 onwards, sometimes staying for several weeks working with Thomas Wardle the brother in law of his works manager George at his dye works at Hencroft.

35. Wardle, Sir Thomas (1831–1909) silk dyer and printer

36. *CL* pp 258-260

37. Sugden, William Larner (1850-1901) architect

38. *The Leek Times*, 28 March 1885

39. A History of Staffordshire, p 114. See British History Online: www.british-history. ac.uk

40. *Pall Mall Gazette,* 19 January 1885

41. *Pall Mall Gazette*, 21 February 1885

42. *Western Mail*, Tuesday February 24 1885

43. *The York Herald*, Monday, February 23, 1885

44. *The Times*, 21 February 1885

45. see *The Correspondence of James McNeill Whistler* at University of Glasgow website at www.whistler. arts.gla.ac.uk/

46. *Whistler, containing Mr. Whistler's 'Ten O'clock'* published London 1888, pp 131-159 plus correspondence pp 161-165

47. *Essays and Lectures*, Ross, Methuen 1913, p x

48. *Miscellanies* Introduction, Ross, pp xiv - xvi

49. *Friendship,* pp 73/74

50. *Pall Mall Gazette*, 24 February 1885 & CL pp250/1.

51. *Self Reliance*, 1841, Ralph Waldo Emerson: Is it so bad, then, to be misunderstood? Pythagoras was misunderstood, and Socrates, and Jesus, and Luther, and Copernicus, and Galileo, and Newton, and every pure and wise spirit that ever took flesh. To be great is to be misunderstood.

52. *Pall Mall Gazette*, 28 February 1885

53. *The Salon of 1846 – XVIII. Of the Heroism of Modern Life*, Trans P E Charvet, Penguin Books, 1972, p 106

54. *Journalism*, pp 44 - 46

55. 'Shakespeare And Stage Costume', May 1885; *The Nineteenth Century: A Monthly Review.* Edited by James Knowles. Vol. XVII. January-June, 1885. pp. 800-18. London: Kegan Paul, Trench, & Co.
'Shakespeare and Stage Costume by Oscar Wilde' sourced from ajdrake.com at www.ajdrake.com/ etexts/ texts/Wilde/Works/shake_ stage_costume.pdf via writersinspire.org. Accessed Tuesday, 15th January 2013

56. *Stage Costume*, p 807

57. *Stage Costume*, p 814

58. *Critic, CW*, p 1050

59. *Stage Costume*, p 815

60. *Stage Costume*, p 816

61. *Stage Costume*, p 817

62. *Stage Costume*, p 811

63. *Stage Costume*, p 818

64. see the 'Chronicling America' web site of the Library of Congress: www.chronicling america. loc.gov/lccn/ sn83030214/1885-04-19/ed-1/seq-9/

65. *Essays and Lectures*, Ross, Methuen 1913, Preface pp ix - xi

66. *Northern Echo*, Saturday, May 2, 1885

67. *The North-Eastern Daily Gazette*, Tuesday April 21 1885

68. *The North-Eastern Daily Gazette*, Monday April 20 1885

69. Holland, Cyril (born Cyril Wilde 1885-1915)

70. *Newcastle Daily Chronicle*, Friday 6 November 1885 & *Pall Mall Gazette,* 15 October 1885

71. *Bell's Life in London*, Thursday October 29 1885

72. *Newcastle Daily Chronicle,* Friday 6 November 1885

73. *Fife Herald*, Wednesday 18 November 1885

74. *The Evening Chronicle*, Wednesday November 11 1885

75. *The Newcastle Weekly Courant*, Friday, November 13, 1885

76. Marillier, Henry Currie (1865–1951) writer and expert on tapestries

77. CL pp 266-282

78. *Aberdeen Weekly Journal*, Saturday December 12 1885

79. *The Dart*, Friday December 18 1885

CHAPTER 7
THE FINAL LECTURES

1. Ellmann p 261

2. Harris, pp 73/4

3. CL p 273/4

4. *The Royal Cornwall Gazette Falmouth Packet, Cornish Weekly News, & General Advertiser*, January 22, 1886

5. *Exeter and Plymouth Gazette*, Thursday 21 January 1886

6. *Son of Oscar Wilde*, Vyvyan Holland, 1954, pp 54/5

7. his reply is dated 11 June 1886. CL p 282

8. *Critic, CW* p 1022

9. *The Bristol Mercury and Daily Post*, Saturday, July 17, 1886

10. *Northern Echo*, Thursday, October 7, 1886

11. *Nottingham Evening Post*, Tuesday 5 October 1886

12. Chatterton, Thomas (1752–1770) poet and forger

13. Wordsworth, William (1770–1850) poet

14. Coleridge, Samuel Taylor (1772–1834) poet, critic, drug addict and philosopher

15. Shelley, Percy Bysshe (1792–1822) poet

16. de Vigny, Alfred Victor (1797 - 1863) was a French poet and playwright

17. Browning, Robert (1812–1889) poet

18. Dunton, (Walter) Theodore Watts- (1832–1914) writer and poet

19. Wallis, Henry (1830–1916) painter and ceramics expert

20. Meredith, George (1828–1909) novelist and poet

21. Norman, Gertrude (1851-1943) actor

22. *Friendship*, pp 43/4

23. de Nerval, Gerard (born Gérard Labrunie)(1808-1855) French poet and essayist

24. Poe, Edgar Allen (born Edgar Poe)(1809-1849) American author, poet and literary critic

25. Horne, Herbert Percy (1864–1916) architect, art collector and art historian

26. CL pp 282 – 484

27. Mackmurdo, Arthur Heygate (1851–1942) architect and social reformer

28. *The Leeds Mercury,* Wednesday, December 30, 1885

29. Brooke, Stopford Augustus (1832–1916) preacher and writer CL pp 289/90

30. CL p 284 n1

31. CL p284 n1 & *Bibliography* p 13

32. Ross, *Reviews,* pp 115-9

33. Noel, Roden Berkeley Wriothesley (1834–1894) poet and essayist

34. CL pp 289/90

35. *Earnest, CW*, p 326

36. *The Dart: The Midland Figaro*, Friday, November 5, 1886

37. Stanley, Sir Henry Morton (1841–1904) explorer and journalist

38. Livingstone, David (1813–1873) explorer and missionary

39. Dickens, Charles John Huffam (1812–1870) novelist

40. *Whistler* p 164

41. CL p 288

42. *Whistler* p 165

43. *The Derby Mercury*, Wednesday, November 24, 1886

44. Campbell (born: Blood) Gertrude Elizabeth (Lady Colin Campbell) (1857–1911) art critic and journalist

45. *CL* pp 286/7

46. Edwards, Herbert Edward Osman (known as Osman) (1864-1936) reviewer, lecturer, translator, and amateur actor

47. *The Hampshire Advertiser*, Saturday, February 5, 1887

48. *CW* p 220

49. *York Herald*, Saturday 11 June 1887

50. McCarthy, Justin (1830–1912) politician and writer

51. *Freeman's Journal*, Friday 23 September 1887

52. *Journalism*, p 10/11, 'A Hand-book to Marriage' (*PMG* 18 November 1885)

53. *London Daily News*, Thursday 27 October 1887

54. Mason pp 130/1

55. Mason pp 21, 40, 237

56. Reid, Sir Thomas Wemyss (1842–1905) journalist and biographer. *CL* pp 297-99

57. *CL* from p 301 onwards

58. *Nottingham Evening Post*, Friday 28 October 1887

59. *The Oscar Wilde Collection*, from the William Andrews Clark Memorial Library, UCLA.

60. *The Graphic*, 4 February 1888

61. This was the Bethnal Green Branch of the South Kensington Museum, opened in 1872.

62. Wilde, Oscar. [Essay on Chatterton]. W.S. Lewins: 1952 MS. Wilde W6721M3 E78 [1886?] Bound 19th century AD. MS Oscar Wilde Wilde W6721M3 E78. William Andrews Clark Memorial Library, University of California, Los Angeles. 82

63. Chatterton: *A Biographical Study* by Daniel Wilson & *Chatterton: A Story of the Year 1770* by David Masson.

64. *Poole & Bournemouth Herald*, Thursday 12 April 1888

65. 'Miner And Minor Poets', *Pall Mall Gazette*, February 1, 1887. *Reviews* Ross, pp 123-7

66. *The English Poets, Selections with Critical Introductions, Volume 3*, ed T. H. Ward, 1880, pp 400-408

67. *The Aesthetic Adventure,* William Gaunt, 1945, p 109

68. National Portrait Gallery. Henry Treffry Dunn, Gouache and watercolour on paper now on card, 1882. www.npg.org.uk/collections/search/portrait Extended/mw05468/Dante-Gabriel-Rossetti-Theodore-Watts-Dunton

69. Swinburne, Algernon Charles (1837–1909) poet

70. *CL* p 290

71. Wilde added a question mark to this quotation which I think indicates he did not know where it came from. The only references I can find for it are all in Watts' own writings: his introduction to Chatterton already referred to, his entry on Poetry in the 1909 *Encyclopedia Britannica* and in his *Poetry and The Renascence of Wonder,* Dutton 1914, p 91.

72. *Mr. W.H. CW* p 1150

73. *Criticism*, p xxxvi

74. 'Olivia at the Lyceum', May 1885, *Journalism* pp 53-56

75. *CW* p 17

76. *CW* pp 987/8

77. Wainewright, Thomas Griffiths (1794–1847) painter, writer on art and poisoner

78. *CW* p 993

79. *CW* p 288

images. (The Oscar Wilde Collection)

80. *The Nineteenth Century*, January 1889.

81. *The Fortnightly Review*, January 1889

82. *English Illustrated Magazine*, with illustrations by Harper Pennington, January 1889

83. *Blackwood's Edinburgh Magazine*, July 1889

84. Barnett (née Rowland) Dame Henrietta Octavia Weston (1851–1936) social reformer

85. *CL* p 415

Introduction to Appendices

1. *Miscellanies*, Ross p 309

2. *Impressions of America*. Edited by Stuart Mason, Keystone Press, Sunderland, 1906.

3. *Essays and Lectures*, Methuen 1913, Ross, p ix

4. *Criticism* pp xxvi – xxvii

Appendix A
Modern Art Training

1. *The Works Of Oscar Wilde - His Life*. The C T Brainard Publishing Co. Edition De Luxe 1909. Chapter VI. Lectures In Great Britain. By W. F. Morse. p 162

2. *Renaissance*, Preface p 3, Many attempts have been made by writers on art and poetry to define beauty in the abstract ... Such discussions help us very little to enjoy what has been well done in art or poetry. ... See also *English Renaissance of Art*, *Miscellanies*, Ross p 243, also *Poison CW* 997 He cared nothing for abstract definitions on the nature of the Beautiful. ... This phraseology is reused in *HB & VAML*.

3. *Dorian Gray, CW* p 31: Nothing can cure the soul but the senses, just as nothing can cure the senses but the soul.

4. *Miscellanies*, Ross p 69: Whatever comes from Mr. Whistler's brush is far too perfect in its loveliness to stand or fall by any intellectual dogmas on art, even by his own: for Beauty ... cares nothing for explanations ...

5. Reused in *VAML*

6. This could be a reference to Ruskin who was Slade Professor of Art at Oxford between 1869-78 & 1883-85. Whistler attacked 'Professors of Art' in his *Ten O'Clock lecture*, February 1885.

7. Perugino, Pietro (born Pietro Vannucci) (c. 1446/1450–1523) Italian Renaissance painter of the Umbrian school. *Renaissance*, Wincklemann p 113: ... the clear loveliness of Perugino ... Also referred to in Leonardo and in *Renaissance* 1961, Raphael (1892): p 147.

8. Rosa, Salvator (1615-1673) Italian Baroque painter and poet (although 'it is of no use to you,' he was born in Arenella, on the outskirts of Naples)

   Pater *Marius* p 164: The picturesque, romantic Italy of a later time—the Italy of Claude and Salvator Rosa—was already forming, for the delight of the modern romantic traveller.

9. *Poison CW* p 997: he never lost sight of the great truth that Art's first appeal is neither to the intellect nor to the emotions, but purely to the artistic temperament, and he more than once points out that this temperament, this 'taste', as he calls it, being unconsciously guided and made perfect by frequent contact with the best work, becomes in the end a form of right judgment.

10. *Renaissance*, p 4: ... all periods, types, schools of taste, are in themselves equal. & *Poison CW* p 996 ... the true harmony of all

really beautiful things irrespective of age or place, of school or manner.

11. Velázquez, Diego Rodríguez de Silva y (1599 – 1660) Spanish painter who was the leading artist in the court of King Philip IV

12. Critic CW p 1030 ...the anecdotage of painting ... scenes taken out of literature or history ... they do not stir the imagination. ...

13. See also *Dress*.

14. *Soul, CW*, p 1090: Now Art should never try to be popular.

15. *Critic CW* p 1018 Plato ... dealt with ... the aesthetic value of appearances, the relation of the visible arts to the external world.

16. *Critic CW* p 1040 It seems to me that with the development of the critical spirit we shall be able to realise, not merely our own lives, but the collective life of the race, and so to make ourselves absolutely modern, in the true meaning of the word modernity. For he to whom the present is the only thing that is present, knows nothing of the age in which he lives. To realise the nineteenth century, one must realise every century that has preceded it and that has contributed to its making.

17. Phidias (c. 480-430 BC) Greek sculptor, painter and architect, commonly regarded as one of the greatest of all sculptors of Classical Greece

18. Leighton, Frederic, Baron Leighton (1830–1896) painter

19. Pericles (c. 495-429 BC) Greek statesman, general of Athens during the city's Golden Age

20. A major Wildean theme and one he would be accused of after the publication of *Dorian Gray* in 1890. See *Art and Morality*, Stuart Mason, Frank Palmer 1912 and

Wilde wrote *The Preface, CW* p 17 as his defence.

21. Aeschylus, Euripides, Socrates: two of ancient Greece's great tragedians and Socrates, the philosopher who was sentenced to death

22. *Critic CW* p 1049 You remember that lovely passage in which Plato describes how a young Greek should be educated, and with what insistence he dwells upon the importance of surroundings, telling us how the lad is to be brought up in the midst of fair sights and sounds, so that the beauty of material things may prepare his soul for the reception of the beauty that is spiritual.

23. see *HB* with Wilde's preference for Gothic architecture as proposed by Ruskin; also *Dress*.

24. see *HB*

25. see *Dress*

26. Ruskin established his Guild of St George in Sheffield which suffered from these 'sordid aspects.' Wilde referred to the beauty of smoke when he spoke in Sheffield in January 1884 (see Chapter 3.)

27. Pisano, Nino (1349 – 1368) Italian sculptor

28. *The Two Paths*, Lect III, p 123 1859

29. *Poison CW* p 998: ... the art-literature of the nineteenth century, that form of literature which has found in Mr. Ruskin and Mr. Browning, its two most perfect exponents. And *Critic CW* p 1028 That mighty and majestic prose of his (Ruskin)...

30. *Masks, CW* p 1065: ... recognises the artistic beauty of ugliness.

31. *Lying, CW* p 978: Art ... is absolutely indifferent to fact ...

32. This statement is the result of Wilde's engagement with Arnold and Pater. See *Renaissance*, p 3, *Poison, CW*

p 997; *Critic, CW* p 1028 & *CW* p 1030 … the primary aim of the critic is to see the object as in itself it really is not …

33. *Lying, CW* p 972 One of the chief causes that can be assigned for the curiously commonplace character of most of the literature of our age is undoubtedly the decay of Lying as an art, a science, and a social pleasure.

34. *Critic,* CW p 1031: For the painter is limited, not to what he sees in nature, but to what upon canvas may be seen.

35. *Preface, CW* p 17: Vice and virtue are to the artist materials for an art.

36. *Lying, CW* p 986 To look at a thing is very different from seeing a thing. One does not see anything until one sees its beauty.

37. Whistler painted many of his nocturnes of the 1870's on the Thames Embankment.

38. *Endymion,* John Keats, at the beginning of first stanza: A thing of beauty is a joy for ever; / Its loveliness increases; it will never / Pass into nothingness…

39. Buonarroti Simoni, Michelangelo di Lodovico (1475-1564) Italian Renaissance sculptor, painter, architect, poet and engineer

40. *Critic, CW* p 1051 … rejecting the tedious realism of those who merely paint what they see, try to see something worth seeing

41. Ruskin, John (1819–1900) art and social critic

42. Wilde made this point in later lectures in industrial cities and was criticised, particularly in Sheffield.

43. Turner, Joseph Mallord William (1775–1851) landscape painter

44. see *PIA* and references to the extremely clear atmosphere in American cities.

45. *Critic, CW* p 1030: It is sometimes said by those who understand neither the nature of the highest Criticism nor the charm of the highest Art, that the pictures that the critic loves most to write about are those that belong to the anecdotage of painting, and that deal with scenes taken out of literature or history.

46. Whistler, James Abbott McNeill (1834–1903) painter and printmaker. Whistler was always referred to in the highest terms in the lectures, see also *VAML* and Wilde's first review of Whistler's 10 o'clock lecture.

47. Wilde concluded his review of *Whistler's Ten o'Clock* with this: For that he is indeed one of the very greatest masters of painting, is my opinion. And I may add that in this opinion Mr Whistler himself entirely concurs (*Journalism*, p 8)

48. Wilde's second review of Whistler's 10 o'clock lecture begins with a quotation from Baudelaire: Great colourists know the secret of creating colour with a black frock-coat and a white cravat and a grey background.

49. *Critic CW* p 1030 … the anecdotage of painting … scenes taken out of literature or history … they do not stir the imagination …

50. *Critic, CW* p 1053: The appeal of all art is simply to the artistic temperament. Art does not address herself to the specialist.

51. Also reused in *VAML*

52. *Critic, CW* p 1054: Technique is really personality.

53. This was an issue in the Ruskin/Whistler trial in 1876, Burne-Jones as a witness for Ruskin gave evidence. Whistler, pp 14-18: '… complete finish ought to be the object of all

artists ... It shows no finish – it is simply a sketch.' Also *VAML*

54. These handcraftsmen are also referred to in *HB*.

55. *Critic, CW* pp 1051/2: Still, the art that is frankly decorative is the art to live with. It is, of all our visible arts, the one art that creates in us both mood and temperament. Mere colour, unspoiled by meaning, and unallied with definite form, can speak to the soul in a thousand different ways. The harmony that resides in the delicate proportions of lines and masses becomes mirrored in the mind. The repetitions of pattern give us rest. The marvels of design stir the imagination. In the mere loveliness of the materials employed there are latent elements of culture. Nor is this all. By its deliberate rejection of Nature as the ideal of beauty, as well as of the imitative method of the ordinary painter, decorative art not merely prepares the soul for the reception of true imaginative work, but develops in it that sense of form which is the basis of creative no less than of critical achievement.

56. Also reused in *VAML*

57. *English Renaissance, Miscellanies*, Ross p 261. Also *HB*.

58. *Renaissance*, p 121: ... art comes to you professing frankly to give nothing but the highest quality to your moments as they pass ...

59. *Critic, CW* p 1029: ...the meaning of any beautiful created thing is, at least, as much in the soul of him who looks at it, as it was in his soul who wrought it.

60. *Critic, CW* pp 1051: Still, the art that is frankly decorative is the art to live with.

APPENDIX B
PERSONAL IMPRESSIONS
OF AMERICA

1. Historical Criticism, *Criticism* p 35 (which is a much amended version of *Rise, CW* p 1127): ... of the influence of climate and temperature in forming the nature of man, (a conception perhaps pressed too far in modern days when ... the latitude and longitude of a country the best guide to its morals,) ... Cousin errs a good deal in this respect: to say like he did 'give me the lat. long. of a country ... and I will deduce the race' is surely a glaring exaggeration. Used also in *HB*

2. *Dorian Gray, CW* p 42 "... What are American dry-goods?" asked the Duchess..."American novels," answered Lord Henry... reused in *A Woman, CW*, p 436

3. See *Dress*.

4. A change in view from *MAT* where Wilde claimed an artist did not need beautiful surroundings.

5. The choice of beautiful English cities did vary slightly. Cambridge, Salisbury, Winchester, Warwick or Gloucester were all mentioned at different lectures.

6. *Soul of Man, CW*, p 1089: On mechanical slavery, on the slavery of the machine, the future of the world depends ... There will be great storages of force for every city, and for every house if required, and this force man will convert into heat, light, or motion, according to his needs

7. The line of beauty is an S-shaped curved line. This is part of William Hogarth's theory of Aesthetics described in his *Analysis of Beauty* (1753).

8. These views upon the wonders of the electric light and machinery together with the previous paragraph's eulogy of inventors and scientists who are to Wilde wonders of American society ('they have applied science to modern life') conflict with our received impressions of Wilde, a point made by Robert Ross in his *A Superfluous Note of Explanation* to the 1919 edition of *The Soul of Man Under Socialism* (Humphreys): 'It may interest some of the author's admirers to note that in this essay he acknowledges, what in his previous writings he pretended to ignore – the potentialities of science...Here he recognises that science, not art, is going to cure consumption and solve the problem of misery.'

9. Footnote in the published version: In a poem published in an American magazine on February 15th, 1882, Wilde wrote: And in the throbbing engine room/Leap the long rods of polished steel. (This is from *La Mer*.) See *CW* p 821 – the poem is, however, about a ship's engine.

10. This argument was heavily criticised when Wilde lectured in Sheffield, January 1884. *Lying, CW* p 986: At present, people see fogs, not because there are fogs, but because poets and painters have taught them the mysterious loveliness of such effects. There may have been f fogs for centuries in London. I dare say there were. But no one saw them, and so we do not know anything about them. They did not exist till Art had invented them. Now, it must be admitted, fogs are carried to excess. They have become the mere mannerism of a clique, and the exaggerated realism of their method gives dull people bronchitis. Where the cultured catch an effect, the uncultured catch cold.

11. Bernhardt, Sarah Henriette Rosine (1844–1923) actor

12. Harte, Francis Bret (1836-1902) American author and poet

13. *The Life of Samuel Johnson, LL.D.* (1791) is a biography written by Boswell, James, 9th Laird of Auchinleck (1740-1795) lawyer, diarist, and author

14. *An Essay Concerning Human Understanding* (1690) Locke, John (1632–1704) philosopher

15. There was no bridge over the strait at this time. It is generally accepted that the strait was named 'Chrysopylae' or Golden Gate after the harbour at Byzantium, Istanbul named Chrysoceras or Golden Horn.

16. Wilde is using the Chinese lifestyle to illustrate William Morris' ideas: William Morris, *The Beauty of Life* (lecture) 1880. ... if you want a golden rule that will fit everybody, this is it: 'HAVE NOTHING IN YOUR HOUSES THAT YOU DO NOT KNOW TO BE USEFUL OR BELIEVE TO BE BEAUTIFUL.' ... and show us the victorious days when millions of those who now sit in darkness will be enlightened by an ART MADE BY THE PEOPLE AND FOR THE PEOPLE, A JOY TO THE MAKER AND THE USER.

17. Wilde uses this description in *HB* as exemplifying William Morris' ideas.

18. Not the line Wilde took under Edward Godwin's influence in *Shakespeare on Scenery* (1885). Wilde developed the theme of this article - supporting archaeological and costume realism in stage productions - reusing parts of it for a broader article on staging Shakespeare, *Shakespeare and Stage Costume* which was published shortly afterwards

19. Young, Brigham (1801-1877) was an American leader in the Latter Day Saint movement

20. Amelia Folsom (1838–1910). There were 55 women that Young was sealed to during his lifetime.

21. In general this is a description of Wilde's view of ideal menswear as he described in his lecture, *Dress*.

22. In *HB* Wilde stated: remember that the morality of art was merely its beauty and the immorality of art merely its ugliness.

23. Cellini, Benvenuto (1500-1571) Italian goldsmith, sculptor, painter, soldier and musician

24. Rabelais, François (1494-1553) French Renaissance writer, doctor, monk and Greek scholar

25. Davis, Jefferson Finis (1808-1889) American statesman serving as President of the Confederate States of America for its entire history, from 1861 to 1865. He lived at a plantation of Beauvoir near Biloxi, Mississippi.

26. See *Journalism*, p 91: Nothing in the United States struck me more than the fact that the remarkable intellectual progress of that country is very largely due to the efforts of American women, who edit many of the most powerful magazines and newspapers, take part in the discussion of every question of public interest, and exercise an important influence upon the growth and tendencies of literature and art (November 1887,'Literary and Other Notes', *The Woman's World)*

27. See *Dress*

28. This was reported extensively. Also see *Dress.*

29. A witticism Wilde used again and made famous in *Dress.*

30. Wilde gave an extensive section of *HB* over to education and handicrafts.

31. Jefferson, Joseph (commonly known as Joe Jefferson) (1829 - 1905) American actor

32. Barrett, Lawrence (1838-1891) American stage actor

33. Morris, Clara (1849-1925) American actor

34. Anderson, Mary (1859–1940) American actor.

35. Rankin, Gladys (married Sydney Drew) (1870-1914) American comic actor

36. Stirling, Mary Anne (Fanny) (nee Kehl)(1815-1895) English actor

37. Prescott, Marie (1850-93) actor of great beauty and wit

38. Marie Prescott would stage *Vera* in New York in August 1883 and Mary Anderson turned down his play *Duchess of Padua* in early 1883.

39. Some newspapers reported that sections of Wilde's audience took this to heart and left before the end of his lecture.

40. Lincoln, Abraham (1809-1865) the 16th President of the United States, serving from March 1861 until his assassination in April 1865

APPENDIX C
THE HOUSE BEAUTIFUL

1. *Renaissance*, Preface p 3: Many attempts have been made by writers on art and poetry to define beauty in the abstract. ... Such discussions help us very little to enjoy what has been well done in art or poetry ... See also 'English Renaissance', *Miscellanies*, Ross p 243, also *Poison CW* p 997: He cared nothing for abstract definitions on the nature of the Beautiful... This phraseology is reused in *MAT* & *VAML*

2. Plato's Republic is Wilde's key reference here. For Wilde's comments upon Plato, see *Critic CW* p 1049/50: You remember

that lovely passage in which Plato describes how a young Greek should be educated, and with what insistence he dwells upon the importance of surroundings, telling us how the lad is to be brought up in the midst of fair sights and sounds, so that the beauty of material things may prepare his soul for the reception of the beauty that is spiritual.

3. See *Dress* for Wilde's comments about the unbearableness of fashionable beauty.

4. *Critic CW* p 1049: But the artist, who accepts the facts of life, and yet transforms them into shapes of beauty, and makes them vehicles of pity or of awe … see also *VAML*.

5. See *PIA* and the San Francisco section.

6. Strictly blue and white pottery made in and around Delft in the Netherlands from the sixteenth century. However, Wilde uses the term here more widely, meaning tin glazed earthenware.

7. *Critic CW* p 1058: Aesthetics, like sexual selection, make life lovely and wonderful, fill it with new forms, and give it progress, and variety and change.

8. Morris, William (1834–1896) designer, author and visionary socialist

9. William Morris, 'The Beauty of Life' (lecture) 1880. Believe me, if we want art to begin at home, as it must, we must clear our houses of troublesome superfluities that are for ever in our way … if you want a golden rule that will fit everybody, this is it: 'HAVE NOTHING IN YOUR HOUSES THAT YOU DO NOT KNOW TO BE USEFUL OR BELIEVE TO BE BEAUTIFUL.'

10. Berlin wool work is a style of needlepoint. Typically it is executed with wool yarn on canvas. Berlin work received a

boost through the Great Exhibition of 1851 and by the advent of ladies' magazines. Subjects to be embroidered were influenced by Victorian Romanticism and included floral designs, Victorian paintings, biblical or allegorical motifs, and quotations such as ' Home Sweet Home' or 'Faith, Hope, Love'.

11. Antimacassars and other household 'ornaments' are also referred to sarcastically in *Dress* and *VAML*.

12. William Morris, 'The Beauty of Life' (lecture) 1880. …and show us the victorious days when millions of those who now sit in darkness will be enlightened by an ART MADE BY THE PEOPLE AND FOR THE PEOPLE, A JOY TO THE MAKER AND THE USER.

13. *Critic CW* p 1049: But the artist, who accepts the facts of life, and yet transforms them into shapes of beauty, and makes them vehicles of pity or of awe, and shows their colour-element, and their wonder, and their true ethical import also, and builds out of them a world more real than reality itself, and of loftier and more noble import …

14. John Ruskin: In chapter II of *Seven Lamps of Architecture*, he defends the pursuit of material and structural 'truth' in architecture. He advocates a rejection of 'deception', 'slander', 'hypocrisy' and 'betrayal'…

15. Ruskin, John (1819–1900) art and social critic

16. *Critic, CW* pp 1038/39: ERNEST: … It seems to me that in everything that you have said there is something radically immoral. GILBERT: All art is immoral.

17. see *MAT* … pass through street after street of the most foolish and stupid architecture that the

world has ever seen

18. Ruskin's major text on this was 'Defence of the Gothic'.

19. The Queen Anne style included fine brickwork varied with terracotta panels or tile-hung upper stories. Other characteristics were white woodwork and blond stonework detailing, oriel windows, corner towers, asymmetrical fronts, deeply shadowed entrances and broad porches.

20. Wilde lectured on *HB* in Derby on 25 October 1883 and made several visits at this time. See *CL* p 223

21. see also *VAML*

22. *Masks, CW* p 1076: For each scene the colour-scheme should be settled as absolutely as for the decoration of a room..

23. 'Mr Whistler's Ten O'clock', *Miscellanies*, Ross, p 66: ...I strongly deny that charming people should be condemned to live with magenta ottomans and Albert-blue curtains in their rooms...

24. see also *Dress*

25. *Renaissance*, Winckelman, p 114: Breadth, centrality, with blitheness and repose, are the marks of Hellenic culture.

26. Wilde disliked patterned wallpapers, see *CL* pp 258/9 about Morris' wallpapers and curtains for Tite Street. The Grosvenor Gallery colour schemes were influential. In *Miscellanies*, 'Grosvenor Gallery' 1877, Wilde describes the gallery as: The walls are hung with scarlet damask above a dado of dull green and gold... The following year this was replaced ... by a quite different "artistic" green. This would inspire Gilbert and Sullivan's famous expression, 'greenery-yallery, Grosvenor Gallery'(Musée d'Orsay website.) This colour

was also described as viridian. Leighton's silk room at Holland Park is lined in sage green silk.

27. *Critic, CW* p 1031/2 Just as on the flowerless carpets of Persia, tulip and rose blossom indeed and are lovely to look on, though they are not reproduced in visible shape or line.

28. See also *VAML. Critic, CW* p 1032: ... the pearl and purple of the seashell is echoed in the church of St. Mark at Venice; just as the vaulted ceilings of the wondrous chapel at Ravenna is made gorgeous by the gold and green and sapphire of the peacock's tail....

29. Sherard, *Friendship*, pp 25/6. When Wilde was in Paris in early 1883 he had a hotel room that looked out over the Seine. Sherard commented on the wonderful view but Wilde's response was: 'A gentleman never looks out of the window.'

30. German stained glass as described was designed to produce a picture in glass. Also *Lying, CW* p 979 The pictorial glass of Germany is absolutely detestable.

31. *Dorian Gray, CW* p 46 describes Lord Henry's library: ... through the small leaded panels of the window streamed the apricot-coloured light...

32. Mashrabiya is the Arabic term given to a type of projecting oriel window enclosed with carved wood .

33. This is another reference to Morris' rules as well as more general issues of beauty and utility.

34. See also *VAML*

35. Also *MAT*. Whistler's Peacock Room was an (expensive) example this arrangement of shelving reaching up to a panelled ceiling.

36. Chippendale, Thomas (1718-1779) cabinet-maker and designer

37. Eighteenth century interior designers and architects from Scotland, Robert Adam (1728–1792) is the more famous.

38. Sheraton, Thomas (1751–1806) furniture designer and author

39. Hepplewhite, George (1727-1786) cabinet-maker and furniture designer

40. Velázquez, Diego Rodríguez de Silva y (1599 – 1660) Spanish painter who was the leading artist in the court of King Philip IV. Velasquez portraits were referred to in *MAT* and *VAML*.

41. These handcraftsmen are also referred to in *MAT*.

42. *Critic, CW* p 1055: We, in our educational system, have burdened the memory with a load of unconnected facts. ... We teach people how to remember, we never teach them how to grow.

43. See also *PIA*

44. Plato's *Republic* is Wilde's key reference here. Also see 'English Renaissance', *Miscellanies*, pp 270/1: [the child] ... will love what is beautiful and good, and hate what is evil and ugly... also *Critic CW* pp 1049/50

45. John Keats, closing lines to *Ode on a Grecian Urn*: 'Beauty is truth, truth beauty'--- that is all /Ye know on earth, and all ye need to know.

46. Now the Victoria and Albert Museum, founded 1852.

47. In October 1885 Wilde began to subtitle *HB* as *The Mission of Art in the Nineteenth Century*.

48. *Renaissance*, Conclusion p 121: ... art comes to you professing frankly to give nothing but the highest quality to your moments as they pass ... See also *MAT*.

49. Keats, John (1795–1821) poet .

This is a quotation from a letter from Keats which Wilde was particularly fond of. He wished to use it in his Poems, published in 1882, and also used a more accurate variant of it in 'English Renaissance' (*Miscellanies*, p 263). In this lecture he quotes it with the – probably judicious, as a public lecturer - omission of a reference to not having the slightest reverence for the public.

APPENDIX D
DRESS &
THE PHILOSOPHY OF DRESS

1. No doubt Wilde reported this tongue in cheek, as representing his own influence through his lectures, particularly through *HB*; see also *VAML*. Also, *Critic, CW* p 1050: What has been done up to now has been chiefly in the clearing of the way. It is always more difficult to destroy than it is to create, and when what one has to destroy is vulgarity and stupidity, the task of destruction needs not merely courage but also contempt. Yet it seems to me to have been, in a measure, done. We have got rid of what was bad. We have now to make what is beautiful. Wilde also considers this point in an extensive section of *Soul of Man*, *CW*, p 1098: And now it is almost impossible to enter any modern house without seeing some recognition of good taste, some recognition of the value of lovely surroundings, some sign of appreciation of beauty. In fact, people's houses are, as a rule, quite charming nowadays.

2. 'House Decoration', *Miscellanies*, Ross p 282: ...that old offender the horse-hair sofa, whose stolid look of indifference is always so depressing.

3. see *HB* where Wilde had decried these items and described antimacassars: ... which really

reduced some rooms to the level of a sort of eternal washing day.

4. *Masks, CW* p 1067: For the stage is not merely the meeting place of all the arts, but is also the return of art to life.

5. Compare with *Phrases, CW* p 1206: Nothing should reveal the body but the body.

6. See *HB*

7. This seems to be self-defence: Wilde was a very large man, tall and at this time newspapers described him as inclining to stoutness.

8. Chaucer, Geoffrey (*c*.1340–1400) poet and administrator

9. Dunbar, William (c1460–1513) poet and courtier

10. see *HB*

11. The First French Empire of Napoleon I and II (1804–1815)

12. Antoinette, Marie (1755-1793) archduchess of Austria, Dauphine of France from 1770 to 1774, Queen of France from 1774 to 1792

13. See *HB*

14. see also *HB*. This comment became very famous.

15. Contrast with *AIH, CW* p 522: Fashion is what one wears oneself. What is unfashionable is what other people wear.

16. A phrase which became very famous.

17. Stuart, Mary (also: Mary, Queen of Scots) (1542-1587) Queen of Scotland

18. Holbein, Hans, the younger (1497/8–1543); Elizabeth I (1533–1603) Queen of England and Ireland.

19. *Masks, CW* p 1074: … whenever in our own day historical accuracy has been disregarded … the result has been that the stage has been turned into that chaos of costume, that caricature of the centuries, the Fancy Dress Ball, to the entire ruin of all dramatic and picturesque effect.

20. Charles I (1600–1649) king of England, Scotland, and Ireland: reigned 1625-1649.

21. Restoration: 1660. Charles II (1630–1685) king of England, Scotland, and Ireland.

22. Medici, Catherine de' (1519-1589) Franco/Italian noblewoman who was Queen consort of France (1547-1559)

23. Hogarth, William (1697–1764) painter and engraver

24. This and the next sentence always raised a laugh from his audience.
Encyclopedia Britannica :
Bustle: …worn at the back, was popular in the 1860s and '70s and revived a fashion that had originated in France in the 1780s. Padded rolls at the hips were known as 'bum rolls' and 'bearers' in the 16th and 17th centuries, as 'cork rumps' in the 18th, and finally as 'dress improvers' in Victorian times.

25. Contrast with: *Lying, CW* p 989: …the ancient Greeks. Do you think that Greek art ever tells us what the Greek people were like? Do you believe that the Athenian women were like the stately dignified figures of the Parthenon frieze, or like those marvellous goddesses who sat in the triangular pediments of the same building? If you judge from the art, they certainly were so. But read an authority, like Aristophanes for instance. You will find that the Athenian ladies laced tightly, wore high-heeled shoes, dyed their hair yellow, painted and rouged their faces, and were exactly like any silly fashionable or fallen creature of our own day. The fact is that we look back on the ages entirely through the medium of Art, and Art, very

fortunately, has never once told us the truth.

26. *Masks, CW* p 1075: The Greek dress was the loveliest dress the world has ever seen, and the English dress of the last century one of the most monstrous …

27. Also *PIA* where Wilde suggests that dresses ought to be sent home 'unfinished' - without bows and flounces.

28. Henry II (1133–1189) King of England, duke of Normandy and of Aquitaine, and count of Anjou. Reigned 1154-1189.

29. Wilde was a supporter of clogs. In both his letters to the *Pall Mall Gazette* on 'Dress' he made positive comments including: … in the England of our own day clogs are still worn in many of our manufacturing towns, such as Oldham. I fear that in Oldham they may not be dreams of beauty; in Oldham the art of inlaying them with ivory and with pearl may possibly be unknown; yet in Oldham they serve their purpose. *Miscellanies*, Ross pp 60/1.

30. Jaeger, Gustav (1832-1917) German naturalist and hygienist: the system of clothing associated with his name originates from *Die Normalkleidung als Gesundheitsschutz* ('Standardized Apparel For Health Protection', 1880) where he advocated the wearing of rough fabrics such as wool 'close to the skin', objecting especially to the use of any kind of plant fibre. The teachings of Jaeger inspired the creation of the Jaeger clothing brand.

31. 'Relation of Dress to Art', *Miscellanies*, Ross, p 71: A nation arrayed in stove-pipe hats and dress-improvers might have built the Pantechnicon possibly, but the Parthenon never.

32. See *MAT*: this became a famous

quote and was reported extensively.

33. Dyck, Sir Anthony van (1599-1641) Flemish artist who became the leading court painter in England

34. *AIH, CW* p 522 where Lord Goring is described – seemingly approvingly - as: He is wearing a silk hat and Inverness cape.

35. This also became a famous quote after Wilde's much reported use of it in Glasgow just before Christmas 1884. Lancashire mill girls or women from Oldham seem to epitomise Wilde's ideas on female dress.

36. *De Profundis, CW* p 938: Charming people such as fishermen, shepherds, ploughboys, peasants and the like know nothing about Art, and are the very salt of the earth.

37. see *HB* which deals with Morris' rules for house decoration.

38. *De Profundis, CW* p 937: People used to say of me that I was too individualistic … my ruin came, not from too great individualism of life but from too little. A theme developed in *The Soul of Man*… e.g. *CW* p 1080: … Socialism itself will be of value simply because it will lead to Individualism.

39. see *MAT*: … even when wearied of the houses you turn to contemplate the street itself, you have nothing to look at but chimney-pot hats …

40. 'Relation of Dress to Art', *Miscellanies*, Ross, pp 70/71 : And so, were our national attire delightful in colour, and in construction simple and sincere; were dress the expression of the loveliness that it shields and of the swiftness and motion that it does not impede … then would painting be no longer an artificial reaction against the ugliness of life, but become, as it should be, the natural

expression of life's beauty. Nor would painting merely, but all the other arts also, be the gainers by a change such as that which I propose; the gainers, I mean, through the increased atmosphere of Beauty by which the artists would be surrounded and in which they would grow up. For Art is not to be taught in Academies. It is what one looks at, not what one listens to, that makes the artist. The real schools should be the streets.

41. Worth, Charles Frederick (1825-1895) English fashion designer widely considered the Father of Haute couture, worked in Paris.

42. Porcelain created by the Capodimonte porcelain factory, established in Naples in 1743

43. Appeal, not to Caesar, but to Caesar's wife. Wilde's amendment of *The Acts of the Apostles*, 25:11 & 12

APPENDIX E
THE VALUE OF ART
IN MODERN LIFE

1. This phraseology is reused from *MAT* & *HB*. *Renaissance*, Preface p 3: Many attempts have been made by writers on art and poetry to define beauty in the abstract ... Such discussions help us very little to enjoy what has been well done in art or poetry... See also 'English Renaissance', *Miscellanies* p 243, also *Poison CW* 997 He cared nothing for abstract definitions on the nature of the Beautiful ...

2. See also *HB*. Plato's *Republic* is Wilde's key reference here. For Wilde's quotations from Plato, see 'English Renaissance', *Miscellanies*, Ross pp 270/1 and *Critic CW* p 1049/50.

3. No doubt Wilde reported this tongue in cheek, as representing his own influence through his lectures, particularly through *HB*; see also *Dress*. Also, *Critic,*

CW p 1050: What has been done up to now has been chiefly in the clearing of the way. It is always more difficult to destroy than it is to create, and when what one has to destroy is vulgarity and stupidity, the task of destruction needs not merely courage but also contempt. Yet it seems to me to have been, in a measure, done. We have got rid of what was bad. We have now to make what is beautiful.

4. see *HB* where Wilde had dealt with all these aspects of 'decoration.'

5. Plato (424BC-348BC) Classical Greek philosopher, student of Socrates. See *Critic CW* p 1049/50: You remember that lovely passage in which Plato describes how a young Greek should be educated, and with what insistence he dwells upon the importance of surroundings, telling us how the lad is to be brought up in the midst of fair sights and sounds, so that the beauty of material things may prepare his soul for the reception of the beauty that is spiritual.

6. Wilde's fascination with aesthetics and ethics. This also derives from Keats, 'Ode on a Grecian Urn', last two lines: 'Beauty is truth, truth beauty,' - that is all/ Ye know on earth, and all ye need to know.

7. Wilde explored art and nature more fully in *Lying CW* p 970+

8. see note 1 above and *Critic, CW* p 1049: But to be purified and made perfect, this sense (temperament) requires some form of exquisite environment. But this was not his point in *MAT* where he decried Ruskin's description of Pisa as a school of art.

9. see *Dress* where Wilde complains of 'added prettinesses.'

10. Michaelangelo quotation. Also used in *MoA19C*.

11. see *Dress* for the rules inspired by William Morris and John Ruskin

12. see 'Handicraftsman', *Miscellanies* p 297

13. see also *HB*

14. *Lying, CW* p 977: … two touches of Nature will destroy any work of Art. & p 982: … it is none the less true that Life imitates art far more than Art imitates life.

15. *Lying CW* p 991: Life and Nature may sometimes be used as part of Art's rough material …

16. *Lying CW* p 979: But wherever we have returned to Life and Nature, our work has always become vulgar, common, and uninteresting.

17. *Critic CW* p 1020 … that spirit of choice, that subtle tact of omission, is really the critical faculty …

18. *Lying CW* p 979 … Orientalism, with its frank rejection of imitation, … its dislike to the actual representation of any object in Nature… in Byzantium, Sicily and Spain…we have had beautiful and imaginative work in which the visible things of life are transmuted into artistic conventions, and the things that Life has not are invented and fashioned for her delight. See also Pater, *Greek Studies*, Macmillan 1928, 'The Marbles of Aegina', p 226: … the Asiatic tendency…in endless play of undirected imagination; delighting in brightness and colour, in beautiful material. Also *HB* on masses of colour.

19. See HB: there would be no flower of our meadows that would not weave its tendrils round our pillows, no little leaf in our woodlands that would not lend itself to design, no single spray of wild rose or briar that would not live for ever over carven doorway or on painted chest.

20. Louis XIV (1638-1715) King of France. Reigned for 72 years

21. see also *MAT*

22. See *HB* which describes William Morris' laws of house decoration.

23. See examples given in *HB*

24. see *Renaissance*, p 4. Also *Poison CW* p 996…he was one of the first to recognise what is, indeed, the very keynote of aesthetic eclecticism, I mean the true harmony of all really beautiful things irrespective of age or place, of school or manner. He saw that in decorating a room, which is to be, not a room for show, but a room to live in, we should never aim at any archaeological reconstruction of the past, nor burden ourselves with any fanciful necessity for historical accuracy. In this artistic perception he was perfectly right. All beautiful things belong to the same age.

25. *Critic CW* p 1050: We have got rid of what was bad. We have now to make what is beautiful. And though the mission of the aesthetic movement is to lure people to contemplate, not to lead them to create…

26. *Critic CW* p 1032: …the highest criticism deals with art, not as expressive, but as impressive purely, and is consequently both creative and independent, is in fact an art by itself, occupying the same relation to creative work that creative work does to the visible world of form and colour

27. *Critic CW* p 1030 … the anecdotage of painting …scenes taken out of literature or history.

28. This is Wilde's view and an argument against Whistler. See

Critic CW p 1030: To the latter (the poet) belongs life in its full and absolute entirety; not merely the beauty that men look at … Also Wilde's review of 'Whistler's Ten O'clock': *Miscellanies*, Ross p 66: But the poet is the supreme artist…and is lord over all life and all arts.

29. See above notes. Also *Critic CW* p 1031: Most of our elderly English painters spend their wicked and wasted lives in poaching upon the domain of the poets, marring their motives by clumsy treatment, and striving to render, by visible form or colour, the marvel of what is invisible, the splendour of what is not seen. Their pictures are, as a natural consequence, insufferably tedious.

30. *Masks, CW* p 1078: … producing that joy in beauty for beauty's sake without which the great masterpieces of art can never be understood

31. reused from *MAT*

32. see also *HB*

33. see *Critic CW* p 1029 … I see that the beauty of the visible arts is, as the beauty of music, impressive primarily, and that it may be marred, and indeed often is so, by any excess of intellectual intention on the part of the artist.

34. Turner, Joseph Mallord William (1775–1851) landscape painter

35. *Poison CW* p 997: He admired Turner and Constable at a time when they were not so much thought of as they are now, and saw that for the highest landscape art we require more than 'mere industry and accurate transcription.'

36. *Critic, CW* p 1051: … rejecting the tedious realism of those who merely paint what they see, try to see something worth seeing

37. Burne-Jones was a witness for Ruskin against Whistler in the trial of 1876, see Whistler pp 14-18: … complete finish ought to be the object of all artists … It shows no finish – it is simply a sketch. Also *MAT*.

38. *Poison CW* p 997: … for the highest landscape art we require more than "mere industry and accurate transcription."

39. see HB on fashionable colour and musical keys

40. *Critic, CW* p 1020 …that fine spirit of choice and delicate instinct of selection by which the artist realises life for us, and gives to it a momentary perfection. Well, that spirit of choice, that subtle tact of omission, is really the critical faculty in one of its most characteristic moods, and no one who does not possess this critical faculty can create anything at all in art.

41. *Masks, CW* p 1073: But subordination in art does not mean disregard of truth; it means conversion of fact into effect …

42. Wilde made a similar point in *MAT* and Whistler responded to Wilde's review of his 'Ten o'Clock' lecture with a letter (CL p 250 n1): You have … left to 'the Poet' the discovery of '*l'horrible*' dans '*le beau*'!

43. Velázquez, Diego Rodríguez de Silva y (1599 – 1660) Spanish painter who was the leading artist in the court of King Philip IV. Velasquez portraits were referred to in MAT and HB.

44. 'Relation of Dress to Art', *Miscellanies*, Ross, p 69: That, under certain conditions of light and shade, what is ugly in fact may in its effect become beautiful…

45. *Critic CW* p 1049: But the artist, who accepts the facts of life, and yet transforms them into shapes

of beauty, and makes them vehicles of pity or of awe, and shows their colour-element, and their wonder, and their true ethical import also, and builds out of them a world more real than reality itself, and of loftier and more noble import...

46. Throughout his written work, Wilde commented favourably many times upon Corot and the Impressionists. At the very beginning of *Lying, CW* p 970: Enjoy Nature! I am glad to say that I have entirely lost that faculty. People tell us that Art makes us love Nature more than we loved her before; that it reveals her secrets to us; and that after a careful study of Corot and Constable we see things in her that had escaped our observation. My own experience is that the more we study Art, the less we care for Nature. And at *CW* p 986: ...Where, if not from the Impressionists, do we get those wonderful brown fogs that come creeping down our streets, blurring the gas-lamps and changing the houses into monstrous shadows? To whom, if not to them and their master, do we owe the lovely silver mists that brood over our river, and turn to faint forms of fading grace curved bridge and swaying barge? The extra-ordinary change that has taken place in the climate of London during the last ten years is entirely due to this particular school of Art... That white quivering sunlight that one sees now in France, with its strange blotches of mauve, and its restless violet shadows, is her latest fancy, and, on the whole, Nature reproduces it quite admirably. Where she used to give us Corots and Daubignys, she gives us now exquisite Monets and entrancing Pissaros. Also, from *Critic, CW* p 1045: All

artistic creation is absolutely subjective. The very landscape that Corot looked at was, as he said himself, but a mood of his own mind... See also AIH CW pp 493/4: CHILTERN: ... Corots seem to go with music, don't they? May I show them to you?

CHEVELEY: I am not in a mood to-night for silver twilights, or rose-pink dawns.

47. This quip is taken directly from *MAT*

48. *Critic CW* p 1053: Art does not address herself to the specialist. Her claim is that she is universal, and that in all her manifestations she is one.

49. Whistler, James Abbott McNeill (1834–1903) painter and printmaker

50. see also *MAT* and Wilde's review of his 'Ten o'Clock': *Miscellanies*, Ross p 67.

51. Browning, Robert (1812–1889) poet. *Critic CW* p 1047: Ruskin put his criticism into imaginative prose, and is superb in his changes and contradictions; and Browning put his into blank verse, and made painter and poet yield us their secret...

52. *Lying CW* p 987: Art never expresses anything but itself. This is the principle of my new aesthetics; and it is this, more than that vital connection between form and substance, on which Mr. Pater dwells, that makes music the type of all the arts. Also *Renaissance*, 'School of Giorgione', p 124: All art constantly aspires towards the condition of music. For while in all other kinds of art it is possible to distinguish the matter from the form, and the understanding can always make this distinction, yet it is the constant effort of art to obliterate it.

53. Wilde's own review of the Grosvenor Gallery, 1877 about Whistler's Nocturnes, *Miscellanies*, Ross , p 18: These pictures are certainly worth looking at for about as long as one looks at a real rocket, that is, for somewhat less than a quarter of a minute.

54. York 9 October 1884. Wilde concluded his review of Whistler's Ten o'Clock lecture with tongue-in-cheek praise of Whistler, *Miscellanies*, Ross, p 67: For that he is indeed one of the very greatest masters of painting is my opinion. And I may add that in this opinion Mr. Whistler himself entirely agrees.

55. Wilde's letter on funeral reform, *CL* p 247: If we are to have funeral memorials at all, far better models are to be found in the beautiful crosses of Ireland, such as the cross at Monasterboice…

56. Ruskin, John (1819–1900) art and social critic

57. see also *MAT, HB*

58. *Critic CW* p 1049: But the artist, who accepts the facts of life, and yet transforms them into shapes of beauty, and makes them vehicles of pity or of awe, and shows their colour-element, and their wonder, and their true ethical import also, and builds out of them a world more real than reality itself, and of loftier and more noble import…

59. *Critic, CW* p 1051: … but seek rather for the imaginative beauty of design and the loveliness of fair colour, and rejecting the tedious realism of those who merely paint what they see…

60. *Poison, CW* p 997: The qualities that he sought for in a picture were composition, beauty and dignity of line, richness of colour, and imaginative power.

APPENDIX F
THE MISSION OF ART IN THE NINETEENTH CENTURY

1. Restatement of Pater's Preface to *Renaissance,* p 4.

2. *Miscellanies*, Ross, p 73

3. *Oscar Wilde in America*, www.oscarwildeinamerica.org/ index.html

4. In 1608–09, the Earl of North-ampton built Northumberland House at Charing Cross. In June 1874, the whole of the duke's property was purchased by the Metropolitan Board of Works for the formation of Northumber-land Avenue. Northumberland Street, off the Avenue, was originally where the Pall Mall Gazette had its offices and where Wilde partook of a thought experiment with Stuart Cumberland in May 1884. The buildings now standing in Northumberland Street have all been erected since 1850.

5. *CL* p 501, Dec 1891, Wilde writes to the Editor of the *Speaker* from Paris and notes: … (I) purchased a copy of the *Speaker* at one of the charming kiosks that decorate Paris; institutions, by the way, that I think we should at once introduce into London … a delightful object, and, when illuminated at night from within, as lovely as a fantastic Chinese lantern, especially when the transparent advertisements are from the clever pencil of M. Cheret.

6. Buonarroti Simoni, Michelangelo di Lodovico (1475- 1564) Italian Renaissance sculptor, painter, architect, poet, and engineer. Also used without reference in *VAML*.

APPENDIX G

CHATTERTON
ESSAY AND LECTURE

1. Wilde, Oscar. [Essay on Chatterton]. W.S.Lewins: 1952 MS. Wilde W6721M3 E78 [1886?] Bound. 19th century AD. MS Oscar Wilde Wilde W6721M3 E78. William Andrews Clark Memorial Library, University of California, Los Angeles. British Literary Manuscripts Online. Web 7 June 2012. © 2012 Gale Previously unpublished material © the Estate of Oscar Wilde 2013

2. Chatterton, Thomas (1752–1770) poet and forger; Coleridge, Samuel Taylor (1772–1834) poet, critic, drug addict and philosopher; Keats, John (1795–1821) poet

3. Emerson, Ralph Waldo (1803-1882) American essayist, lecturer, and poet. *Essays, Second Series, The Poet*: The breadth of the problem is great, for the poet is representative. He stands among partial men for the complete man, and apprises us not of his wealth, but of the common wealth. The young man reveres men of genius, because, to speak truly, they are more himself than he is. They receive of the soul as he also receives, but they more. Nature enhances her beauty, to the eye of loving men, from their belief that the poet is beholding her shows at the same time. He is isolated among his contemporaries by truth and by his art, but with this consolation in his pursuits, that they will draw all men sooner or later. For all men live by truth and stand in need of expression. In love, in art, in avarice, in politics, in labor, in games, we study to utter our painful secret. The man is only half himself, the other half is his expression.

4. Samuel Taylor Coleridge 'Monody on the Death of Chatterton' (1794)

5. At the top of this page of the manuscript, above the title, Wilde has written ' - 4¼ - '. I do not know what this refers to and have omitted it from the transcript.

6. 'Miner And Minor Poets', *Pall Mall Gazette*, February 1, 1887. *Reviews* Ross, pp 123-7 used parts of this introduction.

7. Arnold, Matthew (1822–1888) poet, critic and inspector of schools

8. I have inserted Arnold's sonnet here, the poem is not in Wilde's notes.

9. Wordsworth, William (1770–1850) poet; 'Resolution and Independence': I thought of Chatterton, the marvellous Boy/The sleepless Soul that perished in his pride

10. Blake, William (1757–1827) engraver, artist, and poet

11. Chatterton, Thomas (1713–1752) schoolmaster

12. Nettesheim, Heinrich Cornelius Agrippa von (1486-1535) German magician, occult writer and alchemist

13. Chatterton, Sarah (née Young) (1731–1796) seamstress

14. The text Wilde is copying says 'attery'

15. Cromek, Robert Hartley (1770-1812) English publisher and engraver

16. Plato (424BC-348BC) Classical Greek philosopher, student of Socrates. Unclear what Wilde was to insert here, possibly a passage from Republic which deals with the upbringing and education of children.

17. Unclear what Wilde was to insert here.

18. Worcester, William (1415–1480) topographer and author; Camden, William (1551–1623) historian and herald; Fuller, Thomas (1608-1661) English churchman and historian

19. Canynges, William (c. 1399–1474) was an English merchant and shipper

20. Paraphrase of Wordsworth's *The Wanderer*: So the foundations of his mind were laid/In such communion, not from terror free/While yet a child, and long before his time/Had he perceived the presence and the power/Of greatness; and deep feelings had impressed/So vividly great objects that they lay/Upon his mind like substances, whose presence/Perplexed the bodily sense. He had received/A precious gift; for, as he grew in years,

21. On The Same (Our Lady's Church)

22. 1422-1461 &1461-1470

23. Hoccleve (Occleve) Thomas (*c*.1367–1426) poet and clerk; Lydgate, John (*c*.1370–1449) poet and prior of Hatfield Regis

24. Chaucer, Geoffrey (*c*.1340–1400) poet and administrator

25. Lamb, Charles (1775–1834) essayist

26. Farley, Felix (1708 - 1753) printer

27. Barbour, John (*c*.1330–1395) ecclesiastic and verse historian

28. Shakespeare, William (1564–1616) playwright and poet
Milton, John (1608–1674) poet and polemicist
Dryden, John (1631–1700) poet, playwright, and critic
Prior, Matthew (1664–1721) poet and diplomat
Cowley, Abraham (1618–1667) poet
Gray, Thomas (1716–1771) poet and literary scholar

Pope, Alexander (1688–1744) poet
Thomson, Alexander (1763–1803) poet
Churchill, Charles (1732–1764) poet

29. Hall, Anthony (1679–1723) antiquary
John Hollingshed Camden, William (1551–1623) historian and herald
Stow, John (1524/5–1605) historian
Weever, John (1575/6–1632) poet and antiquary

30. Philips, Ambrose (1674-1749) poet and playwright

31. Burgum, Henry (1739-1789) pewterer

32. Scott, Sir Walter (1771–1832) poet and novelist

33. Gaius Cilnius Maecenas (70 BC-8 BC) friend and political adviser to Octavian (who was to become the first Emperor of Rome as Caesar Augustus) as well as an important patron for the new generation of Augustan poets.
Publius Vergilius Maro (70 BC-19 BC) usually called Virgil was an ancient Roman poet of the Augustan period
Quintus Horatius Flaccus (65 BC-8 BC) known as Horace, the leading Roman lyric poet during the time of Augustus.
Lucius Varius Rufus (c. 74 - 14 BC) Roman poet of the Augustan age. Friend of Virgil and of Horace for whom he and Virgil obtained an introduction to Maecenas

34. Dodsley, Robert (1704–1764) bookseller and writer

35. Walpole, Horatio (Horace) fourth earl of Orford (1717–1797) author, politician, and patron of the arts

36. Coleridge composed a long note to the 'Monody on the Death of Chatterton' which he finally cancelled: 'Walpole writes thus.

All the house of Forgery are relations. Although it be but just to Chatterton's memory to say, that his poverty never made him claim kindred with the more enriching branches yet he who could so ingeniously counterfeit styles and (the asserter believes) hands, might easily have been led to the more facile imitation of prose promissory notes! - O ye, who honour the name of Man, rejoice that this Walpole is called a Lord!'

37. Croft (Crofts, Craftes) Sir Herbert (*c.*1565–1629) administrator and landowner

38. Wilkes, John (1725–1797) politician

39. Beckford, William Thomas (1760–1844) writer and art collector

40. Garrick, David (1717–1779) actor and playwright

41. I assume this is Wilde's instruction to himself.

42. Carey, Thomas 'Elegy to the Memory of Mr. Thomas Chatterton, late of Bristol' *Town and Country Magazine* 2 (October 1770)

43. Goldsmith, Oliver (1728–1774) author

44. Johnson, Samuel (1709–1784) author and lexicographer

45. Boswell, James, 9th Laird of Auchinleck (1740-1795) lawyer, diarist and biographer of Samuel Johnson

46. Tyrwhitt, Thomas (1730–1786) literary editor and critic: *Poems supposed to have been written at Bristol by Thomas Rowley and others, in the Fifteenth Century* (1777) He believed them genuine mediaeval works.

47. In 1782 a new edition of Rowley's poems appeared, with a 'Commentary, in which the antiquity of them is considered and defended,' by Jeremiah Milles, Dean of Exeter.

48. Taken from Theodore Watts, *Critical Introduction to Chatterton, The English Poets, Selections with Critical Introductions*, Volume 3, ed T. H. Ward, 1880, pp 400 – 408: Either Chatterton was a born forger, having, as useful additional endowments, Poetry and dramatic imagination almost unmatched among his contemporaries, or he was a born artist, who, before mature vision had come to show him the power and the sacredness of moral conscience in art, was so dominated by the artistic conscience — by the artist's yearning to represent, that, if perfect representation seemed to him to demand forgery, he needs must forge.

49. see the first aphorisms of *The Preface* to *The Picture of Dorian Gray CW* p 17: The artist is the creator of beautiful things. To reveal art and conceal the artist is art's aim.

50. Homer (probably 7th or 8th centuries BC) author of the *Iliad* and the *Odyssey*.

51. Shelley, Percy Bysshe (1792–1822) poet

52. Petrarca, Francesco (1304-1374) Italian scholar and poet

53. A subject Wilde explored extensively, e.g.in *The Decay of Lying, CW* p 978: Art begins with abstract decoration with purely imaginative and pleasurable work dealing with what is unreal and non-existent... (Then) Art takes life as part of her rough material, recreates it, and refashions it in fresh forms, is absolutely indifferent to fact, invents, imagines, dreams, and keeps between herself and reality the impenetrable barrier of beautiful style, of decorative or ideal treatment.

54. Wilde added a question mark to this quotation which I think indicates he did not know its

origin. The only references I can find for it are all in Watts' own writings: his introduction to Chatterton already referred to, his entry on Poetry in the 1909 *Encyclopaedia Britannica* and in his Poetry and *The Renascence of Wonder*, Dutton 1914, p 91.

55. Junius was the pseudonym of a writer who contributed a series of letters to the *Public Advertiser* from 21 January 1769 to 21 January 1772

56. Smollett, Tobias George (1721–1771) writer

57. Collins, William (1721-1759) English poet

58. Macpherson, James (1736-1796) Scottish writer, poet, known as the 'translator' of the Ossian cycle of poems. He is mentioned, with Chatterton, in the first paragraph of *Mr. W.H. CW* p 1150

59. Observations drawn from Theodore Watts: With regard to octo-syllabics with anapaestic variations, … Chatterton's Unknown Knight, like Christabel, and like Goethe's Erl King, has several variations introduced (as Coleridge says of his own) 'in correspondence with some transition in the nature of the imagery or passion.' The 'new principle,' in short, was Chatterton's. Watts, *Critical Introduction to Chatterton, The English Poets, Selections with Critical Introductions*, Volume 3, ed T. H. Ward, 1880, pp 400 - 408

60. Spenser, Edmund (1552?–1599) poet and administrator in Ireland

61. Tennyson, Alfred, first Baron Tennyson (1809–1892) poet

62. Morris, William (1834–1896) designer, author and visionary socialist

63. *Critic, CW* p 1020: Arnold's definition of literature as a criticism of life was not very felicitous in form, but it showed how keenly he recognised the importance of the critical element in all creative work. *The Study of Poetry*, Matthew Arnold, 1880: For in poetry the distinction between excellent and inferior, sound and unsound or only half-sound, true and untrue or only half-true, is of paramount importance. It is of paramount importance because of the high destinies of poetry. In poetry, as in criticism of life under the conditions fixed for such a criticism by the laws of poetic truth and poetic beauty, the spirit of our race will find, we have said, as time goes on and as other helps fail, its consolation and stay. But the consolation and stay will be of power in proportion to the power of the criticism of life. And the criticism of life will be of power in proportion as the poetry conveying it is excellent rather than inferior, sound rather than unsound or half-sound, true rather than untrue on half-true.

64. *Lying CW* pp 987/8: Even those who hold that Art is representative of time and place and people, cannot help admitting that the more imitative an art is, the less it represents to us the spirit of its age. … The more abstract, the more ideal an art is, the more it reveals to us the temper of its age.

65. Shelley, Percy Bysshe: *A Defence of Poetry*

66. National Portrait Gallery. Henry Treffry Dunn, Gouache and watercolour on paper now on card, 1882.

67. 'Thomas Chatterton' (sonnet) Dante Gabriel Rossetti

68. The poem actually has 'sweet', not 'Dear'

Index